Humanitarian Intervention

An Introduction

Second Edition

Aidan Hehir

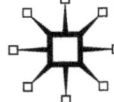

First edition 2010
Second edition 2013

Published by
PALGRAVE MACMILLAN

Palgrave Macmillan in the UK is an imprint of Macmillan Publishers Limited, registered in England, company number 785998, of Houndmills, Basingstoke, Hampshire RG21 6XS.

Palgrave Macmillan in the US is a division of St Martin's Press LLC, 175 Fifth Avenue, New York, NY 10010.

Palgrave Macmillan is the global academic imprint of the above companies and has companies and representatives throughout the world.

Palgrave® and Macmillan® are registered trademarks in the United States, the United Kingdom, Europe and other countries.

ISBN 978–1–137–30156–7   hardback
ISBN 978–1–137–30155–0   paperback

This book is printed on paper suitable for recycling and made from fully managed and sustained forest sources. Logging, pulping and manufacturing processes are expected to conform to the environmental regulations of the country of origin.

A catalogue record for this book is available from the British Library.

A catalog record for this book is available from the Library of Congress.

10 9 8 7 6 5 4 3 2 1
22 21 20 19 18 17 16 15 14 13

Humanitarian Intervention

Also by Aidan Hehir

The Responsibility to Protect: Rhetoric, Reality and the Future of Humanitarian Intervention

International Law, Security and Ethics (co-editor with Andrew Mumford and Natasha Kuhrt)

Kosovo, Intervention and Statebuilding: The International Community and the Transition to Independence (editor)

Humanitarian Intervention After Kosovo

State Building: Theory and Practice (co-editor with Neil Robinson)

Contents

List of Boxes

Abbreviations

AMIS	African Union Mission in Darfur
AU	African Union
CCPDC	Carnegie Commission on Preventing Deadly Conflict
CDR	Coalition pour la Defense de la Republique
DIIA	Danish Institute of International Affairs
DPKO	UN Department of Peacekeeping Operations
ECOMOG	Economic Community of West African States Monitoring Group
FRY	Federal Republic of Yugoslavia
GCC	Gulf Cooperation Council
HRW	Human Rights Watch
ICC	International Criminal Court
ICED	International Commission of Enquiry on Darfur
ICISS	International Commission on Intervention and State Sovereignty
ICJ	International Court of Justice
ICRC	International Committee of the Red Cross
ICRtoP	International Coalition for the Responsibility to Protect
ICTY	International Criminal Tribunal for the former Yugoslavia
IICK	Independent International Commission on Kosovo
IMF	International Monetary Fund
IPA	International Peace Academy
IR	International Relations
JEM	Justice and Equality Movement
KLA	Kosovo Liberation Army
LKCK	National Movement for the Liberation of Kosovo
LPK	Popular Movement for Kosovo
LPRK	Popular Movement for the Republic of Kosovo
MNRD	Mouvement Revolutionnaire National pour le Developpement
MSF	Médecins Sans Frontières
NATO	North Atlantic Treaty Organisation
NGO	Non-governmental organization
NSS	US National Security Strategy
OIC	Organisation for Islamic Conference
P5	permanent five members of the UN Security Council
R2P	responsibility to protect

RPF	Rwandan Patriotic Front
SFRY	Socialist Federal Republic of Yugoslavia
SLA	Sudanese Liberation Army
TNC	Transitional National Council (Libya)
UN	United Nations
UNAMIR	UN Assistance Mission for Rwanda
UNHCR	UN High Commissioner for Refugees
UNMOVIC	United Nations Monitoring, Verification and Inspection Commission
WMD	weapons of mass destruction

Acknowledgements

I would like to thank Steven Kennedy, Stephen Wenham and Cecily Wilson at Palgrave Macmillan. My colleagues in the Department of Politics and International Relations at Westminster University have been as supportive as ever. Thanks in particular to Bola Adediran for his invaluable help with Chapter 14. Thanks, too, to Thomas Weiss, Adrian Gallagher, James Pattison, Robert Murray, Richard Smittenaar, Tom Gregory, Joe Wise, Suzanne Freeman, Elliot Clarke, Colin Jervis and Quintes Kloppers.

As ever special thanks to my family, George, Niamh, Paul, Hazel, Jay, Nial, Rita, Aishling, Aran, Katie, Hannah, Emily, Chris, Lola Bee, Barney, Sue, Lucy and especially my mother, Mary. Finally, the biggest thanks go to my girls, Esmé, Elsie and Iris, and my wife, Sarah … 'let's eat the rich'.

AIDAN HEHIR

Preface

In the concluding chapter of this book's first edition I wrote: 'humanitarian intervention is very much a live issue. As you read this book it is highly likely that there is a crisis somewhere in the world which has generated heated debate about the need to intervene'. That 'a crisis' would erupt in the future was a relatively safe bet; I certainly did not imagine, however, that anything as tumultuous as the (often violent) popular uprisings in Tunisia, Egypt, Libya, Bahrain, Syria, etc. would occur within a year of the book being published.

As a result, throughout the academic year 2011–12 I regularly discussed the Arab Spring in my module on humanitarian intervention. In a number of lectures we watched events in Libya, Syria and Bahrain unfold in real time thanks to Facebook, Twitter and YouTube. At times I wondered what an International Relations academic teaching in 1992 would have made of watching live video feeds from conflict zones, of Facebook, of Twitter, of an entire module on humanitarian intervention. Given the speed of technological innovation in the 20th century it is perhaps the latter that would have been most difficult to envisage.

While these crises propelled the issue of humanitarian intervention back to the top of the international agenda and generated great interest among students, academics and the general public, engagement alone cannot be a cause for cheering; passive observation, even if empathic, will not catalyse change. Unless engagement compels action and ultimately reform we are surely doomed to endure an unending series of crises that repeatedly 'shock the conscience of mankind'.

AIDAN HEHIR

Introduction: Humanitarian Intervention in Contemporary International Relations

As demonstrated by the international reaction to the scenes of state-sponsored violence which all too often characterized the Arab Spring in 2011 and 2012, humanitarian intervention generates intensely divisive debate within academia and amongst policy makers and the general public. It is an issue that directly impacts on the agenda of states, non-governmental organizations (NGOs) and international organizations such as the North Atlantic Treaty Organisation (NATO), the United Nations (UN), the African Union and the Arab League. Academics and students from a wide variety of disciplines – including International Relations (IR), philosophy, political theory, security studies, international law and peace studies – engage with the controversies surrounding this topic. It also, most importantly, affects ordinary people: those suffering 'ethnic cleansing', civil war and genocide, and those moved by these scenes of human anguish who cry out for 'something' to be done.

In the post-Cold War era, debates about humanitarian intervention have become more frequent, more heated and more public, and the issue has moved to the very centre of the international political agenda. This book provides a comprehensive overview of the key concepts central to this debate, an analysis of the major sources of controversy, and an exploration of key case studies which highlight the practical manifestation of these issues. It is designed to act as a key source and guide for students, practitioners and the general reader.

The first section in this introduction comprises an examination of the evolution and nature of the contemporary debate, highlighting the key events and themes that have propelled humanitarian intervention to the forefront of international politics and IR. The second section provides an overview of the structure of this book and a guide on how to use its information to undertake further research in this area.

The contemporary debate

In early 2011 a wave of protests spread across the Middle East and North Africa. While the regimes in certain states, such as Jordan and Morocco,

1

tempered the domestic disturbances by initiating a series of reforms, many others were unable to stem the momentum for change and conflict ensued (see Chapter 14). In Tunisia, Egypt and Yemen long-serving presidents were deposed, while in Bahrain and Libya outside forces intervened, albeit in very different ways: the Gulf Cooperation Council – led by Saudi Arabia – sent troops to support the monarchy in Bahrain, while NATO intervened in Libya in support of the rebels, thereby precipitating the eventual demise of Colonel Gaddafi and his regime. In Syria the conflict between the government of President Assad and the Syrian National Council – a coalition of protest movements – escalated savagely throughout 2011 and 2012. In September 2012 Lakhdar Brahimi, the UN and Arab League envoy to Syria, described the death toll as 'staggering' and 'catastrophic' (BBC, 2012b). Estimates as to the number of deaths ranged from 18,000–30,000 with over 250,000 refugees (CNN, 2012; Reuters, 2012). These crises at their most basic involved egregious violence perpetrated by governments against their own people and calls for the international community to do something. The Arab Spring, therefore, in addition to being arguably the most momentous series of events since the fall of communism, served starkly to cohere many of the disparate themes which had, over the previous 20 years, shaped the debate on humanitarian intervention and graphically demonstrated that a solution to many of the key questions and controversies remains elusive.

The contemporary controversy surrounding humanitarian intervention is not a uniquely modern phenomenon: humanitarian intervention has long been a divisive issue (Bass, 2008). While the terms of the debate may have altered, the actors may have changed and the international context may be radically different, the question, routinely asked during the Arab Spring, 'Should external actors intervene on behalf of suffering people and, if so, how?', has been posed, in some form, for centuries if not millennia.

Accepting this, however, the issue did become more focused and problematic as international society began to organize itself into a community of sovereign states in the 17th century (see Chapter 3). The very idea of sovereignty implies inviolability and the primacy of the principle of non-intervention in international politics. From the 19th century, international law, with sovereignty at its core, increased both its scope and its remit and the status of humanitarian intervention became more ambiguous and contentious (see Chapter 5). Humanitarian intervention necessarily challenges the statist bias in international politics and international law, and, as states have assumed more formal legal powers and entitlements, the tension between the rights of states and the rights of the individuals within them has increased.

This tension has become especially keen in the post-Cold War era. With the implosion of the Soviet Union and the new primacy of the liberal democratic state, three factors have cohered to enliven the issue of humanitarian intervention. They are discussed in the following sections.

The end of history

The end of the Cold War was famously heralded by Francis Fukuyama as 'the end of history'. Fukuyama was of course *not* suggesting that nothing of note would ever happen again; rather he argued that the collapse of communism signalled 'the end point of mankind's ideological evolution and the universalization of Western liberal democracy as the final form of human government' (1992, p. 3). The issues of concern for future generations would centre on improving the functioning of liberal democracy and, crucially for the humanitarian intervention debate, spreading this model across the globe.

During the 1990s the eastward expansion of the European Union and NATO, the sharp turn towards capitalism in China and the increased willingness of the developing world and Russia to implement structural adjustment programmes at the behest of the World Bank and the International Monetary Fund (IMF) were all cited as evidence of a universal appetite for the proliferation of liberal democracy and a general acceptance of the primacy of the liberal state model (Barnett, 2010, p. 21). The events of 11 September 2001 demonstrated, however, that there were some who rejected these changes, although these predominantly non-state actors were largely confined to the shadowy periphery during the 1990s.

As capitalism spread, so too did democracy, as the core group of democratic states, loosely termed 'the West', increasingly tied financial aid and political support to democratic reform. Liberal democracies espoused a commitment to the centrality of human rights in their foreign policy, and the internal character of states thus became an international issue (Chandler, 2002, pp. 1–20). Acceptance into the democratic club was conditional on adherence to notions of individual inviolability and basic standards of human welfare. Those states that refused to reform their domestic system in line with the liberal ideal were increasingly portrayed as 'failed' or 'rogue' states and cast as international pariahs. In contrast to the Cold War, therefore, when a state's relationship with the West was dependent on its disposition towards the Soviet Union, in the post-Cold War era this changed and the domestic dynamics within states became, at least rhetorically, a key factor in determining their association with the West.

Antonio Cassese has noted that human rights are 'subversive' and 'destined to foster tension and conflict among States' (2005, p. 375). The increased focus on human rights certainly heightened international tension in the post-Cold War era; sovereignty became an increasingly contested concept as states subjected to criticism for their record on human rights sought to reject what they described as 'interference' and even 'neo-colonialism'. The West increasingly began to argue that a state's legal entitlements should reflect its adherence to human rights norms – the idea of 'conditional sovereignty' – and this generated a divisive international debate (see Chapter 6). The logical consequences of the march of liberalism were increased tensions between ostensibly liberal and illiberal states, and, occasionally, the determination that particular instances of human rights violations had to be stopped by external military action or 'humanitarian intervention'.

The rise of the 'international community'

A second catalyst for the rise in the contemporary relevance of humanitarian intervention was the structural changes caused by the end of the Cold War. During the Cold War the world was divided between the East and the West, with the Soviet Union and the United States leading their respective spheres of influence. This was commonly referred to as a 'bipolar world order'. When communism collapsed the United States stood as the sole remaining superpower, and we entered the so-called 'unipolar era'.

While this fundamental structural change was considered by some observers to be both temporary and inherently dangerous (Layne, 1993; Mearsheimer, 1990), others believed that the new structure would have positive consequences for international justice and facilitate the promotion of human rights (Shaw, 1994, p. 155; Barnett, 2010, p. 22). The rationale behind this perspective was that the new international order would be less polarized, and hence cooperation amongst states who were against rogue human rights violators would be more feasible than during the era of great-power competition. This cooperation would, it was argued, enable the UN finally to fulfil its mandate and take a more proactive role in international relations. The UN-sanctioned action against Iraq in 1991 seemed to confirm these hopes.

Throughout the 1990s people looked to the 'international community' more and more to solve the pressing issues of the day, and the UN in particular was called upon to extend its influence. This led to a dramatic increase in the number of UN-mandated peacekeeping operations and in interventions sanctioned by the Security Council under Chapter VII of the UN Charter (see Chapter 5). Additionally, the internationalization of previously domestic issues led to significant developments in international law. The International Criminal Tribunal for the former Yugoslavia (ICTY) was established in 1993, and similar tribunals were later established in Rwanda, Sierra Leone, Cambodia and East Timor. The most notable consequence of this process occurred in 1998 when the General Assembly voted to establish the International Criminal Court, with unprecedented powers to prosecute individuals for genocide, war crimes, crimes against humanity and crimes of aggression.

The internationalization of human rights had two major effects. First, it ensured that the domestic human rights record of states became a legitimate issue for discussion at the international level. Previously, during the Cold War, adherence to human rights was essentially deemed a domestic concern, and, strange as it may now seem, the dominant perspective within the discipline of IR was that human rights was not an appropriate issue for research (Lu, 2006, pp. 5–6). Second, it raised expectations about the capacity of the international community to solve intrastate humanitarian crises both within the West and indeed amongst those suffering at the hands of repressive governments (Kuperman, 2003). Since 1945 extensive human rights legislation had been codified in international law, although the suffocating effects of the Cold War negated the enforcement of these laws. With international cooperation now more feasible, the world was said to be entering an era of enforcement (Robertson, 2002).

Yet while human rights became a central issue in IR and expectations were raised about the capacity of the international community, and especially the UN, to enforce these rights, a number of crises demonstrated that the new international order was neither able, nor indeed willing, to act *whenever* egregious human rights violations occurred. The violence in the Balkans in the early 1990s and, most influentially, the genocide in Rwanda in 1994 graphically illustrated the ongoing limitations in human rights enforcement. The international mood had changed, however, and whereas during the Cold War inaction in the face of human rights abuses was often lamented as tragic but prudent, in the 1990s support for such caution declined. The rise of liberalism, as discussed in the preceding section, coupled with the heightened awareness of humanitarian crises caused by the internationalization of human rights and the communication revolution (see the following section), raised expectations, and the demand for action led to the emergence of a conviction that unilateral humanitarian intervention could be legitimate. Many argued that progressive liberal states should not desist from intervening to protect people from their own governments simply because one of the permanent five members of the Security Council vetoed such action (Bellamy, 2002, p. 212). NATO's intervention in Kosovo in 1999 (see Chapter 11) was indicative of this perspective and propelled the issue of unilateral humanitarian intervention to the top of the international agenda; the invasion of Iraq in 2003 ensured that it stayed there (see Chapter 12).

Globalization and the communication revolution

The process of globalization did not begin only when the Cold War ended, for the spread of capitalism which followed the collapse of communism certainly facilitated its acceleration. Open borders, free trade and competition are central to capitalism, and as these principles spread around the world they had significant implications for global communication.

First, increased competition led to rapid technological innovation in the communication sector, leading to advances in satellite communication, the exponential growth of the internet and a greater ability to broadcast live from around the world. Increased global trade meant that events in one part of the world had implications for businesses thousands of miles away. Hence, interest in global events increased due to accelerated economic interdependence. Additionally, the 1990s witnessed a great increase in the sources of information, as new radio and television channels emerged in competition with state-owned media. As the audiences for media sources grew, so did the need to broadcast 24 hours a day to appeal to global audiences in different time zones. With a greater number of channels broadcasting for a longer amount of time, the need for news stories grew, and reporters were sent across the globe to feed this growing appetite.

Human suffering, macabre as it may be, generates great public interest, and thus news reports from crisis areas are a virtual guarantee of high audience ratings. Live 'on the spot' reporting has the benefit of immediacy, though arguably at the expense of context and background; faced with scenes of carnage and death, reporters parachuted into trouble spots have been accused of focusing on the emotive tales of suffering and making ill-founded determinations that X was an aggressor and Y a victim so as to enable audiences to engage quickly with what was happening (Kuperman, 2003). These simple narratives were certainly comprehensible to foreign audiences but often obscured the true causes of conflict. Thus the term 'the CNN effect' was coined to describe the new influence of the media on public opinion: presented with an obvious 'bad guy' and a 'helpless victim', people saw these crises as resolvable if an external force intervened to stop the aggressor from attacking the victim (Hammond, 2002, p. 176). The growth of advocacy journalism in the 1990s witnessed the explicit commitment amongst certain journalists to take sides and proffer policy proposals. Thus the superficial presentation of the dynamics of a conflict, and the explicit support afforded to one party to the conflict, shaped public opinion and led audiences to conclude that the solution was humanitarian intervention. An additional problematic feature of the rise in influence of the media was that, as the International Commission on Intervention and State Sovereignty (ICISS) cautioned, many conflicts in inaccessible or unattractive parts of the world went unreported, and thus the media reportage often 'skew[ed] the response of the international community in an inconsistent and undisciplined manner' (ICISS, 2001a, pp. 5–6).

In tandem with the communication revolution, the number of NGOs increased exponentially during the 1990s, particularly in the first half of the decade (Anheier et al., 2001). A great number of these NGOs were committed to highlighting human rights abuses and raising public awareness so that this would generate domestic pressure for action within Western states. The rapid proliferation of humanitarian NGOs and the increased capacity of the global media had reciprocal benefits: the NGOs exploited the new media, especially the internet, to disseminate their work, while the media used the reports of these NGOs as a source of information and news, thereby spreading the findings of these NGOs.

The result, therefore, was that in the post-Cold War era 'public opinion is better informed (the CNN effect) about geographically remote conflicts, and less tolerant therefore of inactivity on the part of their own governments' (Moxon-Browne, 1998, p. 192). Situations in 'unimportant' parts of the world, such as Kosovo and Somalia, became matters for domestic debate within Western states in the 1990s, in contrast to the Cold War era, in large part because of the communication revolution and the proselytizing of NGOs.

In summary then, we can see that the coincidence of three dynamics – one ideological, one structural and one technological – unique to the post-Cold War era contrived to propel humanitarian intervention to the top of the international political agenda. Events throughout 2011 in the Arab World amply demonstrated the ongoing influence of these dynamics: protestors demanding democracy cried out for Western military support via new technologies, such as Facebook, Twitter and YouTube, while NGOs and media organizations relentlessly broadcast scenes of carnage. While there is much evidence to support the view that the coincidence of these three dynamics explains the rise of humanitarian intervention in the post-Cold War era, it is of course not universally accepted. Certain observers argue that the increased focus on human rights and the new appetite for intervention has had a more nefarious genesis, namely the attempt to further empower Western states by legitimizing intervention through the invention of a new foreign policy rationale which legitimized the armaments industry in the absence of the threat posed by communism and created a conceptual distinction between the civilized core and the barbarous hinterland (Chandler, 2000a; Chomsky, 2011, Orford, 2011). The contested nature of arguably every aspect of humanitarian intervention is, however, one of the reasons that this is such a fascinating subject.

Using this book

This book has three parts. Part I focuses on the foundational concepts central to, and the theoretical basis for, humanitarian intervention. Part II examines the key sources of controversy which have generated the most heated discussion. Part III provides a brief overview of the history of humanitarian intervention and empirical insights into key case studies in the post-Cold War era which have brought together the concepts and controversies noted in Parts I and II.

This book is an introduction to humanitarian intervention, and while I have highlighted as many different perspectives on this issue as possible, what follows is not exhaustive. It is simply not feasible to examine the entire spectrum of perspectives on humanitarian intervention, and although this book is possibly more comprehensive than any other, it is not definitive. Additionally, there are many more case studies which have influenced the trajectory of this debate than the five discussed in Part III (see Wheeler, 2002).

My intention in each chapter is to provide the reader with an insight into differing perspectives on each issue. This book is not designed to support any one viewpoint or privilege a particular school of thought. Rather I consciously aim to provoke the reader's interest by raising more questions than I answer. Understanding humanitarian intervention is not possible by simply accumulating facts, as there are very few uncontested 'facts' as such. The key to engaging with this issue is to read widely, engage with different perspectives and form an opinion based on your accumulated knowledge.

The bibliography lists all the sources used in this book, and following the usual convention there are extensive references throughout each chapter which can be used as a guide to certain perspectives and insights. There are myriad journal articles on this issue, and a number of academic journals are particularly rich sources of information (see Box I.1).

Box I.1   Key journals on humanitarian intervention

American Journal of International Law
Civil Wars
Ethics and International Affairs
European Journal of International Law
European Journal of International Relations
Foreign Affairs
Global Governance
Global Responsibility to Protect
Global Society
Human Rights Law Review
International Affairs
International Journal of Human Rights
International Peacekeeping
International Relations

Journal of Human Rights
Journal of International Law and International Relations
Journal of Intervention and Statebuilding
Journal of Peace Research
Millennium
New Perspectives Quarterly
Political Studies
Review of International Studies
Security Dialogue
Survival
Third World Quarterly
World Politics

Box I.2 Key contemporary authors on humanitarian intervention

Daniele Archibugi	Luke Glanville	Anne Orford
Mohammed Ayoob	Michael Glennon	James Pattison
Alex Bellamy	Eric Heinze	Oliver Ramsbotham
Ken Booth	Stanley Hoffmann	Theresa Reinold
Chris Brown	J. L. Holzgrefe	Nicholas Rengger
Ian Brownlie	Ian Hurd	Adam Roberts
Alan Buchanan	Robert Jackson	Gerry Simpson
Michael Byers	Mary Kaldor	Karen E. Smith
Richard Caplan	Robert O. Keohane	Michael Smith
Antonio Cassese	Alan Kuperman	Jane Stromseth
David Chandler	Anthony Lang	Fernando Tesón
Noam Chomsky	Andrew Linklater	Ramesh Thakur
Simon Chesterman	Mahmood Mamdani	Alex de Waal
Jean Cohen	Richard Miller	Michael Walzer
Philip Cunliffe	Kurt Mills	Thomas Weiss
Neta Crawford	Justin Morris	Jennifer Welsh
Tim Dunne	Terry Nardin	Nicholas Wheeler
Richard Falk	Mary Ellen O'Connell	Paul Williams
Tom Farer	Cian O'Driscoll	Tom Woodhouse

Each chapter has a 'Further reading' section which highlights literature specifically relevant to that chapter. This is not a definitive list, and the references in each chapter should be the primary source of guidance to relevant literature. Many academics specialize in humanitarian intervention, and their lists of publications, usually available through their university websites, should be explored. Box I.2 lists a number of scholars whose work is particularly apposite, although there are many more active in this field. (Apologies to those not listed!) There are additionally a number of key documents – reports, resolutions, declarations, etc. – which are referred to throughout this book and the literature more generally; it is thus useful to familiarize yourself with the content of these and Box I.3 lists many of those commonly cited which are available online (again, this list is not exhaustive, particularly with respects to key Security Council resolutions). The websites of a number of NGOs, such as the International Coalition for the Responsibility to Protect and the Global Center for the Responsibility to Protect, contain links to many of these documents, as well as assorted commentaries.

Box I.3   Key resolutions/reports/agreements

1945   UN Charter. Available at www.un.org/en/documents/charter/index.shtml.

1948   General Assembly Resolution 260, 'Convention on the Prevention and Punishment of the Crime of Genocide'. Available at www.hrweb. org/legal/genocide.html.

1948   Universal Declaration of Human Rights. Available at www.un. org/en/ documents/udhr/index.shtml.

1950   General Assembly Resolution 377, 'Uniting for Peace'. Available at www.un.org/depts/dhl/resguide/r5.htm.

1965   General Assembly Resolution 2131, 'Declaration on the Inadmissibility of Intervention in the Domestic Affairs of States'. Available at www.un.org/depts/dhl/resguide/r20.htm.

1975   Conference on Security and Cooperation in Europe, 'The Helsinki Final Act'. Available at http://chnm.gmu.edu/1989/archive/files/helsinki-accords_f9de6be034.pdf.

1990   Security Council Resolution 688, 'On the Iraq Invasion of Kuwait'. Available at www.un.org/Docs/scres/1991/scres91.htm.

1992   Report of the UN Secretary General, Boutros Boutros-Ghali, 'An Agenda for Peace'. Available at www.unrol.org/files/A_47_ 277.pdf.

1994   Security Council Resolution 940, 'on authorization to form a multinational force under unified command ... to restore the legitimately elected President and authorities of the Government of Haiti'. Available at www.un.org/Docs/scres/1994/scres94.htm.

1995   Report by the Carnegie Commission on Preventing Deadly Conflict, 'Preventing Deadly Conflict: Final Report'. Available at ww.janeliunas.lt/files/Preventing%20Deadly%20Conflict.doc.

1999   Security Council Resolution 1265, 'On the Protection of Civilians in Armed Conflict'. Available at http://www.un.org/en/sc/documents/resolutions/1999.shtml.

→

The questions at the end of each chapter should ideally be answered without referring back to the text of the chapter in which they appear. It is not imperative that these questions be answered immediately: they are indicative of the type of questions asked when discussing the issues raised in the chapter, and therefore should be referred to when more research has been undertaken.

1999 Report by the Danish Institute for International Affairs, 'Humanitarian Intervention: Legal and Political Aspects'. Available at www.diis.dk/graphics/Publications/Andet/ Humanitarian_ Intervention_1999.pdf.

2000 Report by the Independent International Commission on Kosovo, 'Kosovo Report'. Available at www.cfr.org/kosovo/independent-international-commission-kosovo-kosovo-report-executive-summary/p25962.

2001 Report by the International Commission on Intervention and State Sovereignty, 'The Responsibility to Protect'. Available at http://responsibilitytoprotect.org/ICISS%20Report.pdf.

2004 Report of the Secretary General's High-Level Panel on Threats, Challenges and Change, 'A More Secure World: Our Shared Responsibility'. Available at www.un.org/secureworld/report2. pdf.

2005 Report of the UN Secretary General Kofi Annan, 'In Larger Freedom: Towards Development, Security and Human Rights for All'. Available at www.un.org/largerfreedom/.

2005 World Summit Outcome Document. Available at www.un.org/ summit2005/documents.html.

2009 Report of the UN Secretary General Ban Ki-moon, 'Implementing the Responsibility to Protect: Report of the Secretary General'. Available at www.responsibilitytoprotect.org/index.php/edward-luck/2105-secretary-general-ban-kimoon-report-implementing-the-responsibility-to-protect.

2009 General Assembly Debate on the Responsibility to Protect. Available at www.responsibilitytoprotect.org/index.php/component/content/ article/35-r2pcs-topics/2493-general-assembly-debate-on-the-responsibility-to-protect-and-informal-interactive-dialogue-.

2011 Security Council Resolution 1973, 'The Situation in Libya'. Available at www.un.org/Docs/sc/unsc_resolutions11.htm.

2011 Letter from Brazil to the UN Secretary General, 'Responsibility While Protecting'. Available at www.globalr2p.org/media/pdf/ Concept-Paper-_RwP.pdf.

Part I

Concepts and Conceptions

Chapter 1

What is 'Humanitarian Intervention'?

One of the dominant controversies of our time is the question: What is to be done when a state is unwilling or unable to halt a humanitarian crisis within its own territory? Images and accounts of disasters often generate impassioned calls amongst observers to 'do something' and reignite the debate regarding the rights and responsibilities of states, and the international community, to alleviate suffering abroad. The Arab Spring demonstrated once again that 'humanitarian intervention' is an issue of uniquely broad interest which continues to be hotly debated in the international arena, within academia and in the popular media. While there is general consensus as to the importance of humanitarian intervention, it is also one of the most divisive issues in contemporary international relations.

Ideally, an investigation into the controversy surrounding humanitarian intervention and its impact on international relations would start with a definition of 'humanitarian intervention'. Central to the debate surrounding humanitarian intervention, however, is that the very meaning of the term is itself controversial. As Anthony Lang notes,

> The contention over the meaning of ... 'humanitarian intervention' suggests both the difficulty and importance of definitions. In fact, in trying to define this particular term, two issues arise. First, there is no clearly defined understanding of the term. Second, any definition contains within it certain normative assumptions. (2003, p. 2)

The term is used widely in legal, political and philosophical literature, and the definition employed tends to reflect the field of the analyst. Humanitarian intervention is not, of course, unique in this respect: many terms employed in the social sciences, from 'terrorism' to 'sovereignty', evidence similar definitional controversies, and one could plausibly argue that all key concepts in politics are, to some degree, 'essentially contested'. Despite the acknowledged difficulty in determining precisely what 'humanitarian intervention' is, many have, for reasons of expediency, employed the term with a stated degree of caution. A number of definitions have been offered (see Box 1.2: p. 21), and through an analysis of

15

these a composite definition can be formed which, although it might be contentious itself, at least narrows the parameters of the debate. This is the aim of this chapter.

This chapter comprises two sections. The first narrows the scope for ambiguity by outlining what humanitarian intervention is *not*, by differentiating 'humanitarian intervention' from both 'humanitarian action' and 'strategic military intervention'. The second section highlights those aspects of humanitarian intervention that impact on its definition. This section focuses on, in turn, the status of the parties involved, the question of consent, the means employed, the motives and the issue of legality. These issues are examined here only in terms of their impact on the formulation of a *definition* of humanitarian intervention, not on the process of evaluating the *legitimacy* of a given intervention.

'Humanitarian intervention', 'humanitarian action' and 'military action'

Central to the definitional difficulty, as Lang's earlier quote notes, is the word 'humanitarian'. As we shall explore in greater detail in this chapter, the use of an essentially positive adjective – humanitarian – to describe an intervention largely determines the parameters within which the evaluation of this intervention can proceed. An intervening party that declares its actions to be 'humanitarian' is explicitly attempting to legitimize these actions as non-partisan and moral, and hence inherently justified, rather than selfish and strategic, and hence necessarily contentious. Therefore, in a similar way to branding an act of violence 'terrorism', the term 'humanitarian intervention' carries intrinsic normative assumptions. Hence, the application of this term elevates the legitimizing discourse beyond pure description, making it both subjective and contentious. In this respect the statement 'in March 2003 the USA launched a military intervention against Iraq' constitutes a neutral description of Operation Iraqi Freedom, whereas 'in March 2003 the USA launched a humanitarian intervention into Iraq' is necessarily evaluative and subjective. As ICISS stated, '[the] use in this context of an inherently approving word like "humanitarian" tends to prejudge the very question in issue – that is whether the intervention is in fact defensible' (2001a, p. 9).

One of the key distinctions which must initially be drawn is between 'humanitarian intervention' and 'humanitarian action'. 'Humanitarianism' and 'humanitarian action' are terms widely used among aid workers and NGOs. In this context the term 'humanitarian' is used to denote an altruistic, apolitical concern for human welfare. Cornelio Sommaruga, President of the International Committee of the Red Cross (ICRC), outlined this distinction in an address to the UN General Assembly in 1992:

humanitarian endeavor and political action must go their separate ways if the neutrality and impartiality of humanitarian work is not to be jeopardized ... it is dangerous to link humanitarian activities aimed at meeting the needs of victims of a conflict with political measures designed to bring about the settlement of the dispute between the parties. (Lu, 2006, p. 44)

ICISS avoided using the term 'humanitarian intervention' in its 2001 report partly because of the opposition expressed by humanitarian agencies towards the militarization of the word 'humanitarian' (2001a, p. 9). Kofi Annan's address to a symposium organized by the International Peace Academy (IPA) in 2000 is particularly illustrative of this desire to separate humanitarian action from military intervention. Annan, noting the widespread confusion about the meaning of the term 'humanitarian intervention', called for the preservation of the specific role of humanitarianism:

[We must] get right away from using the term 'humanitarian' to describe military operations ... military intervention should not ... in my view, be confused with humanitarian action. Otherwise, we will find ourselves using phrases like 'humanitarian bombing' and people will soon get very cynical about the whole idea. (Annan, 2000)

Despite Annan's plea, the term 'humanitarian intervention' continues to be used widely – though as discussed in Chapter 6 'responsibility to protect' has arguably achieved greater popularity – and the cynicism he foresaw has indeed become a feature of this debate.

Traditionally humanitarian organizations adopted an apolitical stance, refusing to engage with questions of right or wrong, focusing instead on humanitarian need and relief (Barnett, 2010, p. 2). In recent times, however, the avowal of neutrality has been challenged by so-called 'new humanitarians' who reject the traditional approach. As Fiona Fox notes, 'new humanitarian aid provision is overtly political, embracing a politically conscious aid strategy which, it is argued, can positively impact on the politics of a conflict or post-conflict situation' (2002, p. 19). This clash between 'traditional' and 'new' humanitarianism is exemplified by the different strategies employed by the ICRC and Médecins Sans Frontières (MSF). MSF was established by activists frustrated by the ICRC's neutrality and refusal to condemn publicly human rights violators (see Box 1.1). MSF is one of a number of humanitarian organizations that have begun to focus increasingly on 'human rights' rather than 'human needs', thereby necessarily adopting a political strategy (Barnett, 2010, p. 173).

These new humanitarians have at times been amongst the most vocal supporters of military intervention. Bernard Kouchner, founding member

Box 1.1   Médecins Sans Frontières

According to its website, MSF 'was founded in 1971 as the first nongovern-mental organization to both provide emergency medical assistance and bear witness publicly to the plight of the people it assists. A private nonprofit association, MSF is an international network with sections in 19 countries' (MSF, 2008). MSF has a stated commitment to 'intervene in any country or crisis based solely on an independent assessment of people's needs – not on political, economic, or religious interests. MSF does not take sides or inter-vene according to the demands of governments or warring parties' (ibid.). It also, however, publicly condemns offending regimes and seeks to pressure states and international organizations to take certain actions – including military interventions – against these states.

In 1999 MSF was awarded the Nobel Peace Prize. On accepting the award James Orbinski stated:

> Silence has long been confused with neutrality, and has been presented as a necessary condition for humanitarian action. From the beginning MSF was created in opposition to this assumption. We are not sure that words can always save lives, but we know that silence can certainly kill. (Chandler, 2002, p. 31)

of MSF, has consistently championed the merits of external intervention. He was a particularly vocal supporter of NATO's intervention in Kosovo in 1999 and later supported the overthrow of Saddam Hussein in 2003, albeit with certain provisos (Kouchner, 1999; Sciolino, 2007). Similarly, Human Rights Watch (HRW), in its *World Report 2000*, endorsed the interventions in both Kosovo and East Timor in the previous year and offered a very favourable analysis of the 'international community's ... new willingness to deploy troops to stop crimes against humanity'. HRW urged this trend to continue and heralded 'a new era for the human rights movement' (HRW, 2000).

Thus while humanitarian organizations have been critical of the use of 'humanitarian' as an adjective to describe military intervention, many have adopted an approach that necessarily weakens the distinction between humanitarian action and humanitarian intervention, with groups engaged in the former often overtly calling for the latter. This has been criticized by certain observers who see the blurring of the distinction between military action and humanitarian intervention through the human rights discourse as compromising traditional humanitarian princi-ples (ibid., pp. 21–53; Kennedy, 2009). Many argue that the neutrality of humanitarian organizations has been key to their success, and the new dispensation risks the merging of humanitarianism and Western foreign policy, which would necessarily compromise the status of these groups and potentially make them targets in those conflicts where they have explicitly taken a partisan position (Weiss, 1999).

Humanitarian intervention is additionally different from what may be described as strategic military intervention. The UN Charter is clear about the prohibition of the use of force in international relations; this finds its clearest expression in Article 2.4: 'all members shall refrain in their international relations from the threat or use of force against the territorial integrity or political independence of any state, or in any other manner inconsistent with the Purposes of the UN'. While the use of force is therefore clearly outlawed, certain exceptions to this rule do exist.

Article 51 of the UN Charter permits the use of force in self-defence. Chapter VII of the Charter also permits the use of force, but, unlike Article 51, action taken under Chapter VII must receive prior approval from the Security Council (this is dealt with further in Chapter 5). Under Article 51, states are permitted to employ military force when they have been attacked, although the precise meaning of 'self-defence' has become a particularly contentious issue since the launch of the 'War on Terror' in 2001 (Dinstein, 2005; Hehir, 2008c; Gow, 2011; Jones, 2011). The use of force in response to Iraq's invasion of Kuwait in August 1990 was sanctioned by UN Security Council Resolution 660 and constituted a manifestation of collective self-defence (Dinstein, 2005, pp. 273–7). The stated basis for the intervention was therefore not humanitarian but political. States need not advance any humanitarian rationale for the use of force if acting in self-defence. In fact, as Chapter 5 will demonstrate, humanitarian intervention is widely considered illegal and hence the trend has been for states to offer a legal justification based on Article 51 for instances of military intervention rather than a humanitarian justification, even when the latter was the more obvious impetus. A military intervention can thus be legal and legitimate without being humanitarian.

While the US-led intervention in Kuwait constituted a legal intervention sanctioned by the UN, many illegal military interventions and actions have evidenced a similar lack of an expressed humanitarian motivation. A military intervention is judged illegal if it transgresses international law, regardless of whether the aggressors advanced humanitarian motives or whether, if humanitarian motives were advanced, these motives were accepted as genuine.

Lassa Oppenheim's classic definition of war – 'a contention between two or more states through their armed forces, for the purpose of overpowering each other and imposing such conditions of peace as the victor pleases' (2006, p. 202) – makes no mention of humanitarian intent. It is clear, therefore, that a military intervention need not be a humanitarian intervention, though a humanitarian intervention is widely considered necessarily to constitute a form of military intervention. Of course, the issue becomes more complex when states declare their military actions to be motivated by humanitarianism but these claims are not accepted by the wider international community. Infamously, Hitler portrayed Germany's invasion of Czechoslovakia in 1939 as a humanitarian intervention, though few accepted his claims. In recent years the US-led invasion of Iraq has ignited controversy precisely because of the largely, though not exclusively, *ex post facto* humanitarian justifications offered (see Chapter 12). The issue thus becomes a matter of determining the legitimacy of the claims made (which is the focus of Chapter 5). Of course, before the legitimacy of a putative humanitarian intervention can be determined it is necessary to set down a basic definition of 'humanitarian intervention'. It is to this task that I now turn.

Features of humanitarian intervention

Having distinguished 'humanitarian intervention' from 'humanitarian action' and 'strategic military intervention', this section focuses on those features routinely, though not uniformly, identified as fundamental to 'humanitarian intervention'. Box 1.2 provides a number of definitions of humanitarian intervention which form the basis for the analysis that follows.

The status of the parties involved

In the first instance definitions generally insist that the intervener is a third party to the conflict. J. L Holzgrefe's definition refers to states undertaking action 'aimed at preventing or ending widespread and grave violations of the fundamental human rights of individuals other than its own citizens' (2005, p. 18). Many of the other definitions listed similarly focus on interventions where the subjects whose suffering has prompted the intervention are not citizens of the intervening state. In this respect, we can see that there appears to be some consensus over the relationship between the intervening actor and those in distress. Yet Holzgrefe provides the example of Richard Baxter as a counter to this consensus. Baxter's definition, unusually, describes action taken 'for the protection from death or grave injury of nationals of the acting state' (ibid.).

The precise status and composition of the intervening actor is quite ambiguous; few definitions explicitly identify the intervening actor. They offer instead a broad list of potential interveners, such as John Vincent's 'a state, a group within a state, a group of states or an international organization' (1974, p. 13). This aspect of the definition – the precise

Box 1.2   Definitions of humanitarian intervention

'The proportionate transboundary help, provided by governments to individuals in another state who are being denied basic human rights and who themselves would be rationally willing to revolt against their oppressors.' (Tesón, 1988, p. 1)

'The threat or use of force across state borders by a state (or group of states) aimed at preventing or ending widespread and grave violations of the fundamental human rights of individuals other than its own citizens, without the permission of the state within whose territory force is applied.' (Holzgrefe, 2005, p. 18)

'Action taken against a state or its leaders, without its or their consent, for purposes which are claimed to be humanitarian or protective ... including all forms of preventive measures, and coercive intervention measures – sanctions and criminal prosecutions – falling short of military intervention.' (ICISS, 2001a, p. 8)

'A short-term use of armed force by a government ... for the protection from death or grave injury of nationals of the acting state ... by their removal from the territory of the foreign state.' (Baxter, in Holzgrefe, 2005, p. 18)

'Coercive interference in the internal affairs of a state, involving the use of armed force, with the purposes of addressing massive human rights violations or preventing widespread human suffering.' (Welsh, 2006, p. 3)

'The threat or use of armed force by a state, a belligerent community, or an international organization, with the object of protecting human rights.' (Brownlie, 1974, p. 217)

'[When] the "international community" ... intervene[s] in the domestic affairs of one of its members for humanitarian reasons, which can provisionally be defined as "primarily in the interests of the local inhabitants".' (Brown, 2006, p. 135)

'Activity undertaken by a state, a group within a state, a group of states or an international organization which interferes coercively in the domestic affairs of another state. It is a discrete event having a beginning and an end, and it is aimed at the authority structure of the target state. It is not necessarily lawful or unlawful, but it does break a conventional pattern of international relations.' (Vincent, 1974, p. 13)

'Coercive action by one or more states involving the use of armed force in another state without the consent of its authorities, and with the purpose of preventing widespread suffering or death among the inhabitants.' (Roberts, 2002, p. 5) nature of the intervener – is, therefore, seemingly of minor importance. Provided that the intervening party is not based within the state where the crisis is taking place, the identity and composition of this party – be it a substate, state or trans-state actor – is not deemed significant, at least to the definition of humanitarian intervention, though it is of some legal importance.

The question of consent

Definitions invariably identify humanitarian intervention as an act undertaken without the consent of the host state. States experiencing humanitarian crises can appeal, and have appealed, to the international community for help, resulting in many cases in the deployment of troops from abroad, such as the establishment of the UN Mission in Sierra Leone in October 1999 or Bahrain's 2011 appeal to the Gulf Cooperation Council for military support to help put down the pro-democracy uprising (see Chapter 14).

Jennifer Welsh's definition, however, does not stipulate 'non-consent'. This is because she claims that '"non-consent" is in practice very difficult to maintain – particularly when consent is ambiguous or coerced' (2006, p. 3). Indeed, while the Federal Republic of Yugoslavia (FRY) clearly did not consent to NATO's intervention in 1999, technically Indonesia *did* consent to the deployment of an Australian-led force in East Timor in September 1999. The nature of Indonesia's 'consent' does support Welsh's concerns given that extensive international pressure was brought to bear on the government of B. J. Habibie and the consent eventually given was, to a large degree, a function of coercion (Wheeler and Dunne, 2001). Additionally, as Simon Chesterman argues, the issue of consent is 'not legally significant' in the context of an operation mandated by the Security Council under Chapter VII (2011a, p. 2). The Security Council has the power under Article 42 to take action regardless of whether the host state consents. Beyond this legal technicality, the nature of the 'consent' previously given for certain Security Council operations was as Alex Bellamy and Paul Williams note 'coerced and unreliable' (2011, p. 828). Ian Johnstone, likewise highlights previous instances when 'consent' was 'hardly voluntary and bordered on duress' (2011, p. 170), while Antonio Cassese's analysis of UN authorizations finds that many operations involved only 'partial consent' (2005, p. 345). While the question of coerced consent is a valid one, it is nevertheless clear that the majority view assumes consent to be absent.

The means

The focus of this second section of the chapter is not on the debate surrounding the legitimacy of any given intervention, but rather on identifying those features that are generally included in definitions of 'humanitarian intervention'. Therefore, the focus here on the means employed relates only to how they have been conceived in various definitions, rather than the more controversial issue of how the means impact on the perceived legitimacy of any given intervention (see Chapter 8).

Definitions of 'humanitarian intervention' generally emphasize military means as a central component, as evidenced by Iain Brownlie's 'the threat or use of armed force', a formula emulated by many others (1974, p. 217). As with the previous features analysed, however, there are definitions that do not conform to this view. Fernando Tesón's definition stresses that the means must be 'proportionate ... including forcible', thereby suggesting that 'non-forcible intervention' may still qualify as a humanitarian intervention (1988, p. 1). David Scheffer explicitly emphasizes peaceful means, referring to 'non-forcible methods, namely intervention undertaken without military force' (Holzgrefe, 2005, p. 18).

Perspectives on the issue of means are linked to the question of consent; an emphasis on non-consent will naturally encourage a focus on coercive means, and vice versa. In a literal sense, of course, humanitarian organizations such as Oxfam and Save the Children engage in humanitarian interventions insofar as they intervene in a state for humanitarian purposes. This activity has not, however, been the cause of the controversy surrounding 'humanitarian intervention', and, as stated earlier, one of the clearest differences between 'humanitarian intervention' and the work of Oxfam and others is the use of force. Generally, therefore, the popular conception of 'humanitarian intervention' involves the use of force, if only to facilitate the narrowing of the parameters of the debate.

The motives

Whether an intervention must be inspired by humanitarian motives to qualify as a 'humanitarian intervention' is a highly contentious issue, which is dealt with in detail in Chapter 8. It is clear, however, that many definitions do emphasize humanitarian motivations. While Adam Roberts indicatively states that the purpose must be 'preventing widespread suffering or death among the inhabitants' (2002, p. 5), others have gone further, stressing that the intervention must be motivated solely by altruism and the intervening party must have no interests involved (Miller, 2000a, p. 54). This would appear to be an unreasonably onerous requirement; as Thomas Weiss notes, 'motives behind humanitarian interventions are almost invariably mixed', and this, he argues, does not fundamentally undermine an intervention (2007a, p. 7). Chris Brown's requirement that the intervention be 'primarily in the interests of the local inhabitants' possibly best reflects opinion on this aspect of the debate (2006, p. 135). Indicatively, Ramesh Thakur heralded NATO's 2011 intervention in Libya but acknowledged that it occurred because 'the West's strategic interests coincided with UN values' (2011).

Nicholas Wheeler, however, does not place importance on the motives behind an intervention, and focuses instead solely on the outcome. He suggests that interventions motivated by humanitarian intent are certainly more laudable, but interventions impelled by self-interested motives which have positive humanitarian consequences 'should be legitimised by states and not condemned or sanctioned' (2002, p. 39). While this view is endorsed by others, it is a minority position, with most definitions including at least some reference to humanitarian motives. Of course, an individual's perspective on this aspect of the definition of 'humanitarian intervention' will have significant implications on his or her judgement regarding the legitimacy of a given intervention (Heinze, 2009, p. 123).

The issue of legality

One of the primary sources of controversy surrounding humanitarian intervention is its legal status (Hurd, 2011). While there is some disagreement over the legality of humanitarian interventions, the majority of legal scholars consider it to be illegal at present. This, however, does not necessarily have implications for the legitimacy of an intervention; indicatively, NATO's intervention in Kosovo in 1999 was judged by the Independent International Commission on Kosovo (IICK) to have been 'illegal but legitimate' (IICK, 2000, p. 4).

The definitions in Box 1.2 evidence little reference to legality, and those that do mention it are ambivalent. When we examine the definitions provided it is clear that many refer to coercive acts undertaken without the consent of the host state. Given that non-consent implies a breach of sovereignty and, as discussed earlier, such action is prohibited under international law, these acts are by definition illegal as they do not constitute acts of self-defence. If international law is mentioned in definitions it is only to assert that it is not integral to whether a particular act constitutes a humanitarian intervention. In this respect the question of legality has little real impact on the definition of 'humanitarian intervention'.

Conclusion

As Alex Bellamy notes, 'almost every aspect of humanitarian intervention is contested' (2006b, p. 202), and hence defining 'humanitarian intervention' is naturally difficult and contentious. The difficulty that surrounds the definition of the term derives largely from the normative assumptions inherent in the word 'humanitarian'. In this sense, the use of this subjective adjective necessarily complicates the formation of an objective definition, given that the word 'humanitarian', to a large extent, constitutes a positive value judgement. Catherine Lu suggests that the term should be abandoned in favour of 'label[ling] interventions in terms of the substantive activities that define them'. In this way NATO's Operation Allied Force would simply be described as a 'military intervention' (Lu, 2006, p. 139). Similarly Antonio Cassese avoids the use of the term 'humanitarian intervention', preferring the more legally descriptive 'forcible countermeasures to prevent crimes against humanity' (1999, p. 29).

These are valid concerns, yet while attempts have been made to change the terms of the discourse, most notably by the ICISS, 'humanitarian intervention' remains an oft used, though possibly misused, term. This is unlikely to change given how embedded the term has become in the public and academic lexicon though, as discussed in Chapter 6, 'responsibility to protect' is arguably more often used today, though its remit is considerably wider. The pragmatic approach, therefore, is to conform to the prevailing discourse, accept that the term will continue to be used, and try to clarify its distinctive features. To this end, for the sake of further inquiry and based on the above analysis of existing definitions, the following definition constitutes the type of act to which all subsequent uses of the term 'humanitarian intervention' in this book refer:

> Military action taken by a state, group of states or non-state actor, in the territory of another state, without that state's consent, which is justified, to some significant extent, by a humanitarian concern for the citizens of the host state.

This composite definition is clearly not a legal definition, nor is it without contention, but it serves to differentiate 'humanitarian intervention' from 'humanitarian action' and 'strategic military intervention', and thus significantly narrows the parameters of inquiry. The legality, morality, legitimacy and broader implications of such an action for international relations and international law remain outstanding, and these issues constitute the remaining focus of this book.

Questions

- Does the term 'humanitarian intervention' carry intrinsic normative assumptions?
- How can we distinguish 'humanitarian intervention' from 'humanitarian action'?
- How does 'humanitarian intervention' differ from 'strategic military intervention'?
- Based on existing definitions, what are the key features of humanitarian intervention?
- Is 'humanitarian intervention' a useful term or is it inherently flawed?

Further reading

Bellamy, A. and Wheeler, N. (2010) 'Humanitarian Intervention in World Politics' in J. Baylis and S. Smith (eds), *The Globalization of World Politics* (Oxford: Oxford University Press).

Chesterman, S. (2002) *Just War or Just Peace?* (Oxford: Oxford University Press), Chapter 1.

Dinstein, Y. (2011) *War, Aggression and Self-Defence* (Cambridge: Cambridge University Press), Chapter 3.

Holzgrefe, J.L. and Keohane, R. (eds) (2005) *Humanitarian Intervention: Ethical, Legal and Political Dilemmas* (Cambridge: Cambridge University Press), Chapter 1.

International Commission on Intervention and State Sovereignty (2001) *The Responsibility to Protect: Research, Bibliography, Background* (Ottawa: International Development Research Center), Chapter 2.

Lang, A. (ed.) (2003) *Just Intervention* (Washington DC: Georgetown University Press), Chapter 1.

Weiss, T. (2007) *Humanitarian Intervention: War and Conflict in the Modern World* (London: Polity), 2nd ed. 2012, Chapter 1.

Welsh, J. (ed.) (2006) *Humanitarian Intervention and International Relations* (Oxford: Oxford University Press), Chapter 1.

Wheeler, N. (2002) *Saving Strangers* (Oxford: Oxford University Press), Chapter 1.

Chapter 2

The Just War Tradition and Natural Law

The contemporary debate on humanitarian intervention focuses on the question of when it is right – or just – to use force. It is not surprising therefore that those engaged in this debate have drawn upon the rich philosophical lineage of the Just War tradition. The extent to which the contemporary debate employs the language of the tradition is clear; the tradition's key criteria – just cause, right authority, last resort and proportional means – are the central foci of the modern discourse and have been employed by both proponents and opponents of various interventions (O'Driscoll, 2008).

Humanity's propensity to engage in warfare is an obvious feature of our history. This tendency has catalysed many moral and legal texts seeking variously to critique, restrain and justify the resort to force (Evans, 2005a, p. 1). In response to the prevalence of war, certain religious and moral theories have espoused pacifism, the absolute prohibition of force. Conversely some 'realist' perspectives view war as an inevitable feature of human existence which defies moral appraisal (see Chapter 4). As Chris Brown notes, 'neither position sees a moral problem associated with the use of military force; force is either unproblematically wrong (pacifism) or simply morally unproblematic (realism)' (2006, p. 100). The question of whether a war can be 'just' therefore excludes realists and pacifists. Just War theorists do not endorse or promote violence, however. Rather, it is with great reluctance that many have advanced the position that under certain extreme circumstances the use of force is permissible. The tradition represents an attempt, therefore, to delineate these circumstances, and constitutes 'a two-thousand-year old conversation about the legitimacy of war' (Bellamy, 2006b, p. 2).

This chapter is divided into three sections. The first section outlines the key tenets of the tradition and the widely proffered, though controversial, tripartite division of the tradition's principles. The second section traces the evolution of the tradition, outlining the key thinkers, events and themes that have shaped its tenets and contemporary form. The final section addresses the contemporary status of the tradition and the manner in which it has often come to be used controversially as a checklist legitimizing intervention.

The central tenets

The Just War tradition comprises many disparate influences – and there are significant differences between its key proponents. Thus as A. J. Coates argues, 'the unity that is the Just War tradition embraces many formulations that condend one with another and that defy uniform classification' (2006, p. 59). The diversity inherent in the Just War tradition does not undermine its status as a 'tradition', however, as traditions, according to Nicholas Rengger, 'can have many roots ... traditions as I understand them do not have an essence or a central core' (2002, p. 362). The now commonly used term, 'Just War theory', is perhaps less applicable, however; O'Donovan asserts that the Just War tradition is neither a theory nor is it about just wars, but that it is rather a 'proposal for doing justice in the theatre of war' (Rengger, 2005, p. 152).

It is important to outline initially what the Just War tradition is not. The impetus behind the Just War tradition was to create a means by which war could be evaluated, not a means to justify war. The key theorists associated with this tradition conceived of war as always lamentable but justifiable *in extremis*. The fact that certain wars could be judged as justifiable did not constitute an endorsement of those wars, or war more generally, but rather an acknowledgement that 'there are some wrongs that are worse than the wrong of war itself' (Bellamy, 2006b, p. 3).

There are many sub-traditions with very different philosophical orientations and ideological dispositions. These sub-traditions are united, according to Alex Bellamy, by three common factors. First is a shared concern that the recourse to war should be limited and the manner in which it is fought constrained. Second is a common origin in Western traditions of theological, legal and philosophical thought. Third the thinkers involved endorse a common set of rules governing the decision to wage war and the manner in which it is fought, although 'they differ in both their interpretations of the rules and the relative weight they attach to them' (ibid., p. 4).

In relation to the third commonality mentioned, there is, Robert Myers notes, 'little argument about the criteria', and the basic template is clear (1996, p. 118). The tenets of the Just War tradition are invariably divided into two categories of criteria: those governing the resort to force (*jus ad bellum*) and those governing conduct during war (*jus in bello*). A third category concerning justice after war (*jus post bellum*) has more recently been added (Orend, 2000). Rengger rejects the idea of creating a third category, however, arguing that this is already implicit in the tradition (2005, p. 154). Thus, the judgement of war undertaken through this framework comprises an assessment of the motives, the methods and the post-conflict policies pursued by the intervening actors. Each of the three categories contains a series of related criteria as outlined in Box 2.1.

Box 2.1   The Just War criteria

Jus ad bellum

1   Right intention: those using force must be motivated to do so by just rather than expedient intentions.
2   Just cause: force must only be used to correct or prevent a grave injustice.
3   Proportionality of ends: the anticipated benefits of using force must outweigh the injustice being addressed.
4   Last resort: force should only be used after all peaceful means have been exhausted or are clearly not viable.
5   Likelihood of success: force must only be used if there is a strong likelihood of military victory.
6   Right authority: only recognized public authorities have the right to authorize the use of force.
7   Proper declaration: the resort to force must be publicly declared and publicly justified.

Jus in bello

1   Discrimination: force must only be directed against aggressors and never against civilians or non-combatants.
2   Proportionality: the force used should be the minimum necessary to achieve victory and proportionate to the original aggression.
3   Just conduct: all national and international laws governing the use of force must be obeyed in the course of the military action.

Jus post bellum

1   Just peace: the final settlement should be publicly declared, reasonable and fair.
2   Proportionality: the aim of the settlement should be to confirm those rights initially violated.
3   Discrimination: the settlement should discriminate between the leaders, the military and the civilians of that group held responsible for the violence.
4   Responsibility: aggressors, on both sides, must be punished in a fair and accountable manner.
5   Compensation: innocent victims, on all sides, must be compensated for their losses.

The very idea of dividing the tenets of the tradition in this way is rejected by some, who see this as having led to the erroneous separation of *jus ad bellum* from *jus in bello* and the encouragement of a 'checklist' approach in the contemporary era (O'Donovan, 2003, p. 15; Rengger, 2005, p. 153; Connelly and Carrick, 2011, p. 45). The major criticisms and controversies surrounding the utility and application of the Just War tradition are explored in the final section of this chapter. The next section outlines key influences on the evolution of the tradition.

The evolution of the Just War tradition

It is not possible to chart the evolution of the Just War tradition comprehensively here. The tradition spans over 2,000 years of history, has been influenced by a great many thinkers and events, and does not constitute a continuous line of like-minded philosophers working in relay. Rather it comprises 'different streams of thought' which intermittently interweave, collide and separate (Bellamy, 2006b, p. 7). This section seeks only to identify the contribution of certain influential thinkers and highlight the context in which they wrote (see Box 2.2).

The tradition has been strongly influenced by religious thinking and Christianity in particular; indeed, James Turner Johnston describes it as 'the collected consensus of the Christian culture of the West on the justified use of force, set squarely within the normative consensus on the purpose of

---

Box 2.2   Key texts in the Just War tradition

Cicero (106–43 BC): *De officiis*, 44 BC.
St Ambrose (337–97): *De officiis*, 388–90.
St Augustine (354–430): *The City of God*, 413–18.
Gratian of Bologna (birth/death unknown–c. mid-12th century): *Decretum*, 1140.
St Aquinas (1224–74): *Summa Theologiae*, 1265–74.
Francisco de Vitoria (1492–1546): *On the American Indians*, 1539.
Alberico Gentili (1552–1608): *On the Law of War*, 1589.
Hugo Grotius (1583–1645): *On the Law of War and Peace*, 1625.
Samuel von Pufendorf (1632–94): *On The Law of Nature and Nations*, 1672.
Emerich de Vattel (1714–67): *The Law of Nations*, 1758.
Immanuel Kant (1724–1804): *Perpetual Peace*, 1795.
Francis Lieber (1798–1872): *General Orders No. 100*, 1863.
Michael Walzer (1935–): *Just and Unjust Wars*, 1977.

political power' (2005, p. 14). It would be wrong, however, to conceive of the tradition as exclusively Christian or even religious, especially in its later phases (Donnelly, 1989, p. 60; Boyle, 2006, p. 31). Evidence from across the non-Western world shows that the ethics of war have been debated, in some form, for millennia (Nardin, 1998; Christopher, 2004, pp. 9–11). Rengger, however, accepts that the tradition does have a clear Christian and Western foundation but argues that this is unproblematic as it does not preclude its prescriptions from having universal applicability (2002, p. 326).

The oft-quoted progenitor of the Just War tradition is St Augustine of Hippo (354–430), although the tradition's lineage can be traced back further; the work of the Roman statesman and philosopher Cicero (106–43 BC) was of particular influence on Augustine (Bellamy, 2006b, pp. 19–20). Before the 4th century AD the Christian church avowed an outright prohibition on the use of force in keeping with Jesus's instruction: 'if someone slaps you on the right cheek, turn and offer him your left'. Jesus taught that life on earth was but a transitory phase where one's behaviour would determine one's status in the infinite afterlife (Evans, 2005a, p. 2). Hence, death was not to be feared as much as sin, leading to the idealization of sacrifice and martyrdom. The dominant posthumous interpretation of Jesus's teachings emphasized his pacifism and rejected the idea that war could ever be 'just' (Elshtain, 1992, p. 44).

During Augustine's time, however, this principle became increasingly untenable. The adherence to pacifism amongst Christians, epitomized by their stoic sacrifices in the Colosseum at Rome, certainly derived from a strict reading of Jesus's commandments but was also inspired by the belief in the imminent Second Coming (Johnson, 1987, pp. 14–17). By the end of the 2nd century AD, however, belief in the return of Christ had waned, there were many Christians in the Roman army and the Church had begun to find an accommodation with the Empire. Thus, the timing of Augustine's work has led to speculation about the motivation behind the changes wrought by his theory. Augustine wrote at a time when the Roman Empire was under constant threat. Rome was eventually sacked by the Visigoths in 411 and Augustine's own city, Hippo in North Africa, faced the threat of invasion throughout his time there, eventually falling to the Vandals the year after he died. The relative order established by Rome was manifestly more attractive to the Church than the prospect of a Europe divided amongst pagan tribes.

In 312 Emperor Constantine converted to Christianity, which by the end of the 4th century was made the official religion of the Roman Empire by Emperor Theodosius I. Given the Roman Empire's reliance on military might, the conversion to a pacifist religion was problematic. The creation of a framework for legitimizing warfare was obviously attractive to both

Rome and the Church; as Mark Evans notes, 'unsurprisingly, then, it is at this juncture that the Just War tradition is thought to receive its major initial stimulus' (2005a, p. 2). According to Myers the Church was determined to cultivate a relationship with the Roman Empire so as to have some protection against the 'barbarians' massing on the Empire's periphery. To facilitate the union the Church 'turned its back on Christ and the New Testament, and thus Christianity in favour of tales of heroic warriors in the Old Testament and certain creatively interpreted passages of the New Testament (Myers, 1996, pp. 120–1). Augustine, however, was critical of the Roman Empire's lust for *dominium* and the false nature of *Pax Romana* (Elshtain, 2003a, p. 105).

Augustine, building on the work of St Ambrose (337–97), highlighted certain sections of the Bible and pronouncements made by Jesus which suggested that force, though always regrettable, could be legitimate (Deane, 1963, p. 154). He argued that pacifism was neither a divine law nor a reasonable course of action given that earthly life was necessarily fraught with danger and violence:

> Whoever hopes for this so great good [perpetual peace] in this world, and in this earth, his wisdom is but folly ... For in the very great mutability of human affairs such great security is never given to any people, that it should not dread invasions hostile to this life. (Augustine, in ibid., p. 155)

Augustine determined that the sin of violence lay not in the act itself but in the motivations behind the act. He argued that force was justified if the intention was just and if the act was ordered by a just ruler. It followed, therefore, that a soldier carrying out the orders of his ruler was acting justly as it was not he who had decided to kill and he personally took no pleasure in killing. War could be justified if waged on four grounds: in self-defence, to collect reparations or reclaim stolen property, if divinely sanctioned, and to maintain religious orthodoxy (Bellamy, 2006b, p. 28).

The role of the authority ordering the use of force is of paramount importance in Augustine's schema. The state in itself was neither moral nor good but its utility lay in its instrumental value – that of providing the forum for adherence to, and the application of, God's laws. He argued that war could only justifiably be waged by states. This clearly state-centric conception is understandable, however, when one considers that Augustine's religious convictions held that humans can never achieve true justice or righteousness, and that it was God who ultimately rewards and punishes. The temporal abuse of the framework he avows is therefore insignificant given the capacity of God to punish wicked rulers.

In 395 the Roman Empire permanently divided into its Western and Eastern parts, and by 476 the Western Empire had effectively fallen after a defeat to Germanic tribes. The aftermath of Rome's collapse, the so-called 'Dark Ages', witnessed the emergence of many rival groups and widespread violence throughout Europe. This disaggregated order was not a propitious environment in which to preach restraint, and the disposition advocated by Augustine was ignored in favour of a militaristic culture (Johnson, 1987, p. 58). Certain groups adopted the iconography of the church and the idea of divinely sanctioned war but ignored the more restrictive elements of Christian thinking (Bainton, 1986, p. 103). The Church's attempt to reassert its dominance eventually evolved into the launching of the crusades, which 'jarringly fused certain Just War ideas with a sanctioning of morally unmitigated violence against unbelievers' (Evans, 2005a, p. 3). The siege of Jerusalem in 1099 by Christian crusaders led to the massacre of some 70,000 Muslims, after which Raymond of Aguilers declared, 'it was a just and splendid judgment of God that this place should be filled with the blood of unbelievers' (Bellamy, 2006b, pp. 46–7). Augustine's endorsement of divinely sanctioned war had become an abused tenet of his teaching embraced in isolation by warmongering zealots.

Writing during the last years of the crusades, St Thomas Aquinas (1225–74) built on the work of Augustine and those related aspects of canon law to produce 'a short, clear statement [which] provided what is probably the classic statement of the traditional just war theory' (Boyle, 2006, p. 35). Aquinas did not separate *jus ad bellum* from *jus in bello*, and articulated a view clearly based on the earlier Augustinian perspective. Aquinas rejected the notion of a 'crusade' and preached a reactive doctrine (Evans, 2005a, p. 3).

In the *Summa Theologiae* Aquinas stated that war could be justified only if three conditions were met:

> Firstly, the authority of the ruler at whose command war is to be waged ... Secondly, there is required a just cause: that is that those who are attacked for some offence should merit the attack ... Thirdly, there is required, on the part of the belligerents, a right intention, by which it is intended that good may be accomplished or evil avoided. (Boucher and Kelly, 2003, p. 122)

In terms of proper authority, Aquinas stated that only the head of the state (or polity) can rightfully order war as, uniquely, 'rulers have the right to safeguard that public order against external enemies by using the sword of war' (Finnis, 1998, p. 284). Aquinas, like Augustine, argued that private citizens and public officials were bound by different rules (Bellamy, 2006b,

p. 26). Aquinas did not outline a list of potential just causes, but argued that such a cause would involve a reaction to harm done by others to one's state, including, controversially, punitive action. As Joseph Boyle notes, this punitive element is today rejected both by positive law and, perhaps more relevantly, Catholic doctrine (2006, p. 39). With respect to right intention Aquinas draws on Augustine's writing to condemn those who fight for reasons of revenge, hatred or power even if the initial two criteria are met. Self-defence on the part of a state was self-evidently just so long as it was a necessity caused by unprovoked attack (Boucher, 1998, p. 198). His doctrine of double effect (see Box 2.3) additionally sanctioned action which caused unintended harm provided the intention and the outcome were just and the harm caused was unavoidable and unintended. Aquinas's emphasis on right intention, according to Robert Holmes, 'means that one must intend to promote the good and avoid evil; merely having a just cause and legitimate authority is insufficient' (1992, p. 200).

The Western Schism in 1378 divided the Western Christian church and resulted in three separate popes claiming rightful authority. This led to the declaration of crusades against fellow Christians, thus highlighting the subjective nature of 'divinely' sanctioned war. The excesses of the crusades did much to undermine the idea of a divinely sanctioned war and led to the emergence of 'natural law' as the preferred moral reference point (Evans, 2005a, p. 3). The universalism ostensibly inherent in natural law enabled the eventual emergence of international law, conceived as a universally applicable positive expression of natural law.

During the 14th and 15th centuries the conduct of war rather than its inception became the dominant focus with the development of the chivalric code (Bellamy, 2006b, pp. 40–4). The 'discovery' of America in the late 15th century and subsequent European colonization led to increased speculation about how the indigenous peoples – routinely described as

---

Box 2.3   The doctrine of double effect

Unintended negative consequences are excusable if four conditions are satisfied:

1   The desired end must be good in itself.
2   Only the good effect is intended.
3   The good effect must not be produced by means of the evil effect.
4   The good of the good effect must outweigh the evil of the evil effect (proportionality).

(Bellamy, 2006b, p. 124)

savages – should be treated and whether the ethics of warfare then ascendant in Europe should be extended to these peoples.

Francisco de Vitoria's (1492–1546) writings on this issue are of paramount importance to the evolution of Just War thinking Bellamy, 2006b, p. 50). Natural law, according to Vitoria, could be determined without divine revelation. He believed that objectively a war may be just on one side but that only God could truly tell. He wrote:

> where there is provable ignorance either of fact or of law, the war may be just in itself for the side which has true justice on its side, and also just for the other side, because they wage war in good faith and are hence excused from sin. Invincible error is a valid excuse in every case. (Quoted in Bellamy, 2006b, p. 53)

Thus, states could not wage a Just War simply because they felt it was just, and Vitoria suggested that the decision to use force should be taken only after wide consultation, including with those who opposed the use of force. According to David Boucher:

> Vitoria implies that the Law of Nations and customary law are to be equated with human positive law, and not with the Natural Law ... If Natural Law as a dictate of reason prohibits the killing of the innocent, the Law of Nations as a deduction from this determines who are to be regarded as innocent. (1998, p. 200)

Like Augustine and Aquinas, Vitoria argued that citizens should obey their leader and trust their sovereigns. He believed that all commonwealths had the right to declare war provided they were a 'perfect community' – namely self-sufficient and independent (ibid., p. 202). Bellamy notes that this, coupled with the argument that just wars were inherently subjective, 'unwittingly paved the way for later realists and legalists' who used this to claim that, as just wars were impossible to appraise objectively, it should be assumed that wars waged by sovereigns were just (2006b, p. 55).

Vitoria's appraisal of Spain's war on the aboriginals in America contained a provision directly related to the contemporary debate on humanitarian intervention. In outlining permissible grounds for the use of force, he argued that the practice of cannibalism was so contrary to natural law that it was permissible for external forces to intervene to stop it (Boyle, 2006, p. 45). Despite his misgivings about Spanish colonialism, therefore, Vitoria believed that there were certain moral grounds for external interference.

The Dutch lawyer Hugo Grotius (1583–1645) is often referred to as the father of international law. His views were shaped by the holy wars of the 17th century – in particular the Thirty Years War (1618–48) – when opposing sides articulated Just War rationales and claimed divine blessing. Grotius rejected the notion of divinely sanctioned wars and wars to enforce religious orthodoxy and sought to establish a secular natural law basis for the recourse to force. 'Grotius's objective', according to Paul Christopher, 'was to supplant the impotent and corrupt ecclesiastical authority with an external, objective, secular authority that the competing political interests (i.e. nation states) would accept – a corpus of international laws' (Christopher, 2004, p. 67).

Grotius believed in the law of nature, but argued that it was not evidenced through the expression of individual will, but rather 'has an objective existence as a criterion of human action' (Boucher, 1998, p. 212). This natural law, Grotius believed, formed the basis of the law of nations. This law he argued, however, was the product of formal agreement between states, though it was designed for the good of humanity rather than just the states which created it (ibid., p. 213). His criteria for a Just War were self-defence, the punishment of wrongdoers, the enforcement of legal rights, the reparation of injuries, and situations when there was no possibility of effective arbitration (Bellamy, 2006b, p. 73). After the Treaty of Westphalia (1648) and the development of the modern nation state (see Chapter 3), the nature of 'just' wars evidenced a definite state bias and 'national interests became increasingly prominent in Just War theory's concept of justice' (Evans, 2005a, p. 4).

Following Grotius the legalist approach began to dominate. Samuel von Pufendorf (1632–94), though not dismissive of divine law, sought to orientate the regulation of state conduct and warfare more towards positive law. He believed that law was universally valid and not particular to Christian societies. Emmerich de Vattel (1714–67), whose contribution to the development of positive international law is profound, sought to codify the notion of sovereign equality and inviolability. Unlike Grotius and von Pufendorf he argued that war could not be waged justly on behalf of foreign citizens as this created an easily abused pretext for intervention (Boucher, 1998, p. 259). War could only be waged by states on the basis of self-defence to preserve the common good of the state.

Immanuel Kant (1724–1804) was sceptical of the power of natural law and moral persuasion, since states 'are not subject to a common external constraint' (Bellamy, 2006b, p. 82). Kant sought to integrate normative perspectives into clear legally binding treaties between states and was critical of the prescriptions articulated by Grotius, von Pufendorf and Vattel which, he argued, had not and could not restrain states as they lacked a legally constituted framework (Boucher, 1998, p. 269).

Following the French Revolution which began in 1789, the emphasis on the conduct of states meant that the *jus ad bellum* aspect of the tradition was largely sidelined in favour of an emphasis on the conduct of war, and 'from the late eighteenth century onwards little of importance was written in the tradition until the mid twentieth century' (Rengger, 2002, pp. 354–5). Writers such as Hegel, Meinecke and Clausewitz largely dismissed the question of right authority, assuming that states necessarily possessed this right, thus 'the traditional questions of the *jus ad bellum* [were] largely irrelevant' (ibid., p. 359).

The American jurist Francis Lieber (1798–1872) wrote *General Orders No. 100* during the American Civil War, outlining conventions governing the conduct of armies at war. The 'Lieber Code' laid the foundation for the emergence of the laws of war, which became more explicit and international by the end of the 19th century. This codification was contrasted, however, with what Peter Malanczuk describes as 'an almost complete abandonment of the distinction between legal and illegal wars' during the 18th and 19th centuries (2006, p. 307). By the outbreak of the First World War the rules governing the resort to force had lost any real legitimacy and aggression was routinely legitimized as self-defence; indeed this was the spurious justification offered by Kaiser Wilhelm II for the invasion of Belgium in 1914.

Following the carnage of the First World War the League of Nations was established as an attempt to limit the resort to war. While Articles 10–16 of the League Covenant required all disputes to be submitted to the League before force was used, the League manifestly failed to act as a higher authority than its constituent member states. The outbreak of the Second World War and the subsequent Cold War led to the intellectual dominance of the realist perspective, which largely dismissed moralizing about war, preferring instead to focus on explaining the interaction of states and the extent to which a balance of power, rather than abstract moral principles or legal doctrine, could limit the outbreak of war (see Chapter 4). Yet, while realism assumed primacy in the post-Second World War era, the evolution of international law evidenced the formal incorporation of many of the Just War tradition's key prescriptions (see Chapter 5).

The contemporary evolution of Just War thinking has been largely driven by events (Rengger, 2005). Michael Walzer's key modern rendering of the Just War tradition – *Just and Unjust Wars* (1992a) – was written in response to the Vietnam War, and the increase in interest in the tradition in the 1990s was in large part due to the increased exposure afforded to, and incidents of, intra-state crises. Many of the so-called 'new humanitarians' – those concerned with contriving some means by which the suffering of people abroad could be halted – looked to the tradition to justify their advocacy. As the final section of this chapter will demonstrate, however, some argue that the modern usage of the Just War discourse constitutes a misappropriation of the tradition.

Contemporary relevance

The revival of interest in the Just War tradition in the 1990s owed much to those instances of intra-state conflict that challenged both positive international law and the foreign policy preferences of Western states (Hehir, 2008a, pp. 33–52). Interest in the tradition had revived prior to the 1990s, however, when the destruction wrought during the Second World War led many to invoke the *jus in bello* provisions of the tradition (Rengger, 2002, pp. 353–63).

The renaissance in Just War thinking occurred against a backdrop of societal change which was to have significant influence on the contemporary manifestation of the tradition. According to Rengger, the new approach to the Just War tradition, in both scholarship and practice, 'disclosed a character very different from that which the Just War tradition had traditionally displayed'. In identifying the catalysts for this change Rengger points to the 'general hostility to war under any circumstances in liberal public cultures', 'a concept of *jus in bello* largely transformed by both legal instantiation and military habituation', and finally 'the effective secularization of the societies in question' (ibid., p. 358). Jean Elshtain suggests that the modern incarnation of the tradition is based on certain shared principles:

> the current heirs to this way of thinking assume (1) the existence of universal moral dispositions, if not convictions – hence the possibility of a nonrelativist ethic; (2) the need for moral judgments of who/what is aggressor/victim, just/unjust, acceptable/unacceptable, and so on; (3) the potential efficacy of moral appeals and arguments to stay the hand of force. (1992, p. 324)

References to the tradition abound in contemporary discourse. Nicholas Wheeler, in his influential book on humanitarian intervention, *Saving Strangers*, acknowledges that his four criteria for legitimate intervention derive from the Just War tradition (2002, p. 34), while Thomas Weiss describes the International Commission on Intervention and State Sovereignty's (ICISS) criteria as a 'modified just war doctrine' (2007a, p. 106). Tony Blair claimed that NATO's intervention in Kosovo was a 'just war', and his criteria for intervention bear a striking similarity to the Just War tradition's criteria (Blair, 1999).

The two clearest distinctions between modern interpretations of the tradition and its historical antecedents are the contemporary separation of *jus ad bellum* from *jus in bello* and the de-emphasizing of the importance of right intention. Indicative of the separation of the two major categories, Walzer argued that if the indiscriminate bombing of German cities was the only way to stop the spread of Nazism, then this violation of *jus in bello* would yield to the greater good of the defeat of Nazism (1992a, p. 251). This may be a persuasive argument but it is not in accordance with the Just War tradition, which does not permit such selective adherence (Brown, 2006, p. 108).

In the contemporary era the concern with motivation has diminished, with many arguing that it is the outcome rather than the intention that determines whether a war is just (Wheeler, 2002, p. 38; see Chapter 8). The importance afforded to intention by both Augustine and Aquinas belies their religious conviction, in particular the idea of the soul's progression in the afterlife. The emphasis on intention in Aquinas's doctrine of double effect is clear, but from a consequentialist point of view it does not make sense to support one action and condemn another because of the intentions of the actors if the outcomes were similar.

As the tradition has increasingly been used as a template for the discussion on the legitimacy of humanitarian intervention, it has been criticized on a number of grounds. The major criticisms are offered below.

Is the tradition universally applicable?

While it is clear that the tradition's evolution evidences a clear progression away from religious dogma, the question of its Christian character remains. Additionally, while the basis for the tradition may have moved from divine law to natural and positive law, overviews of the tradition's key thinkers rarely include non-Western writers. In what sense then does the tradition's obvious Western and Christian foundation preclude its universal application?

It would seem unreasonable to argue that ideas are limited in their applicability to the cultural origin of their initiators. It is additionally not true that Western culture alone has articulated prescriptions on the use of force and just conduct in war (Hashmi, 2003). Rengger describes the Just War tradition as 'global', arguing that any tradition is 'part of an ongoing and potentially never-ending conversation in which many different assumptions will take centre stage at various points' (2002, p. 362). Hence the dominance of Western Christian voices is conceived as but temporal.

Those who defend the universal applicability of the tradition argue that its basis is natural law, rather than divine law, which, by definition, is applicable to all humanity. Terry Nardin asserts that the contemporary variant of natural law – common morality – constitutes a universal code which informs politics and law, though it is often obscured or ignored by dominant politico-legal systems. 'Common morality', he argues, 'is a critical morality possessing wider authority than the moral practices of particular communities' (Nardin, 2003, p. 18). Thus a belief in the existence of a common morality necessarily enables one to view the Just War tradition as the expression of universal truisms rather than 'any purely particularist and partisan creed' (Evans, 2005a, p. 8). This argument is persuasive if one accepts the underlying validity of a universal moral code knowable to all. Clearly relativists reject such an idea, and hence argue that the applicability of the Just War tradition is limited.

The tradition is inherently statist

The tradition is criticized for its statist bias and for enabling the issue of just authority to be appropriated by states. This issue stems from the earlier proponents of the thesis – Augustine and Aquinas – who have been accused as having delegated great power to the state in authorizing war. Aquinas, like Augustine, viewed the state as a unit of order for the common good rather than an aggregation of individuals (Boucher and Kelly, 2003, p. 113). The state's utility lay in its capacity to promote and facilitate the common good rather than collective individual goods. Individual good was essentially subsumed through the state into the collective good. Aquinas recommended that citizens obey the state in all but the most extreme circumstances and favoured 'passive disobedience' over revolt (Finnis, 1998, p. 290). As with Augustine, the state-centric nature of Aquinas's prescriptions is ultimately explained by his instrumental conception of the state and belief in divine judgement (Canning, 2003, pp. 119–20). Individuals acting out of a duty to the state need not necessarily fear that their own state is commanding an unjust act, as the rulers would face divine retribution while the compliant citizens would not be punished for their obedience.

Aquinas suggested that the 'right authority' is the one which has no authority above it. Those who served a master must seek authorization from that person to use force. The nature of just authority central to his schema, however, is somewhat ambiguous. As John Tooke notes, specifying who this authority might be needs 'serious discussion', yet this is lacking in Aquinas's work (1965, p. 26). Additionally, Tooke notes that 'the "common good" of which Aquinas wrote and which must be the aim of a just war, was rather a limited good, that of a city or province, and never the international good of all' (ibid., p. 27). In his assessment of the implications of this perspective, Holmes notes:

> The net effect is that it is the interests of the state that are paramount and that its laws, so long as they do not directly contravene divine law, should be obeyed unquestioningly. In this one can see the groundwork laid for Hobbes, Machiavelli, Hegel and Treitschke ... Clausewitz ... and of 20th century political realists. (1989, p. 141)

Thus the delegation of just authority to states, evidenced throughout the tradition's lineage, would appear to have facilitated the widespread abuse of the tradition, especially in the 18th and 19th centuries.

Anthony Coates, however, argues that this modern interpretation of the tradition is 'deficient' and a misreading which overlooks the fact that the question of justice was linked to the idea of just authority and sovereign inviolability. Coates's reading of the tradition suggests that 'the internal constitution and practice of the defending state needs to be taken into account' and that the legitimacy of the use of force 'depends on the moral status of those who use it and those against whom it is used' (2006, pp. 63–4). Similarly Rengger argues that the contemporary status of the Just War tradition constitutes a misappropriation of its tenets. He argues that writers such as Johnston and particularly Walzer have portrayed the tradition in a 'state-centric and legalistic' manner and in a form which 'encourages the tendency to think of it in terms of a juristically based calculus' which fails to accurately apply the tradition's conception of right authority (2005, p. 151). Walzer focuses on the state, and his analysis proceeds according to the 'legalist paradigm' which he describes as 'the fundamental structure for the moral comprehension of war' (1992a, p. 61). For Walzer the utility of the Just War tradition lies in its capacity to influence international law as, without legal expression, this code is impotent (ibid., p. 288). Rengger argues that a correct reading of the tradition demonstrates that, while the state may be the right authority in a given context, this should not be assumed (2005, p. 152).

Easily abused/who decides?

The most common critique of the tradition is the charge that its tenets are easily abused. According to Myers, 'these principles ... actually have no meaning, and there are no boundaries to the ways in which they can be manipulated' (1996, p. 126). Reinhold Niebuhr argued that the criteria were inherently indeterminate and values such as 'just' could be easily appropriated and misused (Bellamy, 2006b, p. 107). The tradition is held to articulate principles in an authoritative vacuum, enabling states to act as their own judge, leading inevitably to highly subjective interpretations of the criteria (Kaplan, 2003, p. 130; Buchanan and Keohane, 2004, p. 4). The institutionalization of the criteria would, it is argued, provide a means by which the fulfilment of the criteria could be judged objectively and authoritatively. While the many 'holy wars' and crusades undermined the 'divinely sanctioned' aspect of the early writings on the tradition, the move to a secular legal framework based on states did not eliminate the problem of abuse.

In defence of the tradition, Evans argues that, while there have been many examples of the misuse of Just War rhetoric, such instances cannot be deemed to undermine the utility of the tradition, as all principles can be misused and this in itself is not a viable grounds for rejecting the tradition (2005a, p. 7). Aggressors may invoke the tradition, but equally opponents of the aggression can hold the aggressors to account according to the criteria (2005b, p. 207).

Defenders of the tradition argue that the problem of misuse stems from 'a misunderstanding of the nature of just war thinking itself as essentially a matter of casuistry' (Weigel, 2007, p. 23). Rengger criticizes the contemporary usage of the tradition 'where certain boxes … are ticked or not ticked and in the end one comes out with the view: yes this was/was not a just war' (2005, p. 151). Similarly, James Connelly and Don Carrick caution that the tradition should not be conceived as 'an answer-generating machine operated by turning fact and values into neatly mined outputs … It is a way of reasoning, not a substitute for it' (2011, p. 45). The use of Just War criteria as an apology or excuse for waging war – as many allege Bush and Blair did with respect to the 2003 invasion of Iraq (see Chapter 12) – is a misapplication of the theory. The resort to force is never considered 'good' but rather a regrettable action which can potentially be justified if a set of circumstances – outlined by the Just War tradition – arise. The criteria are not, therefore, a checklist designed to facilitate the use of force, but rather a set of restrictive criteria conceived as a means by which the resort to force can be judged, not enabled (Evans, 2005a, p. 7; Reed and Ryall, 2007, p. 1).

Richard Falk is critical of the contemporary moves towards 'the process of validating war by reference to the Just War doctrine'. This process, he asserts, is problematic because substituting the Just War doctrine for legal doctrine raises the issue of authority; it is plausible that exceptional cases may call for laws to be broken but, he wonders, '[is] the danger of relying on legitimacy to overcome the inadequacies of legality a means to assert the primacy of politics and the subordination of law?' (Falk, 2005a, p. 43). Evans argues, however, that the question of the justness of a war is not dependant on the views of the initiator of the violence but on the objective judgement of others (2005a, p. 8). The problem with this defence, however, is that, while this expands the judgement of a war's justness beyond that of the protagonists, those not directly involved are not necessarily sufficiently dependable judges. Observers may be secretly biased of course but aside from this it cannot be assured that all will be privy to the same information or that this information is correct or complete. This will lead to differing judgements even though the same framework is being applied. Additionally, even if it were possible to find two completely neutral observers, present them with exactly the same information and ask them for their view, there is no guarantee that they would reach similar conclusions. The problem is not that judges will reach different conclusions – this happens regularly in legal trials – but rather the implications of a 'split decision' following the application of the Just War framework: what happens next? This has obvious implications for humanitarian intervention and specifically the appraisal of 'illegal but legitimate' acts (see Chapter 5).

Does the Just War tradition have any real utility?

The very idea of trying to impose rules on warfare is emphatically rejected by some. General Sherman's famous statement – 'war is hell' – points to a certain militaristic perspective on war derived from a 'win at all costs' mentality which accepts no responsibility for the horrors which war is deemed to inevitably cause. As Myers asks, 'why would anyone want to follow rules that interfere with victory and retribution ... once they have crossed the dangerous Rubicon of war?' (1996, p. 119). This critique assumes that, because of the lack of an authoritative international body, states are not constrained by moral principles, or even international law, and act solely to maximize their national interests. According to Robert Kaplan:

> in a world without a universal arbiter of justice, discussions of wars as 'just' or 'unjust' carry little meaning beyond the intellectual and legal circles in which such discussions take place. States and other entities ... will go to war when they decide it is in their interests (strategic, moral, or both), and will, consequently, be unconcerned if others view their aggression as unjust. (2003, p. 130)

Whether the Just War tradition has directly influenced the behaviour of states is thus a contested point. There is clearly evidence that the creation of certain laws of war – such as the Geneva and Hague conventions – owes much to the tradition, and the UN Charter itself contains provisions which can be traced to Just War principles (Evans, 2005a, p. 5). Of course the creation of legal doctrine and the articulation of moral principles do not necessarily lead to lawful or moral behaviour.

Bellamy argues that the tradition fulfils two roles: 'it provides a common language that actors can use to legitimize recourse to force and the conduct of war and that others use to evaluate those claims. It can also inhibit actions that cannot be justified' (2006b, p. 5). Rengger, however, argues that the tradition is not capable of stopping wars, and he accepts the basic realist premise that war is inevitable. He rejects, however, the attendant realist disavowal of moral judgements about war in favour of the Just War tradition: 'it is in the task of continually holding up the mirror of our considered moral judgments in the context of war that the tradition performs its most important role' (Rengger, 2005, p. 160). International law, he argues, often fails to provide guidance and in these situations – such as humanitarian intervention – 'we must surely look to a larger framework in which to embed such judgments' (ibid., p. 147). The tradition is thus vaunted as a framework for examining war, not a means to either prevent or facilitate it (Armstrong and Farrell, 2005, p. 11). Undoubtedly the tradition serves as a comprehensive framework which enables us to examine the legitimacy of a war or intervention. This normative goal, however, has certainly not been the limit of the tradition's actual usage, and it has undoubtedly been employed to excuse the use of force. One may question the normative idea of a framework of legitimacy on the basis that such a goal is quite a modest return on 2,000 years of philosophical inquiry.

Conclusion

The Just War tradition, according to Rengger, 'has retained a remarkable vitality and power well into our own times'. However, he also warns: 'at the opening of the twenty-first century [the tradition] shows some signs of having reached the limit of its elasticity' (2002, pp. 353, 361). A cynic may argue that it is precisely the tradition's elasticity and inherently malleable tenets that have facilitated its longevity. Nonetheless, as long as there are wars there will be moral judgements made about war, and in this sense the tradition is unlikely to lose relevance (Evans, 2005b, p. 203).

The contemporary debate on humanitarian intervention has clearly stimulated a renewed interest in the tradition, and those engaged in this debate must engage with the Just War literature even if only to substantiate their critique of the role of morality in international relations. Those engaging with the tradition as a tool for understanding the contemporary question of humanitarian intervention must be conscious, however, that the tradition should not be conceived of as a homogeneous theory which can be applied unproblematically to contemporary events. Additionally, the context in which many of its key thinkers wrote was very different from our contemporary context. In isolation the tradition cannot reasonably be said to determine the justness of a particular war. 'What is considered "just"', according to Bellamy, 'depends on the interplay between the tradition's legal sub-tradition (positive law), moral sub-tradition (natural law) and political sub-tradition (realism)' (2006b, p. 7). In this sense the tradition is perhaps best seen as a component in a broader framework of legitimacy.

The key sources of contention posed by humanitarian intervention are inherent in the Just War tradition, and much of the contemporary debate on this issue explicitly refers to the tenets of the tradition. While the tradition cannot provide answers to the questions raised by humanitarian intervention, it is an indispensable framework of analysis for this issue, and the historical debates surrounding the tradition's key tenets are highly relevant and informative for scholars engaged in the contemporary debate.

Questions

- Do you consider the criteria outlined in Box 2.1 to be sufficiently comprehensive?
- Does the tradition constitute a Western Christian view of war or does it have universal applicability?
- To what extent has the tradition informed the evolution of international law?
- Has the tradition had any impact on the behaviour of states?
- What would you consider to be the tradition's primary function?

Further reading

Bellamy, A. (2006) *Just Wars: From Cicero to Iraq* (London: Polity), Chapters 1–5.

Christopher, P. (2004) *The Ethics of War and Peace* (Upper Saddle River, NJ: Prentice Hall), Chapters 1–4.

Evans, M. (ed.) (2005) *Just War Theory: A Reappraisal* (Edinburgh: Edinburgh University Press).

Fisher, D. (2011) *Morality and War* (Oxford: Oxford University Press).

Holmes, R.L. (1989) *On War and Morality* (Princeton, NJ: Princeton University Press).

Johnson, J.T. (1987) *The Quest for Peace: Three Moral Traditions in Western Cultural History* (Princeton, NJ: Princeton University Press).

Nardin, T. (ed.) (1998) *The Ethics of War and Peace: Religious and Secular Perspectives* (Princeton, NJ: Princeton University Press).

O'Donovan, O. (2003) *The Just War Revisited* (Cambridge: Cambridge University Press).

O'Driscoll, C. (2008) *Renegotiation of the Just War Tradition and the Right to War in the Twenty-First Century* (Basingstoke: Palgrave Macmillan).

Walzer, M. (2006) *Just and Unjust Wars*, rev. edn (New York: Basic Books).

Chapter 3

The Sovereign State

The controversy surrounding humanitarian intervention centres on the relationship between the state and its citizens. Minimalist conceptions of the state hold that the state must provide its citizens with security from external aggression and ensure that economic activity can thrive. More expansive conceptions hold that the state must provide positive goods such as human rights, education and healthcare. There is, therefore, broad, albeit shallow, agreement that the state has certain responsibilities towards its citizens. Controversy arises, however, regarding the nature of these responsibilities and, crucially, what should be done by other states if a state violates these responsibilities. This latter point is highly contentious precisely because sovereign inviolability – that is, the right of states to non-intervention – has become a key feature of statehood. To understand the dilemma posed by humanitarian intervention it is necessary, therefore, to examine the evolution of the sovereign state and engage with the arguments for and against sovereignty.

In 1999 Kofi Annan, then secretary general of the UN, wrote: 'state sovereignty, in its most basic sense is being redefined' (1999b). Annan cited three main challenges to the sovereign state: the process of economic globalization, international cooperation as manifest through international organizations, and the rise of human rights. While there is no doubt that globalization and international institutions have both impacted on the sovereignty of states to a very significant extent, this chapter focuses on Annan's third challenge, as it is the tension between human rights and state sovereignty that has most relevance to the issue of humanitarian intervention.

Chapter 1's first section outlines the nature of the sovereign state, its history and the legal rights sovereign states currently enjoy. In the second section I examine the argument that the status of sovereignty has always constituted 'organized hypocrisy'. In the final section I outline the critical perspective on sovereignty advanced by the 'new humanitarians' and the counter-position as articulated by those who see sovereignty as both a normative good and a means of preserving international order.

The evolution of the sovereign state

The codification of sovereignty established both the territorial state and contemporary international system (Kratochwil 1995, p. 25). Yet, sovereignty has always been a 'contested concept'. According to Lassa Oppenheim:

> there is perhaps no conception the meaning of which is more controversial than that of sovereignty. It is an indisputable fact that this conception, from the moment when it was introduced into political science, until the present day, has never had a meaning which was universally agreed upon. (2006, p. 129).

Clearly sovereignty is worth having, but what it entails is unclear. It is a fundamental norm of the international system, yet it has been violated routinely since its inception. It is an idea extolled by its supporters as a bulwark against oppression and power politics, yet its critics argue that it in fact facilitates tyranny. In the contemporary era it has come under greater interrogation than perhaps ever before.

It is not possible to chart the evolution of the modern state comprehensively in this section. The aim, rather, is to identify the key catalysts for the emergence of the sovereign state so that we can situate sovereignty in a historical context (see Box 3.1). The guide to further reading at the end of this chapter identifies sources which will provide a more complete history of the state.

From the earliest times humans have formed groups, and these groups have invariably involved some power structure and delegation of responsibilities. The adage 'strength in numbers' has clearly influenced the human propensity towards social organization, as it has for many animals. Unlike animals, however, humankind's agricultural ability and resultant capacity to produce surplus goods, plus our seemingly intrinsic drive to improve our social conditions, led us to engage in economic activity, particularly trade, which catalysed the development of complex social organizations.

War, religion and the modern state

The development of the modern state cannot be traced to one particular event or period and constitutes a long evolutionary process. Large political organizations date back 7,000 years to the city-states and empires based around the Tigris, Euphrates and Nile (Russett et al., 2000, p. 47). These entities evidenced many features of today's 'states' but lacked some or all of those key characteristics that we associate with the modern state, namely distinct borders, centralized authority structures, a bureaucracy and a permanent population of 'nationals'.

The period 1450 to 1650 constituted a transition from the old system of feudal entities to the modern sovereign state system. The old system was characterized by overlapping competencies whereby authority was vested

> **Box 3.1   Key dates in the evolution of the modern state**
>
> | | |
> |---|---|
> | 1439 | Johannes Gutenberg invents the movable type printing press. |
> | 1517 | Martin Luther nails his 95 Theses on the Power of Indulgences to the door of the Schlosskirche in Wittenberg. |
> | 1555 | Peace of Augsburg signed between Ferdinand I and the Schmalkaldic League. Participants agree to respect the principle '*cuius region, eius religio*' ('whose region, his religion'). |
> | 1648 | Peace of Westphalia signed to formally end the Thirty Years War. |
> | 1700–*c*.1804 | The Enlightenment: an era of profound change in Europe, involving governmental consolidation, the growth of nationalism, the diminution of the power of the Church and moves towards the recognition of basic civil rights for all citizens. |
> | 1807–14 | Peninsular War: Napoleon defeats Spain and Portugal, precipitating independence in Latin America. |
> | 1815 | Congress of Vienna: agreement signed between Great Britain, Prussia, Austria, Russia and France on borders within Europe following the defeat of Napoleon. |
> | 1870–1920 | Ottoman, Habsburg, Hohenzollern and Romanoff dynasties in Central and Eastern Europe dissolve. |
> | 1884–85 | Berlin Conference: agreement to regulate the colonization of Africa. |
> | 1899 & 1907 | Hague Conventions: conferences on international humanitarian law and the laws governing the use of force. In 1907 all Latin American states attend. |
> | 1919 | Paris Peace Conference: agreement reached on the formation |
>
> →

in different, often competing, polities and leaders, such as between the Holy Roman Emperor and the Pope. The old system of medieval Christendom was dominated by the power of the Church which necessarily stifled the emergence of individual states. The Church's power, and hence its influence over the composition of political entities, in Europe was undermined by the Reformation (Jackson, 1996, p. 51). In the early 16th century Martin Luther challenged the Pope's authority, and his radical ideas quickly spread throughout Central Europe, where distinct Lutheran churches emerged aligned with particular kings and princes who exploited the situation and consolidated their realm. Europe thus divided into religiously distinct realms, and religious conflict and general disorder followed. By the 17th century territorial units ruled exclusively by one monarch had emerged, and at this point 'the leading principle of legitimacy ... undoubtedly was *Rex est imperator in regno suo*: the King is

	of the League of Nations, including the League of Nations Permanent Mandates Commission.
1926	Imperial Conference: Great Britain acknowledges the right of dominions to participate in international society as equal sovereign states.
1945–80	European decolonization: British, French, Spanish, Portuguese, Belgian and Dutch colonies throughout Africa and Asia gain independence.
1970	General Assembly Resolution 2621: 'reaffirms the inherent right of colonial peoples to struggle by all necessary means at their disposal against colonial powers which suppress their aspiration for freedom and independence'.
1975	Helsinki Accords: 35 states from East and West sign agreement on security and cooperation. Principles of sovereign inviolability and equality are reaffirmed but states additionally commit themselves to respecting human rights.
1989–92	End of the Cold War: communism collapses, precipitating the emergence of new states in Eastern Europe and a rise in intra-state conflict in Africa.
1993	Vienna Declaration and Programme of Action includes 'the solemn commitment of all States to fulfil their obligations to promote universal respect for, and observance and protection of, all human rights and fundamental freedoms for all'.
2001	International Commission on Intervention and State Sovereignty publishes *The Responsibility to Protect*.
2002	International Criminal Court (ICC) established.
2005	World Summit *Outcome Document* endorses certain aspects of *The Responsibility to Protect*.

Emperor within his own realm' (ibid.). Religious conflict in Europe culminated in the extremely violent Thirty Years War which lasted from 1618 to 1648.

The emergence of the state system was driven by two key factors: capital and coercion (Russett et al., 2000, p. 48). To consolidate their realm, monarchs required significant military and economic resources. Economic growth required a centralized bureaucracy capable of collecting taxes, and this necessitated the creation of a coercive force – an army – capable of enforcing compliance. Thus the state can be seen as a function of the quest for economic growth which created a need for centralized control and superior military capability to maintain internal compliance and repel external interference. Without the latter any political entity was liable to be appropriated by foreign powers, hence Charles Tilly's famous statement: 'the state makes war and war makes the state'

(1990, p. 32). The centrality of military force in the growth of the state in Europe is recognized as a key factor in the eventual global dominance of European powers. Military competition within Europe created strong, internally consolidated, political entities. Rivals sought to achieve military preponderance, thus sparking an arms race which spurred economic growth and also, crucially, technological innovation (Russett et al., 2000, p. 49).

Westphalia and the nation-state

The consolidation of the principle of sovereignty is regularly dated to 1648 and the Treaty of Westphalia, more correctly titled the Peace of Westphalia – the collective term for the Treaties of Munster and Osnabrück. While the Peace of Westphalia was clearly significant in terms of ending the Thirty Years War, its significance has possibly been inflated, as the Peace of Augsburg of 1555 had first established the basic template of sovereign inviolability (Brown, 2006, p. 22). Signatories to the Peace of Augsburg agreed to respect the principle *cuius regio, eius religo* (he who rules a region, determines its religion). The Peace of Westphalia reaffirmed this principle and, in essence, set in place the framework for the emergence of independent, territorially defined states, thereby ending the possibility of a united European Empire. In each territory there was no longer multiple loyalties and authorities; rather there was loyalty only to one authority specific to that territory, and external interference was prohibited. Westphalia's chief legacy is the creation of this dual aspect of sovereignty, described by Hedley Bull as internal and external sovereignty (2002, p. 8).

Internal sovereignty is the capacity of state authorities to rule inside their borders. External sovereignty derives from the acknowledgment by other states of a state's right to independence and inviolability (non-interference). International politics after 1648 thus involved the struggle by states, and indeed separatists, to acquire and/or maintain these dual elements of sovereignty which Westphalia acknowledged as central to the legitimacy of a state. Augsburg and Westphalia imbued the state with historically unprecedented power, and according to Jarat Chopra and Thomas Weiss 'transferred to nation-states the special godlike features of Church authority. Nation-states inherited the pedigree of sovereignty and an unassailable position above the law that has since been frozen in the structure of international relations' (1992, p. 104).

It would be wrong, however, to view the Peace of Westphalia as ushering in an era of respect for sovereign inviolability. While the recognition of the external sovereignty of states meant that no national or international entity could legitimately interfere in the activities of another state, state practice after 1648 was not conducted in accordance with this principle. The concept of sovereignty manifest under the 'Westphalian System' was a conspicuously contingent norm. Indicatively, from 1648 to 1815 the number of states actually declined as large ones forcibly absorbed smaller ones (Bull, 2002, p. 17). The 18th and especially the 19th centuries were characterized by the rise of nation-states asserting the *cuius regio, eius religio* principle, yet the more powerful European states systematically ignored the notion of self-determination and sovereign inviolability, especially in their colonial quests through *terra nullius* – no man's land (Clapham, 1999, p. 522). According to Jean Cohen this legal arrangement, *jus publicum europaeum* (public law of Europe), was a conspicuously contingent norm which paradoxically facilitated colonialism (2004, p. 12). The interests of the Great Powers of the 18th and 19th centuries – Great Britain, France, Prussia, the Austrian Empire and Russia – were the primary factor in international relations at this time, and certainly of far greater influence than nebulous legal principles regarding sovereignty.

The idea of the 'nation' constituting the only legitimate source of statehood and governmental authority emerged at the end of the 18th century (Anderson, 1991, p. 3). A number of factors coalesced to precipitate the rise of nationalism as a force in international relations: the reappraisal of the old religious communities and scientific truisms initiated by the Enlightenment, the development of the printing press in the 15th century and subsequent consolidation of language communities, the 1789 French Revolution and its assertion of the people's right to choose their government, and the rejection of empires as political units. The French Revolution catalysed a general rejection of the idea of the monarch as the embodiment of sovereignty in favour of popular sovereignty. The state was thereafter increasingly portrayed as a servant of the people, who came to be conceived as an organic national group.

The conviction that the nation should have its own state led to the fragmentation of existing political units, particularly empires, and the emergence of new 'nation-states'. Thus, sovereignty became the goal of the aspiring nations of this period, much as it would again during the period of decolonization in the mid-20th century. The idea of self-determination as an inherent right was explicitly articulated following the First World War by US President Woodrow Wilson, though this right was certainly not universally applied. Indeed, Bill Bowring argues that Lenin articulated a more 'consistent and revolutionary' avowal of self-determination which, in contrast to Wilson's, sought to catalyse the wholesale disruption of existing states (2008, p. 18). In 1933 at the Seventh International Convention of American States the US agreed not to interfere in the affairs of Latin American states. The Montevideo Convention articulated a set of criteria for statehood which became and remains the universal standard (see Box 3.2).

The modern state, however, clearly comprises more than the technical trappings outlined in the Montevideo Convention. Central to the existence

---

Box 3.2   The 1933 Montevideo Convention

Article 1: The state as a person of international law should possess the following qualifications: (a) a permanent population; (b) a defined territory; (c) government; and (d) capacity to enter into relations with the other states

Source: Convention on the Rights and Duties of States 1933.

---

of the state is what Barry Buzan describes as 'the idea of the state which establishes its legitimacy in the eyes of the people' (1991, pp. 66–7). Functional internal sovereignty allows the people to object to the manner in which the state is being run without questioning the very existence of the state. The willingness of the citizenry to accede to the state's internal sovereignty is dependent on the state's ability to meet their basic requirements and command their loyalty (Kedourie, 1971, p. 12).

The UN Charter

The UN Charter's codification of the sovereign equality of all its members, as detailed in Article 2.1, embedded sovereignty as a universal legal principle. The Charter marked the formal rejection of a hierarchy of states and prohibited the use of force against sovereign equals, except in self-defence. Additionally, Article 2.7 of the Charter prohibits the UN itself from interfering in the domestic affairs of its member-states. Many General Assembly resolutions since 1945 have reaffirmed the principle of non-interference, especially as the number of states grew as a result of decolonization. The effect of the codification of sovereign equality in the Charter and subsequent international legislation, in particular the 1960 General Assembly Declaration on the Granting of Independence to Colonial Countries and Peoples, was that 'it no longer made sense to speak of a hierarchical society of states in which rights of membership and participation were granted in proportion to a society's development and capability' (Bain, 2003b, p. 66). It must be acknowledged, however, that even after its codification in 1945 sovereignty has not been a consistently respected tenet of international law (see Chapter 5).

The number of states has grown exponentially in the post-Charter era, as reflected in the membership of the UN. When the UN was established in 1945 it had 51 members; today there are 192. Between 1973 and 1994 UN membership increased by more than one-third, with 28 states joining between 1990 and 1994 alone. The state clearly remains the unit of currency in international relations although, as later sections highlight, the sovereign rights enjoyed by states have been increasingly challenged in the post-Cold War era. Before examining this challenge in the next section I look at whether the idea of sovereignty has ever been reflected in actual state practice.

Organized hypocrisy?

Sovereignty is a much coveted and protected quality, but it is also ambiguous, having many different meanings and manifestations. 'States', according to Sir Arthur Watts, 'through their rulers or governments, think of themselves as sovereign. They do not, of course, always know what sovereignty means, but it is clearly worth having and keeping' (2001, p. 5). Stephen Krasner, indicatively, identified four ways in which the term has come to be used (1999, pp. 9–25):

- *International legal sovereignty* refers to state practices associated with mutual recognition between territorial entities that have formal judicial independence.
- *Westphalian sovereignty* refers to a political organization based on the exclusion of external actors from the state's internal authority structures.
- *Domestic sovereignty* in turn refers to the organization of political authority within the state and the ability of public authorities to exercise effective control within the borders of their own polity.
- *Interdependence sovereignty* is that ability of public authorities to regulate the flow of information, goods, people, pollutants or capital across the borders of their state.

In practice, international legal sovereignty and Westphalian sovereignty are the key manifestations of sovereignty. In many cases states lack either or both of the last two forms of sovereignty, but by virtue of possessing international legal sovereignty are considered states. This paradox is particularly apparent in the case of Somalia, which has been without a functioning government since 1991 yet remains legally a state. Additionally, while certain states, such as Andorra and Liechtenstein, may possess international legal, domestic and interdependence sovereignty, they are not free from direct external interference and thus lack Westphalian sovereignty. There is an importance distinction, therefore, between *de facto* and *de jure* states; according to the Montevideo Convention, states must exhibit empirical attributes such as population and effective government, but also juridical attributes, such as borders and independence. A failure to meet the *de facto* attributes, for example the inability to govern effectively, does not necessarily impact on the *de jure* aspect of statehood, and thus Somalia is legally a state, despite the internal turmoil.

Therefore, while by definition sovereign states should have a clearly defined territory, be internationally recognized, autonomous and in control of domestic affairs, as Krasner notes, 'only a very few states have possessed all these attributes' (1999, p. 220). In legal terms, sovereignty has meant the recognition by the international community of a state's right to exist and the illegality of unsolicited external interference. Krasner shows, however, that in many cases a state's quest for international recognition has paradoxically had the effect of making it less sovereign. He cites the example of states that emerged from the dissolution of the Ottoman Empire in the early 20th century that were willing to cede certain sovereign rights so as to attain international legal recognition (ibid., p. 139). Many ostensibly sovereign states have not been, and are not, economically, militarily or politically autonomous, but are wholly dependent on external support in one or all of these areas (Jackson, 1996, p. 2). The absence of certain tenets of sovereignty can be camouflaged, however, by achieving international recognition, which automatically bestows these qualities by implication.

The process of decolonization highlighted the often fictitious nature of sovereignty. According to Robert Jackson, while former colonial states acquired the legal status of states, they are 'primarily juridical' as they lack internal capacity (ibid., p. 21). Jackson describes this manifestation of sovereignty as 'negative sovereignty', in contrast to positive sovereignty, which means that the state 'also possesses the wherewithal to provide political goods for its citizens' (ibid., pp. 28–9). The 'sovereign' state created by 20th-century decolonization is, he argues, a break with the historical evolution of sovereignty, as it created 'states' lacking the *de facto* attributes of statehood and which were excessively dependent on external support (ibid., p. 25). These new states are often characterized by authoritarian regimes with poor human rights records, as the new governments did not emerge from organic political communities but were in many cases imposed by former colonial powers on artificial entities. Some 44 per cent of Africa's internal state borders are straight lines based in many cases on astronomical measurements drawn by former colonial powers. Yet in 1964 the Organization of African Unity pledged to respect these arbitrary divisions (Herbst, 1989, pp. 673–6). This endorsement of the principle *uti possidetis, ita possideatis* (as you possess, so may you possess) was designed to prevent the eruption of myriad intra- and inter-state conflicts which would surely have accrued had it been deemed legitimate to contest African borders (Kum, 1990, p. 450).

Thus, while decolonization precipitated a great expansion in the number of sovereign states, it is debatable whether these new states were truly sovereign in the Westphalian sense. Additionally, there is some doubt whether this was an ultimately positive development given the record of intra-state conflict, oppression and corruption in many former colonies. Of course the fact that these post-independence issues are problematic need not lead us to call for the return of colonization, but, as we examine the proliferation of intra-state crises in the post-Cold War era and the resultant calls for humanitarian intervention, we must acknowledge the role decolonization arguably played in the creation of these unviable entities (Jackson, 1996, pp. 23–4).

States possessing international legal sovereignty without Westphalian sovereignty are not unique to former colonies: Bosnia-Herzegovina was recognized as an independent state in 1991 at a time when it demonstrably lacked the trappings of sovereignty (Zaum, 2007, p. 33). Since the 1995 Dayton Accords the internationally appointed High Representative has exercised supreme authority in Bosnia-Herzegovina, even though it is legally a state and a member of the UN (Chandler, 2000b). Kosovo, likewise, has been recognized (at the time of writing) by 96 states and yet its actual 'independence' is empirically dubious (Hehir, 2010b). Thus as Dominic Zaum argues, 'recognition as a state and recognition of sovereignty should not be conflated' (2007, p. 35). Additionally, international financial bodies such as the IMF and the World Bank have imposed many conditions on the provision of monetary aid which compromise the sovereignty of the recipients (Harrison, 2004). Member states of the European Union have voluntarily agreed to relinquish aspects of their sovereignty by ceding key competencies to Brussels. Thus, it is clear that sovereignty can be attenuated in many ways and forms without officially being rescinded.

Sovereignty is less a rigid amalgam of specific tenets but rather, as Chopra and Weiss describe it, 'a quality of a fact' (1992, p. 103). Hence 'sovereign states' may evidence significant dependence upon, or susceptibility to, external forces. The significant aspect of juridical sovereignty, however, is the fact that it derives from recognition by the international community of a state's right to exist, and thus the prohibition on unsolicited external interference. This at least imbues the state with an international legal identity which brings with it the right, though not the guarantee, of inviolability. In those states where Westphalian sovereignty is manifestly lacking, such as Bosnia-Herzegovina and post-2003 Iraq, it could be argued that the involvement of foreign powers is accepted by these states, unlike 19th-century colonialism. It is debatable, however, whether it is inherently contradictory to exercise free will and choose servitude (Bain, 2007).

According to Krasner, 'the principles associated with both Westphalian and international legal sovereignty have always been violated' (1999, p. 24). The key factor is the interests of states and the relative distribution of power, not 'taken-for-granted practices derived from some overarching institutional structures or deeply embedded generative grammars' (ibid., p. 9). Krasner's critique of sovereignty, however, is challenged by Chris Brown, who argues that the currency of the concept imposes significant restraints on the behaviour of states and *does* have real influence. When states violate the sovereignty of others they have had to 'explain how their behaviour can be understood in terms of rules [on sovereignty]'. They proffer these explanations, he argues,

> not as Krasner suggests, as a matter of hypocrisy, but because failure to do so would, as it were, end the 'game', and, at the same time, end their capacity to claim the status of sovereign since this status only exists by virtue of the existence of international society. (Brown, 2006, p. 36)

Certainly all states have an interest in upholding the generic legal rights of states, and in this sense the legal status of sovereignty has some impact, albeit modest.

The actual role played by sovereignty in international relations is manifestly different from its normative precepts. Clearly sovereignty has many meanings, is not uniformly manifest and is regularly violated. Proponents of humanitarian intervention and the responsibility to protect (R2P) have often presented a singularly negative image of sovereignty to the extent that today 'sovereignty has become a dirty word and an endangered concept' (Douzinas, 2009, p. 35). In the next section I outline the extent to which sovereignty has been increasingly challenged in the post-Cold War era by the rise of human rights.

Challenging the sovereign state in the contemporary era

Following the end of the Cold War, intra-state wars became the primary manifestation of global conflict. The domestic and international constraints imposed by the Cold War superpower standoff had marginalized or suppressed many internal disputes. The implosion of the Soviet Union, and the fall of communism generally, lifted these constraints as Moscow no longer propped up communist regimes and the US's interest in previously strategically important states waned. 'The end of the Cold War', according to Francis Fukuyama, 'left a band of weak or failed states stretching from North Africa through the Balkans and the Middle East to South Asia' (2006, p. 2). Within many of these 'failed' and 'weak' states 'new wars' broke out which 'involve[d] a blurring of the distinctions between war, organized crime and large scale violations of human rights' (Kaldor, 1999, pp. 1–2).

The scale of human rights violations caused by these intra-state conflicts generated international attention and in many cases caused popular outrage. Increased economic interdependence caused by globalization meant that intra-state conflicts, with their potential to provoke regional crises, impacted on Western foreign investment and domestic markets, and risked causing 'epidemics of regional disorders', thereby generating international economic instability in addition to political and social disruption (Hoffmann, 2003, p. 23). Thus, intra-state conflicts came to be seen as the greatest threat to international stability; the 1994 UN Commission on Global Governance warned: '[while] war between states is not extinct, in the years ahead the world is likely to be troubled primarily by eruptions of violence within countries' (1995, p. 81).

The rise of human security and global civil society

The end of the Cold War precipitated an upsurge in optimism amongst some over the future of human rights (Shaw, 1994, p. 155; Heinze, 2009, p. 124; Barnett, 2010, p. 22). The new systemic conditions were considered to be more conducive to further codification and, perhaps more importantly, increased enforcement of the existing human rights legislation (de Cuéllar, 1991, p. 2; Berdal, 2003, p. 9). The end of the bipolar stand-off which had suffocated effective human rights enforcement was seen as facilitating an increased focus on 'human security'.

The increasingly globalized media and the rapid proliferation of humanitarian NGOs alerted Western publics to certain conflicts and their humanitarian consequences. The question posed by the *Wall Street Journal*, 'At what point do so-called sovereign governments forfeit their sovereignty through their own despicable acts?' (1992), soon came to encapsulate much of the political debate during the 1990s. Codified international law regarding sovereign inviolability provided an answer that many felt was unconscionable (Robertson, 2002, p. 428). International law on sovereignty was increasingly perceived as outdated, and hence action to alleviate suffering could be illegal but morally legitimate (Kouchner, 1999).

In light of the violence in the Balkans and the genocide in Rwanda (see Chapter 10), a consensus developed that a state's sovereignty should not shield it from external military intervention in cases where it 'brutalises its own people' (Chatterjee and Scheid, 2003, p. 5). The tenets of sovereignty, therefore, came to be regarded as barriers to the preservation of human rights, and there began a 'revolution against unfettered sovereignty' (Hoffmann, 2003, p. 22). Sovereignty came to be construed by many as creating artificial barriers to integration which had become sources of dissonance and contestation (Held, 1995, p. 268; Booth, 2001, p. 65).

Advocates of proactive humanitarianism increasingly focused on the ostensibly anachronistic and immoral aspects of sovereignty (Gow, 1997, p. 155). Sovereignty was deemed to 'reward tyrants' and increasingly portrayed as enabling states to oppress, torture and murder their citizens (Tesón, 1996, p. 342). The universality of human rights and the primacy of human security thus combined to challenge the basis of the existing system and specifically the rights enjoyed by states. Indicatively, Andrew Linklater identified the aim of the human rights movement as 'transcending state sovereignty' (1998, p. 109).

Many argued that the sovereign rights of states were dependent on their human rights record (Robertson, 2002, p. 372). The principle of sovereign equality thus gave way to a conception of a sovereignty hierarchy. While this perspective found no ready manifestation in positive law, this was often dismissed as evidence that international law was outdated and required reform to be more reflective of the new concern for human security.

Mary Kaldor defines human security as 'about the security of individuals and communities rather than the security of states and it combines both human rights and human development, freedom from fear and freedom from want' (2005, p. 177). This perspective is informed by a cosmopolitan framework catalysed and inspired by the end of the Cold War, the effects of globalization, the project of European integration and the increased visibility of transnational actors (Hutchings, 1999, pp. 154–5). The basic rights of individuals, regardless of their nationality, were thus increasingly deemed inviolable and of greater import than the rights of states (Beitz, 1992, p. 125; Kaldor, 1999, pp. 115). The goal of promoting human security was to be realized through global civil society.

Thus, great pressure was exerted by advocates of human security to alter the norms governing international relations. Key to the practical application of this pressure was global civil society (see Box 3.3), which aimed to mobilize international humanitarian actors to 'transform state understandings of their national interests, and alter their calculations of the costs and benefits of particular policies' (Keck and Sikkink, 1998, p. 203). Domestic and global civil society was envisaged as a means to 'counterbalance the state and ... prevent it from dominating and atomizing the rest of society' (Gellner, 1994, p. 5). Via the so-called 'boomerang effect', citizens in repressive states appeal to global civil society to support their cause and highlight their plight. Subsequent coordinated international activism will compel states to pressure the offending state into halting its activity (Keck and Sikkink, 1998, pp. 9–13). Thus the emergence of global civil society constituted 'the domestication of the international' (Kaldor, 2003, p. 78) and a means by which the sovereign rights of states were challenged through normative pressure and humanitarian advocacy (see pp. 137–42 in the context of the strategy adopted by supporters of R2P).

Box 3.3   Global civil society

Two perspectives exist regarding the origins of global civil society. One view suggests that it has been evolving since the mid-19th century, while the second, more prevalent, view sees it as having emerged in the last 30 years as a result of globalization, the spread of Western values and increased communication capacity (Coleman and Wayland, 2006, pp. 242–5). 'Global civil society' is not, however, a precise term or a definite actor; while Helmut Anheier et al. describe it as an 'underlying social reality', they acknowledge that it is 'a fuzzy and a contested concept' (2001, p. 11).

Central to global civil society has been the emergence of a global human rights network, manifest most clearly in the large exponential growth in humanitarian NGOs in the 1990s. Through the mobilization and influence of NGOs, global civil society constitutes 'a source of constant pressures on the state system' (Shaw, 1994, p. 24). According to Kaldor, 'by the end of the 1990s, it could be said that pressure from global civil society had given rise to widespread acceptance of humanitarian norms' (2003, p. 132).

Political developments in the 1990s

Political changes in the 1990s signalled a fundamental revision of the responsibilities of states. On 5 April 1991 UN Security Council Resolution 688 condemned Iraq for its treatment of the Kurds and Shiites, describing the situation as a threat to international peace and security. While this was an important development, Resolution 688 did not include any provisions for enforcing compliance. As the situation worsened, a coalition of states – the Netherlands, France, the UK and the US – launched Operation Provide Comfort, which created 'safe havens' for refugees and imposed no-fly zones over northern, and later southern, Iraq. The coalition justified their intervention as 'consistent' with Resolution 688. This constituted a 'new claim', namely that 'the use of force could be justified to enforce compliance with an existing Security Council Resolution' (Wheeler, 2006, p. 34). The actions of the Security Council and the coalition of states in this case indicated a new dispensation which was to be a feature of Council deliberation and international action in the 1990s: the Council's increased willingness to describe intra-state humanitarian crises as threats to international peace and stability, and an attendant willingness, primarily amongst Western states, to take action – be it multilateral through the UN or unilateral through coalitions of the willing – to halt these crises.

In 1991, in his last *Annual Report on the Work of the Organization*, the then UN Secretary General Perez de Cuéllar called for a reinterpretation of the UN Charter's principles on sovereignty and non-interference in domestic affairs, noting 'an irresistible shift in public attitudes towards the belief that the defence of the oppressed in the name of morality should prevail over frontiers and legal documents (Lyons and Mastanduno, 1995, p. 2). Building on this idea, Boutros Boutros-Ghali, de Cuéllar's successor, outlined a new agenda for states to reflect the increasingly interdependent world and the new, more propitious, systemic conditions:

> The time of absolute and exclusive sovereignty, however, has passed; its theory was never matched by reality. It is the task of leaders of States today to understand this and to find a balance between the needs of good internal governance and the requirements of an ever more interdependent world. (1992, para. 17).

In 1993 at the World Conference on Human Rights, all UN member states adopted the Vienna Declaration and Programme of Action, which declared 'the promotion and protection of human rights is a matter of priority for the international community'. Kofi Annan continued this agenda when he became secretary general in 1997. In a speech in 1998 he argued that the UN Charter 'was never meant as a license for governments to trample on human rights and human dignity' (Roberts, 2006, p. 86), while later, in a widely cited article in the *Economist*, Annan further argued 'state sovereignty, in its most basic sense, is being refined ... individual sovereignty – by which I mean the fundamental freedom of each individual, enshrined in the Charter ... has been enhanced by a renewed and spreading consciousness of individual rights' (1999b, p. 49). These and many other developments in the 1990s – not least Security Council action under Chapter VII (see Chapter 5) – marked a trend whereby the state was deemed responsible for the maintenance of basic human rights; failure to meet this responsibility would result in external sanctions and possibly intervention.

Yet, while many declarations by the three UN secretaries general, by Security Council action and by international commitments made by states in the 1990s suggested an emerging commitment to, and consensus on, the promotion and protection of human rights, significant disquiet remained amongst many developing states and major regional powers such as China, Russia and India (DIIA, 1999, p. 54). This tension came to a head in March 1999 when NATO intervened in Kosovo without explicit Security Council approval, though the Council had previously described the situation as a threat to international peace and security (see Chapter 11). NATO's intervention graphically illustrated the conflict between law and morality and the divisions between states over the permissibility of humanitarian intervention.

Defending the sovereign state

While those critical of sovereignty within the human rights community base their critique on ethical principles, those who defend sovereignty are not necessarily proponents of power and order, averse to the idea of human rights. According to Gareth Evans the debate on humanitarian intervention involves those arguing for the primacy of humanitarian values and those 'defenders of the traditional prerogatives of state sovereignty, who insist that internal events were none of the rest of the world's business' (2008, p. 3). This is an oversimplification: while supporters of an alteration in the nature of sovereignty argue that such change is necessary for the good of the global community, others see ethical merits to sovereignty (Lang, 2003, p. 2; Douzinas, 2009; Cunliffe, 2011;). Michael Byers and Simon Chesterman argue that powerful states have an interest in changing the principle of sovereignty, as it 'operates, in a multitude of contexts, to constrain the law-making influence of the powerful' (2003, p. 194). While sovereignty has clearly been misused by tyrants, the need to transcend sovereignty to protect human rights has also historically been misused.

'Throughout history', John Herz wrote, 'that unit which affords protection and security to human beings has tended to become the basic political unit' (1957, p. 474). In this sense the evolution of sovereignty has much to do with the capacity of the state to protect groups from external aggression. While the notion of the state as an organic expression of national consciousness inflates its genesis (Bloom, 1990, p. 60), the capacity of the tenets of sovereignty, as defined by the UN Charter, to prohibit external interference constituted a major attraction for those determined to extricate themselves from colonialism, as evidenced by the seminal ten-point Declaration on World Peace and Cooperation agreed at the Bandung Conference of 1955 (see Box 3.4). The codification of sovereign equality and inviolability in the UN Charter has thus been conceived as a progressive development insofar as it constituted a means by which entitlements, previously almost exclusively enjoyed by Western powers, were universalized (Cunliffe, 2011). Indicatively, in an address to the General Assembly, Abdelaziz Bouteflika, president of the African Union, described sovereignty as 'our final defense against the rules of an unjust world' (Weiss, 2007a, p. 16).

The prohibition on external interference was a reaction against the historical trend whereby powerful states used military aggression against weaker states or those peoples ostensibly languishing in *terra nullius*. Frequently this aggression was presented as emancipatory and progressive – the so-called 'white man's burden' – rather than as purely self-interested, hence the latter-day suspicion in the developing world towards the 'humanitarian imperative' cited by Western states. According to Bull, the fear of external interference and the determination to maintain the principle of sovereign inviolability as championed by many former colonies is understandable given that this enables these states 'effectively to combat the foreign domination to which they were subjected when they lacked these rights (1984a, p. 6). The prohibition on external interference thus derives from the normative notion that citizens within states should be free to determine their own political system. In this sense, 'restraints to intervention', as noted by Anthony Lang, '[should not] be seen as evil attempts to block the efforts of good humanitarians. Rather, the restraints of sovereignty and the structures of international law that support those restraints serve a moral purpose: the promotion of a community inside clearly defined borders' (2003, p. 2).

The idea of sovereignty as a right conditional on meeting certain criteria, such as human rights, rather than a legal tenet enjoyed by all states, constitutes 'proportionate equality' (Bain, 2003b, p. 63). The conceptualization of international society as a legal order based on proportionate rather than sovereign equality, as stipulated by positive law, would clearly create a hierarchy of states. This is actively championed by certain

---

Box 3.4   Declaration on World Peace and Cooperation, 1955 Bandung Conference

1 Respect for fundamental human rights and for the purposes and principles of the charter of the UN.
2 Respect for the sovereignty and territorial integrity of all nations.
3 Recognition of the equality of all races and of the equality of all nations large and small.
4 Abstention from intervention or interference in the internal affairs of another country.
5 Respect for the right of each nation to defend itself, singly or collectively, in conformity with the charter of the UN.
6 (a) Abstention from the use of arrangements of collective defence to serve any particular interests of the big powers.
   (b) Abstention by any country from exerting pressures on other countries.
7 Refraining from acts or threats of aggression or the use of force against the territorial integrity or political independence of any country.
8 Settlement of all international disputes by peaceful means, such as negotiation, conciliation, arbitration or judicial settlement as well as other peaceful means of the parties own choice, in conformity with the charter of the UN.
9 Promotion of mutual interests and cooperation.
10 Respect for justice and international obligations.

observers: Michael Glennon has defended the right of 'enlightened states' to abandon the UN Charter's codification of sovereign equality and inviolability (1999, p. 2). According to Glennon these enlightened states naturally act in pursuit of international justice, and he concludes that 'if power is used to do justice, law will follow' (ibid., p. 7). Richard Falk, however, has rejected this argument on the grounds that it is similar to the arguments proffered in favour of the civilizing effects of colonialism: 'it seems unavoidable to wonder whether Glennon's use of "enlightened" is not a late 20th century updating of the now unfashionable "civilized"' (2004, p. 41).

The framework of international law established by the UN Charter, with sovereign equality at its centre, can be viewed as comprising legal codes designed to militate the capacity of powerful states to influence weaker states, a so-called 'equalitarian regime' (Reus-Smit, 2005, p. 71). States are clearly not equal in many respects, but international law has sought to emulate pluralist, democratic ideals by fashioning a regime based on the internationalization of 'one man one vote'. A state's international legal rights are thus not dependent on its economic or military capacity, political composition or culture. The advance of positive law and sovereign equality derived from a rejection of the 'natural law' approach to international relations prevalent in the 18th and early 19th century. The conflation of power – be it economic, military or cultural – and legal rights was characteristic of this era of colonialism, when states legitimized their actions as benevolent (see Chapter 5). A potential consequence of this challenge is the 'legitimisation of a new more divisive international framework based on economic and military power' (Chandler, 2002, p. 136). Thus, the pluralist ideal of inter-state relations and rule formation is fundamentally threatened by the regression from sovereign equality.

Sovereignty, it is argued, promotes order and stability in the international system. While it may not necessarily be compatible with certain expansive conceptions of human rights, it at least facilitates non-violent international interaction and even cooperation. According to Gene Lyons and Michael Mastanduno, the emergence of the principle of sovereignty and its widespread acceptance led to the development of four major political institutions which enabled international order to be preserved (1995, p. 8). First, a balance of power developed in Europe that prevented the rise of an overly dominant state. Second, rules of behaviour gradually became codified in international law, and, while a distinct and accepted set of laws for international relations did not immediately emerge, certain state practices were generally accepted as either unlawful or as ingrained customs. Third, the acceptance of sovereignty led to the frequent convening of international conferences to settle major disputes which might otherwise have descended into inter-state conflict. Finally, accepted diplomatic practices and procedures for state-level contact evolved as a result of the greater acceptance of the right of other independent states to exist.

As discussed in the first section, prior to the signing of the UN Charter the recognition of sovereignty was contingent on the whims of the powerful, and was thus less a legal right than a function of power and/or patronage. Without sovereignty enshrined as the legal foundation for international relations, states acted without significant external constraint and relied on more nebulous grounds for their actions, such as natural law: 'positive international law ... derived as a response to the endemic abuse of natural law' (Bellamy, 2004, p. 141). A system based on natural law is, Bellamy states, 'often a more disorderly international society with a much higher incidence of war' (ibid., p. 132). Thus, the historical evidence suggests that in the absence of positive law, warfare increases, particularly when certain states believe themselves to have exclusive rights to act in the interests of humanity. As Bull notes, 'particular states or groups of states that set themselves up as the authoritative judges of the world common good, in disregard of the views of others, are in fact a menace to international order, and thus to effective action in that field' (1984a, p. 12).

States buoyed by an inflated conception of their own benevolence have historically been the cause of much violence. This clearly has significant implications for the contemporary debate on humanitarian intervention and the idea of 'illegal but legitimate' intervention, whereby certain states act as self-appointed guardians of the common good (see Chapter 5).

Aggressive states have, however, proved unwilling to respect the notion of sovereign equality and inviolability even after the signing of the UN Charter. The occasional breach of the Charter's rules on sovereignty need not, however, be taken as evidence of the wholesale ineffectiveness and impotence of the concept or international law generally. According to Chesterman and Byers, the UN framework contributed to the prevention of a major international conflagration and also operated as an international forum for debate (1999). The development of the UN can, in this sense, be seen as a positive derived from the rejection of subjective natural law and great power diplomacy in favour of positive international law based on sovereign equality. Undermining this framework through evoking claims of 'conditional sovereignty' and 'illegal but legitimate' interventionism potentially risks compromising the achievement of the positives that have accrued from the framework's establishment and proliferation. The proliferation of standards or criteria to which states must adhere to qualify as sovereign risks, which destabilize the system through an unanticipated increase in purportedly benevolent interventionism (Vincent, 1986, p. 117).

Many have argued that it is incorrect to conceptualize sovereignty as imbuing the state with the power to do whatever it wants internally. While sovereign inviolability clearly prohibits external interference it does not necessarily separate the individual state from the international system. Sovereignty is better understood as relative – dependent on certain external factors. 'It is relative', according to Gerry Simpson, 'in that this form of sovereignty must constantly treat with the sovereignty of other states'. It is also relative, he notes, in so far as it is 'constrained by the existence of international law itself' (Simpson, 2004, p. 41). This is a view similar to that of Bull who, despite a fundamental endorsement of sovereignty, did not conceptualize sovereignty as synonymous with absolute isolation or complete internal autonomy (1984a, pp. 11–12).

The wholly negative image of the system founded on sovereignty – 'a quagmire of infighting among nations and groups wholly unable to settle pressing collective issues' (Held, 1995, p. 268) – is, therefore, deemed an exaggeration. Jean Cohen notes that, for critics, sovereignty signifies 'a claim to power unrestrained by law and a bulwark against legal, political, and military action necessary to enforce human rights'. She contends, however, that 'the discourse of sovereignty involves normative principles and symbolic meanings worth preserving' (2004, pp. 12–13). The arguments presented by many of sovereignty's critics can only be sustained by presenting an absolutist conception of sovereignty which, Cohen maintains, 'has long since been abandoned' (ibid., p. 13). The image of sovereignty presented by its opponents is, therefore, very often a caricature. As I will demonstrate in Chapter 4, there are few who champion a notion of sovereignty that imbues states with the right to do *whatever* they please internally.

Additionally, it is debatable whether sovereignty is the primary barrier to a more humane world order. Those instances in the 1990s that sparked the greatest moral outcry, the Rwandan genocide in 1994 and the massacre at Srebrenica in 1995, led many to call for a change in the status of sovereignty. It is unclear, however, what influence sovereignty exercised in both these cases. Calls for a diminution of sovereignty in light of these atrocities would make sense only if external actors did not intervene because they did not want to break international law. This, however, was not the case. The ineffective response of the international community to both instances arguably derived from a lack of interest and will on behalf of those with the capacity to intervene rather than any commitment to international law (see Gow, 1997; Bellamy, 2002; Chesterman, 2003).

Conclusion

During the 1990s sovereignty came under sustained criticism from those who believed in the necessity of humanitarian intervention. Those supportive of maintaining sovereign inviolability were accused of being 'complicit in human rights violations' (Linklater, 2000) and recalcitrant 'resisters to change' who 'sponsor a limited and almost irrelevant discussion' (Gow, 2005, p. 122).

By the end of the decade Thomas Pangle and Peter Ahrensdorf wrote: 'the nation-state is today weaker than it has been since 1815, and arguably weaker than it has ever been since its first form was established in the Treaty of Westphalia in 1648' (1999, p. 3). Supporters of humanitarian intervention welcomed this diminution of sovereignty in favour of conditional sovereignty whereby a state's sovereign rights were dependent on its human rights record. The more extreme manifestation of this view held that the West, by virtue of its superior humanitarian record, had a duty to engage in 'a new kind of imperialism, one acceptable to a world of human rights and cosmopolitan values' (Cooper, 2002). The asymmetry between Western states and the rest of the international community was legitimized on the basis that the West was a progressive force in international affairs.

For others, however, the diminution of sovereignty constitutes a regression to the pre-Charter era of Great Power domination (Gibbs, 2009; Cunliffe, 2011). The danger, according to Chesterman, is that the gradual dismantling of the existing restraints on the use of force will make the international security once again reliant 'on the eirenic munificence of the modern Great Power(s)' (2002, p. 236). The negative image of sovereignty, and indeed its supporters, often presented by human rights advocates is thus misleading. Sovereignty is not inherently negative nor has it been created and sustained to facilitate exploitation and the consolidation of power. Equally, however (as is dealt with in Chapters 4 and 5), it would be wrong to view sovereignty as either a legal norm consistently respected since 1945 or a principle inherently subversive of power (Orford, 2003; Simpson, 2004).

The paradox of sovereignty is that, while helping to protect states from external interference, the sovereign-state system has additionally meant that states are not necessarily subject to prevailing international moral norms because of their autonomous status (Held, 1995, p. 79). While few proponents of sovereignty advocate a system based on the absolute autonomy of states, in some cases governments have articulated just such a defence in response to international pressure to halt domestic oppression.

Factors other than human rights have challenged the status of sovereignty in the modern era, and clearly the confluence of these many pressures makes it unlikely that the normative rendering of sovereignty espoused during the period of decolonization can be sustained. Of course, sovereignty has proven to be a remarkably resilient feature of international relations, and while its present political and legal manifestation may alter, support for a system based on sovereign states of some kind is still dominant. In offering an explanation for this, Brown suggests that as sovereignty has become the dominant means of organizing the world a 'lock-in effect' has developed whereby the status quo is maintained because 'the costs of changing it are prohibitively high' (2006, p. 39). In the next chapter I explore theoretical perspectives on the place of human rights in the relationship between the state and its citizens, and the broader issue of what rights and responsibilities the international community has to maintain standards within sovereign states.

Questions

- What were the key events and catalysts for the emergence of the sovereign state?
- To what extent did the Peace of Westphalia alter international relations?
- Is Stephen Krasner correct to claim that sovereignty is 'organized hypocrisy'?
- In what way has the rise of humanitarian advocacy challenged the status of sovereignty in the post-Cold War era?
- How persuasive are the arguments in defence of sovereignty?

Further reading

On the rise and nature of the modern state

Anderson, B. (1991) *Imagined Communities: Reflections on the Origin and Spread of Nationalism* (London: Verso).

Anderson, M.S. (1998) *The Origins of the Modern European State System, 1494–1618* (London: Longman).

Beetham, D. (1991) *The Legitimisation of Power* (Basingstoke and New York: Palgrave Macmillan).

Dryzek, J. and Dunleavy, P. (2009) *Theories of the Democratic State* (Basingstoke and New York: Palgrave Macmillan).

Hobson, J. (2000) *The State and International Relations* (Cambridge: Cambridge University Press).

Kennedy, P. (1987) *The Rise and Fall of the Great Powers* (New York: Random House).

Osiander, A. (1994) *The State System of Europe, 1640–1990* (Oxford: Oxford University Press).

Tilly, C. (1990) *Coercion, Capital and European States, A.D. 990–1990* (Oxford: Blackwell).

On sovereignty

Bain, W. (2003) *Between Anarchy and Society* (Oxford: Oxford University Press).

Bickerton, C., Cunliffe, P. and Gourevitch, A. (eds) (2006) *Politics Without Sovereignty: A Critique of Contemporary International Relations* (London: Routledge).

Brown, C. (2006) *Sovereignty, Rights and Justice* (London: Polity).

Bull, H. (2002) *The Anarchical Society: A Study of Order in World Politics* (Basingstoke: Palgrave Macmillan; New York: Columbia University Press).

Camilleri, J.A. and Falk, J. (1992) *The End of Sovereignty* (London, Elgar).

Held, D. (1995) *Democracy and the Global Order* (London: Polity).

Jackson, R. (1996) *Quasi-states: Sovereignty, International Relations and the Third World* (Cambridge: Cambridge University Press).

Krasner, S. (1999) *Sovereignty: Organized Hypocrisy* (Princeton, NJ: Princeton University Press).

Lyons, G. and Mastanduno, M. (eds) (1995) *Beyond Westphalia: State Sovereignty and International Intervention* (Baltimore: Johns Hopkins University Press).

Miller, D. (2007) *National Responsibility and Global Justice* (Oxford: Oxford University Press).

Scheipers, S. (2009) *Negotiating Sovereignty and Human Rights* (Manchester: Manchester University Press).

Simpson, G. (2004) *Great Powers and Outlaw States* (Cambridge: Cambridge University Press).

Chapter 4

Theoretical Perspectives

The issue of intervention, Martin Wight wrote, 'raises questions of the utmost moral complexity: adherents of every political belief will regard intervention as justified under certain circumstances' (1979a, p. 191). The flipside of Wight's observation, of course, is that what one group views as a just intervention another will consider profoundly unjust. Examining IR theory can help us understand why this is the case by enabling us to (broadly) categorize the differing perspectives and draw out those key beliefs that preclude certain individuals and groups from supporting particular interventions or intervention more generally.

Theory is ostensibly a means by which scholars can understand how and why the international system works as it does. Normatively, therefore, it is a politically neutral tool for inquiry and observation based on certain fundamental tenets (see Box 4.1). It is important to note, however, that this perspective on theory has been increasingly challenged in recent years. According to Robert Cox, 'there is no such thing as theory in itself, divorced from a standpoint in time and space. When any theory so represents itself, it is more important to examine it as ideology, and to lay bare its concealed perspective' (1996, p. 87). Thus, while the theoretical perspectives examined here are not overtly ideological, with the exception of Marxism, and in the majority of cases are proffered as a neutral academic framework for understanding global affairs, this premise is keenly contested.

Box 4.1   Shared theoretical characteristics of Carr's *The Twenty Years Crisis* (2001) and Morgenthau's *Politics Among Nations* (1954)

1   Each developed a broad framework of analysis which distilled the essence of international politics from disparate events.
2   Each sought to provide future analysts with the theoretical tools for understanding general patterns underlying seemingly unique episodes.
3   Each reflected on the forms of political action which were most appropriate in a realm in which the struggle for power was pre-eminent.

Source: Burchill and Linklater (2005, p. 1).

In this chapter I explore those theories of IR that have most to say about humanitarian intervention: realism, Marxism, liberalism, the English School, cosmopolitanism and post-structuralism. It is important to note that it is impossible to cover here the key tenets of each of these theories or even their particular perspective on humanitarian intervention. I seek only to highlight broad trends and key perspectives, and provide an introduction to the basic presumptions which have led observers to reach certain conclusions about humanitarian intervention. The nuances and heterogeneity of each theory cannot be addressed adequately here, and the categorizations are necessarily broad.

Realism

While we may identify 'statism, survival and self-help' as core beliefs of realism, this tradition has a long history and takes a number of forms (Coicaud and Wheeler, 2008, p. 7). Nonetheless, accepting this heterogeneity it is clear that, as Alex Bellamy notes, 'the realist tradition opposes the norm of humanitarian intervention' (2003, p. 10).

Realists argue that states do not act on the basis of moral concerns, such as human rights violations abroad, nor are international institutions significant influences on state behaviour (Mearsheimer, 1994). The classical realist perspective articulates a pessimistic view of human nature whereby egoistic passions incline men and women to evil (Boucher, 1998, p. 93; Donnelly, 2002, p. 86). Thomas Hobbes's widely endorsed rationale for a central authority or 'Leviathan' was that otherwise life would be 'solitary, poore, nasty, brutish, and short' (1968 [1651], p. 186). In the international system there is no overarching authority to impose order, Hobbes argued, 'because there is no Common Power in this world to punish injustice: mutual fear may keep [states] apart for a time, but upon every visible advantage they will invade one another' (Boucher, 1998, pp. 145–6). States are trapped in a security dilemma and in a perennial state of tension and fear, and this, rather than the pursuit of international justice, determines their behaviour (Morgenthau, 1954; Wight, 1966b).

In contrast to classical realists, neo-realists put greater emphasis on the influence of international anarchy rather than human nature, claiming that this compels states to adopt a selfish disposition which curtails altruistic action, such as humanitarian intervention (Waltz, 1991, p. 29). As the international structure is 'probably unchangeable', international politics is characterized by 'continuity, regularity and repetition' (Layne, 1994, p. 11).

In assessing state behaviour realists are guided, Hans Morgenthau claimed, by 'the concept of interest defined in terms of power' (1954, p. 5).

Power has historically been the primary catalyst for state action, and real-ism claims to be 'a recognition of the inevitabilities of power politics in an age of sovereign states' (Herz, 1957, p. 86). The struggle for power and the struggle for survival are seen as identical, and all other interests are secondary (Spykman, 1942, p. 18). Realists assert that law and morality *could* play a role in the behaviour of states if the nature of the international system was such that states felt bound to a wider community. In the absence of this sense of community, however, states are compelled to act strategically, not morally, and aim at all times to maximize their national interest and protect their security (Morgenthau, 1951). Therefore, a concern for those suffering abroad does not motivate states to act unless there are national interests involved (see Chapter 8). This does not mean, however, that states should or do behave aggressively at all times, but rather that they aim to consolidate their position and seek equilibrium or a balance of power (Waltz, 1981).

Morgenthau argued that 'universal moral principles cannot be applied to the actions of states' (1954, p. 9), while neo-realists 'do not even bother with morality', disregarding it as an important factor in international rela-tions (Donnelly, 2002, p. 107). This rejection of morality clearly has signif-icant implications for humanitarian intervention. Realism asserts that morality is not an absolute or universal code, as the Just War tradition suggests (see Chapter 2), and statesmen and women should maintain a situational, case-by-case approach (Rosenthal, 1995, p. xiv). In this respect international issues are dealt with according to prevailing exigencies rather than abstract moral codes (Niebuhr, 1932, p. 174). Moral rhetoric is addi-tionally held invariably to shroud more sectional aims, hence E. H. Carr's famous assertion that 'theories of morality are ... the product of dominant nations or groups of nations' (2001, p. 74). Thus, it is of no surprise to realists that the currently most powerful group of states – the West – have been most vociferous in advocating human rights and humanitarian inter-vention (see Chapter 6). Those who claim to be undertaking humanitarian interventions are indicatively accused by Danilo Zolo of engaging in 'an inherently hegemonic and violent undertaking' (1997, p. 15). Without an agreed international authority to sanction intervention independently, the question 'who decides?' remains outstanding, leading to subjective deter-minations on when to intervene derived from narrow considerations of national interest (see Chapter 7).

Certain realists advance a communitarian ethos, stressing the need to respect diversity and promote the equitable interaction of states as a means of preserving order and promoting peaceful coexistence (Chandler, 2004b, p. 14). Hence the rights enjoyed by citizens within states are deemed an exclusively internal matter, and a plurality of intra-state human rights regimes is to be expected and respected. Anthony Coates describes this strain of realism as 'the morality of states'. He notes that 'because its main object is to safeguard the autonomy of states, it does so in a form that is too limited to accommodate humanitarian intervention' (Coates, 2006, p. 68). Realism, therefore, suggests a clear distinction between the domestic and the international, and the need for a consequent division between the disciplines of politics and IR (Wight, 1966a, p. 18). Nonetheless, while many modern realists have consciously avoided normative theorizing about domestic politics, many of the historical figures touted as realism's antecedents did in fact discuss these issues at length. Hobbes emphasized the state's duty to provide its citizens with the 'good life' (Jackson, 2006), while Machiavelli's extensive writings on republican constitutionalism have often been overshadowed by his more bellicose prescriptions (Brown, 2006, p. 69).

The realist concern with order attributes great utility to the principles of sovereign equality and inviolability, as they limit the extent to which states behave according to subjective considerations of justice and rights (Lyons and Mastanduno, 1995, p. 8). The extent to which sovereignty is respected, however, derives from the distribution of power, and at any given time the existence of states, and the rights they enjoy, are functions of this prevailing distribution. Sovereignty is often not respected and is, as Stephen Krasner famously stated, 'organized hypocrisy' (1999; see Chapter 3).

The preference for order derived from the pursuit of national interest is described as 'rule consequentialism', whereby if all states limit themselves to specific national interests the community of states will benefit, as inherently disruptive interventionism will be reduced (Welsh, 2006, p. 62). Humanitarian intervention necessarily disrupts order, as such action is not a strategic concern and is based on subjective moral judgements (Kissinger, 1992, p. 5). Colin Gray (2001) argues that humanitarian intervention constitutes a policy which will inevitably antagonize the majority who have an interest in the status quo and ultimately catalyse a backlash against the intervening party by other states. Intra-state conflicts, if left alone, will result in a victory for the powerful group, preserve the natural order derived from disparities in power, and 'enhance the peacemaking potential of war' (Luttwak, 1999, p. 36). Thus NATO's intervention in Kosovo in 1999 (see Chapter 11) is criticized as 'a perfect failure' by Michael Mandelbaum (1999) on the grounds that it caused instability in the Balkans and antagonized Russia and China. This preference for strategic goals grounded in the national interest and cognizant of the reality of power echoes Carl Schmitt's critique of Just Wars. Schmitt argued that wars fought for political gain are invariably limited by the strategic goals of the protagonists, while Just Wars, and humanitarian wars in particular, lead to total war because of their inherently expansive goals and moral fervour (1996, p. 36).

Action taken to halt or prevent human suffering will create difficulties for the pursuit of a state's national interest, as there are inevitably occasions when, morally unpalatable as it may be, it is necessary to ally with states with dubious human rights records. To intervene in one state on the basis of human rights will expose the intervening state to the charge of hypocrisy, and it is prudent, therefore, to overlook issues such as human rights for the sake of the preservation of alliances (Bandow, 1999).

Realism, despite its expressed adherence to positivism, does have a normative dimension; states do have a moral duty, but it is to prioritize the welfare of their own citizens (Kennan, 1985, p. 206; Wight, 1966b, p. 128). Thus launching humanitarian interventions for the good of others is a dereliction of duty if the host state has no interests involved and is imperilled by such action (Bellamy, 2003, pp. 9–10; see Chapter 8). Indeed, citizens are held to expect their state to act in the national interest and, as David Hendrickson (1997) notes with respect to the US intervention in Somalia in 1992, have demonstrated a pronounced unwillingness to accept military casualties when national interests are not involved.

Marxism/critical theory

Though Marx himself wrote little specifically on international politics, the Marxist view is universalist and, as with its domestic analysis, events are explained and assessed according to a perceived struggle between the capitalist elite and the oppressed majority (Brown, 2006, p. 54). Marx believed that colonialism was ultimately beneficial, not because he endorsed the 'white man's burden' argument (see pp. 192–3), but because this would accelerate the global transition to capitalism which was a necessary stage on the road to global communism (Marx, 2006 [1867]). Prior to the outbreak of the First World War Marxists such as Rosa Luxemburg and most notably Lenin began to develop a more critical theory of imperialism, which held that inter-capitalist competition was driving Western states to competitive colonialism which would eventually lead to world war. Critical theory, inspired by the Frankfurt School and the writings of Antonio Gramsci, emerged in the 1980s and challenges positivist approaches to IR, seeking instead to act as an emancipatory force (Linklater, 2006).

Marxists broadly agree with the realist analysis of anarchy in terms of the absence of a formal political hierarchy but argue that international systemic composition is a product of the conscious design of the dominant economic powers (Cox, 1986). Powerful states have colluded to create a core–periphery dichotomy, and while there is inter-state rivalry among the elite, this is largely negated by the common goal of proliferating capitalist hegemony (Wallerstein, 1974). Marxism, and critical theory more generally, rejects the idea of the international system constituting a set of 'pre-constituted social actors' and criticizes the realist and liberal perspectives for their ahistorical analysis of the international system and inability to foresee future change (Rupert, 2007, p. 149).

The system of states is considered to be a means by which the global economy can flourish to the benefit of certain actors, and hence Marxist IR theory perceives the present legal status of sovereignty (see Chapter 5) as a function of a top-down consolidation of hierarchy rather than a bottom-up evolutionary process (Rosenberg, 1994, p. 14). The existing constellation of states is held to be a product of power and oppression, and a social order derived from the dominant class's desire, especially during the Industrial Revolution, to perpetuate its hegemony and domination of the means of production. Preserving sovereign inviolability is not, therefore, the goal of Marxists, as states are considered to be inimical to proletariat solidarity, though Marxists do critique intervention as an exercise of power by the strong against the weak. The few genuinely progressive advances in contemporary international law are attributed to the influence of the Soviet Union's promotion of self-determination (Bowring, 2008, pp. 10–11).

The Marxist explanation of the unwillingness of states to act morally is similar to that of realism, though for different reasons. Humans are not inherently selfish or aggressive but become so because they are shaped by the prevailing societal conditions under capitalism, which engenders greed and selfishness (Boucher, 1998, p. 360). This conditioning also occurs in the international system, and thus states behave in singularly self-interested ways so that capitalist exploitation can flourish (Lenin, 1964, pp. 26–8). Marxism anticipates that states will be unconcerned about human suffering in other states and will use the pretext of sovereign inviolability to justify this position, though it rejects relativism in favour of sub-state universalism.

The Marxist view differs fundamentally from that of realism in the sense that Marxism is premised on the need to achieve solidarity between the oppressed classes across states and a belief in progressive evolution towards international communism. For Marxists, international politics is 'intraclass solidarities combined with interclass war waged both across and within state borders' (Coicaud and Wheeler, 2008, p. 10). While Marxists, like realists, consider normative perspectives on international affairs to be inherently partisan, they 'also rely upon an idealist commitment to human welfare that makes the determination of international progress an essential feature of both their scientific explanation and their plan for revolutionary liberation' (ibid.). What Marxist and realist views have in common, Janna Thompson notes, is 'the idea that conflict, injustice, threats of war are embedded in the very structure of relationships in the international world, and that so long as these relationships remain, the peaceful and just world ... will be impossible to achieve' (1992, p. 6).

Marxists argue that humanitarian justifications for intervention hide ulterior motives: for the Marxist, 'morality is ideology, and thus represents the interests of a class' (Brown, 2002, p. 228). Noam Chomsky, indicative of the Marxist approach, argues that the West's increased willingness to undertake 'humanitarian interventions' is part of an escalating Western unilateralism born out of the dramatic extension of Western hegemony in the post-Cold War era. According to Chomsky, 'the right of humanitarian intervention, if it exists, is premised on the good faith of those intervening, and that assumption is based not on their rhetoric but on their record' (1999, p. 74). On the basis of what Chomsky (2011) sees as the West's history of oppression and violence, the moral argument is implausible.

Western interest in humanitarian intervention, it is claimed, stems from the fact that in the post-Cold War era the leaders of these states 'find themselves without effective economic policies to promote the social justice they claim to serve, but still need a virtuous cause to distinguish themselves from "the right"' (Johnstone, 2000, p. 14). Mark Duffield argues 'the strategic complexities of liberal peace ... are part of an already existing system of networked global liberal governance', and thus the spread of liberalism is a means of increasing power (2006, p. 258). The linkage between development and security is considered central to the rise in human security and its adoption by the major Western powers (see Chapter 6). Increasingly, however, Duffield and Nicholas Waddell argue, the discourse has shifted away from development towards 'a "harder" version of security which prioritizes homeland livelihood systems and infrastructures' with a view to providing the West with greater security from threats ostensibly emanating from the developing world (2006, p. 3). Duffield argues that there has been a marked shift from the prioritization of geopolitics during the Cold War to biopolitics in the contemporary era. This manifests as a concern with the social conditions within the periphery and the 'circulatory terrain of human population'. This shift, Duffield argues, has led to the rehabilitation of 'liberal imperialism ... authored by effective states' (2005, p. 144). Human rights have revolutionary potential, but this is denuded when the discourse of human rights is harnessed by the hegemonic powers and expressed in an individualistic as opposed to collective form (Bowring, 2008, p. 126).

Marxist analyses of instances of Western intervention highlight this emphasis on power and capitalism (Gibbs, 2009, p. 10). Western interest in humanitarian crises in the 1990s was described as a function of a quest for new markets and the consolidation of Western dominance, and thus driven by 'the American government and business classes, aided and abetted by their European elites' (Mandel, 2003, p. 293). The overall aim of humanitarian intervention is 'to be able to punish and reward states that defy the contour of political/ideological order advantageous to the hegemonic state' (Chadda, 2003, p. 321). According to Alex Callinicos, 'the real reason' for NATO's intervention in Kosovo was 'the strategic and economic interests of the US and the other Western powers' (2000, p. 176), while Ellen Wood described the intervention as part of the 'new imperialism' whereby intervention is directed towards 'ensuring that the forces of the capitalist market prevail in every corner of the world' (2000, p. 192). In a similar vein, the editorial committee of the Marxist journal *Capital and Class* declared with respect to the 2003 invasion of Iraq: 'rather than being a humanitarian intervention, the invasion is a brutal act of imperialist aggression' (2003). James Tyner argues that the invasion had nothing to do with humanitarian concerns but rather constituted a 'militant neoliberal capitalist imperative ... waged for material gain that – ultimately – would benefit only a select few corporate CEOs, financiers, and bankers' (2006, pp. 32–3). Thus the motivation behind humanitarian intervention for Marxists is not human rights but rather the spread of capitalism and the consolidation of the core–periphery dichotomy (Amin, 2008; Gibbs, 2009; Mamdani, 2009).

Liberalism

Liberalism holds that man is torn between an innate desire for freedom and a competing desire to live in a society. While man is certainly driven by the quest for personal gain (though not necessarily power), this trait is not inevitably detrimental to human interaction, and can in fact be a catalyst for better societal organization. Thus, there is significant scope for contriving rules that benefit the entire society (Keohane and Nye, 1977).

This inherent preference for cooperation over conflict in the pursuit of individual liberty can be transferred to the international realm provided states share certain basic characteristics and hence recognize the utility of cooperation. Thus, in contrast to the realist, and indeed Marxist, analyses, liberalism believes that progressive international cooperation and formal processes of international authority can be developed under certain conditions (see Chapter 7). States that operate according to the principles of free trade will necessarily recognize the benefit of both peaceful interaction and the formal codification of rules to govern trade. This finds its most famous expression in the work of Immanuel Kant. He argued that international trade would lead to a rise in global prosperity, especially amongst 'the peace-loving, productive sections of the population', and financial interdependence amongst states would 'make clear to all of them their fundamental community of interests' (Burchill, 2005, p. 63). This rationale, indeed, underpinned the establishment of the project of European integration after the Second World War. Additionally, because democratic states are ruled by leaders elected by the people whose preference is for peace, the governments of democratic states are unlikely to be aggressive and 'wars become impossible' (Doyle, 1986, p. 1151). This is the basis of the democratic peace theory which holds that democracies do not go to war against other democracies (Levy, 1989, p. 88)

Liberalism holds that as the evolution of human society is characterized by progress the current international system is transitory; democracy will gradually spread and the quality of life will increase (Fukuyama, 1992; Howard, 2000, p. 31). Michael Barnett's definition of liberalism emphasizes this belief:

> [Liberals are] ... intellectuals who believe in progress; the capacity of individuals to learn from the past; the construction of new political institutions to increase freedom and reduce the likelihood of physical violence; and thus the ability to improve the moral charter and material welfare of humankind. (2010, p. 26).

Unlike Marxists, of course, liberalism seeks to proliferate the Western capitalist system on the grounds that liberal democracy is 'the end point of mankind's ideological evolution' and 'the final form of human government' (Fukuyama, 1992, pp. xi–xii). The fact that there is a correlation between the best political system and the currently most powerful group of states is not a cause of concern for liberals in the way it is for realists and Marxists. Rather than a modern manifestation of the union of power and dominant moral norms, the post-Cold War coincidence between liberal democracy and power is what makes the current systemic configuration so potentially progressive (Shaw, 1994, p. 155; Frost, 2001, p. 42). This desire to see the West spread liberal values has obvious implications for humanitarian intervention, as such action is considered part of the march of human progress and a means by which the global transition to liberal democracy can be facilitated.

Marshall Cohen's perspective is typical of the broad liberal approach to morality: 'it is entirely appropriate to judge both a nations and its statesmen's conduct by pertinent moral standards' (Cohen, 1984, p. 300). While warning against excessive moralism, Cohen argues that states are duty bound to be concerned about the plight of people resident in other states (ibid., p. 324). Michael Walzer dismisses the realist belief that behaving amorally in international relations is excusable on the grounds that there is a systematic bias against such action, and notes:

> If we had all become realists like the Athenian generals or Hobbists in a state of war, there would be an end alike to both morality and hypocrisy. We would simply tell one another brutally and directly, what we wanted to do or have done. But the truth is that one of the things most of us want, even in war, is to act or to seem to act morally. (Walzer, 1992a, p. 21)

Walzer seeks to bring order *and* justice back to international relations so that statesmen and women can no longer excuse amoral action by taking solace in the realist assertion that international society is irrevocably anarchical. He, like a number of 'institutional liberals', advocates codified international laws which give legal expression to moral norms (ibid., p. 288; see also Chapter 5 and Conclusion).

Although the state is considered a necessary guarantor of individual liberties, liberalism favours limiting the influence of the state in the 'private' affairs of citizens. Internationally this manifests as an underlying preference for laws and practices that privilege the individual over the state, but, unlike cosmopolitanism, not to the extent that the state is fundamentally undermined. Indicatively, Marc Weller states that the rise of human rights as an international issue has challenged the fictitious notion that states are international subjects, arguing 'the state only exists to the extent that the people out of which it is composed have transferred to it the competence to exercise public powers on their behalf' (1999, p. 24). The sharp distinction between internal and international as advanced by realism is thus rejected, although, as with the normative conception of the domestic system, there is a preference for state autonomy and international pluralism.

The liberal respect for pluralism, however, necessarily encourages the inside/outside distinction on one level, suggesting as it does tolerance for the difference inherent in other states and cultures. However, there are limits to this tolerance, and the extension of this privilege to others is in key respects dependent on political and ideological symmetry. Thus, the liberal perspective is often characterized by what Gerry Simpson describes as 'liberal anti-pluralism', which manifests an intolerance for different regimes and international institutions that do not reflect liberal values (2004, p. 280). In this sense there is a clear unwillingness to accept that a state is entitled to inviolability by virtue of being a state; sovereignty is therefore 'conditional' (Gowan, 2003, p. 51; see Chapter 6). Ann-Marie Slaughter, a proponent of this idea, admits: '[liberal theory] permits, indeed mandates, a distinction among different types of states based on their domestic political structure and ideology' (1995, p. 509), while self-described liberal Geoffrey Robertson claimed: the reality is that states are not equal' (2002, p. 372). Non-intervention is described by Fernando Tesón as 'a doctrine of the past' based on relativism and statism (2005a, p.

358). Hence, in the post-Cold War era liberals have, somewhat paradoxi-cally, been to the fore in advocating the subversion of the UN in cases where humanitarian intervention is deemed necessary, such as in Kosovo in 1999, because of the Security Council's dependence on the assent of non-democracies (see Chapter 7 and Conclusion).

Liberalism does not privilege order, and like Marxism is in fact predi-cated on the necessity of progressive change and in this sense is 'inherently disorderly' (Freedman, 2005, p. 101). Liberalism refutes the validity of realism's exclusive concern with order, arguing that 'order without a mod-icum of justice can only lead to disaster' (Hoffmann, 2003, p. 24). The con-temporary liberal perspective on intervention, often described as 'liberal internationalism', is at times bellicose and militaristic, stressing the imperative of intervention for the good of humanity (Cooper, 2004). This modern variant of 'disorderly' liberalism is, however, different from older forms; for instance, Walzer highlighted John Stuart Mill's classical liberal perspective on intervention and his belief that nations must achieve self-determination *without* external involvement. Mill did assert, however, that there were three cases when intervention may be permissible. The first is when a state clearly contains two or more separate communities and one is engaged in a struggle for independence. The second is when boundaries have already been crossed and the issue is counter-intervention. The third is 'when the violation of human rights is so terrible that it makes talk of community or self determination or "arduous struggle" seem cynical and irrelevant' (Walzer, 1992a, p. 90). Mill did not, however, give a precise definition of a sufficiently terrible violation of human rights that would warrant intervention, thus leaving the issue open to discretion.

This preference for non-intervention, however, is less apparent in con-temporary liberal theory. Interventionism was particularly championed in the wake of the Soviet Union's collapse as the new systemic conditions were seen as enabling greater Western intervention without threatening international war. The West, it is argued, has elevated itself to a new level of consciousness characterized by a rejection of violence and conquest and unencumbered by old-fashioned, legalistic notions of sovereignty (Cooper, 2002). The intervention in Kosovo (see Chapter 11), for example, was 'an action fought for principles ... to enforce certain minimum values on a state unwilling or unable to accept them' (Cooper, 2004, p. 59). Prior to the invasion of Iraq (see Chapter 12), Michael Ignatieff argued that the use of force by progressive liberal states was historically often progressive, noting that 'there are many peoples who owe their freedom to an exercise of American military power'. The choice facing the West in March 2003, Ignatieff claimed, was 'between containing and leaving a tyrant in place and the targeted use of force, which will kill people but free a nation from the tyrant's grip' (Ignatieff, 2003). More recently, many championed the intervention in Libya in 2011 as indicative of liberalism in action: Roger Cohen (2011) rejoiced that '"liberal interventionist" has now become the proud badge of a generation discovering the good war', while Paul Heinbecker (2011) claimed the intervention upheld liberal values and demonstrated that 'human progress is possible'.

The English School

The English School constitutes something of a mid-point between realism and liberalism. International politics is considered to be anarchical, and this forces states to behave in particular ways, but this systemic condition does not preclude the formation of an international society which adheres to mutable shared norms and laws. Hedley Bull notes that a plurality of sovereign states with a limited degree of interaction among them constitutes a system, whereas a society is characterized by 'a degree of acceptance of common rules and institutions' (2002, p. 225). These societal rules, usually termed norms, 'both constrain and enable actors', thereby limiting the decision-making autonomy of states (Wheeler, 2002, p. 6). While these norms may not constitute laws presided over by a judicial system with the power of enforcement analogous to that in domestic systems, they determine a state's international status and its relationship with other states. Nicholas Wheeler argues that realist and Marxist perspectives overlook the extent to which 'the pursuit of international legitimization' binds state actions, noting that 'even the great powers seek approval from their peers and domestic publics' (2006, p. 32). States are not, therefore, conceived of as autonomous actors devoid of external restraint, although the extent to which the force of norms can influence state behaviour has limits. Nonetheless the English School makes both the empirical observation that norms do influence states to a significant extent and the normative claim that states should be bound by these rules: Chris Brown indicatively assets: 'if diversity entails that states have the right to mistreat their populations, then it is difficult to see why such diversity is to be valued' (1992, p. 125).

Within the English School a division exists between the solidarist, or Grotian, view and the pluralists who are closer to de Vattel (Bellamy, 2005b, p. 9). Pluralists stress the importance of the state, arguing that it provides for both order in the international sphere and, depending on the particular internal composition, for justice and the protection of human rights domestically (Dunne, 1998, p. 100). Individuals enjoy legal rights only to the extent that the state enables them to do so, through the provision of security and domestic legal structures, and thus states are of greater import than individuals. Thus, the basic presumption of non-intervention should be maintained (Jackson, 2000).

Solidarists, however, argue that states, though clearly important, are instrumental – a means by which the individual's rights are upheld – and if this normative duty is not fulfilled, 'collective humanitarian intervention' is legitimate in response to 'extreme human suffering' (Wheeler, 1992, p. 468). Solidarists argue that international regulation of a state's human rights record is both right and necessary, and a means by which the coherence of the society is upheld (Falk, 2005b). The solidarist view is based on the idea that an international society can coalesce around shared norms and values, and hence the violation of one of these norms – such as respect for human rights – is potentially legitimate grounds for intervention (Wheeler and Dunne, 1998, 2001). Alex Bellamy argues that while pluralists insist that intervention must only take place when the host state consents, lest the fundamental rule of the international system be subverted, solidarists by contrast 'claim that the principle of consent is a circumscribed rule with important exceptions in times of massive human suffering' (Bellamy, 2003, p. 5). International society simply could not function if the norms governing intra-state human rights were routinely flouted, and thus intervention is not disruptive, rather it is an occasionally warranted means by which order is in fact restored.

Though Bull is essentially a pluralist, aspects of his work have been highlighted by solidarists to support their perspective. Bull argued that the rule of non-intervention prevailed because unilateral intervention threatened harmony and order within the society of states, although he additionally noted that when an intervention 'expresses the collective will of the society of states' it may not jeopardize international harmony (1984b, p. 195). Given that Bull was writing during a period when the international system was arguably more fractured than it is today, it is possible that the contemporary systemic configuration and the greater integration apparent within the West means that this 'collective will of the society of states' may be stronger (Dunne, 1998). Solidarists argue that there is evidence that norms regarding humanitarian intervention have indeed changed; the many human rights treaties signed since 1945 and the emerging consensus that states cannot treat their citizens any way they please are held as examples of the ascendency and increasingly binding power of international human rights norms (Greenwood, 1993; Bellamy, 2009b). The post-Cold War ascendency of these norms is, therefore, indicative of the fluidity of norms and the potential for a 'norm cascade' to force a shift in the prevailing normative rules influencing the behaviour of states (Finnemore and Sikkink, 1998, p. 893). Governments within states might not naturally act morally in pursuing their foreign policy but through pressure exerted from below by the general public – 'the shaming power of humanitarian norms' – they may be compelled to do so (Wheeler, 2006, p. 39). In this way states become 'rhetorically entrapped' by virtue of adhering to treaties and norms they may not intend to abide by (Glanville, 2011, p. 471).

Solidarism does not suggest, however, that national interests play no role in the decision as to whether to intervene, and, while humanitarian intervention is morally permissible under certain circumstances, it is not necessarily morally required once these circumstances arise (Wheeler, 2002, p. 49).

The pluralist perspective, by contrast, argues that even within an international society states remain the rightful authority on, and guarantor of, human rights. Thus while norms and indeed laws on human rights and intervention exist, they are subjectively interpreted and invariably applied in practice only by powerful states (Bellamy, 2003, p. 3). According to Robert Jackson:

> The ethics of human rights have to be fitted into the pluralist framework of international society and cannot sidestep that framework. That is the only operational context within which human beings can be defended in contemporary world politics. Human rights and humanitarianism have no actuality outside that pluralist framework. Solidarism is clearly subordinate to pluralism. (2000, p. 289)

Similarly, Bull argued that the international society implied by the discourse of universal human rights 'exists only as an ideal, and we court great dangers if we allow ourselves to proceed as if it were a political and social framework already in place' (1984a, p. 13). Bull was sceptical of the power of norms and the existence of an international society generally, and argued that if such a society exists it enjoys 'only a precarious foothold' (2002, p. 248). Bull stressed that it was untenable to claim that sovereignty can be enjoyed without qualification, but argued that promoting ostensibly 'universal human rights' in a context in which there is no consensus over their meaning or the mechanisms for their enforcement 'carries the danger that it will be subversive of coexistence among states, on which the whole fabric of world order in our times depends'. States that declare themselves to be acting in the common interest for the benefit of all humanity are thus 'a menace to international order, and thus to effective action in that field' (1984a, pp. 12–13). This privileging of order over justice in the specific case of humanitarian intervention leads pluralists to espouse what at times appear to be cold-hearted prescriptions. In discussing the crisis in the Balkans, Jackson wrote, in my view, that the stability of international society, especially the unity of the great powers, is more important, indeed far more important, than minority rights and humanitarian protections in Yugoslavia or any other country – if we have to choose between the two' (2000, p. 291).

While this may appear morally unconscionable it is important to remember that this preference is born from a normative conviction that stability is itself a significant moral good, as it prevents war and destruction. Yet, the prevailing systemic composition has clearly altered, and in the post-Cold War era there is an emerging acceptance amongst pluralists that, at the very least, action taken by the Security Council in response to intra-state humanitarian tragedy now has a strong degree of legitimacy and reflects a limited consensus on humanitarian intervention (Bellamy, 2003, p. 12).

Solidarists welcomed NATO's intervention in Kosovo in 1999, with Bellamy asserting that it highlighted 'the extent to which international values and interests have begun to come together during the 1990s' (2002, p. 214). While this intervention appeared to affirm the solidarist conception, the 2003 invasion of Iraq highlighted the extent to which the ascendency of the norm of humanitarian intervention facilitated the abuse of humanitarian rhetoric, and arguably the accuracy of the pluralist concern that intervention was inherently destabilizing and likely to be abused by the powerful (Thakur and Sidhu, 2006; Job, 2006).

Cosmopolitanism

Cosmopolitanism believes in a progressive evolution towards a universal order based on common morality. It constitutes a 'break with the assumption of territorially-based political entities' and explicitly disavows statist conceptions of international politics in favour of an agenda predicated on 'the existence of a human community with certain shared rights and obligations' (Kaldor, 1999, pp. 115, 147). Catherine Lu argues that realists have overlooked the 'transformative potential' that exists when the barriers between states diminish in importance and the distinction between international and domestic politics is removed (2006, p. 50). This merging of the internal and the external has ostensibly accelerated in the contemporary era as states, albeit primarily Western states, have increasingly developed mutually dependent relationships, pooled their sovereignty and contrived new norms on the use of force for humanitarian purposes (Levy et al., 1995; Kaldor, 2003, p. 17). Cosmopolitanism asserts that the maintenance of an internal/external distinction is no longer tenable because of the effects of globalization and the general internationalization of post-Cold War interstate relations (Keane, 2003, pp. 4–8; Held, 2004, p. 189; Hayden, 2005, p. 91). States are no longer the dominant force in the international system and are increasingly constrained by domestic publics, global civil society and transnational organizations such as the European Union (Sørensen, 2001; Brown, 2006, p. 3). The international system is therefore considered to be evolving towards a radical new alignment characterized by the diminution of the centrality of the state, increased interdependence, respect for human rights and, perhaps most ambitiously, mechanisms of global governance involving international military capabilities (Woodhouse and Ramsbotham, 2005, p. 140).

The cosmopolitan perspective comprises a normative vision of the responsibilities of states towards their citizens and, significantly, the responsibilities of the international community to citizens in states that fail to meet these responsibilities. Human rights were thus deemed an international concern and not the sole jurisdiction of sovereign states (Linklater, 1998, p. 109). In this sense, cosmopolitanism rejects the international/domestic distinction in both IR theory and actual state practice as anachronistic and untenable, and seeks greater international coordination on human rights legislation and enforcement, and the diminution of the power of the state in respect to the rights of its own citizens.

'Intervention' occurs when an outside entity intervenes in the internal affairs of another, and thus discussing 'intervention' presupposes an inside/outside distinction. In the specific case of humanitarian intervention we are confronted with a conceptual distinction between the private sphere of the state and the public domain of the international community (Lu, 2006, p. 4). The guiding premise behind this distinction has been questioned in relation to humanitarian intervention. Mervyn Frost argues that humanitarian intervention should not, in fact, be considered a violation of the principle of non-intervention, but rather 'an act directed towards upholding the non-intervention norm of civil society, which protects an area of freedom for individuals'. The principle of non-intervention relates firstly to individuals, and only democratic collectivities of individuals can be afforded the international right of inviolability (Frost, 2001, p. 51). In the same vein Kaldor suggests rethinking humanitarian intervention as an action analogous to domestic police work (2003, pp. 134–6).

The cosmopolitan perspective seeks to increase intervention by fashioning greater interdependence and altering the tenets of sovereignty to reflect a preference for human rights. The statist system has encouraged the singular pursuit of national interests and the privileging of order over justice. This has created a world plagued by instability, violence and 'the callous indifference towards the interests of persons beyond (and perhaps even within) the borders of each state' (Hayden, 2005, p. 70). Cosmopolitanism argues that the international system of states has created false divisions in the international community and allowed relativist claims of morality to thrive. Given that humanity is not singularly motivated by self-interest, as realists suggest, the projection of this negative (and flawed) diagnosis of motivations onto the international system overlooks the capacity of individuals, and hence states, to act in defence of others (Janzekovic, 2006, p. 26). There is, therefore, a need fundamentally to reorganize the international system so as to reflect the underlying universal morality which is humanity's true nature (Küng, 1991, pp. xv–xvi).

Proponents of cosmopolitanism prioritize 'human security' (see Chapter 6) and articulate a trans-state vision of international relations where the individual's rights trump those of the state and thus order and stability amongst states is a secondary concern (Falk, 1995; Kaul, 1995). Andrew Linklater identified the aim of human-centred advocacy as 'transcending state sovereignty', which he considered 'essential to promoting narratives of increasing cosmopolitanism' (1998, p. 109). Humanitarian intervention is therefore conceptualized as 'an act directed towards upholding the non-intervention norm of civil society, which protects an area of freedom for individuals' (Frost, 2001, p. 51). Human rights violations are 'legitimate concerns of individual men and women everywhere, communities in all parts of the world, and the society of states as a whole' (Lu, 2006, p. 112). Rather than viewing intra-state conflicts as a potential threat that needs to be contained, cosmopolitanism 'would seek to understand the underlying reasons behind human rights conflicts and apply positive measures to solve them' (Archibugi, 2003, p. 11).

In addition to this normative defence of humanitarian intervention, trends in the contemporary era have added a practical rationale for increased trans-state humanitarianism. Globalization has undermined state autonomy and fused political, social and cultural interdependence, and therefore humanitarian crises within one state will not be confined to that state. This key supposition mirrors the cosmopolitan maxim proposed in the 18th century by Kant, who held that if the suffering of people abroad were tolerated it would threaten international peace and security because of 'the interconnectedness of the parts that form the whole' (Jackson, 2006, p. 30). In stark contrast to realism, therefore, cosmopolitanism argues that increased humanitarian intervention 'will make for a more peaceful world' (Janzekovic, 2006, p. 190).

As the UN constitutes 'the creature of an unreconstructed system of sovereign nation states' which promotes 'state interest and militarised power', cosmopolitanism has generally called for an adherence to ostensibly less politicized natural law when dealing with intra-state humanitarian crises (Woodhouse and Ramsbotham, 2005, p. 141). Many have compiled lists of criteria that states *should* adhere to for their interventions to be deemed legitimate (see Chapter 2). This attempt to constrain intervention is predicated on the assumption that democracies will intervene only with the endorsement of their domestic populace and global civil society, who can ensure compliance with the criteria (Buchanan and Keohane, 2004, p. 19). The emergence of global civil society poses a 'trans-formative challenge to the customary role of states' (Falk, 1995, p. 206) and has, cosmopolitanism holds, transformed the international system to the extent that it no longer makes sense to theorize about a world of self-contained states evolving according to the principle of non-intervention (Farer, 2003, p. 146). These groups coordinate international activism which constitutes a 'pervasive, significant, positive influence on the policies of the states' (Hensel, 2004, p. ix). Through the mobilization of NGOs, global civil society had become 'a source of constant pressures on the state system' (Shaw, 1994, p. 24) and as a consequence of this pressure 'policy makers are more likely to act ... in the interests of the human community' (Kaldor, 2003, p. 102). The preference for moral norms is not shared by all cosmopolitanists, however, with Fred Dallmayr arguing that while these norms are progressive they require legal expression and a clear means of consistent and impartial enforcement to be truly effective (2003, p. 434).

NATO's intervention in Kosovo was heralded by many cosmopolitanists (Fuller, 1999; Janzekovic, 2006), and though many were highly critical of the lack of coercive military intervention in Darfur (see Chapter 13), the West's engagement with the crisis has been identified as an improvement on the record in Rwanda and a function of international pressure by NGOs (Mayroz, 2008). The US and UK's attempts to secure a Security Council resolution prior to the invasion of Iraq is also cited as evidence of the power of international mass movements (Cortright, 2006, p. 75).

Post-structuralism

The post-structuralist approach, in so far as a coherent approach exists (Devetak, 2009, p. 183), sees the discipline of IR as part of a wider movement in social thought and seeks to 'unsettle established categories and disconcert the reader' (Brown and Ainley, 2005, p. 53). Thus, post-structuralist IR scholars have stressed the necessity of an interdisciplinary methodology (Der Derian and Shapiro, 1989).

The theory derives much of its inspiration from Michel Foucault, who argued that power and knowledge are intimately linked, with one implying the other. Using the example of the prison system Foucault (1991) suggested that a generic set of assumptions, derived from particular societal power relations, can be identified as underpinning all aspects of society. A dominant discourse or a 'regime of truth' is held to impose critical limits upon our ability to think politically about particular problems faced (Foucault, 1980, p. 131). Post-structuralist analyses, therefore, interrogate discourse on a particular theme to highlight the inherent assumptions which perpetuate a particular dominant belief (Malmvig, 2001, p. 251). Challenging the prevailing discourse and especially those ideas and institutions presented as axiomatic, Jean Elshtain argues, implies 'a recognition of the ways in which received doctrines ... may lull our critical faculties to sleep, blinding us to the possibilities that lie within our reach' (1992, p. 276).

Post-structuralists seek to identify how the primacy of the sovereign state has been maintained by a discourse which overlooks the true evolution of the state and presents state sovereignty as a pre-existing neutral reality (Edkins and Pin-Fat, 1998). Rather than seeing violence as something states are forced to employ in exceptional circumstances by virtue of the international structure or human nature, post-structuralism argues that violence created the state and is central to the system of states (Hoffman, 2009). Therefore, the periodic eruption of violence between or within states enables them to constitute themselves and is a means by which the state system is perpetuated (Klein, 1994). Attempts to limit violence that advocate the maintenance of the basic system of states, such as the dominant discourse of humanitarian intervention whereby states 'solve' problems in other states, are therefore futile (Campbell, 1994, p. 456).

The discourse of 'intervention', as much as it is often represented as a violation of sovereignty, presupposes the existence of sovereignty and therefore helps to reaffirm the idea (Weber, 1995, pp. 1–29; Malmvig, 2001, p. 252; Edkins, 2003, p. 255). Rob Walker argues that, despite the often divisive nature of the debate on humanitarian intervention, the dominant opposing positions take the state for granted. The state is conceived as worthy, albeit for differing reasons, and therefore debates about humanitarian intervention since the 1990s have not addressed the real problem – state sovereignty (Walker, 2003, p. 280). Humanitarian activism of the sort espoused by global civil society (see Chapter 6) requires the assent of states to undertake interventions, be they military or not, 'and thus rather than challenging state power these actors act as an instrument and rationality of statecraft' (Campbell, 1998b, p. 519).

Helle Malmvig argues that the manner in which the discourse of intervention is framed involves a strategy whereby egregious humanitarian violations are portrayed in a way so that 'they constitute the need to do something as evident' and 'work as justifications in and of themselves' (2001, p. 257). The popular portrayal of humanitarian crises lacks political analysis and facilitates the idea that the solution can be found in externally coordinated administrative, as opposed to political, action (Edkins, 2000; Hoffman, 2009). While these strategies do not necessarily compel intervention they can be used to frame the debate according to 'zero-sum logic' where actors are presented with an exceptional choice between action and inaction, humanitarian intervention or passivity (Malmvig, 2001, p. 267). Likewise Jenny Edkins suggests that the discourse presupposes a distinction between 'we' and 'they' which narrows the debate to a focus on 'whether and how "we" should help "them"' (2003, p. 255). While the rhetoric of humanitarian intervention implies a need to 'do something' and 'get involved', David Keen argues that the idea of external involvement occurring only *after* a disaster has erupted is false (2001, p. 19). Likewise Anne Orford asserts that the debate about the merits of intervention in Yugoslavia in the 1990s obscured the extent to which the international community 'had itself contributed to the humanitarian crises that had emerged' (2003, p. 13).

The discourse of humanitarian intervention reproduces power asymmetries; the West is portrayed as the powerful saviour while the 'other' is cast as the needy victim inhabiting a chaotic distant world (Hoffman, 2009; Orford, 2011, pp. 27–34). Victims of humanitarian tragedy live in 'an official faraway place' which is 'morally distinct' to the West (O'Tuathail, 1996, p. 171). David Campbell (1998a) argues that the framing of the international response to the conflict in Bosnia created a conceptual division between 'them' and 'us', whereby the 'other' is represented as lacking the traits that characterize the hegemon and thus the decay in the periphery affirms the good life in the core. The fate of the 'rescued' other, Patricia Owens claims, is portrayed in a way that 'conform[s] to (usually liberal) sentimental fantasy norms about the "American way of life"'. This discourse means that national myths and the pervading sense of moral benevolence 'appeared upheld and invigorated via representations of these "foreigners"' (Owens, 2004, p. 287). Thus the liberal notion of spreading the good life is in fact a means by which the 'other' is further mystified and the homeland is venerated. Likewise David Kennedy sees the project of the new humanitarians as inspired more by the sense of purpose and self-worth it inspires in the actor than the actual good it does for the 'victim' (2006, p. 87). Humanitarian activists have, Kennedy argues, increasingly aligned with Western state interests in the misplaced belief that they can maintain a neutral role and influence foreign policy; in reality 'humanitarians increasingly provide the terms in which global power is exercised' (Kennedy, 2009, p. 132).

As much as humanitarian intervention suggests a merging of the national and international, Orford argues that the discourse serves to reassure the international community that there is a differentiated other and to locate this other 'somewhere else, outside' (Orford, 2003, p. 124). The appropriation of human rights by Western states, it is claimed, has facilitated the image of a barbarous hinterland and a civilized core, and resulted in human rights becoming a means by which the legitimacy of the present order has in fact been bolstered (Douzinas, 2000, p. 129–41). The discourse of humanitarian intervention has therefore stripped human rights of their revolutionary potential.

Conclusion

Explaining the new concern with humanitarian intervention in the post-Cold War era is of significant concern for theorists of IR, and it is clear that consensus is manifestly lacking. By the latter half of the 1990s virtually all major Western states articulated a commitment to 'ethical foreign policies' which seemed to contradict the realist focus on power and the national interest, and appeared to constitute the death knell for realism (Zakaria, 1992). Some have argued that the popular conception of realism purportedly vanquished by recent events is a truncated version of the theory which overlooks its many normative dimensions (Bain, 2006; Molloy, 2006; Williams, 2007). Liberals, cosmopolitanists and solidarists suggest, albeit in differing ways, that this change in foreign policy priorities was the result of humanitarian advocacy whereby academics, human rights organizations and NGOs successfully convinced Western powers to include moral considerations in their foreign relations. Realists, Marxists and post-structuralists, by contrast, view the discourse as essentially a rhetorical facade designed to obscure the true power-political motivations.

The utility of examining IR theory when studying humanitarian intervention stems from the capacity of theory to provide a framework for understanding the motivations driving states to behave in certain ways. Whether theory comprises prescriptions as to how states should act, or objective explanations of how states *actually* act, is a source of contention. It is increasingly argued that the theorist cannot be seen as an entirely dispassionate observer of international events, and thus all theory is, to some extent, subjective and partisan (Edkins, 2005b, p. 68). This idea that the theorist's personal bias inevitably influences his or her theoretical beliefs echoes Cox's famous claim: 'theory is always for someone and for some purpose' (1981, p. 128). An individual's view on this perspective on theory necessarily influences his or her opinion on the utility of theory. Nonetheless, a comprehensive understanding of humanitarian intervention must involve some engagement with theory regardless of the perspective on the accuracy and utility of the various theories here described.

Questions

- What is the function of IR theory?
- Can IR theory ever be truly objective?
- Outline and assess the perspectives of realism, Marxism, liberalism, the English School, cosmopolitanism and post-structuralism on the following issues: the role of morality in international relations; the place of human rights; the relationship between order and justice.

Further reading

Realism

Carr, E.H. (2001) *The Twenty Years Crisis* (Basingstoke and New York: Palgrave Macmillan).
Morgenthau, H.J. (1954) *Politics Among Nations: The Struggle for Power and Peace* (New York: Alfred Knopf).
Niebuhr, R. (1932) *Moral Man and Immoral Society: A Study in Ethics and Politics* (New York: Charles Scribners).
Waltz, K. (1979) *Theory of International Politics* (Toronto: McGraw-Hill).
Williams, M. (2007) *Realism Reconsidered* (Oxford: Oxford University Press).

Marxism and critical theory

Chomsky, N. (1999) *The New Military Humanism: Lessons from Kosovo* (London: Pluto).
Cox, R. (1996) *Approaches to World Order* (Cambridge: Cambridge University Press).
Duffield, M. (2006) *Global Governance and the New Wars: The Merging of Development and Security* (London: Zed).
Mamdani, M. (2009) *Saviors and Survivors: Darfur, Politics, and the War on Terror* (London: Pantheon).
Rosenberg, J. (1994) *Empire of Civil Society* (London: Verso).

Liberalism

Cooper, R. (2004) *The Breaking of Nations* (London: Atlantic).
Fukuyama, F. (1992) *The End of History and the Last Man* (New York: Avon).
Holmes, R.L. (1989) *On War and Morality* (Princeton, NJ: Princeton University Press).
Keohane, R. and Nye, J. (1977) *Power and Interdependence: World Politics in Transition* (Boston, MA: Little, Brown).
Walzer, M. (1992) *Just and Unjust Wars* (New York: Basic Books).

The English School

Bellamy, A. (ed.) (2005) *International Society and its Critics* (Oxford: Oxford University Press).
Bull, H. (2002) *The Anarchical Society: A Study of Order in World Politics* (Basingstoke: Palgrave Macmillan and New York: Columbia University Press).
Dunne, T. (1998) *Inventing International Society* (Basingstoke and New York: Palgrave Macmillan).
Vincent, J. (1986) *Human Rights and International Relations* (Cambridge: Cambridge University Press).
Wheeler, N. (2002) *Saving Strangers: Humanitarian Intervention in International Society* (Oxford: Oxford University Press).

Wight, M. (1979) *International Theory: The Three Traditions*, ed. G. Wight and B. Porter (Leicester: Leicester University Press).

Cosmopolitanism

Archibugi, D. (ed.) (2003) *Debating Cosmopolitics* (London: Verso).
Hayden, P. (2005) *Cosmopolitan Global Politics* (Aldershot: Ashgate).
Held, D. (1995) *Democracy and the Global Order* (London: Polity).
Kaldor, M. (2003) *Global Civil Society: An Answer to War* (London: Polity).
Lu, C. (2006) *Just and Unjust Interventions in World Politics: Public and Private* (Basingstoke and New York: Palgrave Macmillan).

Post-structuralism

Campbell, D. (1998) *National Deconstruction: Violence, Identity and Justice in Bosnia* (Minneapolis, MN: University of Minnesota Press).
Der Derian, J. and Shapiro, M.J. (eds) (1989) *International/Intertextual Relations: Postmodern Readings of World Politics* (Lexington, KY: Lexington Books).
Douzinas, C. (2000) *The End of Human Rights* (Oxford: Oxford University Press).
Edkins, J. (2005) *Poststructuralism and International Relations: Bringing the Political Back In* (Boulder, CO: Lynne Rienner).
Kennedy, D. (2005) *The Dark Side of Virtue: Reassessing International Humanitarianism* (Princeton, NJ: Princeton University Press).
Orford, A. (2003) *Reading Humanitarian Intervention* (Cambridge: Cambridge University Press).

Part II

Controversies

Chapter 5

International Law and Human Rights

One of the most divisive controversies surrounding humanitarian intervention is the tension between natural and positive law. Positive law has developed steadily since the end of the Second World War, and, though its effectiveness is debatable, the expansion of its tenets and remit has been marked. The manner in which international law has evolved, specifically with respect to sovereign inviolability and equality, has resulted in the exclusion of humanitarian intervention from the canon of positive law. This illegality has been strongly criticized by humanitarians outraged by what they regard as an amoral, if not immoral, anachronism.

Owing to the nature of some of the humanitarian crises that have occurred in the post-Cold War era, there has emerged a conviction that interventions can be 'illegal but legitimate'. Proponents of positive law suggest that it has developed in response to the endemic abuse of the necessarily nebulous and subjective natural law. Conversely, advocates of natural law assert that its universality and timelessness make it a higher source of guidance than temporal and invariably contrived positive law (see Chapter 2). The nature of this debate is the focus of this chapter.

In this chapter I begin by outlining the evolution of international law regarding the use of force, charting its development from the 17th century to the present UN Charter system. I then provide an overview of development of laws on state responsibility contrasting the "traditional" with the contemporary manifestation. I then examine the legal status of humanitarian intervention and assess the various arguments asserting its legality. In the next section I analyse the rationale behind the 'illegal but legitimate' perspective which holds that, in the case of humanitarian crises, positive law occasionally yields to moral or natural law. I additionally outline the counter-argument presented by those opposed to natural law. In the final section I analyse whether there is a need for legal reform to reconcile the tension between legality and legitimacy highlighted by humanitarian intervention.

The legal status of humanitarian intervention is a highly contentious issue (Hurd, 2011). On the one hand it would appear that humanitarian intervention is manifestly contrary to codified international law, though as we shall see this is not a universally held view. On the other hand, even accepting this illegality, the legal proscription against humanitarian intervention has increasingly been deemed anachronistic and morally untenable. This aspect of the controversy has meant that humanitarian intervention, more so than any other issue, highlights the tension between international law and morality.

The evolution of international law

The legal status of humanitarian intervention is a function of the evolutionary trajectory of international law following the First World War, and particularly after the signing of the UN Charter in 1945. The contemporary tenets of international law derive from the process of law formation orientated towards defining the rights afforded to states and the remit of the international institutions established to regulate them. As discussed in Chapter 3, the emergence of the sovereign state in the 17th century led to the gradual development of rules governing relations between these political entities. While international law expanded in the 18th and 19th centuries, the legal system at this time was undermined, being abused by the more powerful states and lacking a constitutional base. Prior to the First World War, 'the dominant powers determined the criteria by which non-European political communities could be admitted to membership of international society, including the degree to which the laws of armed conflict were to apply to the non-European world' (Hurrell, 2005, pp. 20–1).

States essentially acted without restraint, apart from that derived from domestic considerations and the policies of their rivals and allies (Bellamy, 2006b, p. 93). Legal codes certainly existed and states often committed themselves to behave in certain ways, but the malleability of these codes was routinely exploited. For example, it was agreed that self-defence was a permissible basis for the use of force, hence effectively all acts of aggression during this period, including even Germany's invasion of Belgium in 1914, were legitimized as such. Important progress was made with respect to international humanitarian law, however, particularly at the Hague conventions of 1899 and 1907. War was, nonetheless, in essence considered inevitable, akin to natural disasters; the point of law was to limit its consequences, not its occurrence.

Following the First World War, steps were taken to address the resort to force. The Industrial Revolution had imbued modern armies with the capacity to destroy on a historically unprecedented scale, and states now faced the prospect of annihilation. The arms race and the division of Europe into rival pacts prior to the First World War led many to determine that a more developed international forum based on universal legal codes was required. The establishment of the League of Nations in 1919 was the product of this idea and was championed by its proponents as a force for peace. As we know, the League was ultimately unable to prevent the redivision of Europe and the outbreak of total war. While the political aspirations of the League manifestly failed to materialize, significant developments in international law with long-term implications did occur during the League's existence. The Permanent Court of International Justice was established in 1922, later becoming the International Court of Justice (ICJ) in 1946. The Kellogg–Briand Pact in 1928 constituted a significant renunciation of war as an instrument of foreign policy, and the pact's key provisions were incorporated into key articles in the UN Charter. The normative remit of international law thus expanded to constrain not just the conduct of war but the grounds on which it could legitimately be waged.

As discussed in Chapter 4, the Second World War catalysed a shift from idealism to realism in IR theory, which largely mirrored international politics during the Cold War. In terms of international law, however, the Second World War accelerated the process of law formation regarding the use of force. The UN Charter constituted an ambitious attempt to constrain the recourse to force and for the first time codified sovereign equality as the basis of the international legal system. As discussed in Chapter 3, the new legal regime attempted to restrict the use of force through the creation of inviolable states of equal legal status, thereby preventing, at least in legal terms, the overt use of power in international politics. Andrew Hurrell argues that the evolutionary trajectory of international law in the 20th century has been orientated

> towards a system in which norm creation becomes an increasingly complex and pluralist process, in which ideas of equality become more powerful and pervasive, and in which specific rules come to be understood and interpreted in the light of general legal principles and shared foundational values and as part of an increasingly integrated normative order. (2005, p. 18)

The normative goal of pluralist law creation and peaceful inter-state relations could only be realized if the legal subjects of this new regime were afforded equal rights and, crucially, empowered with the right to determine their own fate, hence the need for sovereign equality and inviolability. The impermissibility of humanitarian intervention is, therefore, arguably an unintentional function of this goal.

The establishment of the UN and the legal rights granted to states should not be seen, however, as a bottom-up process whereby major powers bowed to pressure exercised by smaller states demanding equality.

Gerry Simpson cites the special powers reserved for the permanent five members (P5) of the Security Council as evidence of what he terms 'legalised hegemony' (2004, p. 68). Additionally, Anne Orford believes the international legal order has been constructed so as to privilege those militarily and economically powerful states and facilitate domination by the powerful (2003, pp. 46–7). Indeed, according to Hedley Bull, 'any historical system of rules will be found to serve the interests of the ruling or dominant elements of the society more adequately than it serves the interests of the others' (2002, p. 53). The UN framework was of course constructed by the victorious Allies, who did reserve significant competencies for themselves, some of which still remain, notably the veto powers of the P5 (Bourantonis, 2007, p. 6). Additionally, aside from the evidence of formal hierarchy, actual state practice since 1945 has certainly not evidenced consistent respect for sovereign equality and inviolability. While we can point to the many achievements of international law in terms of the widening and deepening of its remit, the codification of laws and the delimitation of the permissible grounds for the use of force do not in themselves constitute evidence of the effectiveness of international law. It remains debatable whether, for all the many impressive advances in international law made since 1945, state behaviour is constrained, to any significant extent, by legal codes (Mearsheimer, 1994). Indicatively, when planning US military strategy following the 11 September 2001 attacks, President Bush declared, 'I don't care what the international lawyers say; we are going to kick some ass' (Coicaud, 2006, p. 426). Yet, while international law has been routinely derided as impotent, significant developments in the post-Cold War era, such as the establishment of the ICC and various ad hoc war crimes tribunals, testify to the emerging vitality of international law. High-profile violations of international law should not obscure the fact that states obey it most of the time (Malanczuk, 2006, p. 6).

State responsibility

The responsibility a state has towards its citizens has been one of the dominant themes in political thought; the spectrum ranges from communism to fascism, and between these poles there are many differing perspectives, though all agree that states have *some* responsibilities to their citizens (Brown, 2006, p. 2).

The term 'state responsibility' has a different meaning in international law from that used in IR and refers to the legal responsibilities of states towards other states and to the nature of state responsibility for breaches of international law (see Crawford and Olleson, 2006, p. 451; Dixon, 2007, p. 242). In terms of IR, the question of state responsibility was until quite recently deemed an exclusively domestic issue and thus not a topic for discussion within the discipline of IR (Wight, 1966a, p. 33). This distinction between the domestic and the international has increasingly been challenged in the post-Cold War era, however, and state responsibility, once the preserve of political theory, is now a key issue in IR.

Traditional approaches to state responsibility

As discussed in Chapter 3, the emergence of the modern state began in the 16th century and accelerated after the Peace of Westphalia in 1648. In the modern era the state has come to be considered a reflection of national consciousness, though this normative union of nation and state really only emerged in the 18th century and flourished after the French Revolution in 1789. The initial impetus for the formation of states had little to do with nationalism and was more a function of the rivalry between monarchs. The system of sovereign states was created to limit the recourse to war, consolidate the realms of the existing hierarchy and facilitate economic growth (see Chapter 3).

With the growth of nationalism after 1789, states gradually began to be conceived of as servants of the people, rather than institutions to enable the proliferation of monarchical dynasties. The rise of national consciousness necessarily created a sense of community, albeit in most cases 'imagined' (Anderson, 1991), which brought with it heightened expectations about what the state should do for its people. Logically, if a community believes its state to be a servant of the nation, it will expect its institutions to provide certain goods for all members of this nation (Bloom, 1990, p. 60). The rights of citizens, however, was not a key concern for many state leaders until the 20th century. Indeed, the emergence of socialism as a political force in the 19th century was a response to the conditions endured by the majority of people, formally disenfranchised from the political system, who suffered from poor housing, inadequate healthcare and oppressive labour practices.

While the nature of the rights afforded to citizens and the state's responsibility to uphold these rights have arguably been primary concerns in domestic politics for over 200 years, these issues were largely absent from the IR agenda until recently. The international debates generated by the formation of the system of sovereign states essentially centred on inter-state relations, particularly the laws governing the use of force. The inability of states to agree on their duties to their citizens led to an agreement amongst states to omit this divisive issue from international law so as to forestall disorder (Bull, 2002, p. 146). Occasionally certain atrocities, or practices such as cannibalism, committed abroad were deemed morally unacceptable, and action was taken, up to and including military intervention (Bass, 2008). In the majority, if not all, of these cases, however, geopolitical motives were the more pressing concern (see Chapter 9). Certain European states, particularly Great Britain and France, justified their colonies on the basis that their administration was morally superior and more respectful towards the rights of individuals than the previous indigenous system (Carr, 2001, pp. 71–5). This was, of course, debatable to say the least, and in many cases European empires were responsible for extreme brutality (Amin, 2008; Hoffman, 2009; Chomsky, 2011).

Before the First World War the nascent international legal system imposed only modest constraints on inter-state relations, although international humanitarian law had begun to develop by the end of the 19th century. A small number of states did provide some human rights protection through their constitutions and related domestic legislation, but even where these laws existed there were few effective means of enforcement (Armstrong et al., 2007, p. 151). During this period, therefore, 'individuals were mere "appendices" of the state to which they belonged, simple pawns in its hands, to be used, protected, or sacrificed according to what State interests dictated' (Cassese, 2005, p. 376). What international action was taken to stop domestic oppression was limited to 'remedying particular abuses or on protecting particular minority groups or aliens' (Malanczuk, 2006, p. 209).

As discussed above, the First World War led to a number of significant developments in international law, though predominately in respect to inter-state relations. Indeed, the Covenant of the League of Nations makes no mention of human rights, although under Article 23(b) members committed to the 'just treatment of the native inhabitants of territories under their control'. The Second World War demonstrated horrifically that more needed to be done to strengthen international law, and this was reflected in the new international political and legal system enshrined in the UN Charter. This dual goal of limiting the recourse to war by strengthening the sovereign inviolability of states and protecting the rights of individuals through human rights legislation has become, however, one of the major tensions since the establishment of the UN.

State responsibility and the UN Charter

During the drafting of the UN Charter at the San Francisco Conference (April–June 1945), three groups formed, with different views on the new rules regarding human rights and state responsibility (Cassese, 2005, pp. 377–9). The first group – comprising mostly Latin American states plus Australia, New Zealand, India and Norway – advocated the inclusion of specific obligations to respect human rights. The second group, of major Western powers, opposed the inclusion of any definite obligations on human rights and favoured clear proscriptions against the new international organization interfering with 'domestic' affairs (Roberts, 2006, p. 72). The third group comprised socialist states which also sought to limit the UN's powers, but looked too to bolster the language regarding self-determination and non-discrimination. The outcome of the negotiations constituted a compromise between the last two of these groups, resulting in four key elements within the Charter:

- There were no specific obligations to act to promote or protect human rights.
- The right of self-determination was proclaimed but only as a guiding principle.
- The power of the General Assembly was limited.
- Respect for human rights should only be furthered as a means of safe-guarding peace.

As a consequence of this compromise the Charter has struggled to reconcile its provisions on human rights with its proscription against intervention, both multilaterally through the Security Council and (more explicitly) unilaterally by individual states or coalitions of states. While the Charter's Preamble, Article 1 and particularly Article 55 proclaim human rights to be a concern for the UN and all its member states, the proscriptions against intervention in Articles 2.4 and 2.7 appear to override these principles. The Charter contains no provision explicitly sanctioning intervention for the purpose of upholding human rights and does not specify the human rights that states must uphold. During the course of the drafting of the Charter the French negotiating team proposed the inclusion of a passage authorizing states to intervene in other states without Security Council authorization when 'the clear violation of essential liberties and of human rights constitutes threats capable of compromising peace' (Franck, 2005, p. 207). This was rejected by both Western and socialist states. As a result, 'it is generally recognized that the legal obligation to respect and observe human rights for all in the UN Charter is too general in provenance' (Armstrong et al., 2007, p. 156).

The 1948 Declaration of Human Rights went some way towards clarifying the nature of human rights, but failed to advance any effective enforcement mechanism (Malanczuk, 2006, p. 213). The judgements in the Tokyo and Nuremberg trials, however, did advance a prohibition against 'crimes against humanity', applicable to all states in their treatment of both their own citizens and foreigners, which constituted definite progress in the prohibition of intra-state human rights violations (Robertson, 2002, p. 203).

The onset of the Cold War limited the possibility of further clarification of what would be done in response to a violation of human rights. Consensus *was* reached, however, on certain issues leading to conventions on genocide (1948), racial discrimination (1965), discrimination against women (1979) and torture (1984). Additionally, significant developments were made in more contentious areas that had traditionally been considered domestic political issues (Landman, 2005, p. 14). Of course, the increased codification of human rights did not readily translate into greater respect for, or enforcement of, these rights. In certain egregious cases, most notably the racist regimes in South Africa and Southern Rhodesia, the General Assembly and/or the Security Council *did* condemn the oppressive policies of states towards their own citizens (DIIA, 1999, p. 53), but these cases were exceptional. In general, while human rights law espoused lofty humanitarian aims, the actual mechanisms of enforcement relied on states. International law continued to recognize states as having the primary responsibility for their citizens, which could only be bypassed if they failed to provide an effective remedy to the original problem; therefore 'there cannot be a violation of international human rights law unless state authorities fail to provide adequate remedies' (Armstrong et al., 2007, p. 164).

The legal status of humanitarian intervention

The Kellogg–Briand Pact outlawed war as an instrument of state policy except when fought in self-defence or sanctioned by the League of Nations. This principle was incorporated into the UN Charter and finds its clearest expression in Article 2.4 (see Box 5.1). Additionally under Article 2.7 the UN itself is prohibited from unsolicited involvement in the domestic affairs of its member states. Many subsequent treaties, resolutions and statements reaffirmed this principle. Articles 53 and 64 of the 1969 Vienna Convention on the Law of Treaties state that this particular provision is *jus cogens* and therefore accepted by the international community as a principle from which no derogation is permitted. General Assembly Resolution 2131 in 1965 affirmed the Assembly's opposition to all forms of intervention 'for any reason whatsoever' and declares: 'armed intervention is synonymous with aggression'. In 1970 the General Assembly passed Resolution 2625 which reaffirmed the prohibition on 'the threat or use of force against the territorial integrity or political independence of any State'. Clause IV of the Helsinki Accords Final Act of 1975 notes: 'the participating states will respect the territorial integrity of each of the participating states. Accordingly they will refrain from any action ... against the territorial integrity, political independence, or the unity of any

Box 5.1   Key Articles of the UN Charter related to humanitarian intervention

Article 1.1
[The purposes of the UN are] to maintain international peace and security, and to that end: to take effective collective measures for the prevention and removal of threats to the peace, and for the suppression of acts of aggression or other breaches of the peace, and to bring about by peaceful means, and in conformity with the principles of justice and international law, adjustment or settlement of international disputes or situations which might lead to a breach of the peace.

Article 2.4
All Members shall refrain in their international relations from the threat or use of force against the territorial integrity or political independence of any state, or in any other manner inconsistent with the Purposes of the UN.

Article 2.7
Nothing in the present Charter shall authorize the UN to intervene in matters which are essentially within the domestic jurisdiction of any state.

Article 24.1
In order to ensure prompt and effective action by the UN, its Members confer on the Security Council primary responsibility for the maintenance of international peace and security, and agree that in carrying out its duties under this responsibility the Security Council acts on their behalf.

Article 39
The Security Council shall determine the existence of any threat to the peace, breach of the peace, or act of aggression and shall make recommendations, or decide what measures shall be taken in accordance with Articles 41 and 42, to maintain or restore international peace and security.

participating state'. The Charter, and supplementary international law, therefore explicitly recognize the inviolability of the state and outlaws the use of force.

There are two exceptions to the prohibition on the use of force. Article 51 of the UN Charter reads: 'nothing in the present Charter shall impair the inherent right of individual or collective self defense if an armed attack occurs against a member of the UN'. This is premised, however, by the declaration that the use of force in self-defence is only permissible 'until the Security Council has taken measures necessary to maintain international peace and security', and that this right of self-defence 'shall not in any way affect the authority and responsibility of the Security

Council'. The ICJ ruled in the 1986 case of *Nicaragua v the United States* that the notion of self-defence should be understood restrictively (Guicherd, 1999, p. 21).

The other grounds on which the use of force is permissible are outlined in Chapter VII of the Charter. Article 39 gives the Council the power to determine whether 'any' situation constitutes a threat to peace and precedes action ordered under Articles 41 and 42. Article 41 gives the Security Council the power to determine non-military responses to a perceived threat; Article 42 comes into effect if measures taken under Article 41 prove inadequate and enables the Security Council to sanction more robust measures 'as may be necessary to maintain or restore international peace and security'.

Under Article 24 of the Charter, member states acknowledge that the Security Council has 'primary responsibility for the maintenance of international peace and security'. The one possible derogation from this rule is the 1950 General Assembly Resolution 377, 'Uniting for Peace' (see Box 5.2). This resolution enables the General Assembly to act when the Security Council is unable to sanction action unanimously, or to demand a cessation to ongoing military action when there is a threat to international peace and stability. The General Assembly may take up the issue under two conditions. The first is when nine members of the Security Council vote to move the issue to the General Assembly and this vote is immune from the P5 veto. The second is when a majority of UN member states vote to move the issue to the General Assembly (Krasno and Das, 2008, p. 175). The General Assembly can only take the lead on an issue that is not under consideration at the Security Council, though, provided this condition is met, technically the General Assembly could sanction a military intervention if two-thirds of its members so agreed.

Box 5.2   'Uniting for Peace': General Assembly Resolution 377, 3 November 1950

'*Resolves* that if the Security Council, because of lack of unanimity of the permanent members, fails to exercise its primary responsibility for the maintenance of international peace and security in any case where there appears to be a threat to the peace, breach of the peace, or act of aggression, the General Assembly shall consider the matter immediately with a view to making appropriate recommendations to Members for collective measures, including in the case of a breach of the peace or act of aggression the use of armed force when necessary, to maintain or restore international peace and security.'

The procedures outlined in Resolution 377 were first used in 1950 regarding the conflict in Korea, although the first explicit reference to 'Uniting for Peace' occurred during the Suez Canal crises in 1956. However, the ineffectiveness of this principle was evidenced later that year when the General Assembly's declaration that the Soviet Union should discontinue its military action in Hungary was ignored. The Danish Institute of International Affairs (DIIA) found that the 'Uniting for Peace' resolution 'has lost much of its importance [and] is no legal basis for the authorization of humanitarian intervention' (1999, p. 61). Additionally moving divisive issues like those posed by humanitarian intervention to the General Assembly is no guarantee that they will be dealt with swiftly. At times use of the 'Uniting for Peace' resolution simply created another forum for unproductive rhetoric and division (Krasno and Das, 2008, p. 189). Nonetheless, as discussed further in Chapter 6, an increased role for the General Assembly, specifically through the utilization of the 'Uniting for Peace' resolution, has been suggested as a possible solution to an impasse at the Security Council (ICISS, 2001a, p. 53; Evans, 2008, p. 136).

Under existing codified international law, therefore, there is no law explicitly sanctioning humanitarian intervention. In its key ruling in the 1949 *Corfu Channel* case the ICJ declared that it could:

> only regard the alleged right of intervention as the manifestation of a policy of force, such as has, in the past, given rise to most serious abuses and as such cannot, whatever be the present defect in international organization, find a place in international law. Intervention ... would be reserved for the most powerful states and might easily lead to perverting the administration of international justice itself. (DIIA, 1999, p. 86)

In its ruling in the 1986 case *Nicaragua v the United States*, the ICJ further declared: 'while the US might form its own appraisal of the situation as to respect for human rights in Nicaragua, the use of force could not be the appropriate method to monitor or ensure such respect' (ibid., p. 83). In 1986 the UK Foreign Office gave its opinion as to the legal status of humanitarian intervention, which found against its legality, noting: 'the scope of abusing such a right argues strongly against its creation' (Holbrook, 2002, pp. 140–1). Similarly, the US 1987 Restatement of Foreign Relations Law noted: 'whether a state may intervene with military force in the territory of another state without its consent not to rescue the victims but to prevent or terminate human rights violations, is not agreed or authoritatively determined' (Burton, 1996, p. 428). This apparent consensus on the illegality of humanitarian intervention, however, dissipated in the post-Cold War era.

The provisions of Chapter VII of the Charter have been cited as a possible source of legality. Humanitarian intervention could be sanctioned by the Security Council if intra-state conflicts were deemed a threat to international peace and stability, as increasingly they have been in the post-Cold War era. Security Council Resolution 688 in 1991 declared that the Security Council 'condemns the repression of the Iraqi civilian population in many parts of Iraq, including most recently in Kurdish populated areas, the consequences of which threaten international peace and security in the region'. Security Council practice in the 1990s reflected the emergence of the view that economic, social, ecological and humanitarian instability were grounds for acting under Chapter VII.

Simon Chesterman, however, notes that Security Council action under Chapter VII during the 1990s was haphazard, leading to 'ambiguous resolutions and conflicting interpretations [of Chapter VII]' (2002, p. 5). The sanctioning of action, according to Chesterman, 'depended more upon a coincidence of national interest than on procedural legality' (ibid., p. 165). Additionally, it is questionable whether the Security Council has the authority to apply Chapter VII to intra-state crises. According to DIIA:

> it was hardly the intention of the framers of the Charter that internal conflicts and human rights violations should be regarded as a threat to international peace. There is no evidence that they might have envisaged a competence for the Security Council under Chapter VII to take action to cope with situations of humanitarian emergency within a state resulting from civil war or systematic repression. (1999, p. 62)

Indeed in 1946 the Security Council refused to describe Franco's Spain as a threat under Chapter VII, noting that this Charter provision constituted 'a very sharp instrument' and that care should be taken so that 'this instrument is not blunted or used in any way which would strain the intentions of the Charter or which would not be applicable in all similar cases' (Chesterman, 2002, p. 130). The IICK found that 'at present the Charter does not explicitly give the UN Security Council the power to take measures in cases of violations of human rights' (2000, p. 196).

Nonetheless, during the 1990s the remit of Chapter VII was stretched to facilitate interventions in situations where the threat to international peace and security was relatively minimal. Following a military coup in 1991 the democratically elected president of Haiti, Jean-Bertrand Aristide, was ousted. The UN imposed economic sanctions, which by 1994 were said to have had no effect. In July 1994 the Security Council passed Resolution 940, which determined that the situation in Haiti constituted a threat to international peace and stability, and ordered an intervention to restore the democratically elected president. In practice, however, as the ongoing situation in many other states attested, non-democratic regimes and benefactors of military coups were not considered to constitute this grave threat in every instance. In addition, in keeping with other uses of Chapter VII during the 1990s, this Security Council ruling was officially deemed an exception. Resolution 940 recognized 'the unique character' of the situation and stated that Haiti's 'extraordinary nature ... [required] an exceptional response'. Similarly the sanctioning of action in Somalia in 1992 under Chapter VII was premised on it being 'an exceptional response', and the deployment of troops in Rwanda in 1994, through Resolution 929, was described as 'a unique case'. This inconsistent use of Chapter VII has angered many states who accuse the Security Council of hypocrisy (Cassese, 2005, p. 347). Interventions sanctioned under Chapter VII have thus clearly become more commonplace, but the selective application of this provision has been a cause for concern (Chesterman, 2011a, p. 2; Hehir, 2012, p. 211).

Whether the Security Council has acted in accordance with international law in its use of Chapter VII is a moot point; some have noted that it is not authorized to interpret the Charter in any way it pleases (White, 2004). Despite these valid concerns about the politicization and legality of Security Council action under Chapter VII, interventions authorized by the Council have a very strong legal case, which have not, historically, been sources of great legal contestation. Few, indeed, claimed that the intervention against Libya in March 2011 was illegal, precisely because the Security Council had sanctioned it (see Chapter 14). It is action taken without Security Council authorization – namely unilateral humanitarian intervention – that has proved far more controversial.

Essentially three justifications have been articulated for defending the legality of unilateral humanitarian intervention. The first relates to a particular interpretation of Article 2.4 of the UN Charter (see Box 5.1). It is claimed that a true humanitarian intervention would not be directed against 'the territorial integrity or political independence' of the targeted state and would thus not be 'inconsistent with the Purposes of the UN' (Tesón, 1988, p. 150; Weiss, 2007a, p. 17). The IICK rejected this argument, noting that 'Charter provisions relating to human rights were left deliberately vague, and were clearly not intended when written to provide a legal rationale for any kind of enforcement, much less a free-standing mandate for military intervention without UN Security Council approval' (2000, p. 168). Chesterman's analysis of the preliminary meetings held to discuss the UN Charter determines that the 'dominant' legal opinion as to the meaning of Article 2.4 holds that it does not provide any scope for humanitarian intervention (2002, p. 53).

Secondly, there is the 'link theory' justification as proffered in particular by Richard Lillich (1967), who argues that, while under Article 24.1 the

Security Council has 'primary responsibility for the maintenance of international peace and security', under Article 1.1 UN member states have a responsibility to maintain international peace and security when the Security Council is unable to carry out its duties in this respect. Under certain circumstances, therefore, the onus is on member states to act and the prohibition on the use of force as outlined in Article 2.4 is suspended. Geoffrey Robertson similarly argues that Article 2.4 'really means to prohibit any armed attacks which are inconsistent with Charter purposes, and does not necessarily exclude those which are directed to uphold those purposes' (2002, p. 434).

In its assessment of the merits of the link theory, the DIIA (1999, p. 82) identified three flaws. Firstly, there is no explicit basis for this rationale outlined in the Charter. Although Article 24.1 states that the Security Council has *primary* rather than *exclusive* responsibility for the maintenance of international peace and security, according to the DIIA '[this] refers to a subsidiary responsibility of other organs of the UN, notably the General Assembly, but not of the Members states'. Secondly, it is not legally sound to assert that the Charter must be suspended when the Security Council fails to act, as there is no legal basis for this assertion. Thirdly, the prohibition on the use of force is a tenet of customary international law and has evolved independently of the UN Charter, and therefore 'can hardly be conditioned upon the effectiveness of collective security under Chapter VII'. This view is supported by Thomas Franck and Nigel Rodley, who note that those who drafted the human rights legislation never intended it to be used as a justification for unilateral action. Such action would, in fact, 'bring to a standstill' the very process of defining and codifying human rights (Franck and Rodley, 1973, p. 300).

The third justification relates to customary international law. The *Paquete Habana* case (1900) established that in addition to codified doctrines, treaties and court judgments, international law is based on established customary behaviour of states, and this is codified in Article 38 of the Statute of the ICJ. By definition customary law begins with a breach of existing positive law followed by what Cassese describes as 'the fundamental elements constituting custom', namely 'state practice (*usus* or *diuturnitas*) and the corresponding views of states (*opinio juris* or *opinio necessitates*)' (2005, p. 157). In this sense, there may be a legal basis to a principle, such as humanitarian intervention, that has not been formally codified, and states may be considered bound by a customary law even if they have not signed a treaty to that effect. For example, in 1986 the ICJ ruled that the Geneva Convention applied to all states, even those who had not signed it, as it had become part of customary international law.

An analysis of customary international law prior to and since the inception of the Charter, however, suggests that there is no customary international law on humanitarian intervention. In relation to the pre-Charter era, Chesterman's analysis concludes: 'pre-Charter state practice illustrates the paucity of evidence of a general right of humanitarian intervention in customary international law' (2002, pp. 24–5). This view is supported by Franck and Rodley, who argue that the pre-Charter record of intervention does not support the existence of a customary norm (1973, p. 285). Citing India's invasion of East Pakistan in 1971, however, they do not discount the possibility that such a norm could emerge, and note that international law is not immutable (ibid., p. 303). Therefore, given the lack of any evident norm pre-1945, the only possible legal justification for unilateral humanitarian intervention is that state practice since 1945 has established a customary right of humanitarian intervention.

Fernando Tesón argues that India's intervention in East Pakistan and France's intervention in the Central African Republic in 1979 constituted examples of humanitarian intervention (1988, pp. 207, 199). He accepts that in both cases the intervening parties did not offer a humanitarian justification for their actions, but he argues that it 'matters little' what states say; the consequences of their actions are the basis upon which any claim of humanitarian intervention can be made (ibid., p. 193). Anthony Arend and Robert Beck's analysis concludes, however, that 'between 1945 and 1990 there were no examples of a genuinely humanitarian intervention' and, in addition, during this period there was 'no unambiguous case of state reliance on the right of humanitarian intervention' (1993, p. 137). In those cases during this period where the greatest case for a 'humanitarian' justification could have been made, such as India's intervention in East Pakistan in 1971, Vietnam's 1978 intervention in Cambodia, and Tanzania's intervention in Uganda in 1979 (see Chapter 9), none of the intervening states relied exclusively on a humanitarian justification. 'Thus', according to Philip Hilpold,

> it can be inferred from these events and reactions that the necessary elements for the formation of a customary rule allowing measures of humanitarian intervention were not only not present but relevant state practice was a thorough confirmation of the rule which excludes the permissibility of such interventions. (2001, p. 445)

It is widely accepted, therefore, that humanitarian intervention was not a customary norm at the time of NATO's intervention in Kosovo (Ambos, 1999; ICISS, 2001a, p. 12). Yet the significant international support afforded to NATO in 1999 suggested that Operation Allied Force was 'a potential harbinger of future legality' (Rodley and Cali, 2007, p. 278). Nicholas Wheeler similarly notes that the debate on the legitimacy of humanitarian intervention at the UN post-Kosovo altered as 'norms had clearly changed', although, he cautions, not to the extent that unilateral humanitarian intervention was widely supported (2002, p. 286). An analysis of state practice since 1999 suggests that Operation Allied Force fails to constitute a precedent given that NATO's action failed the two tests outlined by Cassese on customary law formation, namely state practice and the views of states (2005, p. 157; Hehir, 2009b). In the aftermath of NATO's intervention the 133 states comprising the Group of 77 (2000) declared: 'we reject the so-called "right" of humanitarian intervention, which has no legal basis in the UN Charter or in the general principles of international law'. Even the states that participated in Operation Allied Force distanced themselves from suggesting that a new norm had been established, and in terms of consistent practice it is relatively clear that similar humanitarian crises have not received the same attention afforded to Kosovo in 1999 (Hehir, 2008a).

On balance it seems fair to conclude that the dominant view on the legal status of unilateral humanitarian intervention is that it is illegal. There has been no fundamental change in either positive or customary international law that can be said conclusively to have legalized such action. This illegal status, however, has become a source of considerable controversy, not least because, as the next section attests, human rights legislation has increased dramatically since 1945 – yet this growing legal corpus lacks the attendant means of enforcement.

Human rights law

Many human rights treaties have been signed since the UN Charter came into force in October 1945, although the impact of these treaties has been limited. States have demonstrated a willingness to publicly support human rights, increasingly so in the post-Cold War era, but this has not led to an increased adherence to these treaties (Armstrong et al., 2007, p. 157). Indeed, the proliferation of these expressions of concern for, and commitment to, human rights have not been accompanied by an attendant alteration in the Charter's provisions for dealing with violations of human rights (Chesterman, 2011b). The result is a large body of both treaty and customary law related to human rights which lacks clear means by which these laws can be enforced (Peters, 2009). States are subject to scrutiny by UN bodies such as the Human Rights Council (formerly the UN Commission on Human Rights), the Human Rights Committee and the Office of the UN High Commissioner for Human Rights. Compliance with even the supervisory role of these organizations, however, is poor and their enforcement capacity and effectiveness is minimal.

The nature of human rights differentiates this area of international law from the laws governing inter-state relations. As Malgozia Fitzmaurice states, 'human rights treaties are not contractual in nature and do not create rights and obligations between States on the traditional basis of reciprocity; they establish relationships between States and individuals' (2006, pp. 205–6). States, therefore, may well agree amongst themselves the standards they should uphold domestically, but ultimately the necessarily domestic nature of compliance with these agreements limits the effect the inter-state context of the original treaty can have. Non-compliance with these treaties results in negative consequences only for the domestic citizenry and not other signatories to the treaty. In this respects, as Louis Henkin notes, 'compliance with human rights law ... is wholly internal' (1990, p. 250).

This leads to a key problem with the existing system. The vast corpus of human rights law lacks independent enforcement mechanisms, and the laws are reliant on the Charter's provisions. These provisions, covered under Chapter VII, are essentially ill-suited to being applied to intra-state crises. Even if it is maintained that Chapter VII, imperfect as it is, can be applied to intra-state crises, there remains a key barrier to enforcement, namely the interests of the P5. Unless the P5 agree, no enforcement action can be ordered. An example is provided by the provisions of the 1948 Genocide Convention. Article 8 of the Convention states:

> Any Contracting Party may call upon the competent organs of the UN to take such action under the Charter of the UN as they consider appropriate for the prevention and suppression of acts of genocide or any of the other acts enumerated in article III.

In practice the 'competent organ' of the UN is the Security Council. Thus if states believe that genocide is occurring and wish to stop it, the matter is referred to the Security Council. The crisis in Darfur was described as genocide by many states, including the United States, and by UN missions to the region. The matter was referred to the Security Council, and while it determined that the situation constituted a threat to international peace and stability, and certain members agreed that the Sudanese government was orchestrating the genocide, no effective action was taken by the P5 (see Chapter 13.) Even if it is widely agreed that genocide is taking place, states do not have the legal right to intervene unilaterally to stop the killing (Dinstein, 2005, pp. 72–3).

There is, therefore, a paradox at the heart of international law regarding human rights. Laws prohibiting certain human rights violations have increasingly been ratified in the post-Second World War era, yet the mechanisms for enforcing these laws have failed to evolve, and enforcement remains largely the preserve of the Security Council and the signatories themselves. Frustration at the unwillingness of the Security Council to use the powers at its disposal consistently and swiftly has led to increasing calls for unilateral action and, more fundamentally, the wholesale reform of the international legal system.

'Illegal but legitimate'?

Demonstrating the illegality of humanitarian intervention, though not without contention, is relatively unproblematic, and many pro-intervention advocates would readily acknowledge this legal proscription. The major contention surrounding humanitarian intervention does not, however, focus on its legal status. Human rights campaigners argue that the legal proscription is morally untenable and should be violated when humanitarian need is great. NATO's intervention in Kosovo in 1999 dramatically illustrated this controversy and highlighted the gulf between contemporary legal doctrine and evolving conceptions of human rights and ethical state behaviour. The conclusion reached by the IICK – 'the NATO military intervention was illegal but legitimate' – is succinctly illustrative of the central problem (2000, p. 4).

The idea that ending suffering is a higher priority than adhering to international law has gained momentum in the post-Cold War era. The dependency of international law on the Security Council – itself considered a body of low moral standing – led to the conviction that, as Robertson argued, 'humanitarian intervention cannot be the prerogative of the UN' (2002, p. 382). The rejection of the UN, and international law generally, demands an alternative source of authority and legitimacy; according to Terry Nardin the basis for regulating humanitarian intervention must be 'common morality' rather than international law, because the latter 'rests on custom and agreement, not moral reasoning' (2003, p. 19). This preference for moral reasoning over international law evidences faith in both the objective existence of universal morality and the efficacy of moral norms. As discussed in Chapter 2, this embrace of moral or natural law led to renewed interest in the Just War tradition, and many compiled criteria for intervention based on the tradition's central tenets.

The fixation on the legality of an act is seen by some as obscuring the more important question of its moral quality, which is deemed more relevant to determining its legitimacy. In the case of the US-led invasion of Iraq, much of the debate focused on the legality of the intervention. Nicholas Rengger notes:

> what was perhaps oddest, at least to my eye, was that the general discussion both amongst politicians and in the media ... was almost exclusively focused on whether or not the war was 'legal'. At no point that I

am aware of, did anyone seriously discuss the surely related question that even if it was legal, was it morally justified? (2005, p. 145)

It is indeed true that a significant portion of the anti-war movement, particularly those opposed to the war within mainstream political parties such as the Liberal Democrats in the United Kingdom, justified their opposition on the grounds that the intervention was not approved by the Security Council. Many 'anti-war' protestors, therefore, called for a second UN resolution before the deployment of troops. Yet, as Rengger notes, it is difficult to understand why the assent of the P5 would affect the underlying moral legitimacy of the invasion.

The preference for moral law over positive law clearly has many attractions. International law is certainly deficient in many areas, particularly enforcement, and it is undeniably oriented towards states rather than the people who inhabit them. Moral laws by contrast are human-centred and not restricted by the temporal state system. Additionally many of the more progressive movements and events in human history have been driven by people unwilling to respect the laws of the day. The suffragettes, Gandhi, Martin Luther King and many others consciously rejected their legal systems on moral grounds, and we now generally regard their actions as trailblazing. Additionally, international law is not static and *has* demonstrated its capacity to change. Therefore, as Franck notes, 'even an illegal action, if instrumental in bringing about results widely desired by a community, will not seriously undermine a resilient legal system, one with the elasticity to make allowances for mitigating circumstances' (1999, p. 859). Action, such as humanitarian intervention, could thus be deemed illegal but, provided the ethical merits of the action were endorsed by the international community, the intervening party would not be punished. Ian Brownlie, using the example of euthanasia, argues that mitigation is already a feature of domestic law. In certain cases, such as when a father smothers his severely handicapped son, the law has exercised a 'discretion not to prosecute', which means that the principle prohibiting murder remains firm but the punishment takes account of the context of the criminal act (1973, p. 146). Humanitarian intervention, therefore, could similarly be justified as an extraordinary remedy to a great wrong.

As I have discussed above, international law has developed in a manner designed to prevent powerful states from arbitrarily using force. The 18th and 19th centuries were eras when, in the absence of legal codes, states claimed to act in accordance with natural law and their own conceptions of morality. The result was colonialism and the subjugation of millions throughout the world, primarily legitimized on the grounds that the 'savages' in Africa, Asia, the Americas and indeed within Europe – particularly Ireland and the Balkans – required the civilizing presence of their

European masters. Central to imperialism was the conviction that 'certain territories and peoples require and beseech domination' (Said, 1993, p. 76). As noted in Chapter 3, before the codification of sovereign equality and inviolability there was no legal proscription against imperialism, and, while natural law was routinely invoked, the system at this time was disorderly and prone to violence. Rejecting international law in favour of natural, and ostensibly moral, norms, therefore, risks regressing to this earlier system.

In tandem with the privileging of natural law is the assumption that certain states have more legitimacy to act in certain ways than others by virtue of their superior human rights record. As noted in Chapter 3, this has been manifest as the idea of conditional sovereignty and proportionate equality. Contemporary moves towards recognizing a hierarchy of states, especially manifest in the renewed interest in trusteeship, are, according to William Bain, 'fundamentally irreconcilable with a universal society of sovereign states ordered according to the principle of universal equality' (2003b, p. 75). The contemporary shift towards proportionate equality, or 'the formal rehierarcitisation of international society', thus contradicts both the doctrine and direction of positive international law (Reus-Smit, 2005, p. 72).

Another concern with the pro-morality perspective is the exact nature of the code being championed. The natural law argument outlines the grounds on which states may violate the law to help others but fails to impose enforceable duties to so act. This thus appears to create only a discretionary right or entitlement (Berman, 2007, p. 161; Chesterman, 2011b, p. 21).

While the risks of a move towards natural law are great, there are limits to the parallels between the era of colonialism and the contemporary discourse of cosmopolitan human rights. As discussed in Chapter 4, cosmopolitan human rights theory not only espouses universal moral norms, it additionally questions the very idea of the sovereign state, and thus, unlike colonialism, does not (generally) act as advocate for a particular state or culture. The debate can thus be seen as a clash between adherents of two codes: those who adhere to 'constitutionalist' principles and those who privilege 'cosmopolitan moralist, rules' (Hurrell, 2005, p. 21).

The criticisms made of international law perhaps fail to acknowledge the extent to which it is largely a reflection of prevailing moral norms. Morality informs law, and therefore the ascendancy of a moral norm, such as the perceived need to alleviate suffering in foreign lands, need not constitute grounds for rejecting positive law, but rather stands as an argument in favour of amending the law. The existing system therefore may accommodate change, even fundamental change, and act as a means by which emerging ideas are incorporated into a universally legitimate legal structure. Arguably the many positives that have accrued from the strengthening of international law in the past 60 years should not be jeopardized through the abandonment of the core proscription on the unilateral use of force and the basic principle of sovereign equality. It is additionally unlikely that the creation of an 'illegal but legitimate' loophole will meet with widespread international approval given that this kind of action is realistically only available to certain powerful states and their key allies. The legitimacy of such a development is thus questionable.

The need for legal reform

The IICK's conclusion that Operation Allied Force was 'illegal but legitimate' has become an oft-quoted appraisal of NATO's intervention; one aspect of the IICK's report that received less publicity was the corollary, 'allowing this gap between legality and legitimacy to persist is not healthy' (2000, p. 186). The disjuncture between international law and legitimate action exemplified by NATO's action concerned many who argued that reform was required lest international law lose its credibility (ICISS, 2001a, p. 3). Allowing states to determine independently when force should be used for humanitarian reasons is certainly inherently problematic. According to the UN High-Level Panel on Threats, Challenges and Change, diminishing the UN monopoly on the use of force would fundamentally undermine the authority of the UN and cause a chain reaction of unilateral aggression (2004, p. 63).

The feasibility of reform

Reforming international law, especially in the highly sensitive areas of the use of force and sovereignty, is far from straightforward (Chesterman, 2011b). In 1969 the International Law Commission established a sub-committee on the legal status of humanitarian intervention. The committee examined the potential for drafting a list of criteria for humanitarian intervention which could be incorporated into international law. This process was abandoned, however, in 1976 because the issue 'proved too controversial' and consensus was impossible (DIIA, 1999, p. 105). At the World Summit in 2005, states attempted to achieve consensus on new rules regarding the use of force specifically in the areas of self-defence and 'the responsibility to protect' that is incumbent on all states. The acrimony caused by the invasion of Iraq contributed to the impasse, and the prospects for substantive legal reform remain remote. The final 'Outcome Document' did contain two paragraphs related to humanitarian intervention, although concerns remain that little substantive progress was actually made (Wheeler, 2005; Bellamy, 2006a; Weiss, 2007a, p. 117).

Nonetheless, there is some evidence that reform is possible. In its findings ICISS noted: 'even in states where there was the strongest opposition
to infringements on sovereignty, there was a general acceptance that
there must be limited exceptions to the non-intervention rule for certain
kinds of emergencies' (2001a, p. 31). This suggests that there is not widespread opposition to the principle of the international community having
a role in upholding universally agreed human rights domestically.
Indeed, Article 4(h) of the Constitutive Act of the African Union recog-
nizes 'the right of the Union to intervene in a Member State pursuant to
a decision of the Assembly in respect of grave circumstances, namely:
war crimes, genocide and crimes against humanity'. This provision highlights that, even amongst those states most suspicious of and hostile
towards the idea of humanitarian intervention, there is an acceptance
that sovereignty does not imbue states with the right of complete domestic impunity.

Potential legal reform

Regardless of the political obstacles, the desirability of reform and the
nature of this change remain issues for discussion (Christopher, 2004, p.
248). Sir Arthur Watts frames the issue in stark terms:

> there is a choice: the international community must either establish an
> international force to maintain order, or let states perform that function
> themselves. The framers of the UN Charter attempted the former, but
> their good intentions have never really been carried through ... one is
> left in practice with self-appointed guardians of the peace. However,
> that cannot be a satisfactory basis on which to organize a legal order.
> (2001, p. 10)

Potential reforms range from codifying a right to unilateral humanitarian
intervention (Burton, 1996) to the establishment of new international
bodies empowered to deploy troops when situations deteriorate to certain
levels (Woodhouse and Ramsbotham, 2005, p. 152; Held, 2005, p. 25;
Buchanan and Keohane, 2011; Hehir, 2012, p. 228). Additionally, there
have been arguments in favour of clarifying the grounds on which the
Security Council can authorize humanitarian intervention to overcome the
problem of the inconsistent use of Chapter VII. The UN High-Level Panel
on Threats, Challenges and Change outlined 'five basic criteria of legitimacy' (see Box 5.3) which they argued should guide the Security Council.
The criteria reflect many of the sets of criteria previously articulated, and
have obvious parallels with the Just War tradition (see Chapter 2). The UN
Panel acknowledged that these criteria did not constitute 'agreed conclu-

Box 5.3   Five basic criteria of legitimacy

- Seriousness of threat
- Proper purpose
- Last resort
- Proportional means
- Balance of consequences

Source: UN High-Level Panel on Threats, Challenges and Change (2004, pp. 57–8).

sions with push-button predictability' and offered them as a means to 'maximise the possibility of achieving Security Council consensus around when it is appropriate or not to use coercive action' (2004, p. 57). The problem, however, is that the Panel's criteria do not address the key problem with respect to the use of force, namely, who decides whether these criteria have been met? (see Chapter 7). The Security Council will doubtless consider the UN Panel's criteria but these have no obvious power to constrain the Council's deliberations and overcome the central tension between interests and pressing humanitarian need (Hurrell, 2005, p. 30).

In addition to the obvious difficulty of ever achieving substantive reform, many oppose establishing a new rule on humanitarian intervention. Oscar Schachter argued that a new law is 'highly undesirable' because it could 'provide a pretext for abusive intervention' (1991, p. 126). While this is a widely held view (Chesterman, 2002, p. 231; Stromseth, 2005), it has been argued that this potential for abuse is far less damaging to international law than the current status. Jarat Chopra and Thomas Weiss acknowledge the potential for abuse in any new law, but point to the adverse consequence derived from the argument that codification should be avoided:

> since no definition could be sufficiently comprehensive, it was argued … that potential aggressors would be able to navigate between provisions and circumvent the letter of any prohibition. Instead, without any defined parameters states found that they did not have to navigate at all to contravene the spirit of the prohibition. (1992, p. 97)

Thus, viewed in the context of its current status, codifying humanitarian intervention is deemed likely to diminish rather than exacerbate the problem of the misuse of humanitarian justifications for intervention (Burton, 1996, p. 422).

Political will or legal obstacles?

While the need for legal reform is often presented as pressing, it is not necessarily the solution. If the problem posed by humanitarian intervention was singularly derived from legal restrictions and constitutional inadequacies, then clearly relevant reform would be apposite. An examination of the impediments to intervention, however, suggests that they are primarily political rather than legal. States, according to John Mueller, will intervene 'only when their interests seem importantly engaged or where they manage to become self-entrapped' (2005, p. 123). If Mueller is correct, and there are strong grounds for endorsing his analysis, then legal reform will not address what Chesterman describes as 'inhumanitarian non-intervention' (2003, p. 54). The idea that international law has prevented willing saviours from helping suffering innocents is, Chesterman notes, a misreading of history:

> Implicit in many arguments for a right of humanitarian intervention is the suggestion that international law currently prevents interventions that should take place. This is simply not true. Interventions do not take place because states choose not to undertake them. (ibid.)

It is difficult to think of any case where a state wanted to intervene but did not because it would have been illegal to do so. State power and interest, not international law, have therefore been the key variables influencing the decision not to intervene (Hehir, 2010a).

Conclusion

According to Cassese, 'the system envisaged in the UN Charter for the maintenance of international peace and security ... has substantially failed' (2005, p. 339). This failure has arguably manifested itself in the various inter-state wars which have occurred since the organization's inception. It is additionally arguable that the UN's paralysis in the face of egregious human rights violations perpetrated by states against their own citizens has highlighted the failings inherent in the post-1945 legal system.

As I have noted in this chapter, international law contains no explicit provision for sanctioning humanitarian intervention. Chapter VII of the Charter is the closest approximation to such a code, and it has been used increasingly since the end of the Cold War. However, the Security Council's composition, the influence of national interest and the questionable legality of applying Chapter VII to intra-state humanitarian crises have undermined support for the Chapter. Clearly in certain cases the Security

Council has failed to act, and thus, humanitarians argue, this body cannot be relied upon to act when necessary.

Unilateral humanitarian intervention is deeply contentious. While the dominant view is that such action is fundamentally illegal, this has not precluded further discussion. Three responses to this finding of illegality are discernible. First are the counter-claims that there *is* a legal basis for such action. Second is the claim that law must yield to ethics when it comes to halting massive suffering, and interventions should be judged on their morality rather than their legality. Third is the view that the disjuncture between legality and legitimacy must be addressed. Different legal reforms have been proposed in an effort to address what is considered the shameful spectacle of inertia in the face of human suffering. As we have seen, however, it is debatable whether international law has ever been responsible for inaction. More commonly inaction has been a function of the 'triumph of the lack of will' (Gow, 1997).

The legal status of humanitarian intervention derives from the rights afforded to sovereign states. These rights, as discussed in Chapter 3, are a function of the attempt to mitigate the impact of power in international politics and move beyond the 'might is right' ethos of the 19th century. Facilitating unilateral humanitarian intervention, even if motivated by the desire to 'save strangers', is seen as posing a risk to the 'fragile normative edifice' separating the post-1945 system from that of the 19th century (Chesterman and Byers, 1999). And yet it seems hard to deny that, regardless of the egalitarian motives responsible for the composition of the present system, the current legal framework cannot be deemed effective if atrocities such as those that have occurred in Rwanda, Darfur and Syria go unchecked. Jean Cohen outlines the choice facing the international community:

> we can either opt for strengthening international law by updating it, making explicit the particular conception of sovereignty on which it is now based and showing that this is compatible with cosmopolitan principles inherent in human rights norms; or we can abandon the principle of sovereign equality and the present rules of international law for the sake of human rights, thus relinquishing an important barrier to the proliferation of imperial projects and regional attempts at Grossraum ordering (direct annexation or other forms of control of neighbouring smaller polities) by great powers who invoke (and instrumentalize) cosmopolitan right as they proceed. (2004, p. 3)

Humanitarian intervention, Tom Farer notes, 'has subsisted on the shadowy periphery of international law' (2003, p. 143). It is surely doubtful whether this shadowy periphery can be sustained for much longer.

Questions

- To what extent did the evolution of international law in the 19th and 20th centuries preclude a right of humanitarian intervention?
- What is the basis for suggesting that humanitarian intervention is currently illegal?
- How convincing are the arguments that humanitarian intervention is in fact legal?
- Is legal reform of the status of humanitarian intervention required? What should this legal reform involve?

Further reading

On the evolution and role of international law

Armstrong, D., Farrell, T. and Lambert, H. (2007) *International Law and International Relations* (Cambridge: Cambridge University Press).

Brown, C. (2006) *Sovereignty, Rights and Justice: International Political Theory Today* (London: Polity).

Bull, H. (2002) *The Anarchical Society: A Study of Order in World Politics* (Basingstoke: Palgrave Macmillan and New York: Columbia University Press).

Byers, M. (ed.) (2001) *The Role of International Law in International Politics* (Oxford: Oxford University Press).

Chesterman, S. (2002) *Just War or Just Peace?* (Oxford: Oxford University Press).

Chesterman, S., Franck, T. and Malone, D. (2008) *Law and Practice of the United Nations* (Oxford: Oxford University Press).

Danish Institute of International Affairs (1999) *Humanitarian Intervention: Legal and Political Aspects* (Copenhagen: Danish Institute of International Affairs).

Gazzini, T. (2005) *The Changing Rules on the Use of Force in International Law* (Manchester: Manchester University Press).

Orford, A. (ed.) (2009) *International Law and its Others* (Cambridge: Cambridge University Press).

Simpson, G. (2004) *Great Powers and Outlaw States* (Cambridge: Cambridge University Press).

On the tension between law and morality

Armstrong, D., Farrell, T. and Maiguashca, B. (eds) (2005) *Force and Legitimacy in World Politics* (Cambridge: Cambridge University Press).

Fisher, D. (2011) *Morality and War* (Oxford: Oxford University Press).

Jokic, A. (ed.) (2004) *Lessons of Kosovo: The Dangers of Humanitarian Intervention* (Toronto: Broadview Press).

Lang, A. (ed.) (2003) *Just Intervention* (Washington, DC: Georgetown University Press).

Tesón, F. (1998) *Humanitarian Intervention: An Enquiry into Law and Morality* (New York: Transnational).

On codifying humanitarian intervention/UN reform

Buchanan, A. and Keohane, R. (2011) 'Precommitment Regimes for Intervention: Supplementing the Security Council', *Ethics and International Affairs*, 25/1, 41-63.

Burton, M. (1996) 'Legalising the Sublegal', *Georgetown Law Journal*, 85, 417–54.

Byers, M. and Chesterman, S. (2003) 'Changing the Rules About Rules?' in J. Holzgrefe and R. Keohane (eds), *Humanitarian Intervention: Ethical, Legal and Political Dilemmas* (Cambridge: Cambridge University Press).

Chesterman, S. (2011) 'The Outlook for UN Reform', New York University School of Law, Public Law & Legal Theory, Research Paper Series, Working Paper No. 11-55, August. Available at: http://ssrn.com/abstract=1885229.

Cohen, J. (2004) 'Whose Sovereignty? Empire Versus International Law', *Ethics and International Affairs*, 18/3, 1–24.

Hehir, A. (2012) *The Responsibility to Protect: Rhetoric, Reality and the Future of Humanitarian Intervention* (Basingstoke: Palgrave Macmillan), Chapter 8.

Pattison, J. (2010) *Humanitarian Intervention and the Responsibility to Protect* (Oxford: Oxford University Press), Chapter 8.

Chapter 6

The Responsibility to Protect

The 'responsibility to protect' (R2P) has become a remarkably ubiquitous term in both international political discourse and academia. In the past five years an extraordinary number of books and articles have been published on the subject; as the former UN Special Adviser on R2P Ed Luck (2010) exclaimed, 'the ever-expanding literature on the responsibility to protect could now fill a small library. The number of graduate theses alone devoted to the topic has been nothing less than staggering'.

R2P is also a very controversial term, one which inspires widely divergent reactions. Its proponents claim it is a revolutionary concept posed to alter radically the international system so that mass atrocities are a thing of the past; many, indeed, heralded the 2011 intervention in Libya as evidence of R2P's efficacy and the harbinger of a new era (see Chapter 14). Others, however, see the concept as a means of perpetuating Western hegemony and a threat to international peace and stability. In recent years an increasing number of scholars have dismissed the concept as an inherently nebulous political slogan.

In the first section below I examine the origins of R2P and its key tenets, focusing in particular on those who argue that the concept is revolutionary. I then examine the international reception to the ICISS report and the development of the concept. The main critiques of R2P are examined and assessed in the final section.

The origins of the responsibility to protect

If one wishes to conceptualize R2P as a modern rendering of those movements and advocates who have called for action to redress suffering abroad – the so-called 'atrocitarians' (Bass, 2008, p. 345) – then the origins of R2P can be traced back many centuries; as discussed in Chapter 2, the Just War tradition boasts a long historical lineage. The work of Francis Deng and Roberta Cohen in the 1990s, however, is generally cited as the first coherent rhetorical conflation of sovereignty and responsibility and thus the direct progenitor of R2P (Weiss, 2007a, p. 22). In 1993 Deng was appointed UN Special Representative on Internally Displaced People and, in the course of his work, he argued that sovereign states had a responsibility to protect their neediest citizens. Where a state was unable to fulfil this responsibility, he argued, it should accept international support (Deng et al., 1996, p. 1). The immediate catalyst for the emergence of R2P was, however, the controversy surrounding NATO's 'illegal but legitimate' intervention in Kosovo in 1999 (see Chapter 11). Following the intervention, Kofi Annan asked, 'if humanitarian intervention is, indeed, an unacceptable assault on sovereignty, how should we respond to a Rwanda, to a Srebrenica – to gross and systematic violations of human rights that affect every precept of our common humanity?' (ICISS, 2001a, p. vii). This led to the establishment of ICISS which began its work in August 2000 and published *The Responsibility to Protect* in December 2001. Gareth Evans claims to have invented the actual term 'the responsibility to protect' while in the shower prior to one of the ICISS meetings (Evans, 2008, p. 5).

Key tenets

ICISS was determined that its recommendations would have practical influence and declared: 'we want no more Rwandas and we believe that the adoption of the proposals in our report is the best way of ensuring that' (2001a, p. xiii). A key aim of *The Responsibility to Protect* was to reformulate the terms of the debate on responding to mass atrocities. 'Humanitarian intervention' was deemed inappropriate as it favourably prejudiced any intervention so described and was also routinely criticized by humanitarian aid workers as an unacceptable conflation of militarism with humanitarianism (ibid., p. 9). Rather than pose the issue in terms of the rights of intervening states, ICISS sought to place the onus on states to meet their responsibilities to their own citizens (ibid., p. 13). The 'responsibility to protect', therefore, resides first with individual states and only secondly with the international community.

ICISS employed the concept of 'human security' as the basic framework for its approach (ibid., p. 15). Building on the 'emerging principle' inherent in this idea, ICISS argued that intervention is legitimate when 'major harm to civilians is occurring or imminently apprehended, and the state in question is unable or unwilling to end the harm, or is itself the perpetrator' (ibid., p. 16). Intervention need not necessarily imply military intervention, however, and was not considered limited to action undertaken to stop an ongoing atrocity. Rather, ICISS put forward three aspects to this responsibility: the responsibility to prevent, the responsibility to react and the responsibility to rebuild.

The responsibility to prevent and the responsibility to rebuild are the least contentious aspects of R2P, although they cannot be divorced from the overall argument (Evans, 2008, p. 57). The idea of a 'responsibility to prevent' is that states have a responsibility to ensure that domestic tensions are addressed before they escalate (ICISS, 2001a, pp. 19–27). Failure by a state to take appropriate or effective preventive measures means the responsibility transfers to the international community. This responsibility also requires more effective early warning systems and implementing measures aimed at tackling the root causes of domestic disquiet, such as economic inequality and political disenfranchisement. The 'responsibility to rebuild' places a responsibility on an intervening state, or states, to contribute to the post-conflict recovery process in the form of monetary aid and political support to ensure a lasting settlement to the original conflict (ibid., pp. 39–45).

The 'responsibility to react' is most related to the central dilemma posed by humanitarian intervention and is the aspect of R2P that has attracted greatest attention. ICISS noted that 'above all else' R2P constitutes 'a responsibility to react to situations of compelling need for human protection' (ibid., p. 29). If a state is either unable or unwilling to meet its responsibility to protect its citizens, ICISS argued, the responsibility transfers from the state to the international community.

International intervention to stop human rights abuses need not take the form of military intervention, which, ICISS warned, is legitimate only in extreme cases (ibid.). ICISS offered six 'Principles for Military Intervention', criteria that must be met for an intervention to be legitimate: right authority, just cause, right intention, last resort, proportional means and reasonable prospects (ibid., p. 32). In terms of 'just cause', ICISS suggested two thresholds:

> large scale loss of life, actual or apprehended, with genocidal intent or not, which is the product either of deliberate state action, or state neglect or inability to act, or a failed state situation; or large scale 'ethnic cleansing', actual or apprehended, whether carried out by killing, forced expulsion, acts of terror or rape. (Ibid.)

ICISS acknowledged that these thresholds exclude racial discrimination, tyranny and the rescue of foreign nationals, but argued that, grave though these are, they did not warrant external intervention (ibid., p. 34).

By 'right intention' ICISS suggested that the intervening party must be motivated primarily, though not exclusively, by humanitarian aims (ibid., p. 36). This is most likely to be achieved if the intervention is multilateral in composition. Regarding 'last resort', the report advises that every diplomatic and non-military avenue must have been explored, though not necessarily exhausted, provided there are good grounds for discounting these options (ibid.). On 'proportional means', ICISS advised that all interventions must be executed in strict adherence with international humanitarian law and employ the minimum degree of force possible. The final criterion – 'reasonable prospects' – advises that interventions should only be undertaken if the action is likely to be successful (ibid., p. 37).

'Right authority' is clearly the most important criterion given the implications this has for determining whether the other criteria have been met. Reflecting this importance, an entire chapter of *The Responsibility to Protect* is devoted to this question. Regarding 'right authority', ICISS clearly privileges the UN, and within the UN the Security Council. All those seeking to launch an intervention must seek the Security Council's approval, and the report warns that acting without explicit UN approval runs the risk of undermining the UN and international law generally (ibid., p. 48). Membership of the UN, ICISS claimed, carries an obligation not to use force unilaterally, but also an obligation to use force on behalf of the UN if so sanctioned (ibid., p. 49). While ICISS was clear as to the importance of the Security Council, the unrepresentative nature of the P5 was criticized, as was its lack of accountability to the General Assembly (ibid., p. 51). In terms of addressing the biggest issue regarding the Security Council's record on humanitarian intervention – the veto power of the P5 – ICISS suggested a 'code of conduct' whereby 'a permanent member, in matters where its vital national interests were not claimed to be involved, would not use its veto to obstruct the passage of what would otherwise be a majority resolution' (ibid.).

If, however, the Security Council does not act when a crisis passes the just cause threshold, ICISS highlighted a number of alternatives. First, the matter should be taken to the General Assembly, which could employ the powers vested in it through the Uniting for Peace resolution (ibid., p. 53; see Chapter 5). Additionally, ICISS suggested that regional organizations could undertake an intervention and seek to have retrospective legitimacy bestowed on their actions by the Security Council, as happened with the Economic Community of West African States Monitoring Group's (ECOMOG) interventions in Liberia in 1992 and Sierra Leone in 1997 (see Chapter 9).

Of course, the most obvious alternative, and that which caused the furore about Kosovo in 1999, was intervention without explicit approval from the Security Council or the General Assembly. *The Responsibility to Protect* acknowledged that this was a particularly divisive issue and accepted that 'it would be impossible to find consensus … around any set of proposals for military intervention which acknowledged the validity of any intervention not authorized by the Security Council or General Assembly' (ibid., pp. 54–5). *The Responsibility to Protect* outlines 'two lessons' which must guide thinking in respect to this dilemma. First, it states that, in the face of Security Council inaction, 'it is unrealistic to expect that concerned states will rule out other means and forms of action to meet the gravity and urgency of these situations'. Such interventions 'may not be conducted for the right reasons or with the right commitment to the necessary precautionary principles' (ibid., p. 55). Second, if action is taken without the Security Council's approval and this action proves successful, 'then this may have enduring serious consequences for the stature and credibility of the UN itself' (ibid.).

Thus, *The Responsibility to Protect* constituted a key statement on humanitarian intervention which aimed at embedding the idea of sovereignty as responsibility and, crucially, the principle that the international community has a responsibility to act when individual states are unwilling or unable to do so. The next section outlines the international response to ICISS's report and the evolution of R2P thereafter.

International reception and evolution

As Bellamy notes, R2P has 'changed in important respects from the way it was originally conceived by the ICISS' (2009, p. 195). It does not make sense, therefore, to equate 'R2P' only with the ICISS report, though obviously the latter inspired the contemporary manifestation. The evolution of R2P has comprised two main themes: first, the dramatic rise in popularity of the term in international political discourse; and second, the gradual alteration of its content and focus. While proponents of R2P have naturally welcomed the former, many have lamented the latter (Weiss, 2007a, p. 117).

ICISS's report was initially favourably received by most Western states and many traditional allies (Bellamy, 2006a, p. 151). East Asian countries were 'more cautious' in their response, while, perhaps most importantly, the Security Council was quite negative (Macfarlane et al., 2004, p. 982). In May 2002 the Security Council discussed ICISS's report. The US 'was noticeably unenthusiastic' and 'there was widespread opinion in the meeting that if new situations emerged ... the five permanent members and broader Council would lack the political will to deliver troops and would limit themselves to condemnatory resolution' (Welsh, 2006, pp. 185, 210). The US rejected the idea of being bound to commit troops should a set threshold be breached, while the Chinese opposed any diminution of the Security Council's monopoly on the legitimization of the use of force, a perspective shared by Russia (Bellamy, 2006a, pp. 151–2).

The Non-Aligned Movement rejected the basic premise behind the ICISS report, while the G-77, though it offered no joint position, suggested amending the provisions to strengthen the principles of territorial integrity and sovereignty (ibid., p. 152). In 2003 the African Union (AU) formally replaced the Organization of African Unity, and its Constitutive Act contained provision 4(h) which established 'the right of the Union to intervene in a Member State pursuant to a decision of the Assembly in respect of grave circumstances, namely war crimes, genocide and crimes against humanity'. Thus the AU appeared to adopt formally the key principle behind *The Responsibility to Protect*, though the position later taken by many AU states undermined the idea that African states had come to endorse the doctrine of R2P (ibid., pp. 157–62).

At the July 2003 Progressive Governments Summit the prime ministers of both Canada and the UK attempted to include the basic principles of *The Responsibility to Protect* in the final communiqué, but this was rejected, with Argentina, Chile and Germany being particularly opposed. This marked 'a surprising new kind of hostility among countries that earlier might have been counted among the supporters of the concept (Macfarlane et al., 2004, p. 984). The fallout from the invasion of Iraq and the general rhetoric of the Bush administration after 11 September 2001 created a new unwillingness on the part of many Western states to facilitate interventionism, while in the non-Western world any change to the status of sovereignty was viewed with great suspicion. The invasion of Iraq had led to a 'poisonous' atmosphere in the General Assembly, and thus the potential for the kind of reform suggested by ICISS was greatly reduced (Weiss, 2007a, p. 125).

In September 2003 Kofi Annan commissioned a High-Level Panel on Threats, Challenges and Change to examine the UN's role in addressing international security concerns. Their report recognized the principle that both sovereignty and membership of the UN imposed certain responsibilities (2004, p. 17). The report further explicitly acknowledged the notion that the international community had a 'responsibility to protect' citizens in other states (ibid., p. 66). It adopted the just cause thresholds and precautionary principles contained in *The Responsibility to Protect* with some minor amendments (Bellamy, 2006a, p. 156). Additionally, the report generally advanced a cautious perspective on revising the rules governing the use of force, though it did suggest that the Security Council needed to 'enhance its capacity and willingness to act in the face of threats' (High Level Panel on Threats, Challenges and Change, 2004, p. 80). The report 'significantly changed the normative context' within which the debate surrounding R2P had proceeded (Wheeler, 2005, p. 99). Kofi Annan welcomed the findings and included the recommendations in his report *In Larger Freedom* (2005a), which he presented to the General Assembly in March 2005.

The 2005 World Summit, held in New York from 14–16 September, marked the 60th anniversary of the UN and was billed as an opportunity for the organization to 'undergo the most sweeping overhaul in its 60 year history' (Annan, 2005b, p. 66). Representatives from all of the world's states attended and engaged in negotiations in an atmosphere clouded by the US-led invasion of Iraq. Two paragraphs – 138 and 139 (see Box 6.1) – were included in the final 'Outcome Document', explicitly endorsing the notion of a responsibility to protect. The fact that this agreement was reached suggests on one level a success on the part of the advocates of R2P. Others have argued, however, that the compromises that secured the inclusion of these paragraphs undermined the essence of the original proposal.

In terms of explaining how the idea of a 'responsibility to protect' came to be included, Bellamy (2006a) suggests that three major amendments to

---

Box 6.1　Paragraphs 138 and 139 of the World Summit 'Outcome Document'

138: Each individual State has the responsibility to protect its populations from genocide, war crimes, ethnic cleansing and crimes against humanity. This responsibility entails the prevention of such crimes, including their incitement, through appropriate and necessary means. We accept that responsibility and will act in accordance with it. The international community should, as appropriate, encourage and help States to exercise this responsibility and support the UN in establishing an early warning capability.

　139: The international community, through the UN, also has the responsibility to use appropriate diplomatic, humanitarian and other peaceful means, in accordance with Chapters VI and VIII of the Charter, to help protect populations from genocide, war crimes, ethnic cleansing and crimes against humanity. In this context, we are prepared to take collective action, in a timely and decisive manner, through the Security Council, in accordance with the Charter, including Chapter VII, on a case-by-case basis and in cooperation with relevant regional organizations as appropriate, should peaceful means be inadequate and national authorities manifestly fail to protect their populations from genocide, war crimes, ethnic cleansing and crimes against humanity. We stress the need for the General Assembly to continue consideration of the responsibility to protect populations from genocide, war crimes, ethnic cleansing and crimes against humanity and its implications, bearing in mind the principles of the Charter and international law. We also intend to commit ourselves, as necessary and appropriate, to helping States build capacity to protect their populations from genocide, war crimes, ethnic cleansing and crimes against humanity and to assisting those which are under stress before crises and conflicts break out.

Source: UN General Assembly (2005).

the ICISS version of R2P were made. First, regarding the question of authority, the idea of the Security Council members agreeing not to use their veto powers – the 'code of conduct' – was jettisoned early in the negotiations, while the notion of legitimate intervention without explicit Security Council approval was 'sidestepped' (ibid., p. 155). Second, the just cause threshold included in the 'Outcome Document' actually restricted the instances when the Security Council could legitimately intervene. Security Council practice in the 1990s had substantially broadened its remit to act (see p. 106). With authority being once again clearly vested in the Security Council, and the criteria for intervention limited to 'genocide, war crimes, ethnic cleansing and crimes against humanity', the scope for intervention was restricted (Byers, 2005b). Third, while ICISS stated that the responsibility to protect transferred from the state to the international community when the host state was deemed 'unable or unwilling' to exercise its responsibilities, in the 'Outcome Document' this was amended to cases where the host state was guilty of a 'manifest failure' – a semantic change but one that raised the threshold for international action.

Supporters of R2P sought to convince the General Assembly to make a commitment to the tenets of the original ICISS document and persuade the Security Council to do three things: first, to adopt a resolution committing it to act whenever the just cause thresholds were crossed; second, to submit its decisions to public deliberation; and third, for the P5 to agree not to use the veto in cases of humanitarian emergencies where they did not have clear national interests at stake (Bellamy, 2006a, p. 153). None of these aims was realized. The consensus on R2P was, therefore, achieved by conceding key aspects of the ICISS report. Thus, the 'Outcome Document' constituted for some 'a step-backward ... R2P lite' (Weiss, 2007a, p. 117).

The 2005 World Summit certainly did not precipitate an immediate improvement in the international response to intra-state crises: the slaughter in Darfur raged before, during and after the 'Outcome Document' was agreed (Heinze, 2009, p. 126). Certain states, most notably the US, seemed determined to ignore the agreement and consign it to the same fate as dozens of previous forgotten commitments (Bassiouni, 2009, p. 34; Feinsten and De Bruin, 2009, p. 189). Additionally, certain states that had signed the 'Outcome Document' somewhat curiously later suggested that they hadn't in fact agreed to the idea of a 'responsibility to protect' (Evans, 2008, p. 52).

To discuss the implementation of R2P the General Assembly convened a special session which began on 21 July 2009. Six months prior to the debate, UN Secretary General Ban Ki-moon presented his report, 'Implementing the Responsibility to Protect', in which he stressed that R2P constituted a commitment that could not be retracted – and he also cautioned against broadening the remit of R2P beyond the 'four crimes' listed in the 'Outcome Document': genocide, war crimes, ethnic cleansing and crimes against humanity (2009a, p. 8). He described R2P as comprising three pillars:

- Pillar 1: The protection responsibilities of states.
- Pillar 2: International assistance and capacity building.
- Pillar 3: Timely and decisive response.

Over the course of three days UN member states gave their views on the Secretary General's report and R2P more generally. In total over 90 governments made presentations and more were represented by international regional organizations such as the Non-Aligned Movement and the Caribbean Community. Following the debate a number of very positive appraisals lauded the event as a significant achievement (ICRP, 2009, p. 1; Global Center for R2P, 2009, p. 1). UN Secretary General Ban Ki-moon described the debate as 'heartening' and 'forward-looking' (2009b).

Many states highlighted the AU's 2000 Constitutive Act as a significant development in the evolution of R2P. The Act was cited as indicative of the move from 'non-interference' to 'non-indifference' and of the willingness of states in the developing world to adhere to, and advance, principles on human rights protection often characterized as culturally specific or 'Western'. R2P was, therefore, generally endorsed as a universal principle in keeping with the cultural norms in the developing world and not simply 'Western'.

It was also consistently stressed that prevention was a key component of R2P; many states emphasized that R2P involved much more than military intervention and, further, that its greatest potential efficacy lay in its capacity to prevent, rather than halt, humanitarian crises. States additionally overwhelmingly reasserted that R2P could only apply to the four crimes listed in the 2005 'Outcome Document'; in May 2008 certain international observers, such as the then French Foreign Minister Bernard Kouchner, claimed that the humanitarian crisis caused by the hurricane in Myanmar was being exacerbated by the ruling military junta's inability, if not unwillingness, to provide aid to the needy and thus the situation demanded external intervention (Reuters, 2008). This was criticized in many parts of the world, by both R2P sceptics and supporters, as an unjustifiable expansion of R2P's remit (Evans, 2008, p. 65). There was also widespread agreement that R2P was not a new legal principle, as Ban Ki-moon had emphasized in his pre-debate report (2009a, p. 5). The impetus for this line of argument was the perceived need to counter the charge that R2P was not in conformity with existing international law and thus that it should be rejected. This was very much the minority position, however, as even states such as

North Korea, Sudan, Myanmar and Iran acknowledged that the basic principles underpinning R2P could be found in existing international law. As will be argued later in this chapter, however, the fact that R2P does not constitute a new legal principle has been one of the main criticisms levelled against its potential efficacy. Finally, there was general agreement on the need for the mobilization of political will. This call for a new will to act echoed paragraph 138 of the 2005 World Summit 'Outcome Document' and Ban Ki-moon's pre-debate report (2009, pp. 8–9). The debate's proceedings were summarized and endorsed in General Assembly Resolution 63/308 in September 2009.

In 2010 the General Assembly again discussed R2P this time in the context of prevention; though a smaller number of states took part, the debate again evidenced general support for both the idea of bolstering the UN's preventative capacity and the basic principle that the international community had the right to play a role in intra-state affairs. In July 2011 the General Assembly discussed the role of regional and sub-regional arrangements under the R2P umbrella and the UN Secretary General published a report on the issue (Ban Ki-moon, 2011b).

In addition to these various debates at the General Assembly two new offices have been created which directly link to R2P: first, on the tenth anniversary of the Rwandan genocide the then UN Secretary General Kofi Annan established the Office of the Special Adviser on the Prevention of Genocide; the Special Adviser's role was recognized in paragraph 140 of the 2005 World Summit 'Outcome Document'. Second, in 2008 the Secretary General appointed Ed Luck as the 'Special Adviser to the Secretary General with a Focus on the Responsibility to Protect'. The title originally put forward ('Special Adviser on the Responsibility to Protect') was opposed by a number of member states who argued that R2P's meaning remained unclear (ICRtoP, 2012a). Nonetheless, Ed Luck essentially focused exclusively on R2P. In his report prior to the 2009 General Assembly debate Ban Ki-moon suggested the two offices should work more closely and in 2010 they officially merged. While concerns have been raised as to the utility of the new position (Hehir, 2011b) many have argued that the appointments constitute an encouraging sign of intent and a platform to build on (Ramcharan, 2008, p. 180; Hamburg, 2008, p. 226). Both Luck and Deng regularly issued public statements as crises erupted across the Middle East and North Africa in 2011, and their very presence at UN meetings and international conferences at the very least provided a tangible expression of R2P's existence. Adama Dieng became the new joint Special Adviser in July 2012.

Challenging the responsibility to protect

The debate about R2P naturally echoes the earlier debates in the 1990s about the limits of sovereignty and the merits of external intervention. Given both the importance and the sensitive nature of sovereignty it is hardly surprising that R2P has not been greeted with unanimous support. The concept has also suffered from what Evans describes as 'the misdirected enthusiasms ... of self-described friends of R2P whose attentions have ... been less than entirely welcome' (2008, p. 55). Certain NGOs, journalists, politicians and academics have indeed advanced a wildly expansive version of R2P; in November 2011, for example, Thor Halvorssen, citing R2P, called for military action against Russia to stop domestic oppression, particularly in Chechnya (Henry Jackson Society, 2011). Whatever we may wish to identify as the 'real' or 'sober' face of R2P – and it *is* possible to identify aberrant extremism such as Halvorssen's rallying cry – R2P has come under sustained critique for a number of reasons, and its claim to be a 'revolutionary principle' (Feinstein, 2007) is widely disputed. The following sub-sections outline the key objections raised against it.

Prevention

A very obvious trend in the evolution of R2P has been the increased focus on prevention; indeed, Weiss, a vocal supporter of R2P, has railed against what he describes as the 'virtually exclusive emphasis on prevention' after the 2005 World Summit (2011, p. 1). Naturally, the shibboleth 'prevention is better than cure' applies to intra-state crises and thus the inclusion of prevention in the R2P canon is not illogical. Many have argued, however, that this shift to emphasizing prevention rather than intervention stems from the fact that the former is far less contentious then the latter (ibid., p. 2; Chandler, 2009). In a bid to avoid contention by tackling the core of problem, prevention has thus been advanced, some claim, because it is the 'lowest common denominator' (Hehir, 2012, p. 54).

The 'responsibility to prevent' was one component of ICISS's tripartite conception of R2P and the focus of an entire chapter of their report. ICISS, indeed, described prevention as 'the single most important dimension of the responsibility to protect' (2001a, p. xi). Both *The Responsibility to Protect* and the supplementary research volume (ibid., 2001b, p. 27) outline a wide array of policy choices available to the international community to address the causes of conflict, including political, diplomatic, economic and judicial measures incorporating both coercive and non-coercive action (ibid., 2001a, pp. 23–7). Paragraphs 138, 139 and 140 of the 2005 World Summit 'Outcome Document' also affirmed the centrality of prevention while, in the course of the 2009 General Assembly debate on R2P, states consistently stressed that prevention was the key component of R2P; this was in fact arguably the most commonly articulated sentiment (Hehir, 2011a). A number of R2P's more prominent supporters have certainly come to champion its preventative dimension (Evans, 2008, p. 79; Bellamy, 2009a, p. 198).

While it is certainly true that *The Responsibility to Protect* described prevention as the 'single most important aspect of R2P', the report also stated that 'the "responsibility to protect" implies *above all else* a responsibility to react to situations of compelling need for human protection' (ICISS, 2001a, p. 29). The first sentence of the report likewise outlines its primary focus:

> This report is about the so-called right of 'humanitarian intervention': the question of when, if ever, it is appropriate for states to take coercive – and in particular military – action against another state for the purpose of protecting people at risk in that other state (ibid., p. vii).

Chapter 7 of the ICISS report, 'The Operational Dimension', refers briefly to prevention but primarily discusses reaction and in particular military intervention. Additionally, despite its ostensible importance, prevention is the focus of only nine of the 85 pages of the whole report (Bellamy, 2009a, p. 65).

The sections on prevention are, it has been argued, hardly revelatory: ICISS articulated a number of eminently sensible general prescriptions but few concrete policy options or suggestions for reform. The scope of preventative action identified is enormous, ranging from education and economic development to peacekeeping. As Michael Lund warns with respect to such expansive approaches, 'with so much varied activity now being lumped under conflict prevention there is also a risk it will lose its distinctive meaning' (2004, p. 122). Research on conflict prevention may not receive the acclaim and attention it deserves but it is certainly not lacking and there is no shortage of detailed studies examining this issue in far greater depth than R2P has done. Indeed, in a 2003 article Bellamy criticized ICISS's treatment of prevention, noting that 'the need to pay more attention, and more money, to prevention and post-conflict rebuilding has long been identified' (2003, pp. 6–7). Later he described the sections on prevention as 'brief, confused and unoriginal' and asserted that 'I would go as far as to argue ... that the commission should rewrite its chapters on prevention and rebuilding' (Bellamy, 2009a, pp. 52–3).

Aside from the fact that R2P is charged with having little new to offer to the prevention canon and evading the central question by concentrating on prevention, there are a number of other broader concerns. As Henry

Huttenbach noted, 'the capability to predict wars, civil strife and revolutions, let alone specific genocides, with any kind of reasonable, rational certitude escapes even the most knowledgeable' (2008, p. 472). Indicatively, as will be discussed in Chapter 14, the crises which erupted across the Middle East and North Africa in 2011 were a surprise and eluded the various early warning mechanisms; thus, if the identification of future crises to be prevented is often impossible, surely emphasis should be placed on reaction? There is a further argument that early intervention, even if preventative in nature, is not always welcome and in certain cases, such as Rwanda, exacerbates underlying societal tensions (see Chapter 10).

As Tom Malinowski of Human Rights Watch stated, 'presidents get more credit for stopping atrocities after they begin than for preventing them before they get out of hand' (HRW, 2011a). Statesmen, indeed, have proven time and time again to be reluctant to expend resources on foreign wars; they are arguably less likely to do so in cases of *potential* war. According to Bruce W. Jentleson, 'almost every study of conflict prevention concludes that when all is said and done, the main obstacle is the lack of political will' (2009, p. 293). The ICISS report itself even noted: 'it is possible to exaggerate the extent to which lack of early warning is a serious problem ... lack of early warning is an excuse rather than an explanation, and the problem is not a lack of warning but of timely response' (2001a, p. 21). Simply reiterating the 'prevention is better than cure' mantra does not, therefore, necessarily advance the debate – this has long been proclaimed and accepted but rarely acted upon.

According to Weiss, the 'mumbling and stumbling' regarding prevention is a 'superficially attractive but highly unrealistic way to try and pretend that we can finesse the hard issues of what essentially amounts to humanitarian intervention' (2007a, p. 104). The major issue is, he maintains, the responsibility to react. Prevention, he claims, 'obscures the essence of the most urgent part of the spectrum of responsibility, to protect those caught in the crosshairs of war' (ibid., p. 107). Weiss describes the strategy of those R2P supporters, such as Bellamy, who cite prevention as the key focus of R2P, as simply 'hard to fathom' (2011, p. 2).

A tool of the powerful

The most vociferous champions – in terms of states, academics and NGOs – of R2P are predominantly Western, and the rationale underlying the idea is a basic principle of Western liberal democracy. Beyond just the particular origins of R2P, there is scepticism in the developing world regarding the motivation driving this pressure for change, with many members of the 133 states comprising the G-77 arguing that the focus on human rights is designed to facilitate Western expansion. At the 2005 World Summit, the President of Venezuela, Hugo Chavez (2005), described R2P as part of a movement whereby 'a few countries try to reinterpret the principles of international law in order to impose new doctrines'. Likewise, in 2012 the Venezuelan Ambassador to the UN declared:

> The 'responsibility to protect' is only intended to be applied to militarily weak countries, in order to invade developing countries ... Why isn't the 'responsibility to protect' mentioned when the Palestinian people is slaughtered? Why isn't the 'responsibility to protect' mentioned when imperial powers assassinate, with impunity, Iraqis, Afghans and Pakistanis? (Venezuela, 2012, p. 2)

As noted in Chapter 3, sovereignty is considered by many states in the developing world to be a bulwark against colonialism, and the rhetoric of human rights and 'sovereignty as responsibility' is reminiscent of the arguments proffered by European empires in the 19th century – thus R2P 'raises the spectre of a return to colonial habits and practices on the part of the major Western powers' (Ayoob, 2002, p. 85). Mindful of the history of Western interference in the developing world, many are naturally sceptical of the ethical foreign policy espoused in the post-Cold War era (Fake and Funk, 2009). 'Africans and Asians', Ramesh Thakur observed, 'are neither amused nor mindful at being lectured on universal human values by those who failed to practice the same during European colonialism and now urge them to cooperate in promoting "global" human rights norms' (2004, p. 197).

In explaining this need to contrive new norms conducive to hegemonic proliferation, Chandler argues that the post-Cold War systemic configuration, though favourable to the West and particularly the US, provided no 'framework which can legitimize and give moral authority to new, more direct forms of Western regulation'. This 'crisis' led to the assertion of the liberal peace thesis which constitutes 'the convergence of morality and Realpolitik' (Chandler, 2004a, p. 75). R2P is ostensibly part of this liberal peace thesis and thus a means by which the tenets of international law can be manipulated to facilitate the national interest of Western states. Noam Chomsky (2011) similarly discounts the humanitarian rhetoric employed by Western proponents of sovereignty as responsibility as entirely cynical and designed to erode the restrictions international law places upon them. Christian Reus-Smit likewise argues that the increased focus on the internal human rights record of states and attendant desire to determine a state's sovereign rights according to this record is part of 'the liberal hierarchy thesis' which suggests that liberal democracies should be afforded greater rights under international law (2005, p. 76).

Drawing on the historical record many have asserted that prevailing norms and laws favour the dominant powers (Orford, 2009). The emergence of R2P should not be seen, therefore, as a challenge to the powerful but rather as a means of enabling the hegemonic powers to further their aims. R2P may well thus cause further disorder as the powerful seek to exploit the new framework for intervention which challenges the old proscription against the use of force (Jackson, 2000, p. 291; Ayoob, 2002, pp. 82–3; Reus-Smit, 2005, p. 92; Reinhold, 2012).

Many have raised concerns about R2P's capacity to be employed consistently. ICISS's consultations in Egypt reported that there existed a belief that 'the mechanisms and procedures of the intervention process must be subject to objective international regulation' (2001b, p. 375). Likewise in Latin America participants did not reject intervention outright but did express concern that political interests would continue to impact on the consistent authorization of intervention if the present system was not reformed (ibid., p. 372). The 'code of conduct' suggested for the P5 has also been criticized as inherently nebulous. The question of the P5's veto power is central to the controversy surrounding humanitarian intervention, yet the solution advanced by R2P, many argue, amounts to a nonbinding gentleman's agreement which appears to overlook the fact that the national interests of the P5 are invariably involved and, if a case arises where they are not, there is unlikely to be a major problem anyway (Hehir, 2008a, pp. 121–2).

It is additionally claimed that the potential increase in military intervention could stem from the actions of not just the militarily powerful but also the militarily weak. The potential for intervention may well induce certain groups to provoke their government into using excessive military force in the hope that the ensuing repression would compel the international community to intervene to protect the victims of the government's reprisals. An escalation imperative – described as a 'moral hazard' – is thus created, predicated on the logic that the greater the tragedy, the more likely it is that intervention will occur (Belloni, 2006; Kuperman, 2006, p. 19). The problem is thus twofold: first, while the possibility of intervention exists, rebel groups that ordinarily would not have used military force may do so; second, once they have attacked the state and provoked a retaliatory attack, there is no guarantee that intervention will take place, therefore rebels may create and then endure a humanitarian crisis. This, Kuperman argues, was precisely the strategy employed by the Kosovo Liberation Army in 1995–9 (Kuperman, 2006) and the rebels during the conflict in Libya in 2011 (Kuperman, 2013). This has been subjected to in-depth critique, however, by Bellamy and Williams. They argue that this theory lacks supporting evidence, is based on a theory imported from economics which does not apply, and ultimately 'guides analysts towards simplified explanations that ignore or misinterpret significant pieces of information that do not correspond to the theory' (Bellamy and Williams, 2012, p. 541).

A norm or nebulous?

Many have argued that while R2P may not be a legal principle it is a 'norm' (Evans, 2008, p. 16; Slaughter, 2011b). Others assert, however, that the term 'norm' has been used loosely with respects to R2P, cautioning that a distinction must be made between genuine 'norms' and 'political catch-words' (Stahn, 2007, p. 120). There is a large body of academic literature which interrogates the meaning of 'norms' and the process by which a norm is established (Focarelli, 2008). True norms are certainly more than just popular terms. Martha Finnemore and Kathryn Sikkink's seminal work on the evolution of norms, for example, warns of the need to 'think seriously about the microfoundations on which theoretical claims about norms rest, and evaluate those claims in the context of carefully designed historical and empirical research' (1998, p. 890). Where there is evidence that, despite a term's ubiquity, there is confusion as to its meaning and contestation surrounding its tenets, its putative standing as a 'norm' is in doubt.

As discussed throughout this chapter, certain commentators – and indeed states – have claimed that R2P is not a new legal principle – which even its supporters accept – but also that it is inherently nebulous. Observers have noted that there are a number of ambiguities within R2P itself: both threshold criteria in *The Responsibility to Protect* use the term 'large scale', and ICISS stated it wished to 'make no attempt to quantify "large scale" [as this] will not in practice generate major disagreement' (ICISS, 2001a, pp. 32–3). In fact, Bellamy argues that this indeterminacy can enable the P5 to block interventions by claiming that the thresholds have not been breached (2006a, pp. 148–9). The 2005 World Summit did nothing to clarify this seminal ambiguity, to the disappointment of R2P's supporters (Evans, 2008, p. 48). This charge of indeterminacy can be applied to a number of other aspects of R2P: how do we determine that human protection is the 'primary purpose' behind a state's desire to intervene or that the use of force is truly the last resort, given that all alternative means do not have to be attempted so long as there are 'reasonable grounds' for believing that they would not have succeeded? (Wheeler, 2005, p. 97; Focarelli, 2008, p. 209). In particular, how does the Security Council decide when and where to intervene? As noted above, in 2005 R2P's supporters failed to convince the Security Council to increase its transparency by engaging in public deliberation (Bellamy, 2006a, p. 153). In fact, during the crisis in Sri Lanka in 2008, key meetings of the Security

Council were held behind closed doors in the basement of the UN head-quarters.

As Theresa Reinhold notes, beyond the general, and relatively modest, consensus that states should not commit certain acts against their citizens and that the international community *may* get involved if they do, R2P is underdeveloped. She argues that R2P lacks both conceptual clarity and consistent application in state practice and therefore 'norm internalisation cannot occur ... the responsibility to protect clearly has not evolved into a norm, that is, an intersubjectively shared standard of appropriate behavior' (Reinhold, 2010, p. 74). Carlo Focarelli, indeed, argues that there is 'extreme ambiguity surrounding the responsibility to protect' (2008, 210). While the intervention in Libya in 2011 was heralded by many as evidence of R2P's efficacy, others pointed to the fact that the term was conspicuously missing from the resolutions authorizing action; Jennifer Welsh argues that the absence of any reference to the international responsibility to protect in both resolutions on Libya suggests that R2P is 'still contested by some members of the Security Council' (2011, p. 1). The acrimony which erupted during and after NATO's intervention, as the meaning of 'no-fly zone' was stretched considerably, has arguably only increased opposition to R2P-type action and further eroded consensus (see Chapter 14).

In November 2011 Brazil introduced a new term, 'responsibility while protecting'. While this 'concept note' – delivered as a letter to the Secretary General – did not amount to a rebuke of R2P, it did highlight a number of concerns Brazil and other 'developing world' states have with the concept. The letter stated: 'the world today suffers the painful consequences of interventions that have aggravated existing conflicts, allowed terrorism to penetrate into places where it previously did not exist, given rise to new cycles of violence and increased the vulnerability of civilian populations' (Brazil, 2011, p. 3). Reflecting the concerns which emerged in the wake of the intervention in Libya, Brazil further stated: 'there is a growing perception that the concept of the responsibility to protect might be misused for purposes other than protecting civilians, such as regime change' (ibid.). The concept note, though couched in diplomatic rhetoric, is further evidence that consensus on R2P remains elusive.

The emperor's new clothes?

It is one thing to assert that sovereignty carries with it a responsibility to protect and that failure to meet this responsibility legitimizes external intervention; it is quite another to create the means by which the latter aspect of this assertion is realized. There is certainly little doubt but that states are today considered to have responsibilities towards their citizens and that there are certain human rights violations which cannot be considered exclusively domestic matters. But we could reasonably ask: 'Is there anything new about this?'. While many have welcomed the increasing number of references made to R2P in official treaties, resolutions and declarations, others point to the long and undistinguished history of rhetorical commitments and the 'disconnect between political reality and pious rhetoric' (Weiss, 2007b, p. 7). Perhaps indicative of the actual importance afforded to rhetorical commitments, following the publication of the World Summit 'Outcome Document' the then US Ambassador to the UN, John Bolton, stated: 'I plan to never read it again. I doubt many others will either' (Bellamy, 2009a, p. 92).

At the conclusion of the 2005 World Summit Tony Blair declared: 'for the first time at this summit we are agreed that states do not have the right to do what they will within their own borders' (Fisher, 2007, p. 109). This is a questionable claim. Since at least the Nuremberg trials in 1945 it has been clear that states could not do whatever they wanted to their own citizens. The concept 'crime against humanity' is formulated in a way that explicitly describes certain actions as affecting more than just the victims themselves, and hence is not purely a domestic matter. Many developments during the Cold War, such as the Genocide Convention and the Universal Declaration of Human Rights, outlined the responsibilities states had towards their citizens. Indeed the 1966 International Covenant on Civil and Political Rights committed states to 'respect and to ensure to all individuals within its territory and subject to its jurisdiction the rights recognised in the present Convention, without distinction of any kind'. Thus even before the rise of human security, and later R2P, in the post-Cold War era, no state could reasonably claim that it was legally or morally entitled to do whatever it wanted to its own citizens.

Indeed, each of the four crimes proscribed by R2P were illegal prior to its emergence; if the 1948 Genocide Convention, the Universal Declaration of Human Rights and the literally dozens of other human rights treaties, declarations and resolutions signed, proclaimed and ratified since 1945 have been unable to prevent or halt mass atrocities, why should R2P not suffer the same fate, given it merely restates existing laws? According to Chesterman, 'by the time RtoP was endorsed by the World Summit in 2005, its normative content had been emasculated to the point where it essentially provided that the Security Council could authorize, on a case-by-case basis, things that it had been authorizing for more than a decade' (2011a, p. 2). Likewise, in his 2009 report 'Implementing the Responsibility to Protect' the UN Secretary General acknowledged that Pillar 1 'rests on long-standing obligations under international law' (Ban Ki-moon, 2009a, p. 10). In the absence of any real legal innovation or structural reform R2P's efficacy is thus seen by some as negligible (Focarelli, 2008).

What was/is potentially innovative about R2P was not the principle that states have responsibilities to their citizens, but that, in the event that a state fails to meet these responsibilities, the responsibility to protect transfers to the international community. Yet, R2P does not suggest a means by which this latter responsibility can be actualized. It does not outline specific reforms to the Security Council that would compel it to act, nor does it support the creation of a new organ – such as a UN police force – that would act whenever humanitarian crises erupted (Bain, 2010, p. 26). As noted in the previous chapter, the adoption of aspects of the responsibility to protect in the 'Outcome Document' of the 2005 World Summit was conditional on the removal of any reference to a duty incumbent on states to intervene. In his letter to the president of the General Assembly prior to the World Summit, John Bolton (2005) outlined his country's position on R2P:

> we agree that the host state has a responsibility to protect its populations from such atrocities, and we agree in a more general and moral sense that the international community has a responsibility to act when the host state allows such atrocities. But ... we want to avoid formulations that suggest that the other countries are inheriting the same responsibility that the host state has.

It is debatable, therefore, whether the variant of 'responsibility to protect' adopted at the 2005 World Summit made intervention more likely or actually constituted a delineation of responsibility which put the emphasis on the host state rather than the international community (Focarelli, 2008, p. 209). The language of R2P can thus be employed by those wishing to avoid intervening and those wishing to block an intervention. As Bellamy noted in relation to Darfur, '"responsibility to protect" language enabled anti-interventionists to legitimize arguments *against* action by claiming the primary responsibility in certain contested cases still lies with the state and not (yet) with an international body' (2006a, p. 33). Therefore the rhetorical shift from 'humanitarian intervention' to 'the responsibility to protect', described by some as 'ingenious' (Tanguy, 2003, p. 142), creates significant scope for states to utilize the new discourse to legitimize both non-intervention and domestic oppression.

The end point of R2P is thus seen by some as inherently weak, creating merely a 'discretionary entitlement' (Berman, 2007, p. 161). The main obstacle to external intervention historically has not been the legal status of sovereignty or barriers to intervention generally, but rather the lack of political will (Chesterman, 2003, p. 54). Thus, given the system hasn't changed and the 'international community's' response to intra-state crises remains as dependent as ever on political will, and hence on geopolitical concerns and political machinations at the Security Council, some have branded R2P 'the emperor's new clothes' (Strauss, 2009). The response of the international community is dependent on the will of the Security Council and this will is heavily contingent on political exigencies. Indeed, as the Benin ambassador noted during the 2009 General Assembly debate:

> The real problem does not relate to the existence of a legal basis for UN enforcement action, but rather to the inconsistent practice of the Council. We know the reasons for this. It is because of geo-strategic rivalries that have paralyzed the work of the Council and that have made the Council incapable of taking the decisions that were expected of it in circumstances that called for its decisive action.

Without substantial reform of the decision making process within the Security Council, the Benin ambassador argued, R2P would be a 'mere scarecrow'.

R2P's many supporters dismiss this critique, however, as ahistorical and a (perhaps wilful) misreading of their strategy. A minority have suggested that R2P does in fact constitute a new legal development which, though in its infancy, amounts to evolving legal reform (Arbour, 2008; Glanville, 2012). Many others, however, readily acknowledge that R2P has not altered the legal system but claim that its efficacy is predicated on its capacity to act as a means to 'mobilise political will'; this, indeed, has become the dominant clarion cry of R2P supporters and the *raison d'être* of a number of NGOs such as the Global Center for R2P and the International Coalition for R2P. Indicatively, Evan's belief in R2P is sustained by his conviction that 'good people, good governments, and good governance will eventually prevail over bad' (2008, p. 7). He acknowledges: 'without the exercise of political will, by the relevant policy makers at the relevant time, almost none of the things for which this book has argued will actually happen' (ibid., p. 223). Likewise, Bellamy warns that if political will evaporates, R2P will falter (2009a, p. 119). Indicative of the strategy advocated for generating this political will, David Scheffer suggests that the message of R2P should be '[championed by] school children and their parents ... stamped on bumper stickers and broadcast through enlightened corporate sponsors' so that 'policymakers ultimately comprehend this siren call of their peoples' (2009, p. 95). Many, indeed, have explicitly rejected the idea of legal reform: when asked if legal reform was required to operationalize R2P, Sapna Chhatpar Considine, Project Manager for the International Coalition for the Responsibility to Protect (ICRtoP), replied: 'no, personally I don't feel that way ... I don't look at it as something that needs to actually become a treaty or international law ... my personal belief is that it doesn't have to become international law for it to work'.

Rather, she argued, the better strategy was to work towards 'strengthening normative consensus' (Considine and Sonner, 2009). This strategy has found its most explicit expression in the 'Will to Intervene Project' launched by the Montreal Institute for Genocide and Human Rights Studies (Chalk et al., 2010).

Many, however, have questioned the logic of this strategy, asking whether states, even Western democratic states, are receptive to popular advocacy when it comes to foreign affairs. History suggests that states are quite willing to ignore popular calls for action – the response to the slaughter in Darfur and Syria being cases in point – and thus R2P's endpoint, that of a means to 'mobilize' popular support for action, has been deemed foolhardy; the latest manifestation of a hubristic and utopian understanding of state interests and strategy that is doomed to fail (Hehir, 2012, p. 260).

In response R2P advocates argue that in the past 200 years great strides have been made towards protecting individuals which have invariably been catalysed, it is argued, by pressure groups and advocacy (Bass, 2008). International law and international political institutions are not static; they evolve and are impelled do so by changes in the prevailing norms. Thus, the strategy of generating consensus around R2P through advocacy with a view towards the gradual evolution of law, and the institutions that enforce it, is, many argue, prudent, albeit often slow and punctuated by success *and* failure (Evans, 2008; Bellamy, 2009a; Weiss, 2011). To rebuff the critiques many point to a number of cases, such as the intervention in Libya in 2011, as evidence of the strategy's efficacy (Bellamy and Williams, 2011). Indeed, in the wake of the intervention in Libya in 2011, Evans claimed that, had R2P been around in 1994, '800,000 men, women and children murdered in Rwanda might still be alive today' (Evans, 2012, p. 2). The disconnect between appraisals of R2P is, thus, often enormous. The coming decade will no doubt determine which view is correct.

Conclusion

Since 1945, inspired by the depravity of the Holocaust, international law has greatly expanded its rules on human rights and codified an increasing number of proscriptions on domestic state behaviour. Yet millions continued to be killed at the hands of their own states and action taken to halt atrocities was inconsistent. During the 20th century, 35 million people died in all civil and international wars; 150 million people, however, were killed by their own governments (Lu, 2006, p. 54).

With the end of the Cold War, many hoped that the gap between the tenets of international law and the enforcement of international law would be closed. The new power wielded by Western states, ostensibly those most respectful of human rights, led to great optimism that substantive action could now take place. A new resolve swept across the West as states rushed to declare their new understanding of the world; indicatively, Tony Blair declared that 'the most pressing foreign policy problem we face is to identify the circumstances in which we should get actively involved in other people's conflicts' (Stromseth, 2005, pp. 239–40). Such commitments emboldened those who sought to reorder international relations and international law in favour of human security rather than state security.

With the rise of human security has come the idea of sovereignty as responsibility. Today it is almost inconceivable that states would claim the right to do whatever they please to their own citizens. Significant disagreement remains about the scope of 'purely domestic matters', but complete inviolability appears an untenable defence. Cassese suggests that there are now five principles on which all states agree (2005, p. 398):

- The dignity of the human being is a basic value that every state should try to protect.
- It is necessary to aim at the achievement of fundamental rights of groups and peoples.
- Racial discrimination is universally condemned.
- Large-scale violations are universally condemned.
- The international community can intervene when large-scale violations occur.

It must be acknowledged that while these principles leave much to be clarified they do constitute progress when we consider the situation 100 years ago (Dixon, 2007, p. 341). Clearly, however, although the state has lost its status as a 'supreme ungovernable entity', this does not mean that it is no longer the primary actor in international relations. The reaction by the international community of states to R2P and the nature of the 2005 World Summit 'Outcome Document' testify to the power of states to reject change that substantially undermines their autonomy.

Some argued that R2P, and humanitarian intervention, was a victim of the post-11 September 2001 preoccupation with terrorism and self-defence (Welsh, 2006, p. 181). Yet the term 'responsibility to protect' is today routinely used and, as evidenced by the Arab Spring, the debate about humanitarian intervention continues and ICISS's report remains a key work on the issue. Many have argued that as R2P seeks to alter fundamentally the international system, in a way that amounts to a veritable revolution, it is too early to judge its efficacy (Weiss, 2011). What is clear is that R2P has sparked a debate about the responsibility of states internally and externally that is likely to remain at the heart of the international political agenda for some time.

Questions

- Identify the sources of tension between the rights of the individual and the rights of states in the UN Charter.
- Assess the key tenets of the ICISS report *The Responsibility to Protect* (2001).
- How convincing are the key critiques of R2P? In particular, is legal reform necessary for R2P to work?
- Is there evidence that R2P has influenced international politics?

Further reading

Bellamy, A. (2009) *Responsibility to Protect* (London: Polity).

Cooper, R.H. and Kohler, J.V. (eds) (2009) *Responsibility to Protect: The Global Moral Compact for the 21st Century* (Basingstoke and New York: Palgrave Macmillan).

Cunliffe, P. (ed.) (2011) *Critical Perspectives on the Responsibility to Protect* (London: Routledge).

Evans, G. (2008) *The Responsibility to Protect: Ending Mass Atrocity Crimes Once and For All* (Washington, DC: Brookings Institution Press).

Hehir, A. (2012) *The Responsibility to Protect: Rhetoric, Reality and the Future of Humanitarian Intervention* (basingstoke: Palgrave Macmillan).

Orford, A. (2011) *International Authority and the Responsibility to Protect* (Cambridge: Cambridge University Press).

Pattison, J. (2010) *Humanitarian Intervention and the Responsibility to Protect* (Oxford: Oxford University Press).

Reinhold, T. (2012) *Sovereignty and the Responsibility to Protect* (London: Routledge).

Weiss, T. (2007) *Humanitarian Intervention* (London: Polity), 2nd edn 2012.

Chapter 7

Who Decides? Authority and Legitimacy

Central to controversy surrounding humanitarian intervention is the question: who decides whether a particular situation requires external intervention? It is one thing to agree upon inviolable human rights which states *should* respect, but it is far more difficult to contrive a universally agreed means to enforce these human rights. Such enforcement requires not just agreement on the thresholds for intervention and the means by which intervention should occur, but also, more problematically, an authority imbued with the right to determine when these thresholds have been breached and the power to authorize intervention. Despite its centrality to the debate surrounding humanitarian intervention, 'the criterion of legitimate authority has become the most neglected of all the criteria that have been traditionally employed in the moral assessment of war' (Coates, 1997, p. 123).

Authority is notably elusive in international politics, and thus the justification of power is more arbitrary and contested in the international arena than it is in domestic political systems. The UN Security Council constitutes an institution with the greatest claim to act as an international authority, but the Council suffers from a perceived lack of legitimacy. Authority without legitimacy is inherently weak, and it is precisely this conundrum that has undermined the Council's capacity to resolve the 'who decides' question.

States routinely reject the authority of the Security Council: former US President George W. Bush outlined his views on the United Nations' authority by declaring, 'we don't really need the United Nation's approval to act ... When it comes to our security, we really don't need anyone's permission' (White, 2004, p. 660). Additionally, states, and many humanitarian NGOs and activists, have criticized the inconsistency and moral bankruptcy of the Security Council and called for unilateral interventions to address pressing humanitarian need. Yet, many of those who endorsed NATO's actions in 1999 in Kosovo were uncomfortable with the implications of the unilateral use of force (see Chapter 11). At the time Kofi Annan warned: 'unless the Security Council is restored to its preeminent position as the sole source of legitimacy on the use of force we are on a dangerous path to anarchy' (Hurd, 2007, p. 130). These concerns appeared to be confirmed when the US-led coalition invaded Iraq in 2003. The question of authority, often posed starkly as 'who decides?', clearly has implications beyond international law. In Chapter 2 I noted that the tripartite division of the Just War tradition is not, in itself, especially contentious. Determining whether these sets of criteria have been met, however, *is* highly contentious, and in the absence of a recognized authority figure, the discussion regarding adherence to the criteria is necessarily subjective and potentially interminable.

The first section of this chapter constitutes an assessment of legitimacy, authority and power, highlighting the interdependent nature of these concepts. The second section examines the powers vested in the Security Council, noting the formal limitations on the Council derived from the UN Charter, and the Council's reliance on the assent of states. The final section analyses alternative sources of authority suggested as a means by which humanitarian intervention can consistently and effectively be executed when the need arises.

Legitimacy, authority, power and rights

As noted in Chapter 6, there is now general agreement among states that sovereignty does not entitle a state to treat its citizens in any way it pleases. States, particularly in the post-Cold War era, have generally not opposed external intervention on the basis that sovereign inviolability is absolute; many indeed maintain that they never really did (Cohen, 2004, pp. 12–13; Nolan, 2006, pp. 82–3; Stahn, 2007, p. 111). Rather states have claimed – albeit often spuriously – that a particular crisis was a domestic concern which they were capable of dealing with. In such situations there is a clash between the state's perception of a particular crisis and that of external actors (Hehir, 2012, p. 200). This clash derives from differing interpretations of the nature and scale of a crisis rather than from a state claiming an unlimited right to treat its citizens however it pleases and an external perspective countering that certain acts are never justified. For example, throughout 2012 the Syrian government disputed the scale of its own military assault and the nature of both the crisis and the rebels; it never claimed that it has the right to arbitrarily kill, torture and displace its citizens. In the case of Syria, and many other similar crises, certain actors called for intervention while others have cautioned against such action. The question of legitimacy arises in this context when we assess whose perspective carries greater weight.

Legitimacy

The term 'legitimacy' is widely used in IR, yet it is also recognized as an underdeveloped concept (Wheeler, 2002, p. 4; Hurd, 2007, p. 1). Legitimacy is central to the issue of 'who decides', as the perceived legitimacy of prospective arbiters is a crucial factor in this inquiry. People and states follow rules under three circumstances: coercion, consent and self-interest. Forcing an actor to follow a certain code depends on the utilization, overtly or covertly, of a power asymmetry. Conversely, actors voluntarily obey rules if they are convinced of a rule's inherent legitimacy and the legitimacy of the organ that created and enforces this rule (Armstrong and Farrell, 2005, p. 5). For example, compliance with the law in Chile following Augusto Pinochet's coup in 1973 was, to a large extent, a function of the deployment of the army and the violent oppression of dissent. Compliance with the law in contemporary Norway, however, is a function of the widespread – though of course not unanimous – belief in the legitimacy of the Norwegian government and judiciary amongst the general population. Clearly a system of rules is more effective and stable if compliance derives from consent rather than coercion. This consent is ultimately dependent on the perceived legitimacy of the organs which administer the legal system.

Self-interest, however, is another potential motivation for lawful action which does not constitute consent. We may well support a legal regime provided we feel it furthers our interests, but this does not mean we perceive the regime to be legitimate. Such a coincidence between self-interest and lawful action is, however, unlikely to be sustained; while a certain clique in Pinochet's Chile benefited from the laws then enforced, the majority of the population did not. 'Legitimacy therefore refers to a particular kind of rule-following or obedience, distinguishable from purely self-interested or instrumental behaviour on the one hand, and from straightforward imposed or coercive rule on the other' (Hurrell, 2005, p. 16). In his defence of law and a hierarchical judicial system, Martti Koskenniemi (2006, p. 69) argues that without law 'the acting persons or entities exist as subjects of interests and preferences, both liberated and weighed down by their irreducible particularity'. Without law, or an authority to enforce law, we may imagine we would enjoy more freedom, but individuals would actually be forced to adopt an instrumental worldview driven by pure interest-fulfilment; the result would be chaos and violence. The existence of both law and a legitimate authority, therefore, facilitate individual freedom while tempering destructive individualism.

The perceived legitimacy of a particular institution encourages actors to abide by the rules of that institution even when these rules are inconvenient. Key to this is the sense that the procedures that facilitate the functioning of the legal regime are inclusive and fair. An actor formally involved in the process of decision making is likely to consider the outcome of the process to be legitimate (Cronin and Hurd, 2008, p. 8). This applies, crucially, even to those situations where the actor's aims are not realized. The proposal to grant a veto to the P5 was strongly opposed by other states during the San Francisco conference on the UN Charter. While the non-permanent members ultimately failed to have this controversial provision removed they nonetheless endorsed the final Charter because, Ian Hurd argues, they were convinced of the procedural correctness of the deliberation process (2007, pp. 91–5). Similarly, opposition parties in democracies throughout the world accept the legitimacy of the elected government despite its passing legislation they oppose.

Hurd argues that 'legitimation and internalization of a rule or institution have taken place in states' when three traits are observable. First, citizens treat the rule in question as a necessary part of the strategic landscape for decision making. Second, citizens cease making cost–benefit calculations about the effects of breaking the rule as they consider future behaviours. Third, citizens use the symbols that derive from the rule or institution as resources (ibid., p. 79). Whether these traits are observable in terms of the Security Council is discussed later in this chapter. Key to the above is the active incorporation of rules and norms into the behaviour of states. It is not enough, clearly, to acknowledge the legitimacy of an institution and concomitantly act contrary to its rules and procedures.

International politics is characterized by weak authority structures, hence the oft-quoted concept of 'international anarchy' (see p. 70). The international institution with greatest claim to act as international authority – the Security Council – suffers from a perceived lack of legitimacy. This derives from a number of issues, not least its composition and inconsistent record of law enforcement. In light of this perceived absence of a legitimate arbiter, some have sought to shift the focus from assessing the legitimacy of the paramount international authority and its judgements to the legitimacy of the act itself. Thus the lack of a universally recognized legitimate authority does not necessarily render the appraisal of the legitimacy of an action impossible.

Alex Bellamy, drawing on the earlier work of Ian Clark (2005, pp. 18–19), notes that there are primarily two ways of understanding legitimacy (2006b, pp. 5–7). The first is the substantive approach, which holds that an act is legitimate if it conforms to a particular set of rules. The second is procedural, and this focuses on the manner in which decisions are reached rather than their relationship with a codified set of rules; for example, decisions taken on the basis of consensus. Each perspective is difficult to apply to international politics. With respect to the substantive approach, rules require authoritative bodies, and, given that the international system is widely regarded as anarchic, this appears to foreclose this process. In terms of the procedural approach, Bellamy states that the present composition of the international system renders this impossible (ibid., p. 6). This does not mean that legitimacy is fundamentally elusive: Bellamy argues that the legitimacy of an act can be deduced by examining what the 'judges and juries' say. Judges are those 'capable of backing up their judgments with material rewards or punishments' while juries 'comprise the rest of world opinion' (ibid.). Bellamy asserts that the claims made by actors can be assessed according to the three subordinate sets of norms: legality, morality and constitutionality. Thus the appraisal of the legitimacy of an act is possible outside of both formal authoritative structures and consensus-based procedures.

There are, however, a number of problems with this approach. First there is clearly enormous scope for disagreement amongst the judges; if we assume that Russia and the US constitute 'judges capable of backing up their judgments with material rewards', we must accept that it is highly likely that these judges will form different opinions about the legitimacy of a particular action, as was clearly evidenced during the conflict between Russia and Georgia over South Ossetia in August 2008 and the situation in Syria throughout 2012. Given the propensity of these judges to differ so fundamentally, it is unlikely that any clarity will be provided by deferring to their opinion. The powerful global judges will determine their position on a particular case, Bellamy accepts, according to considerations based on natural law, positive law and national interest, with particular emphasis on the latter (ibid., p. 128). Second, there is something fundamentally problematic about an actor being deemed a judge by virtue of its material power. It is difficult to justify the proposition that a state constitutes a judge of legitimacy because of its capacity to exercise leverage via its large military and/or economic wealth. Finally, as Bellamy acknowledges, global juries will always be less powerful than global judges. International mass movements raise awareness of issues and constitute a source of pressure on the architects of unpopular policies. There is little evidence, however, that such movements have the capacity to 'shame' governments into desisting from unpopular action (Hehir, 2008a, pp. 81–4).

Authority and power

If we obey the law because we believe that the governmental and judicial institutions are legitimate, we may say that these particular institutions have authority. If we obey the law solely because we are forced to do so, we may say that the institutions in this case have power but lack authority. Authority implies power, but power does not imply authority. Bruce Cronin and Ian Hurd define authority as 'a relation among actors within a hierarchy in which one group is recognized as having both the right and the competence to make binding decisions for the rest of the community' (2008, p. 6). Key to this definition is the focus on right and competence rather than capacity. Following Iraq's invasion of Kuwait in 1990, Saddam Hussein exercised power in Kuwait but he lacked authority in the eyes of both the Kuwaitis and the international community. Authority, therefore, differs from power because of the legitimacy inherent in the former.

As discussed earlier, the international system is widely regarded as primarily characterized by the lack of centralized authority. While IR theorists disagree over the extent to which international anarchy impacts on the behaviour of states, the underlying presumption of anarchy is common to the majority of theoretical perspectives (ibid., p. 4). This assumption, however, is challenged by Hurd, who argues that it is based on 'untested premises' and that a form of authority is identifiable in the international arena (2008, p. 24). His analysis resonates with the English School view on the role of norms (see Chapter 4), as he suggests that states, including the P5, invariably justify their actions according to the UN Charter and Security Council resolutions, conduct their foreign policy in accordance with international laws and norms, and seek to utilize the symbols of legitimacy inherent in organs such as the Security Council (2007, p. 187). Hurd does not discount the role played by strategic interests in foreign policy, but challenges the perception of a system devoid of constraint characterized by the singular pursuit of self-interest.

That states seek to justify their acts as lawful is certainly clear (Watts, 2001, p. 7). Yet, accepting this, does the desire amongst states to be seen to be acting lawfully translate into a finding that authority does in fact exist in international relations? Indeed, Arthur Watts acknowledges that international law is sufficiently malleable to enable states to justify their foreign policy on legal grounds even in extremely dubious cases, because they know legal censure can be ignored, thus highlighting law's inherent weakness (ibid., p. 8). Few people in domestic societies wish to be seen as habitual law breakers. Regardless of whether people desire their peers to perceive them as law abiding, compliance with the law is also enforced. Can we identify a similar enforcement mechanism in the international system? It is not at all clear that we can. In this sense, while we may accept that state behaviour is shaped by international law, and thus outright anarchy is a misrepresentation, the fact that these rules are not enforced surely undermines the notion that there is authority in international politics. For surely a quality of authority requires not simply that the subjects of the authority believe that authority to have legitimacy, but also that that authority has the capacity, and the will, to enforce its rules; indeed, according to Hans Kelsen the capacity to enforce the law is 'the most important, the essential stage in any legal procedure' (1972, p. 13). This enforcement gap casts some doubt on the importance of the fact that states justify their actions as being in accordance with international law and specifically seek to have their actions endorsed by the Security Council, for this may be 'little more than high-sounding tokenism' (Watts, 2001, p. 8). The desire to seek Security Council approval certainly demonstrates that states attach significant importance to the Council as a legitimate international institution. If, however, states fail to receive the endorsement of the Council and act regardless, then the Council's status as a recognized authority is surely undermined. This lends credence to Cherif Bassiouni's reflection on the efficacy of international human rights legislation: 'legal experience demonstrates that the enunciation of rights without concomitant remedies are pyrrhic pronouncements, and that remedies without enforcement are empty promises' (2009, p. 41).

An alternative way of looking at international law bridges the gap between authority and anarchy. Armstrong and Farrell argue that international law is best seen 'as a site of legitimation for state action'. The structures of international law such as the Charter, the Security Council and the General Assembly are, they maintain, not analogous to domestic institutions but rather are 'political spaces where states engage in normatively bounded deliberation about legitimate action' (2005, p. 10). In this respect states seek approval from, and justify their behaviour to, the institutions of international law, especially the Security Council, and their actions are judged by the international community in the light of this deliberation, and thus constrained by the framework of international law. States may choose to disregard the opinion of the international institutions and the community of states, but they will be thereby identified as law breakers more obviously than if the 'site of legitimation' did not exist.

Right or duty?

The controversy surrounding humanitarian intervention derives much of its divisiveness from the question: is there a right to intervene? Whether this is posed in terms of a right of the Security Council or 'coalitions of the willing' to intervene, the nature of this right remains problematic, for how do we understand a 'right'? This question can only be answered by first clarifying the status of the actor. For example, as an individual I have no formal authority. I have the right to own a dog but I am under no obligation to do so. A police officer has the right to ask me to control my dog in public places. Additionally, however, because of their status, the police officer also has an obligation to ensure that my dog is under control in public places. Legally they are not entitled to choose not to enforce their right in this instance. In the context of humanitarian intervention, then, if we identify that the Security Council has the right to act under Chapter VII of the Charter, to intervene to halt humanitarian atrocities, can we also say that the Security Council actually has an obligation to do so? Similarly, if we seek to identify an alternative source of legitimate authority – namely coalitions of states – can we assume that, failing action by the Security Council, they have a duty to intervene as well as a right? As Franck Berman asks, 'if we are genuinely in the presence of a "right" … where is the correlative obligation, and who has the legal quality to enforce it?' (2007, p. 160). The danger is that identifying rights without obligations facilitates selectivity and leads to inconsistency (Bassiouni, 2009, p. 34). In this sense the legitimacy of a legal order, and the recognized authority within that order, diminish if the subjects of this order believe that enforcement will occur only when there is a coincidence between the interests and the rights of the authority. There is, therefore, a need to identify not only that an authority has the right to act, but also that the authority has duties to act, otherwise we are left with an unsatisfactory 'discretionary entitlement' (ibid., p. 161).

As will be explored in the final section of this chapter, there are many who argue that the Security Council cannot be the final arbiter when it comes to cases of egregious human rights violations. This argument is necessarily based on morality rather than procedural legality as international law does not permit unilateral humanitarian intervention (see Chapter 5). The moral principle upon which the perspective in favour of action taken without Security Council authorization depends asserts that in the face of human suffering we have a duty – not just a right – to act. The underlying principle is, according to Terry Nardin, that 'you shall not stand idly by, whoever you are, if you can provide effective assistance at reasonable cost and without neglecting other duties' (2003, p. 21). Thus we are hereby enjoined to act not because we can but because we must. Failure to act is therefore not perceived as unwillingness to exercise one's right but, more seriously, a dereliction of duty (Janzekovic, 2006, p. 74).

The question 'who decides?' is thus influenced by our understanding of legitimacy, authority and power and complicated by the need to distinguish between a discretionary entitlement (a *right* to act) and an obligation (a *duty* to act) (Bain, 2010). As is explored in the final section of this chapter, states have proved unwilling to assume the latter.

The UN Security Council

One might be forgiven for wondering why the question 'who decides?' is asked at all; surely it is obvious that the UN Security Council performs this function. Two issues have contrived to undermine the Security Council's status as ultimate international authority. First is the fact that the Council's powers derive from states and the Council is dependent on the assent of states to execute these powers. Second, the Security Council suffers from a poor international perception because of the unrepresentative nature of the P5 and the extent to which the P5 have consistently afforded primacy to political rather than legal considerations. These factors, dealt with in the following sections, have encouraged the formulation of alternative sources of authority, an issue examined in this chapter's final section.

Nature of the Security Council's powers

Under Article 24 of the Charter the Security Council has the 'primary responsibility for the maintenance of international peace and security'. The Council's status as a legal authority is, however, limited. The Council's powers are exercised in response to breaches of the peace and acts of aggression, and thus 'the powers of the Council are designed primarily to preserve the peace rather than to enforce the law, although these can coincide' (Dixon, 2007, p. 7). The Council lacks the authority to 'enforce international law, create binding legal precedents, or legislate new legal norms' (Cronin, 2008, p. 61). The Council does not have the power to create law but rather 'simply interprets and applies existing law' (de Brichambaut, 2000, p. 275). Resolutions passed by the Security Council are not considered binding law; rather, they are material or evidential *sources* of law. Council resolutions are also not indicative of customary law, as the Council is not considered to reflect *opinio juris* – evidence of a general acceptance of a new legal norm (Gowlland-Debbas, 2000, p. 300).

The Security Council is formally constrained by the Charter and exercises its power within the framework stipulated therein. The Council's powers, therefore, 'cannot be unlimited' (White, 2004, p. 646). In 1948 the ICJ acknowledged the formal constraints upon the Security Council: '[the] political character of an organ cannot release it from the observance of the treaty provisions established by the Charter when they constitute limitations on its powers or criteria for its judgments' (Gowlland-Debbas, 2000, p. 304). More recently in the 1995 *Tadic* case the Appeals Chamber of the ICTY declared that the Security Council must only take action 'within the limits of the Purposes and Principles of the Charter' (ICTY, 1995, p. 43). Nonetheless, despite these legal constraints, in reality the Council has acted as the principal interpreter of the Charter's rules and hence its own powers. During the course of the negotiations at San Francisco in 1945 Greece proposed that the ICJ be designated as the sole interpreter of the Charter, but this was rejected. This has meant that in practice 'the Charter is what the principal organs do' (Franck, 2005, p. 206).

Regardless of formal limitations the Security Council is also dependent on its constituent member states, and as such the Council 'cannot enforce its decisions without the cooperation of others and does not have exclusive jurisdiction over its issue area. In other words the power of states outside the institution matters a great deal' (Voeten, 2008, p. 54). Richard Falk notes that there are no 'governmental institutions beyond the state that can claim "sovereignty" in the sense of autonomous and ultimate authority to pronounce the law'. The UN is, thus, best conceived as a 'club of states' and the role of the Security Council is constrained by this relationship between the UN and its members (Falk, 2005a, p. 35). This dependence on member states is, of course, most evident in the veto powers of the P5.

Voting at the Security Council is regulated by Article 27 of the Charter; the term 'veto' is not used in the Charter but is implicit in Article 27(3). In practice, while the veto has been deployed by the P5 on many occasions, the threat of it has often meant that issues have not even been brought before the Council because a veto was considered inevitable, as was the case in 1999 when NATO did not submit its intervention in Kosovo to a vote. Article 27 stipulates that the veto only applies to non-procedural matters. Determining whether an issue is procedural or not is, however, itself a non-procedural matter, hence the 'double veto': a permanent member can veto any attempt to treat an issue as procedural, then veto any proposal on this matter when it is set before the Council as a non-procedural matter (Malanczuk, 2006, p. 374). Of course, the veto power has additionally ensured that conflicts involving one of the P5 were 'practically excluded from the reach of the Charter's system of collective security' (Dinstein, 2005, p. 292).

Action by the Security Council is thus dependent on the assent of states, especially its permanent members. In addition the Council is reliant on states to provide it with military resources when action is authorized. Article 43 of the Charter was intended to provide the UN with an organized military force at the Security Council's disposal. This never materialized and thus the Council has not been able to enact Article 42, which enables the Council to *authorize* and *require* the use of force (Dixon, 2007, pp. 330–1). The Council has authorized the use of force at times, such as in response to Iraq's invasion of Kuwait in 1990, but has not as such *required* such action. The Council's role in deploying troops during the 1990s was, in many respects, limited to legitimizing action taken by coalitions rather than actively authorizing action itself (Job, 2006, p. 63). Articles 45 and 47 outline the scope and structure of the Military Staff Committee which was designed as a means by which the UN would have something akin to a standing army, but this entity was a victim of the Cold War and has no significant role (Malanczuk, 2006, p. 389).

Council action is thus constrained by the Charter and heavily dependent on states. The P5 have used their veto power to limit the scope of Council action and have consistently adjudicated on matters with political considerations to the fore. Despite the provisions contained in Articles 42 and 43, the Council has avoided any requirement to take action and has not taken steps to empower the Military Staff Committee.

International perception

The veto power and composition of the P5 are today widely criticized. Three of the P5 are members of NATO yet none are from Africa, Latin America or the Middle East. This obviously limits its perceived ability to represent global opinion, and while non-permanent seats increased from six to ten in 1965, this has not resolved the issue of the Council's composition (Chesterman, 2011b). In 1993 the General Assembly established an 'Open-ended Working Group on the Question of Equitable Representation on and Increase in the Membership of the Security Council'. The work of this group is ongoing, although there have been no concrete steps taken to expand Council membership. Via the General Assembly's Millennium Declaration all states pledged 'to intensify our efforts to achieve a comprehensive reform of the Security Council in all its aspects' (UN General Assembly, 2000, para. 30). This commitment was followed by more definite proposals in the 2004 report published by the High-Level Panel on Threats, Challenges and Change, which proposed two models for reforming the membership of the Council (see Box 7.1). Kofi Annan's 2005 report – *In Larger Freedom* – endorsed the choice posed by the High-Level Panel, although his recommendation that the Security Council be 'broadly representative of the international community as a whole, as well as of the geopolitical realities of today' constitutes a concession to the influence of power on the Council's composition (2005a, p. 42). The 'G4' – Germany, Japan, Brazil and India – have long campaigned for a permanent seat as well as the election of a representative from Africa and the Arab League. Despite significant effort no reforms were agreed at the 2005 World Summit.

In tandem with the obviously unrepresentative nature of the Council is the charge that it is undermined by the P5 members' narrow pursuit of their national interests (Rodin, 2002, pp. 179–80; Buchanan and Keohane, 2011, p. 51). As was noted in Chapter 5, the Council began to be more active following the end of the Cold War, but action taken by it under Chapter VII during the 1990s was inconsistent and motivated by the interests of the P5, especially the US (Chesterman, 2002, pp. 160–2; Graubart, 2008, p. 154). The Security Council-sanctioned intervention in Libya in 2011 was conceived by many as in keeping with this trend, particularly in light of the subsequent inaction in the face of the carnage in Syria (see Chapter 14).

Hurd designed three tests of whether an entity has authority, namely 'compliance, justificatory discourse and unavoidability' (2008, pp. 35–7),

Box 7.1   Two models for reforming the UN Security Council

Model A provides for six new permanent seats, with no veto being created, and three new, two-year-term, non-permanent seats, divided among the major regional areas as follows:

Regional area	No. of states	Permanent seats (continuing)	Proposed new permanent seats	Proposed two-year seats (non-renewable)	Total
Africa	53	0	2	4	6
Asia and Pacific	56	1	2	3	6
Europe	47	3	1	2	6
Americas	35	1	1	4	6
Total model A	191	5	6	13	24

Model B provides for no new permanent seats but creates a new category of eight four-year, renewable-term seats and one new two-year, non-permanent (and non-renewable) seat, divided among the major regional areas as follows:

Regional area	No. of states	Permanent seats (continuing)	Proposed four-year renewable seats	Proposed two-year seats (non-renewable)	Total
Africa	53	0	2	4	6
Asia and Pacific	56	1	2	3	6
Europe	47	3	2	1	6
Americas	35	1	2	3	6
Totals model A	191	5	8	11	24

Source: UN High-Level Panel on Threats, Challenges and Change (2004, pp 67–8).

and applied these to the Security Council. In terms of compliance with the UN, and specifically the Security Council, he notes that there is little evidence that states consistently comply with Council resolutions. Nonetheless, he argues, absolute compliance with an authority is unrealistic as it would require 'subordinates who are automatons'. Of greater import is the fact that states feel the need to justify their decisions to the Council and 'frame their behaviours in ways that they believe will bring approval from the institution' (ibid., p. 35). This, of course, does not readily imply compliance – and hence Council authority – as such justificatory discourse may well be proffered cynically. Finally, he notes that there are signs that the Security Council has entered into the decision-making calculus of states. The US attempt to gain Council approval for its invasion of Iraq suggests that even powerful states are 'forced to frame their policies around the existence of the Council' (ibid.). Although it is undeniably true that the US sought Council approval, this is, Hurd admits, not a conclusive indicator of Council authority. He argues that the behaviour of the Great Powers 'suggests that they sometimes approach the Council with the intention of "laundering" their favored policies through the legitimating machine of the Council' (Hurd, 2007, p. 129). Indicatively, William Cohen, US Secretary of Defense 1997–2001, described Security Council authorization as 'desirable, not imperative' (Voeten, 2008, p. 52). The P5 know that their own contentious polices have a limited chance of avoiding the veto at the Council and so, paradoxically, have a vested interest in downplaying the authority of the very institution they constitute and/or manipulating the resolutions it has previously passed. Indeed, at its Fiftieth Anniversary NATO states announced that they would 'prefer' to act with Security Council backing but 'must not limit themselves to acting only when such a mandate can be agreed' (Caplan, 2000, p. 31). Yet as noted earlier three of the P5 are members of NATO, and hence NATO was downplaying the importance of an institution it numerically dominates.

Despite the problems identified above, and the prevailing negative image of the Council, there is evidence that people still consider it to be the most legitimate international authority (Cronin and Hurd, 2008, p. 15). The international support afforded to the intervention in Libya in 2011 was in large part a function of the fact that the P5 sanctioned it. It is indeed striking that the Council has managed to retain this level of international support although, given the dangers obviously inherent in indiscriminate unilateral action, the Council may well be a beneficiary of the fact that, though deeply flawed, it is the least worst option.

A source of order, not justice

Disappointment with the performance of the Security Council derives from a normative view of the Council's role. It is debatable, however, whether this normative role was ever the guiding rationale behind the establishment of the Council. The idea behind the Security Council, and particularly the special powers of the P5, was that these states were, at least in 1945, the dominant world powers and should have this status reflected in the new legal regime (Briggs, 1945, p. 670; Bosco, 2009, pp. 10–38). It was agreed at the Yalta conference among the 'big three' (the US, the UK and the Soviet Unon) prior to the San Francisco Conference that the proposed UN organization must act in accordance with the wishes of these powers to prevent instability and potentially war. Conflict between the UN and one or a number of these states had to be avoided, hence the need for the veto power (Bourantonis, 2007, p. 6). In this respect the composition of the Security Council and its mandate had more to do with considerations of order than justice. Given this it is, one could argue, unsurprising that the record of the Council evidences a preference for stability and order rather than justice.

Following the Second World War it was perhaps somewhat inevitable that the victorious powers would contrive a new system which served their interests. Political systems are not, many contend, designed by impartial actors based on abstract considerations of justice (Bull, 2002, p. 53). Thus, in assessing the record of the Security Council we must be realistic about the rationale behind its creation and the interests of those who designed it. Anne Orford criticizes those who imagine that the laws governing the use of force and the architecture of the international legal system are designed to challenge hierarchy and power, asserting that the legal regime was actually designed to facilitate and maintain the prevailing power asymmetry (2003, pp. 46–7). Likewise, Gerry Simpson challenges what he describes as the 'orthodox approach' (2004, pp. 26–37) to the evolution of sovereign equality. While this narrative holds that sovereign equality has emerged as a normative challenge to hierarchy and power, Simpson notes that this 'equality' is fundamentally undermined by what he terms 'legalised hegemony', that is

> the existence within an international society of a powerful elite of states whose superior status is recognised by minor powers as a political fact giving rise to the existence of certain constitutional privileges, rights and duties and whose relations with each other are defined by adherence to a rough principle of sovereign equality. (Ibid., p. 68)

The powers vested in the P5 are the most obvious manifestation of this phenomenon. Nigel White describes the veto as 'a realist core in an institutionalist framework – a political core in a legal regime' (2004, p. 666). Thus, the Security Council can be seen in this context as a means by which the great powers perpetuate their primacy and general order is maintained (Gowlland-Debbas, 2000, p. 303). Changes in the nature of the powers exercised by the Security Council are, therefore, not initiated by the subjects of Security Council authority but rather constitute a conscious process designed to facilitate the P5's own agendas. Hence, Jonathan Graubart argues that the Council's increased willingness to authorize interventions under Chapter VII in the 1990s was a means of 'legitimizing interventions of regional or global powers into the affairs of weaker, mostly Southern, states' (2008, p. 169), a view shared by Orford (2011, p. 4). Likewise, Vittorio Parsi suggests that the Security Council is itself dominated by the US and hence its action is essentially a product of US power (2006, p. 121).

Alternative authorities

The perceived limitations of the Security Council were manifest emphatically in March 1999 when NATO launched Operation Allied Force. NATO's actions were deemed 'illegal but legitimate' by the IICK, thereby confirming the gap between law and morality. The intervention appeared to some to confirm the redundancy of the Security Council (Welsh, 2006, p. 182).

The lack of Security Council authorization for such an act of ostensible moral worth was deemed of secondary importance by those who, as discussed in Chapter 2, champion moral laws over temporal positive laws. This perspective holds that actors should not be constrained by the prevailing legal system from acting morally. As Terry Nardin argues:

> interventions should be approved by a recognized international authority acting in accordance with reasonably just international laws. But if such an authority does not exist or is substantially unjust or ineffective, either in general or in a given situation, states may act without its approval. Whether the UN is a just and effective international authority is a judgment that those contemplating intervention will have to make – and defend. (2003, p. 23)

Such an approach does not eliminate the need for an authority per se, and alternative authorities to the Security Council have been advanced. Alternatives to the Security Council are examined below, although it is worth noting that there are many who argue that while the Council is fundamentally flawed and can thus occasionally be bypassed legitimately, such a situation does not require an alternative authority to the Council. They advocate a position, described as 'mitigation', whereby the law is broken, and the Council bypassed, but, as the cause is just, the intervening party's case is deemed illegal but nonetheless tolerated (see Conclusion).

International morality

Disenchantment with the Security Council's approach to matters placed before it has led to calls from humanitarian activists to bypass the Council if it fails to discharge its duties (Evans, 2005b, p. 83). Evans acknowledges that this approach to Security Council authorization is inherently dangerous and potentially facilitates unilateralism of the kind witnessed in 2003 when the US invaded Iraq. His counter-argument, however, is that the Just War theory comprises more criteria than merely right authority, and so any action will be judged on the basis of its adherence to other criteria and could be condemned on this basis (see Chapter 2). Similarly, Alex Bellamy explicitly rejects reformulating positive law, instead advocating a policy orientated towards constructing criteria which will act as constraints on state action. If states abuse the new scope for intervention, global civil society will 'expose the abuse as such, and ... confront the perpetrators with the unjustness of their actions in order to constrain potential abusers through normative pressure at the domestic and international level' (2004, p. 134).

Martha Nussbaum also rejects the statist basis of international law; she argues that 'we should give our first moral allegiance to no mere form of government, no temporal power' but rather should pledge allegiance to 'the moral community made up by the humanity of all human beings' (Dallmayr, 2003, p. 435). This perspective, central to cosmopolitanism (see Chapter 4), asserts that action should be assessed, therefore, on moral rather than legal grounds and judged by the international community rather than the unrepresentative and politically motivated P5.

Appeals to international morality are certainly attractive, and there is clearly merit to the suggestion that law is often an imperfect reflection of deeper universal moral norms. It is additionally difficult not to agree that international law as presently organized is deeply flawed (Franck, 2005, p. 212; Meyer, 2009, p. 56; Hehir, 2012, p. 210). Yet, there are significant problems inherent in this perspective. Firstly, it is debatable whether beyond very broad parameters there is a universal moral code. There is much to suggest that moral pluralism exists, but how do we then adjudicate between two genuinely different moral arguments? Beyond this obvious difficulty lies a greater problem. As Fred Dallmayr argues:

> Even assuming widespread acceptance of universal norms ... rules do not directly translate into praxis but require careful interpretation and application. At this point eminently political questions arise: who has the right of interpretation? And in cases of conflict: who is entitled to rule between different interpretations? This right or competence cannot simply be left to 'universal' theorists or intellectuals – in the absence of an explicitly political delegation or empowerment. (2003, p. 434)

Thus universal agreement on basic moral principles does not necessarily achieve the aim of a consistently responsive, morally conscious, international system. It is quite possible even for people who share a set of narrow moral codes to disagree about real-world events, as evidenced by the many differing perspectives within the world's religions. Contriving rules and codes on which all agree does not eliminate the need for some clear means by which disagreements regarding the implementation of these codes are resolved, and thus there is a need for a recognized authority. The underlying dilemma intrinsic to humanitarian intervention is, Anthony Lang maintains, 'not one between amoral politicians and moralistic humanitarians, but one between competing moral claims' (2003, p. 2).

Liberal hierarchy thesis

Linked to the idea of reliance on ostensibly universal moral principles is the view that certain states have a greater moral status than others. These states, by virtue of their superior moral rectitude, are championed as arbitrators of global affairs and hence worthy of formal authority. This necessitates endorsing a form of proportionate equality in the state system, and adherents to this view, Christian Reus-Smit notes, 'advocate the formal rehierarchisation of international society, whereby democratic states would gain special governance rights – particularly with regard to the legitimate use of force and other states would have their categorical rights to self-determination and non-intervention qualified' (2005, p. 72).

This 'liberal hierarchy thesis' asserts that liberal democracies are distinguished by characteristics such as their passivity towards one another, their constitutional commitment to the protection of civil and political rights, and their 'comparative moral reliability' (ibid., p. 76). Given these characteristics, liberal democracies are the most advanced political actors and thus deserve special rights to adjudicate on international affairs.

There is evidence to suggest that certain prominent figures within Western states, and the US in particular, adhere to this hierarchical vision. A central tenet of the national mythology of the US is its ostensible 'manifest destiny' to spearhead progressive global change. Madeleine Albright, secretary of state under President Clinton, described the US as the 'indispensable nation' and legitimized US leadership on the basis that 'we stand tall and we see further than other countries into the future' (Malone, 2006, p. 13). Similarly President George W. Bush justified launching the war on terror on the basis that 'this is the world's fight. This is civilisation's fight', which is to be prosecuted on behalf of all 'civilised nations' (Kinsella, 2005, pp. 181–2). Likewise in his speech to the nation on the intervention in Libya President Barack Obama described the US as the world's 'leader' playing a 'unique role as an anchor of global security' and impelled by 'different' motivations to other states (White House, 2011). As discussed in the concluding chapter, it has been suggested that a formal hierarchy of rights is particularly apposite with respect to humanitarian intervention, and that something akin to a 'concert of democracies' should be imbued with unique powers. The desired evolution of the norm of humanitarian intervention, it is argued, requires that progressive states explicitly usurp existing international law regarding the use of force for the protection of human rights and ultimately fashion a new norm for others to follow. The liberal hierarchy thesis does not, therefore, advocate the development of a rigid two-tiered system, but rather a temporary hierarchy which will compel others to reform both their domestic system and foreign policy so as to gain advanced rights (Elshtain, 2003b; Buchanan and Keohane, 2004; Ikenberry and Slaughter, 2006, pp. 25–6; Orford, 2011).

Western states are certainly characterized by an adherence to democracy and relatively advanced constitutional commitments to human rights. Nonetheless, there is much counter-evidence which suggests that liberal democracies are motivated by self-interest and willing to ignore human rights when this is deemed necessary. The history of Western colonialism, variously legitimized as 'the white man's burden' and *mission civilisatrice*, testifies to how dangerous and easily abused the idea of moral hierarchy can be. Additionally, as noted in Chapter 4, even if states are genuinely motivated by a sense of moral purpose and believe themselves to be a force for good, action taken on this basis is inherently dangerous. Such a view is akin to zealotry and leads to implacable behaviour on the basis that dissent is irrational (Hurrell, 2005, p. 25; Koskenniemi, 2006, p. 65). Thus a sense of inflated moral standing and an attendant belief in one's own legitimacy to rule in defiance of the objections of 'lesser' moral actors threatens the assumption of a dictatorial disposition.

Reform of the Security Council

There is much evidence to suggest that there is widespread consensus on the need for some reform of the present international legal system and specifically the Security Council. This was a key aspect of the Millennium Declaration signed by all the world's states and which has featured in the recommendations of all major commissions into the working of the UN since 2000. Specifically in relation to humanitarian intervention it has been suggested that legal reform is required to enable more consistent and efficient enforcement of existing human rights laws (Simma, 1999, p. 6), greater clarity regarding those violations of human rights that demand intervention (UN Commission on Global Governance, 1995, p. 90) and also, more controversially, to legalize unilateral humanitarian intervention in the event of Security Council inaction (Burton, 1996).

ICISS asserted that the problem posed by humanitarian intervention necessitated not finding alternatives to the Security Council but rather initiating reforms to enable the Council to function more efficiently (2001a, p. 49). ICISS warned that it was unrealistic to expect that states would not act in the event of Council inaction in the face of a humanitarian tragedy, and that if an intervention was undertaken without Council approval, but subsequently deemed legitimate by the international community, this would have 'enduring serious consequences for the stature and credibility of the UN itself' (ibid., p. 55). To prevent such a situation

ICISS recommended that the Council agree a set of guidelines specifying when military intervention should take place and additionally that the P5 commit to an agreement not to use their veto in matters of humanitarian need when their national interests are not involved.

As noted in Chapter 6, however, this 'code of conduct' for the P5 has been criticized as unrealistic and ultimately weak. At the 2005 World Summit the P5 rejected any proposals which would have limited their powers or their formal monopoly on the authorization of the use of force, a point reiterated by the P5 during the 2009 General Assembly debate on R2P (Hehir, 2011a). Additionally, the P5, and the US in particular, refused to countenance any proposals that would have constrained their capacity to choose when to use force. In a letter to the President of the General Assembly prior to the World Summit, John Bolton suggested amending the section in the draft document regarding the responsibility to protect because 'we note that the Charter has never been interpreted as creating a legal obligation for Security Council members to support enforcement action in various cases involving serious breaches of international peace' (2005). The provisions related to humanitarian intervention in the final 'Outcome Document' have done little to address the controversy surrounding who has the authority to take military action and in effect constitute a reassertion of the status quo (Wheeler, 2005; Stahn, 2007; Peters, 2009; Reinold, 2010).

Given the failings of the Security Council it has been proposed that greater powers be devolved to the General Assembly. Jean Krasno and Mitushi Das suggest the 'Uniting for Peace' provision (see p. 104) as a potential alternative to the Security Council. They note that this provision has been long overlooked and has become 'essentially useless' (2008, p. 186), but argue that it should be reconsidered and strengthened. The General Assembly is certainly a more representative body than the Security Council, and has been to the fore in spearheading progressive human rights legislation. Yet, while processes that rely on the opinion of the international community of states are clearly more inclusive than the Security Council, they are not necessarily fairer (Lu, 2006, p. 150; Chesterman, 2011b).

More far-reaching structural legal reform has also been proposed in the form of the creation of a new body for judging the need for military intervention if the Security Council is deadlocked. David Held argues that the UN is inherently ineffective and that there is a need for 'new bodies at the global level' independent of states (2005, p. 25). He states: 'the establishment of an independent assembly of democratic peoples, directly elected by them and accountable to them, is an unavoidable institutional requirement' (ibid., p. 273). Similarly Allan Buchanan and Robert O. Keohane have advocated the creation a new body with formal authority comprising 'a coalition of reasonably democratic states' (2004, p. 18).

Creating a new body for such authorization, however, potentially flounders on the issue of troops (Wolf, 2005). While a new institution may well authorize an intervention it will have no independent military capacity and will therefore be reliant on states to supply their national forces (Kinloch-Pichat, 2004, p. 211). This has led to proposals for an international army of some kind (Watts, 2001, p. 10; Langille, 2002; Weiss, 2009, p. 180; Pattison, 2010, p. 229). Clearly this would require wholesale reform of the existing system and is highly unlikely to come to pass. The major powers have demonstrated a pronounced unwillingness to countenance the creation of any body with the power to authorize force independently or develop an independent military capability (Thakur and Sidhu, 2006, p. 6). In terms of a coalition of democracies, while this would clearly be favourable to the West, and hence highly unlikely to be supported by the developing world, it is not at all clear that Western states have any real appetite for substantive reform (Archibugi, 2003, p. 8).

More fundamental reform involves transforming the statist structure of both the international system and international law. Tom Woodhouse and Oliver Ramsbotham describe the UN as 'the creature of an unreconstructed system of sovereign nation states'. They argue that this present organizing principle is antithetical to human rights and thus reforms which do not address the primacy of the state will have limited impact as they do not reflect 'genuine cosmopolitan values' (2005, p. 141). Such a perspective leads, in effect, towards a world state. This radical idea is widely rejected as undesirable; Kant argued that a universal state will quickly descend into a 'soulless despotism' and 'after crushing the germs of goodness, will finally lapse into anarchy'. David Rodin however rejects this diagnosis, arguing that a world state need not involve a centralized authority with extensive global power. Instead such an entity might comprise 'an extremely minimal form of sovereign power ... [and] consist solely in the establishment of a world monopoly of military force with a minimal judicial mechanism for the resolution of international and internal disputes' (2002, pp. 186–7). Hans Kelsen, by contrast, argued that delegating authority to a non-state international judicial body would be a step towards 'the pacification of the world' (1972, p. 13).

Again this proposal is so radical that it is difficult to imagine how such change could ever evolve. Nonetheless, we cannot discount the possibility of a major change to the structure of the international political and legal systems (Thompson, 1992, p. 94). Today's UN, World Bank and ICC would doubtless have seemed inconceivable to people in the 19th century. Parsi asserts, however, 'to consider a reform of the UN that could reduce the power of the US is pure fantasy' (2006, p. 118). Hegemons, indeed, have historically (unsurprisingly) resisted any legal reforms which temper their power (Koskenniemi, 2001, p. 34). It is difficult to see, therefore, how substantive change could occur without a seismic event such as a world war or global economic catastrophe that would obliterate the present system and the power asymmetries inherent in it.

Conclusion

To date the question 'who decides?' has remained highly controversial, and it seems unlikely that a solution is imminent. This is unsurprising given that creating an international authority with the power to sanction intervention is such a sensitive issue. Yet, since the end of the Cold War, and especially after the genocide in Rwanda in 1994, an unprecedented momentum in favour of reform has been generated and it is, therefore, of significant concern that no resolution to this issue has been found in this context.

The UN Charter gives the Security Council significant powers but does not outline how its effectiveness should be measured (Cronin and Hurd, 2008, p. 11). Thus, despite near universal agreement that the Council suffers from a legitimacy deficit and is not functioning as it should be, there is no obvious means by which this problem can be resolved (Gowlland-Debbas 2000, p. 312; Chesterman, 2011b; Weiss, 2011). A vicious circle is thus created; the Council's lack of legitimacy continues to impact negatively on its effectiveness, which further erodes its legitimacy.

In an effort to overcome the Council's failings, alternative sources of authority have been championed. Those supportive of the reassertion of the Just War tradition and the application of common morality argue that this provides a universally applicable standard beyond the reach of politically motivated states. It is not clear, however, that the development and utilization of a moral framework such as the Just War tradition constitutes a viable solution to the 'who decides?' question (Berman, 2007, p. 163). Similarly the idea of empowering liberal democracies with unique rights suffers from the charge of subjectivity; on what objective, empirical basis can this group make a claim to deserve this authority? Such a hierarchy goes against the evolutionary trajectory of international law, and the majority of the world's states vehemently oppose such a change. It is also potentially very dangerous: this perspective is indicative of what Oliver Richmond describes as 'a liberal and cosmopolitan faith on the part of the interveners in the infallibility of their approach' (2005, p. 90). Moral righteousness and zealotry have been the catalysts for some of the more destructive episodes in human history.

If the Security Council continues to be seen as no more than a desirable but discretionary stamp of approval, it is likely to become little more than a 'debating society' (Falk, 2005a, p. 42). There are doubtless many who will not lament the demise of the Security Council, and there are few who advance unconditional support for its record and present composition. Whatever our views on its performance and structure, however, its possible demise must be a source of concern given the manifold lack of an obviously better alternative.

Questions

- How can we judge the legitimacy of a particular authority?
- What differentiates authority from power?
- What legal competencies are vested in the Security Council?
- Why does the Security Council suffer from a negative international image?
- Do you believe reform of the Security Council is required? If so what should such reform involve?

Further reading

On the question of legitimate authority

Berman, F. (2007) 'Moral Versus Legal Legitimacy' in C. Reed and D. Ryall (eds), *The Price of Peace* (Cambridge: Cambridge University Press).

Clark, I. (2005) *Legitimacy in International Society* (Oxford: Oxford University Press).

Hurd, I. (2007) *After Anarchy: Legitimacy and Power in the UN Security Council* (Princeton, NJ: Princeton University Press).

Hurrell, A. (2005) 'Legitimacy and the Use of Force: Can the Circle be Squared?' in D. Armstrong, T. Farrell and B. Maiguashca (eds), *Force and Legitimacy in World Politics* (Cambridge: Cambridge University Press).

International Commission on Intervention and State Sovereignty (2001) *The Responsibility to Protect* (Ottawa: International Development Research Centre), Chapter 6.

On UN reform

Annan, K. (2005a) 'In Larger Freedom: Towards Development, Security and Human Rights for All', UN document A/59/2005, 21 March. Available at: www.un.org/largerfreedom/.

Chesterman, S. (2002) *Just War or Just Peace?* (Oxford: Oxford University Press), Chapter 6.

Cronin, B. and Hurd, I. (2008) *The UN Security Council and the Politics of International Authority* (London: Routledge).

Falk, R. (2005a) 'Legality and Legitimacy: The Quest for Principled Flexibility and Restraint' in D. Armstrong, T. Farrell and B. Maiguashca (eds), *Force and Legitimacy in World Politics* (Cambridge: Cambridge University Press).

Hehir, A. (2012) *The Responsibility to Protect: Rhetoric, Reality and the Future of Humanitarian Intervention* (Basingstoke and New York: Palgrave Macmillan), Chapter 8.

Pattison, J. (2010) *Humanitarian Intervention and the Responsibility to Protect* (Oxford: Oxford University Press), Chapter 8.

UN High-Level Panel on Threats, Challenges and Change (2004) *A More Secure World: Our Shared Responsibility*, 2 December. Available at: www.un.org/secureworld/report.pdf.

Weiss, T. (2009) *What's rong With the United Nations and How to Fix It* (Cambridge: Polity).

Chapter 8

Motives and Means

As demonstrated by the controversy surrounding NATO's intervention in Libya in 2011, one of the key areas of contestation in the debate on humanitarian intervention has been the importance of the intervener's motives: for some the intervention was motivated by laudable humanitarian aims (Cohen, 2011), others alleged geopolitical concerns impelled the action (Ali, 2011). The Just War tradition (see Chapter 2) puts strong emphasis on right intention, but many modern analyses suggest that complete disinterest and purity of motives are unreasonably onerous requirements. They argue that actors will always have mixed motivations, but provided these motivations do not actively contradict humanitarianism they are unproblematic. Others go further, suggesting that motives are, in essence, irrelevant and that an intervention can be considered humanitarian even if the intervening party was motivated purely by self-interest provided the action had positive humanitarian consequences.

Additionally, further controversy surrounds the means employed during a humanitarian intervention. NATO's intervention in Kosovo in 1999 highlighted this dilemma: while certain observers supported the intervention, they criticized the manner in which it was executed. There exists a tension, therefore, between those who argue, largely in line with the *jus in bello* thinking outlined in Chapter 2, that the means used must be just (and that the interveners must be prepared to expose themselves to some risk) and those who maintain that a preference for force protection is acceptable.

This chapter begins with an analysis of the question of motives, initially highlighting the normative code presented by adherents to the Just War tradition. I then assess the arguments of those who maintain that some self-interest is unproblematic or even irrelevant. In the second section I examine the differing perspectives on the issue of the appropriate means employed during a humanitarian intervention. While both international humanitarian law and the Just War tradition advance clear prohibitions on certain tactics, others maintain that states have a duty to privilege their own soldiers' lives above those of others, and ultimately, restraint and the adherence to laws and norms are impossible because 'war is hell'.

Motives

On the day NATO launched air strikes against the FRY, President Clinton outlined his motivations for taking action:

> We act to protect thousands of innocent people in Kosovo from a mounting military offensive ... we act to prevent a wider war, to defuse a powder keg at the heart of Europe that has exploded twice before in this century with catastrophic results. By acting now, we are upholding our values. Ending this tragedy is a moral imperative. (Chatterjee and Scheid, 2003, p. 6)

Many supported Operation Allied Force because of its purportedly humanitarian intent, but the articulation of a parallel security interest – 'to prevent a wider war' – highlighted that NATO was not motivated purely by the 'moral imperative'. Likewise, President Barack Obama declared that he ordered the military action against Libya in 2011 'because our *interests* and values are at stake' and noting that the US 'has an important strategic interest' at stake (White House, 2011). For some this mixture of self-interest and altruism is troubling: would NATO have intervened in the absence of self-interest? We could point to notorious instances of non-intervention, in particular the genocide in Rwanda in 1994, to argue that national interests must be involved before any state will undertake an intervention. Yet, others counter that while some degree of national interest will always be involved, this does not preclude an intervention from being deemed humanitarian. Pure altruism is unrealistic, and an intervention can be described as humanitarian, provided it has positive humanitarian consequences. The following sections explore and analyse these contrasting positions.

The humanitarian imperative

As noted in Chapter 2, the origins of the Just War tradition are invariably traced back to the Christian Saints Ambrose, Augustine and later Aquinas. In contrast to the pacifist position of earlier Christians, these thinkers argued that there were occasions when violence, though always regrettable, was necessary. Ambrose argued that Jesus's injunction to 'turn the other cheek' constituted a proscription on the use of force in self-defence, but Jesus did not disapprove of the use of force in defence of others. In fact Ambrose argued that the use of force to protect others was occasionally a duty, stating: 'he who does not keep harm off a friend, if he can, is as much in fault as he who causes it' (Bellamy, 2006b, p. 24). Thus, provided the intention is altruistic, the use of force is potentially just. This idea influenced

Augustine, who stressed that the motivation driving a person to act in a particular way, including the use of force, was a key factor in determining the justness or otherwise of the act, and thus 'restraining men from sin' potentially justified the use of force (Deane, 1963, pp. 164–5). Thus, the key concern for Augustine was 'the inward disposition that drove one to war' (Bellamy, 2006b, p. 27).

Aquinas also emphasized the importance of right intention, arguing that we must always intend to do good. Thus for Aquinas, 'merely having a just cause and legitimate authority is insufficient' (Holmes, 1992, p. 200). Right intention and just cause are, therefore, separate criteria within the Just War tradition. This has significant implications for the judgement of 'just wars': such an emphasis on right intention potentially precludes certain purportedly 'humanitarian interventions'. If such actions were undertaken for the wrong reasons they would be potentially deemed unjust even if a humanitarian crisis had been occurring prior to, and was subsequently halted by, the intervention. So 'right intention', as Bellamy states, 'stands at the very heart of the Just War tradition's justifications for killing' (2006b, p. 122).

In the contemporary era, and arguably since the Second World War, interventions have invariably been justified, to some extent, as motivated by moral concerns. These justifications have often been spurious or very much secondary to the dominant geopolitical motivation. Some interventions, however, though motivated by self-interest have had positive humanitarian consequences: for example, Vietnam's invasion of Cambodia in 1978 (Wheeler, 2002, pp. 78–110). Those uncomfortable with applying the label 'humanitarian' to such interventions, where the positive humanitarian consequences of the act appear to be coincidental, have sought to distinguish between such action and true 'humanitarian intervention' by focusing on the intention of the intervening party. An essential quality of a humanitarian intervention for some, therefore, must be right intention. According to Richard Miller, humanitarian intervention is 'a form of altruism writ large, a kind of self-sacrificial love' (2000a, p. 54). While many of the definitions listed in Box 1.2 refer to humanitarian motives, few ascribe to Miller's high ideal. Frank Berman argues that '[altruism] is inherent in – or necessarily implied by – the fact that the justification for resorting to force is a humanitarian one' (2007, p. 165). He additionally notes, however, that while a necessary component of a humanitarian intervention is that the stated aim of the intervener is humanitarian, such a claim may be cynical and must be objectively judged.

Bhikhu Parekh describes humanitarian intervention as an act 'wholly or primarily guided by the sentiment of humanity, compassion or fellow feeling, and in that sense disinterested' (Wheeler, 2003, p. 194). This is a less stringent position on right intention; clearly the intention is important, and it must be at least the primary motivation, but it need not be the only motivation. Similarly to Parekh, ICISS argued that 'the primary purpose of the intervention, whatever other motives intervening states may have, must be to halt or avert human suffering' (2001a, p. xii). They note that complete disinterestedness may be preferable but caution that 'mixed motives, in international relations as everywhere else, are a fact of life' (ibid., p. 36). Nonetheless, the primacy of right intention is asserted and thus, according to ICISS, the ratio of right intention to self-interest must strongly favour the former.

In defence of interests

In contrast to those who argue that motives must be purely or even primarily humanitarian, there are many who assert that the motivations of the intervening party do not undermine the humanitarian aspect of an intervention, even if there is compelling evidence that considerations of national interests were a major factor in the decision to intervene. Tony Blair's famous Doctrine of the International Community speech in April 1999 outlined the criteria he assessed before making a judgement on whether to intervene (see Box 8.1). As the final criterion makes clear, national interests had to be at stake before he would countenance taking any action.

Chris Brown describes as 'bizarre' the idea 'that actions can only be described as ethical if motives are absolutely pure' (2001, p. 23), while, according to Michael Walzer, 'political motivations are always mixed ... A pure moral will doesn't exist in political life, and it shouldn't be necessary to pretend that kind of purity' (2006, p. 26). The nature and centrality of right intention, as proffered by the Just War tradition, is therefore rejected. The fixation with 'pure' motives is seen by some as a distraction from the more important issue. According to Thomas Weiss, 'looking for parsimony in motives does not really advance the discussion, because not all political motivations are evil ... While the ethical humanitarian rationale need not be exclusive or even foremost, it should be explicit and prominent' (2007a, p. 7).

Such a perspective rests on the belief that self-interest is not antithetical to moral action. For example, a person attends a fundraising dance in aid of a local homeless charity because they wish to meet their friends and enjoy themselves and because they know that doing so helps homeless people. The fact that this person's motivation for attending the dance was not purely, or even primarily, altruistic does not mean, many would argue, that this was not a humane act, as it had positive humanitarian consequences.

> ## Box 8.1   'Doctrine of the International Community': speech by UK Prime Minister Tony Blair, 24 April 1999
>
> First, are we sure of our case? War is an imperfect instrument for righting humanitarian distress; but armed force is sometimes the only means of dealing with dictators. Second, have we exhausted all diplomatic options? We should always give peace every chance, as we have in the case of Kosovo. Third, on the basis of a practical assessment of the situation, are there military operations we can sensibly and prudently undertake? Fourth, are we prepared for the long term? ... having made a commitment we cannot simply walk away once the fight is over ... And finally, do we have national interests involved? The mass expulsion of ethnic Albanians from Kosovo demanded the notice of the rest of the world. But it does make a difference that this is taking place in such a combustible part of Europe.
>
> *Source*: Blair (1999).

A further extension of this logic, however, holds that the motivation need not be altruistic in any way for the act, or intervention, to be deemed humanitarian. Nicholas Wheeler, in contrast to the Just War tradition, discounts right intention from the evaluation of whether a particular use of force qualifies as a humanitarian intervention. He argues: 'if an intervention is motivated by non-humanitarian reasons, it can still count as humanitarian provided that the motives and the means employed do not undermine a positive humanitarian outcome' (2002, p. 38). Occasionally the use of force by states for reasons of self-interest, such as self-defence, has had positive humanitarian consequences, he argues, and these can therefore be considered humanitarian interventions. Wheeler cites India's intervention in East Pakistan in 1971, Vietnam's intervention in Cambodia in 1978 and Tanzania's intervention in Uganda in 1979 as evidence. In each case these interventions were acts of self-defence, yet all resulted in significant humanitarian benefits (2003, p. 195). Wheeler is satisfied if, as in the case of Vietnam's intervention in Cambodia, there is a 'happy – if purely inadvertent – coincidence among motives, means, and a positive humanitarian outcome' (ibid., p. 197). Similarly Fernando Tesón argues that non-humanitarian motives are not relevant and that the 'true test' is 'whether the intervention has put an end to human rights deprivations' (1988, pp. 106–7).

Additionally, some argue that self-interest is in fact a necessary component of any successful humanitarian intervention. According to Taylor Seybolt, states motivated to intervene purely by humanitarian concern are likely to withdraw their troops once they sustain casualties, whereas if there is some degree of national interest involved, such difficulties will be tolerated (2007, p. 27). The US's retreat from Somalia in 1995 is cited as evidence to support this (Docking, 2008, pp. 215–16). DIIA similarly argues that 'states may need more than humanitarian motives to be willing to intervene in a substantial way' (1999, p. 111). In fact, some argue that any state articulating a purely altruistic justification for the use of force is likely to meet with domestic opposition. In this sense it may be that justifications asserting some self-interest are in fact a cover for humanitarian justifications (Berman, 2007, p. 166). Nicholas Wheeler and Justin Morris, indeed, argue that Tony Blair was forced to downplay his humanitarian intent in supporting the invasion of Iraq and that this intent was a far greater influence on his support than he admitted prior to the invasion (2006, p. 454). Many of those who supported the intervention in Libya on humanitarian grounds had no problem admitting that the intervening coalition were motivated by self-interest as well as humanitarianism (Thakur, 2011; Bellamy, 2011)

It would certainly seem too onerous to argue that motivations must be purely altruistic to pass the right-intention test. A degree of self-interest is perhaps inevitable, but what about pure self-interest? Returning to the first hypothetical example, the rationale behind hosting charity dances is that people are more likely to give money to charities if they receive something in return for their donation. It is perhaps unproblematic that certain people who attend these functions want to enjoy themselves while they help the homeless. However, it is less clear that acts can be deemed humanitarian if self-interest is the sole motivation. For example, we might wonder at the motivation driving certain celebrities to pay huge sums to attend Elton John's annual 'White Tie and Tiara Ball' to raise money for AIDS research. Do they attend because of a genuine desire to support AIDS research, or do they want to enjoy a lavish party and be photographed by the media? Indeed, it could be argued that it would be easier, and more cost-effective, simply to donate the money without the huge expense. If we can be sure that a celebrity, whose fame is on the wane, is motivated to pay to attend this ball purely to achieve publicity and resurrect their career, then can we really describe them as 'charitably minded'?

To assert that uncovering *any* degree of national interest on the part of the intervening state automatically negates any possible humanitarian motivation seems extreme. Yet an exclusive focus on consequences is also problematic. For example, state A discovers that state B has huge oil reserves in its eastern provinces. State A invades state B and occupies these provinces to exploit the oil. The government in state B had previously been involved in a campaign of ethnic cleansing against the minority population of non-nationals in these oil-rich provinces, and this oppression ceases when state A assumes control. In this hypothetical situation, despite the fact that the actions of state A bring an end to ethnic cleansing, can we really describe this use of force as a humanitarian intervention? It would surely be more accurate to describe such action as a military intervention with positive humanitarian consequences. This is a semantic difference, but if humanitarian intervention is to have any distinct meaning, then motivations must surely be taken into account. Avoiding both extremes – absolute purity of motivation and the outright disregard for motivation – perhaps enables us to come to terms more accurately with the importance of right intention. As Anthony Lang argues, the motivation of the actor cannot be the sole factor analysed when assessing an intervention, but it must at least be one of the factors assessed (2003, p. 3).

'He who invokes humanity wants to cheat'

The focus on intention is regarded by many as essentially a redundant exercise. As noted in Chapter 4, the realist and Marxist perspectives assert that the motivations of states are never altruistic, and thus agonizing over the balance between humanitarian intent and self-interest is a waste of time.

President Clinton outlined his intentions in intervening in Kosovo in often emphatically moralistic ways, claiming that the intervention was aimed at 'preventing another holocaust' and halting 'genocide at the heart of Europe' (Jackson, 2000, p. 281). Yet Ellen Wood highlights one of Clinton's other statements which points to more selfish intents: 'if we're going to have a strong economic relationship that includes our ability to sell around the world, Europe has got to be a key … that's what this Kosovo thing is all about'. Wood thus concludes, 'forget humanitarian motives, this is all about US global hegemony' (2000, p. 190). Few supporters of Operation Allied Force argue that NATO was entirely disinterested, and, as noted earlier, many are unconcerned about these mixed motivations. For those such as Wood, however, there are always underlying selfish motivations driving states, and it is a question of uncovering these truths. Carl Schmitt's famous maxim, 'he who invokes humanity wants to cheat', captures the essence of this suspicious, if not cynical, disposition (1996, p. 54).

In their analysis of ten cases of intervention, the Research Directorate of ICISS found 'the rhetoric of humanitarianism had been used most stridently in cases where the humanitarian motive was weakest' (Weiss, 2007a, p. 37). This is certainly a troubling finding and clearly adds credence to the notion that there is a difference between states' claimed motivations and their actual motivations. The increased use of humanitarianism as a justification for Western foreign policy and Security Council interventionism in the post-Cold War era is thus seen by some as a cover for geopolitical aims (Graubart, 2008). According to Michael Wesley:

interventionism gained momentum on the back of an interplay between norms and self-interest that allowed developed states to provide legitimating normative cover for interventions by casting developing states' weaknesses in terms of overarching and supposedly universal and economic, political, humanitarian and security principles. (2006, p. 24)

Portraying foreign interventions as humanitarian ostensibly enabled states to justify the use of force in the absence of the 'Soviet threat'. The idea of fighting for human rights has meant, according to Anne Orford, that 'high-violence options ... [are] now once again marketable to citizens of the USA and other democracies' (2003, p. 12).

This of course presupposes that domestic publics are ill-disposed to their states going to war for explicitly selfish reasons. There is much evidence to support this proposition particularly within the West. Even when the US led a coalition against the Taliban in Afghanistan in response to the 11 September 2001 attacks, the use of force was justified on moral as well as security grounds. We might have assumed that the nature of the atrocities committed against the US would have enabled the Bush administration to articulate a one-dimensional rationale for the intervention, but, interestingly, it was evidently felt that a humanitarian rationale had to be additionally proffered (Hehir, 2008a, pp. 57–9). Evidence suggests that the US domestic public is uncomfortable with a foreign policy based purely on self-interest (Cook, 2003, p. 146; Wesley, 2006, p. 43).

Thus for many, the issue of motives is clear: states will only intervene if they have significant interests at stake or if they have no other option but to take action (Mueller, 2005, p. 123). Wondering whether humanitarian motivations outweighed self-interest is thus a futile exercise as the latter will always outweigh the former. Humanitarian motivations are seen as either wholly cynical or entirely secondary.

If we expect absolute purity of motives, then clearly there has never been a humanitarian intervention. If we believe that mixed motives are inevitable, this record does not constitute the death of humanitarian intervention. Provided we accept that mixed motivations are inevitable and unproblematic, it is possible to reject the realist/Marxist critique as overly deterministic and empirically unsound. Indeed, why must we assume that all those involved in determining the foreign policy of states are necessarily unconcerned with morality or human rights? It is difficult to accept that, upon assuming power, statesmen and stateswomen undergo a highly effective socialization process which filters out all altruistic impulses. We can surely accept that those in power afford primacy to the national interest, though prioritization need not be a zero-sum game. Empirically, can we prove that Tony Blair lied consistently when he claimed that at least part of his reason for supporting the invasion of Iraq was the humanitarian benefits he believed would accrue? We may certainly form our own view about the extent to which this concern for the Iraqi people's freedom outweighed other motivations, but it is not possible to prove that Blair was actively unconcerned about the humanitarian motivations he so emphatically espoused – unless, of course, he admits this himself.

Means

The use of force by states, whether for humanitarian or selfish reasons, constitutes action that necessarily causes destruction and usually death. The laws of war – *jus in bello* – apply to all instances when force is used, but some argue that, when force is used for ostensibly just or moral reasons, these rules acquire a unique importance. The Just War tradition comprises both *jus ad bellum* and *jus in bello*, and failure to adhere to the criteria in the latter undermines the justness of the entire intervention (see Chapter 2).

War is, however, conducted by the military rather than the government: while overall responsibility for ordering the use of force lies with the government of a state, the strategy employed is primarily determined by the army. This delegation of competencies, many argue, precludes the notion of a 'humanitarian war' because the intent of the military is always force protection and victory at any cost, hence the maxim *inter arma silent leges* (in the time of war the law is silent). Additionally, governments have demonstrated a pronounced unwillingness to agree to any military strategy that will endanger troops and potentially create domestic mobilization against the war.

'Bombing for humanity'

Attempts to outlaw the use of force are manifest in those tenets of international law that outlaw aggression and generally attempt to minimize the resort to violence. International law, however, does not prohibit the use of force in all circumstances; under Article 51 of the UN Charter states may legitimately use force if attacked, and Chapter VII of the Charter empowers the Security Council to sanction military action (see Chapter 5). The laws governing the use of force emerged in the 18th and 19th centuries when attempts to restrain the recourse to force were essentially abandoned, although restraints on the actual conduct of war were increasingly agreed, if not always honoured (Malanczuk, 2006, p. 342). During this period the nature of war differed significantly from the 'total war' which evolved in the late 19th century, resulting in the heavy death toll during both World Wars in the 20th century. Previously wars were fought between armies with relatively little adverse consequences for civilians. Agreements and protocols such as the Lieber Code in 1863 and the three Hague conventions of 1899 sought to establish rules on the conduct of armies, such as the treatment of wounded soldiers and prisoners of war, and the prohibition on the use of certain weapons like gas and, for a time at least, aerial bombing (Laughland, 2002, p. 44). International laws governing the permissible means by which states may wage war pre-date the laws outlawing the resort to force, but nonetheless are arguably the least respected aspect of international law. As Hersch Lauterpacht observes, 'if international law is, in some ways, at the vanishing point of law, the law of war is, perhaps even more conspicuously, at the vanishing point of international law' (1952, p. 382).

For some the very idea of killing for human rights is an irreconcilable contradiction. Geoffrey Robertson, describing this as the 'Guernica paradox', asks: 'When can it be right to unleash terror on terrorists, to bomb for human rights, to kill to stop crimes against humanity?' (2002, p. 402). As noted in Chapter 2, the Just War tradition argues that force is permissible under certain circumstances. A key aspect of the tradition, however, is those tenets contained within the *jus in bello* framework: discrimination (non-combatants should never be targeted); proportionality (targets should only be destroyed if their military value is greater than the destruction that will accrue); and observance of the laws of war. Implementation of these criteria is influenced by the doctrine of double effect, derived from the writings of Aquinas. This doctrine asserts that harmful consequences of military action can be excused if certain circumstances pertain (see Box 2.3). Thus even the death of civilians does not fundamentally compromise the justness of a particular instance of the use of force, provided the intention was just and the civilians were not deliberately targeted. This does not mean, however, that people can claim that killing civilians was justified for the greater good: Michael Walzer's argument that the destruction of Dresden and other German cities by Allied bombardment was excusable because this hastened the end of Nazism has been criticized as contrary to the Just War tradition because this consequentialist approach is explicitly rejected by the tradition (Brown, 2006, p. 108). One may therefore both fight a Just War unjustly and an unjust war justly (McMahan, 2005).

There is, therefore, a consequentialist rationale at play: if using force and unavoidably killing ten people results in the prevention of the deaths of one hundred people then surely this is acceptable, if always lamentable? This does not mean that it is acceptable to use ten people to save a hundred – here the Kantian rejection of the instrumental use of individuals applies (Anscombe, 1981, pp. 78–9; Donaldson, 2002, pp. 136–9). Rather, if it is demonstrably impossible to avoid the deaths of ten to save a hundred then the use of force is defensible, though always regrettable.

There have been many instances, of course, when the idea that it is necessary to cause *some* damage and inflict *some* casualties to prevent greater loss of life has been cynically employed. According to some, those claiming to be engaged in a humanitarian intervention have a greater duty to ensure that they adhere to the laws of war (Hayden, 2005, p. 90; Janzekovic, 2006, p. 109). ICISS argues that in the course of a humanitarian intervention international humanitarian laws should be 'strictly' followed and adds that 'an argument can be made that even higher standards should apply in these cases' (2001a, p. 37). ICISS adapts the Just War tradition's *jus in bello* criteria in outlining the permissible means by which war may be waged:

> The scale, duration and intensity of the planned military intervention should be the minimum necessary to secure the humanitarian objective in question. The means have to be commensurate with the ends, and in line with the magnitude of the original provocation. (Ibid.)

Therefore, the means employed during a humanitarian intervention are regarded by some as exceptional and of greater importance in the judgement of the intervention than the means employed during a traditional war. The following sections examine those counter-perspectives that argue that, regardless of whether a war is fought for human rights, self-defence or acquisition, certain generic principles of military engagement will always prevail, and thus the means employed 'may not be a pretty sight' (Brown, 2006, p. 154).

Force protection

'Countries that champion humanitarian values such as the USA', according to Robert Jackson, 'are unwilling to risk the lives of their soldiers to defend human rights' (2000, p. 289). While this may be something of an exaggeration, given that US troops have been killed during certain ostensibly humanitarian interventions, there is no denying that there is a clear reluctance to send troops abroad for humanitarian missions. Writing in 2000, future Secretary of State Condoleezza Rice stated that while 'there is nothing wrong with doing something which benefits all humanity', this is 'a second order effect' and American foreign policy should be based on the national interest (2000, p. 47). During the 2000 US presidential election, candidates Al Gore and George W. Bush both endorsed President Clinton's decision not to send troops to Rwanda in 1994 (Wheeler, 2003, p. 192). While Clinton himself has lamented this decision (to some extent at least – see Chapter 10), it seems fair to conclude that presidential candidates, and indeed presidents, do not want to be seen as prepared to endanger the military by fighting wars on behalf of others. Rather, candidates and presidents aim to project a conservative vision for the use of force based on national interests.

While this disposition has led to much criticism it is not necessarily immoral, or even amoral, to prioritize the safety of one's own troops. According to Walzer, 'the leaders of states have a right, indeed they have an obligation, to consider the interests of their own people, even when they are acting to help other people' (1992a, p. 26). Martin Cook argues that individuals enter into a 'military contract' with their state when they join the army which obliges them to take risks and give their lives if necessary. Cook notes, however:

> They do these things on the basis of the implicit promise that the circumstances under which they must act are grounded in political leadership's good faith judgment that the defense of the sovereignty and integrity of the nation (or by careful extension, the nation's vital interests) requires their action. The farther a particular engagement or deployment departs from this clear contractual case, the more difficult it is for political leadership to offer moral and political justification for any killing and especially dying that their military forces experience. (2003, pp. 150–1)

Seen from this perspective the unwillingness of Western states to, for example, deploy troops in Rwanda in 1994 or Syria in 2012 potentially drew on a reasonable appraisal of the likely consequences of such an intervention. The lesson of the US-led intervention in Somalia in 1992 appeared to be that the US domestic public had little appetite for sustaining casualties on behalf of a state thousands of miles away. This led to the so-called 'vietmalia' syndrome, whereby US policy makers, conscious of the effects of the interventions in both Vietnam and Somalia, developed a great reluctance to order troops oversees (Hehir, 2006, p. 74).

The US, though supportive of the idea of humanitarian intervention, has clearly been unwilling to countenance any external control over US troops. Presidential Directive 25 (see Box 8.2), issued five months after the deaths of 19 Rangers in Mogadishu in 1993, emphasizes the preference for independent control and selectivity, and this logic continues to guide US policy, as well as that of arguably the vast majority of states (Cook, 2003, p. 149). This determination to maintain control over the deployment and use of one's own forces derives in large part from the fact that troop casualties create domestic unease. So long as the state retains command over the deployment of its troops, it can minimize potential domestic uproar. Thus in 1995 the United States was able to pull its troops out of Somalia when public support for the operation plummeted, and during the intervention in Libya the US resisted calls for the deployment of ground troops and,

---

Box 8.2   Presidential Directive 25 (PDD-25), 1994: 'The Clinton Administration's Policy on Reforming Multilateral Peace Operations'

The President retains and will never relinquish command authority over U.S. forces. On a case by case basis, the President will consider placing appropriate U.S. forces under the operational control of a competent UN commander for specific UN operations authorized by the Security Council. The greater the U.S. military role, the less likely it will be that the U.S. will agree to have a UN commander exercise overall operational control over U.S. forces. Any large scale participation of U.S. forces in a major peace enforcement mission that is likely to involve combat should ordinarily be conducted under U.S. command and operational control or through competent regional organizations such as NATO or ad hoc coalition.

Source: Cook (2003, p. 147).

---

within two weeks of the commencement of military operations, President Obama withdrew all US troops from combat operations, thereby minimizing potential US casualties (Barry, 2011, p. 5).

Therefore, given the not necessarily immoral preference for force protection among states, the normative guidelines and international laws governing the means employed during an intervention are likely to be afforded secondary importance. The challenge posed by humanitarian intervention, according to Wheeler, is 'to find a strategy that protects civilians without exposing military personnel to excessive dangers' (2003, p. 194).

'War is hell'

Peacekeeping troops are deployed with a mandate to keep the peace and not to kill, but such missions differ fundamentally from humanitarian interventions because they are undertaken with the consent of the host state. Humanitarian interventions by definition are not launched with the approval of the host state, and therefore conflict is inevitable. Once we accept that military force is going to be used, we may have to accept that a 'win at all costs' mentality assumes primacy and that the result will be nasty (Myers, 1996, p. 119; Boucher, 1998, p. 62). Carl von Clausewitz, the 19th-century military strategist and historian, argued that 'we can never introduce a modifying principle into the philosophy of war without committing an absurdity' (quoted in Walzer, 1992a, p. 23), thereby suggesting that, once war begins, restraint is impractical (see Box 8.3).

> **Box 8.3   The violence and the lethality and the destruction ...'**
>
> The speed and the violence and the lethality and the destruction that is going to occur is beyond anything that you can imagine. If, indeed, you're not going to accept my terms, we need to break this meeting right now. I suggest you go outside, get into your car and ride around the city of Belgrade. Remember it the way it is today. If you force me to go to war against you, Belgrade will never look that way again – never in your lifetime, or your children's lifetime. Belgrade and your country will be destroyed if you force me to go to war.
>
> *Source*: Lieutenant General Michael Short, United States Air Force in negotiations with Yugoslav military officers, October 1998 (quoted in Shue, 2003, p. 110).

Even though humanitarian intervention is different from self-defence and wars for acquisition, there are certain similarities. A state intervenes with the aim of deploying sufficient military power to force another to behave a certain way. Brown contends, therefore, that 'effective humanitarian intervention' constitutes:

> an act of power; it involves taking sides, choosing which of the various parties to support and enforcing one's choice by superior strength ... the behaviour of the successful intervener may not be particularly attractive, and may indeed involve temporarily contributing to humanitarian distress. (2006, p. 154)

Therefore, much as we may wince at the idea of 'bombing for humanity' and implore armies to show particular restraint when engaged in such missions, it is possibly naïve to expect that such considerations will factor in the strategy of intervening forces. This contrast between *jus ad bellum* and *jus in bello* were arguably manifest most emphatically during NATO's intervention in Kosovo in 1999 (see Chapter 11). During Operation Allied Force the UN High Commissioner for Human Rights, Mary Robinson, criticized NATO's methods and, highlighting the general dangers of unilateralism, stated that 'NATO remains the sole judge of what is or is not acceptable to bomb' (Roberts, 1999, p. 114). NATO's intervention in Libya was, perhaps unsurprisingly, deemed to have been precise and proportionate by both NATO and the Libyan rebels, but a report by the UN Human Rights Council pointed to a number of instances where civilians were killed by NATO bombs (Human Rights Council, 2012, p. 17). The report did note that NATO appeared to have taken great measures to avoid these casualties and for the most part succeeded (ibid., p. 22). This is, of course, cold comfort to those innocents killed, but perhaps a sober reminder that even the most powerful military coalition in the world cannot avoid civilian casualties even during a purportedly humanitarian intervention.

According to George Lucas, humanitarian interventions 'are seriously compromised if the intervening forces themselves deliberately, or even inadvertently, behave unjustly, violate rights, infringe liberty, or destroy the rule of law' (2003, p. 77). If we endorse this view, which is indeed embedded in the Just War tradition, then it appears clear that NATO's tactics, particularly the strategy of undertaking military action by bombing from 15,000 feet, compromised the purportedly 'humanitarian' nature of their intervention. According to David Rieff, the use of humanitarian rhetoric by NATO during its intervention in Kosovo 'constituted one more demonstration of Napoleon's maxim that in war the moral was to the material as three to one' (2004, pp. 292–3).

Of course, as noted earlier, we could argue that force protection is both a necessity and a duty. In both the intervention in Kosovo and Libya no NATO personnel were killed; as Michael Ignatieff argued, however, the danger is that this kind of risk-free, or 'virtual', warfare will desensitize the domestic public within the intervening state and increase the propensity to use force (2000, pp. 179–80). What appears to be clear from the example of NATO's operation in Kosovo is that even interventions undertaken for high ideals will be prosecuted according to generic rules of military engagement which appear to afford little consideration to normative moral codes or even international humanitarian law. This is, of course, a troubling finding for anyone supportive of humanitarian intervention.

Conclusion

Despite the protestations of those who disavow the importance of motives, the motivation behind an intervention, particularly a purportedly humanitarian intervention, will inevitably be taken into consideration when people come to judge the merits of a particular instance of the use of force. It seems unrealistic to expect that a putative humanitarian intervention must be motivated purely by altruism. We are thus faced with the problem of trying to determine a means by which we can assess the place of humanitarianism within a hierarchy of motives. We can only do this, of course, if we believe statesmen and stateswomen when they say that they were motivated to some extent by 'moral imperatives'. Clearly realists and Marxists reject this very premise on the basis that morality is not a factor in the foreign policy of states: only national interest prevails, although certain realists argue that the pursuit of the national interest is a moral aspiration (Morgenthau, 1951). Hedley Bull, instinctively sceptical and critical of humanitarian intervention, rejects the idea that asserting the dominance of national interest forecloses all debate about moral intent. This belief in the dominance of national interest, he argues, 'does not even provide a basis for distinguishing moral or ideological considerations in a country's foreign policy from non-moral or non-ideological ones' (2002, p. 63). It may be possible that humanitarianism becomes part of the national interest (Pasic and Weiss, 2003, p. 108). We shall doubtless continue to disagree whether the espousal of humanitarian intent in any given case was the 'true' motivation.

Writing in the 19th century Clausewitz claimed that the laws of war are 'almost imperceptible and hardly worth mentioning' (Malanczuk, 2006, p. 343). This statement appears to continue to have credence given the scale of atrocities and war crimes committed in the period since then. What is perhaps more dispiriting, however, is that this appears to apply even to ostensibly humanitarian interventions. Robertson notes: 'as with modern war of any kind, the result of NATO's bombing [in 1999] was tragedy and terror, the greatest anguish being that much of it was inflicted on the very people that the West had intervened to save' (2002, p. 402). States perhaps justifiably retain a pronounced unwillingness to risk their soldiers' lives on behalf of others. Cook argues that until international organizations develop their own military capacity, 'humanitarian intervention and peacekeeping operations will be piecemeal, inconsistent, and dependent on coalitions of the willing. They will be (and morally need to be) risk averse and highly focused on force protection' (2003, p. 152).

While the reluctance to put troops in harm's way may appear immoral in light of some of the horrifying humanitarian tragedies that have occurred in the past 20 years alone, it is worth noting that this reluctance is born in no small part from prudential reasoning and the sense that domestic publics have a very limited tolerance for casualties and expenditure in the cause of 'saving strangers'. The US's withdrawal from Somalia in 1994 was, to a large extent, a consequence of the domestic backlash against the deployment following the deaths of 19 troops in October 1993 in Mogadishu (Mayall, 2006, pp. 132–5). It is therefore far from certain that the reluctance to put troops in harm's way is solely a function of unwillingness at the governmental level.

Questions

- Can we expect states to behave in purely altruistic ways in their international affairs?
- Does the presence of some self-interested motivations disqualify an intervention from being described as humanitarian?
- Do states have a duty to always act in the national interest?
- Is 'bombing for humanity' an oxymoron?
- Must states risk their own troops if they are to undertake a humanitarian intervention?

Further reading

Bellamy, A. (2006) *Just Wars: From Cicero to Iraq* (London: Polity), Chapter 6.

Chomsky, N. (1999) *The New Military Humanism: Lessons from Kosovo* (London: Pluto), Chapter 1.

Cook, M. (2003) '"Immaculate War": Constraints on Humanitarian Intervention' in A. Lang (ed.), *Just Intervention* (Washington, DC: Georgetown University Press).

Fisher, D. (2011) *Morality and War* (Oxford: Oxford University Press), Chapter 1.

Ignatieff, M. (2000) *Virtual War: Kosovo and Beyond* (New York: Picador), Chapter 8.

International Commission on Intervention and State Sovereignty (2001) *The Responsibility to Protect* (Ottawa: International Development Research Centre), Chapter 4.

Lebow, R.N. (2010) *Why Nations Fight: Past and Future Motivations for War* (Cambridge: Cambridge University Press).

Pattison, J. (2010) *Humanitarian Intervention and the Responsibility to Protect* (Oxford: Oxford University Press), Chapter 6.

Robertson, G. (2002) *Crimes Against Humanity* (London: Penguin), Chapter 11.

Walzer, M. (1992) *Just and Unjust Wars* (New York: Basic Books), Chapters 7 and 8.

Wheeler, N. (2002) *Saving Strangers* (Oxford: Oxford University Press), Chapter 1.

Part III

Cases

Chapter 9

Humanitarian Intervention in History

The resort to war has always been justified by its instigators, although these justifications have not always been based on ethical claims. The attempt to legitimize the use of force on ethical and moral grounds distinguishes 'just wars' from strategic warfare. The Athenians' justification for their invasion of Melos during the Peloponnesian War (431–404 BC) (see Box 9.1) was based solely on what the Athenians considered to be an immutable law of nature: the strong do what they can and the weak suffer what they must. While in the modern era this rationale has rarely been advanced in such emphatic (and honest) terms, realists maintain that the logic of power lies behind all military actions (see Chapter 4).

Whether realists are correct is certainly debatable; what is clear, however, is that at certain times in history states have advanced ethical arguments as justification for military action. The Just War tradition has evolved as an attempt to create a framework for discussion about the legitimate grounds on which force may be used (see Chapter 2). The contemporary debate surrounding humanitarian intervention can, therefore, be seen as the latest manifestation of this attempt to evaluate the ethical claims advanced by states for their use of force.

In this chapter I provide a (necessarily) brief overview of the history of humanitarian intervention – with a particular focus on the post-Second World War era – building on the more extensive treatment of the evolution

---

Box 9.1   The Melian dialogue

Our opinion of the gods and our knowledge of men lead us to conclude that it is a general and necessary law of nature to rule whatever one can. This is not a law that we made ourselves, nor were we the first to act upon it when it was made. We found it already in existence, and we shall leave it to exist forever among those who come after us. We are merely acting in accordance with it, and we know that you or anybody else with the same power as ours would be acting in precisely the same way.

Source: Thucydides (1972 [43BC], pp. 404–5).

---

of humanitarian intervention in the chapters in Part I of the book. I identify the evolution of international attitudes towards humanitarian intervention and provide contextual insight to explain these trends. In this chapter I demonstrate that, in the overwhelming majority of cases, states undertaking purportedly humanitarian interventions have had some significant national interest at stake. Additionally, where there has been no clear national interest there has been no intervention, regardless of the scale of the suffering involved.

Humanitarian intervention: trends and changes

Humanitarian intervention was the primary issue in international relations in the immediate post-Cold War era. Though its pre-eminence undoubtedly waned in the wake of the 11 September 2001 attacks, the Arab Spring has given the issue a new vitality and political importance. The contemporary currency of this issue, however, should not obscure its historical lineage. Though the actors and international context may well have changed, this issue has been debated for centuries, and if we conceive of humanitarian intervention as derived from the Just War tradition, which many do, then the issue dates back over two millennia (Bellamy, 2006b; Bass, 2008, p. 4)

The state and the evolution of humanitarian intervention

The contemporary controversy surrounding humanitarian intervention can only be understood, as Simon Chesterman notes, in the context of the transformation of international law in the 19th century and the emergence of positive legal doctrine, specifically the notion of non-interference (2002, pp. 7–8). The term 'humanitarian intervention' was first used by William Edward Hall in 1880, though similar expressions had been employed earlier in the 19th century (ibid., pp. 23–4). Following the expansion of positive international law in the 19th, and especially the 20th, centuries, an act of intervention could not be readily justified according to the existing legal codes unless in self-defence. Hence, interventions were at various times justified as expressions of 'moral norms' or 'natural laws' which ostensibly transcended or preceded legal doctrine (Bass, 2008, p. 3). In Chapter 5 I outlined the evolution and nature of the legal proscriptions against the use of force and how these codes have impacted on the legitimacy of a given intervention.

When people speak of the controversy surrounding humanitarian intervention they speak, therefore, of the clash between two codes, one legal, the other moral. Questions regarding the morality of war have been posed for thousands of years, but while this Just War tradition certainly informs contemporary debates about humanitarian intervention, Just War thinking is an explicitly moral evaluation of the use of force and one that is not confined to the question of helping those in other states. Humanitarian intervention, therefore, is a controversy derived from the emergence of positive law in the 19th century and especially the codification of sovereign inviolability.

Boxes 9.2 and 9.3 comprise a chronology of key events since the 19th century which have come to form part of the historical narrative of humanitarian intervention. It is important to note, however, that the vast majority of interventions listed are not widely considered to have been genuine ones. Chesterman notes that the examples provided by those authors seeking to

---

Box 9.2 A chronology of humanitarian intervention: 1827–1939

1827	Great Britain, France and Russia attack the Ottoman Empire at the Battle of Navarino ostensibly to aid Greek insurgents. British and French motives include a desire to prevent Russia from gaining strategic advantage in the region.
1860–1	France occupies Syria following the deaths of thousands of Maronite Christians. An earlier intervention by Turkey is largely responsible for the eventual end of the oppression.
1877–8	Russia declares war on the Ottoman Empire supposedly to protect Christians in Bosnia, Herzegovina and Bulgaria. It was widely believed that the intervention was actually motivated by Russian desire to acquire new territory in the Balkans.
1898	The US invades Cuba during its war with Spain. Some 200,000 Cubans had died in Spanish concentration camps since 1895. Seen as the closest example to humanitarian intervention in the pre-Charter era.
1900	The US and Great Britain intervene in China during the Boxer Rebellion ostensibly to protect nationals. Their shared desire to maintain trade links with China is more likely to have been the primary impetus.
1904–17	France, the US and others call on Turkey to cease oppression of the Armenians. No intervention occurs and one million Armenians are killed.
1913	Bulgaria, Greece and Serbia invade Macedonia ostensibly to protect Christians although few endorse these claims.
1939	Germany invades Czechoslovakia ostensibly to protect the German minority. Hitler's claims of Czech oppression are widely discounted.

Box 9.3 A chronology of humanitarian intervention since the Second World War

1971   India invades West and East Pakistan (Bangladesh) following air strikes launched by the Pakistani government. India also claims to be acting in defence of the people of East Pakistan, one million of whom had been killed by the West Pakistani military in the previous year. Neither the UN Security Council nor the UN General Assembly explicitly support or condemn the intervention.

1978   Following border skirmishes Vietnam invades Cambodia with the support of the United Front for National Salvation of Kampuchea. Pol Pot, responsible for the deaths of a million or more people, is eventually overthrown. Vietnam claims to be acting in self-defence. The Soviet veto blocks a Security Council resolution, supported by the United States, United Kingdom, France and China, condemning Vietnamese 'aggression'.

1979   Tanzania invades Uganda following Uganda's attempted annexation of the Tanzanian province of Kagera. With the support of Ugandan exiles the Tanzanian army overthrows Idi Amin. Neither the Security Council nor the UN General Assembly explicitly support or condemn the intervention.

1991   To enable the provision of humanitarian aid to Kurds in Northern Iraq the United States, United Kingdom and France impose 'no-fly' zone restrictions on the Iraqi air force and station some 20,000 troops to guard 'safe havens' in the region.

1992   The UN Security Council passes Resolution 794 characterizing the situation in Somalia as a 'threat to international peace and stability' and sanctions the deployment of a US-led military force. Following the deaths of 18 soldiers the US pulls out in March 1994.

1993–5 In April 1993 the UN establishes 'safe areas' around five Bosnian towns. In July 1995 Srebrenica is overrun by Bosnian Serbs and some 7,000 civilians are killed. In August 1995 NATO launches air strikes against the Bosnian Serb military.

1994   The UN Security Council passes Resolution 940 which authorizes a 'multinational ... to use all necessary means' to remove the military junta. Ultimately coercive force is unnecessary as junta steps aside.

1994   Despite extensive media coverage, and pleas from UN officials within Rwanda, 800,000 people are slaughtered by Hutus in 100 days.

→

1999	NATO launches Operation Allied Force against the Federal Republic of Yugoslavia, claiming to be acting to protect Kosovo's ethnic Albanians. The intervention is neither condoned nor condemned by the UN Security Council, while it is widely supported in the West. China, Russia and the G-77 condemn the unilateral use of force.
1999	Australia leads a UN-mandated force into East Timor to restore order following a referendum on independence. Indonesia consents to the intervention.
2001	The US launches Operation Enduring Freedom against Afghanistan. Great emphasis is placed on justifying the intervention on humanitarian grounds.
2003	The US launches Operation Iraqi Freedom, citing the emancipation of Iraq's citizens as one of its goals. As the claims regarding Iraqi weapons of mass destruction prove false, the humanitarian aims are retrospectively inflated.
2003	Government-sponsored militias carry out massacres in Darfur, Sudan. Despite numerous UN reports throughout 2003–4 no intervention takes place. By 2007 the UN claims some 450,000 people have died.
2008	Protests by Buddhist monks in Burma are violently repressed by the ruling military junta, leading to calls for external intervention, though no action is taken.
2008	President Mugabe of Zimbabwe is accused of initiating the nationwide oppression of opposition party supporters and activists. Many NGOs call for external intervention, although a power-sharing deal brokered by South Africa leads to fragile peace.
2008–9	The government of Sri Lanka defeat the separatist group 'The Tamil Tigers'. Reports from NGOs and UN bodies accuse the government of using excessive force and perpetrating crimes against humanity.
2011	In response to the escalating crisis in the state the Security Council passes resolution 1973 authorizing the imposition of a no-fly zone over Libya. NATO's military operation leads to the overthrow of Colonel Gaddafi's regime.
2011–2	Violence rages between the Syrian government and opposition groups; Russia and China twice cast their veto to block resolutions sanctioning Assad's regime. By September 2012 the UN estimates over 20,000 people have been killed and 250,000 displaced.

claim that humanitarian interventions did occur prior to the UN Charter have had motives retrospectively attributed to them that were not articulated at the time (2002, p. 25). Additionally, Anthony Arend and Robert Beck's analysis of interventions during the Cold War concludes that there were no examples of a genuine humanitarian intervention, nor did any state proffer a legal claim based exclusively on humanitarian justifications (1993, p. 137). In the post-Cold War era, however, the record appears less definitive. Since 1991, with the establishment of no-fly zones over Iraq, a number of cases have challenged the preceding historical narrative. The interventions in Somalia (1992), Kosovo (1999) and Libya (2011) in particular have been identified by some as indicative of a new willingness to undertake humanitarian interventions. This view is disputed, however, and it is the intensity of this dispute, and the importance of the issues involved, which have propelled humanitarian intervention from the periphery to the very centre of contemporary international relations.

Humanitarian intervention in historical context

The growth of interest in humanitarian intervention in the post-Cold War era is often erroneously portrayed as evidence of an unprecedented disposition amongst states to act morally. In fact states have offered humanitarian justifications for their actions for centuries. Gary Bass, indeed, notes: 'the basic ideas go all the way back to Thucydides, who, horrified at bloody ancient civil wars, hoped for the endurance of "the general laws of humanity which are there to give a hope of salvation to all who are in distress"' (2008, p. 4). Martin Cook notes that the US 'has always tended to speak in universalizing terms of fighting wars to end all wars, advancing human rights and democratic political order, and opposing tyranny and despotism' (2003, p. 146). As discussed in Chapters 3 and 6, the emergence of the modern sovereign state in the 17th century sharpened the humanitarian intervention debate, as clear legal and political distinctions were made between states and individuals. The primacy of non-intervention necessarily contrived against cross-border humanitarian action yet, paradoxically, as the non-intervention norm grew it compelled states undertaking interventions to contrive a humanitarian rationale for their actions.

Colonialism was routinely justified as being beneficial to the 'savages' and portrayed as 'the white man's burden' or, in French, *mission civilatrice*. Similarly James Tyner highlights the historical tendency of the US to justify its expansion in humanitarian terms. Following the annexation of 50 per cent of the territory of Mexico in 1848, President James Polk argued that had these territories remained part of Mexico they would have been 'little value to her or any nation, while as part of our Union they will be productive of vast benefits to the United States, to the commercial world, and the general interests of mankind'. President William McKinley stated, on ordering the intervention in the Philippines in 1899:, 'we intervene not for conquest. We intervene for humanity's sake [and to] earn the praises of every lover of freedom the world over' (Tyner, 2006, p. 35–6).

In the modern era the debate about humanitarian intervention has been shaped by the framework of modern international law established in 1945 with the birth of the UN. The horror of the Holocaust catalysed significant new developments in international law and international organizations designed, at least to some extent, to ensure that egregious intra-state human rights violations could be prevented or at least halted by the international community. The UN statement of purposes included a commitment 'to save succeeding generations from the scourge of war' and 'reaffirm faith in fundamental human rights'. Rhetorical support for human rights, however, is one thing; implementing measures to constrain the capacity of states in this regard is quite another. States may well have routinely espoused their support for the idea of human rights, but they have also consistently rejected measures which they deem an infringement of their sovereignty. For example, Antonio Cassese notes that the US was one of the most vocal proponents for the inclusion of human rights in the Charter. Yet, once this was accepted the US became one of the more cautious voices during the drafting process, not least because of its racist domestic laws at that time (Cassese, 2005, pp. 377–8).

During the Cold War the norm of non-intervention was championed by the many newly independent states that saw sovereign inviolability as a bulwark against external interference. The ICJ ruled on two cases during the Cold War that involved assessing the legality of humanitarian intervention: in both the *Corfu Channel* case in 1949 and *Nicaragua v. US* in 1986 the ICJ came down in favour of the principle of non-intervention. In legal terms, therefore, the principle of non-intervention maintained primacy throughout the Cold War, although the political context was less absolute. While the norm of non-intervention was periodically abused by the rival superpowers, Robert Jackson notes that both the US and the Soviet Union always sought to justify their interventions to the wider international community as something more than pure realpolitik, as they 'could not arbitrarily cast the conventional morality of international society aside' (2000, p. 254).

Thomas Franck notes that when India invaded East Pakistan in 1971 it claimed to be doing so primarily on the basis of self-defence, but it also, though less vocally, justified the intervention as an act of humanity. Despite the fact that it was clear that India's actions had brought an end to a humanitarian crisis and facilitated the eventual independence of Bangladesh, the international community of states overwhelmingly condemned the action.

These states, Franck claims, 'felt directly threatened: not by the action itself, which elicited widespread sympathy, but by a precedent that appeared to condone the invasion of a country by a more powerful one' (2005, p. 217).

In December 1978 Vietnam invaded Cambodia, bringing an end to the genocidal regime of Pol Pot's Khmer Rouge. Like India in 1971 Vietnam claimed to be acting in self-defence, and attributed the overthrow of the Khmer Rouge to an indigenous uprising. While there was some basis for the self-defence justification, the 'two wars' idea was widely rejected and seen as a means by which the Vietnamese could justify not only taking military action to defend itself but also the more contentious decision to remove Pol Pot's regime (Wheeler, 2002, p. 88). Wheeler notes that Vietnam distanced itself from any formal humanitarian justifications, though it did describe the Khmer Rouge regime as 'inhuman' and 'monstrous' (ibid.). Vietnam's justifications for its use of force were greeted unfavourably within the United Nations, and for years after the General Assembly continued to recognize the Khmer Rouge as the rightful government of Vietnam, despite the evidence that over a million Cambodians had been killed by the government from 1975–9. Suspicions about Vietnam's motivations and its links to the Soviet Union contributed to the international opprobrium which followed the intervention.

In April 1979 Tanzania invaded Uganda and toppled the regime of Idi Amin. The international community 'responded with mute, but evident, satisfaction' (Franck, 2005, p. 219), though there were some dissenting voices (Jackson, 2000, p. 259; Wheeler, 2002, pp. 122–32). The nature of Amin's regime and the democratic credentials of President Julius Nyerere of Tanzania facilitated this reaction, as did the fact that Tanzania justified its intervention as an act of self-defence – Ugandan forces had indeed invaded Tanzania first – so as to assuage fears that a precedent would be set. This tacit support for Tanzania's actions is evidence of what Adam Roberts describes as the 'trends and disjointed moves [during the Cold War] which pointed, often ambiguously and always controversially, in the direction of accepting the legitimacy of intervention in support of an oppressed and threatened population' (2006, p. 80).

Clearly the different reactions to the Vietnamese and Tanzanian actions suggested that the context and the actors involved influenced international reaction to intervention more than the humanitarian consequences of the action. Likewise the UN was willing to acquiesce when ECOMOG militarily intervened in Liberia in 1989 and again in Sierra Leone in 1997, despite the fact that these actions did not have explicit UN authorization at the time they were launched.

As discussed in Chapter 6, many felt that the structural changes wrought by the end of the Cold War provided the context within which humanitarian intervention could become a more established and consistent practice in international relations. In 1991 the then UN Secretary General Pérez de Cuéllar stated:

> The extinction of the bipolarity associated with the cold war has no doubt removed the factor that virtually immobilized international relations over four decades. It has cured the Security Council's paralysis and helped immensely in resolving some regional conflicts. (1991, p. 2)

The UN-sanctioned action against Iraq's invasion of Kuwait in 1991 and the subsequent intervention to protect the Kurds and Shiites in northern and southern Iraq suggested that this optimism was well founded. Apart from earlier resolutions on Rhodesia and South Africa in 1977, Resolution 688 which sanctioned the collective use of force against Iraq was the first time the Security Council had described a humanitarian crisis as a threat to international peace and stability (Malone, 2006, p. 88). The action of the Security Council in this instance, coupled with the deployment of UN-mandated troops to Somalia in 1992, led to further optimism about the future of humanitarian intervention, and as Michael Smith notes, 'from about 1991–3, there existed a sort of Dudley Do-Right euphoria' (1998, p. 66). The Security Council mandated an unprecedented number of interventions under Chapter VII in the 1990s, further suggesting that a new humanitarian dispensation had achieved ascendancy. The UN, to the dismay of many in the developing world, thus appeared to be changing from an organization committed to the principles of non-intervention and the non-use of force into one associated with forceful intervention (Roberts, 2006, p.71).

This widely held belief in the imminence of a new era for the UN has been described by Mats Berdal as 'the great illusion' (2003, p. 9). As Michael Barnett notes, the proliferation of reports and commissions which enthused about the 'transformational possibilities for global politics and about the role of the UN as the prospective global deliverer' proved misplaced; soon the UN found itself unable to stop a number of situations from 'descending into chaos if not hell' (2010, pp. 21–2). As explored in Chapter 5 even the Security Council-mandated actions in the 1990s evidenced a strong correlation between action taken and the national interests of the P5. The intervention in Haiti in 1994, for example, appeared on one level to herald a new intolerance of military coups against democratically elected governments. In fact the US had an interest in stemming the flow of refugees from Haiti, while China agreed to the operation because the US promised it support for a World Bank loan (Voeten, 2008, p. 51). The response of the international community to the genocide in Rwanda and the ethnic cleansing in the former Yugoslavia also dashed nascent hopes that there was a new will to act to halt suffering. Additionally the US's retreat from Somalia in 1993 suggested that any commitment that did exist was shallow. Increased interventionism by the Security Council since 1991, Roberts cautions (2006, pp. 96–7), has additionally led to a number of 'worrying developments' which have negatively impacted on international peace and security (see Box 9.4). As Roberts's analysis highlights, many developing world states have greeted the increasingly active role of the UN with both disappointment and concern.

At the end of the 1990s, however, the intervention by NATO in Kosovo reinvigorated the optimists. Here, it seemed, was a case where states had transcended both their narrow national interests and the restrictive provisions of international law to halt suffering (see Chapter 11). The fact that the intervention was technically illegal but widely seen as legitimate dealt a blow to the system of international law and the credibility of the UN itself, as both appeared anachronistic and unacceptably restrictive. Jennifer Welsh speculated that 'historians may come to view the Kosovo intervention as the first step on the road to a post Security Council era' (2006, p. 182). Operation Allied Force sparked renewed interest in humanitarian intervention and led directly to the ICISS report, *The Responsibility to Protect*, which claimed to constitute a new formulation for the relationship between states, their citizens and the international community (see Chapter 6). This report undoubtedly had, and continues to have, an impact

---

Box 9.4 Six 'worrying developments' arising from the practice of intervention since 1991

1   The great majority of member states, having long seen the UN as an institution in which their sovereignty can be protected, are worried about any doctrine or practice that would challenge that vital UN function.
2   States may augment their national armaments to reduce their vulnerability to intervention.
3   There is a risk of the UN building up expectations of its capacity to protect threatened civilians, only to preside once again over another Rwanda.
4   Actual cases of humanitarian intervention leave the UN having to manage a series of difficult territories.
5   [Disputes over this issue add] to the mutual suspicion among states.
6   The governments of many developing countries suspect that the Western powers have down played the economic and social agenda ... because of their preoccupation with the peace and security agenda in general and military interventions in particular.

Source: Roberts (2006, pp. 96–7).

on the humanitarian intervention debate (Evans, 2008; Bellamy, 2009a), though the events of 11 September 2001 displaced this issue from the top of the international political agenda.

During the 'war on terror' the crisis in Darfur and the invasion of Iraq eroded optimism in humanitarian intervention. Many – including the Secretary General of the UN – lamented that Darfur was evidence that nothing had really changed since Rwanda, and that state interest remains the primary factor in determining when and where states will intervene (see Chapter 13). The invasion of Iraq arguably had much more of a negative impact, increasing scepticism towards any humanitarian claims made by intervening states. Following the difficulties experienced in Iraq appetite for international military intervention within the US waned. Many feared 'the Iraq Syndrome' would mean that 'persecution by [rogue] regimes of their own people will be wistfully tolerated and ignored' (Mueller, 2006, p. 189).

The intervention in Libya in 2011, however, reinvigorated the pro-interventionists. The intervention was widely heralded as ground-breaking, not least because of the nature of the authorization granted by the Security Council (Bellamy and Williams, 2011). As discussed in Chapter 14, the Council's actions were unquestionably robust, rapid and unusually unified. Debate has raged as to whether this constituted an aberration or a new disposition; the Security Council's subsequent lamentable, and very publicly divided, response to the horrific violence in Syria certainly tempered the nascent optimism prevalent after Libya. For some, the fact that Syria was an issue that the Security Council couldn't avoid discussing was progress of a kind; others, however, saw this, and the intervention in Libya, as consistent with the Council's record of inconsistency (Hehir, 2012, p. 17).

Conclusion: assessing the record

Chesterman notes that the cynical invocation of humanitarian concerns is prevalent throughout the history of interventionism: 'the rare cases of intervention that might plausibly be regarded as humanitarian in character have tended to coincide with other motives' (2006, p. 163). According to Nicholas Wheeler and Justin Morris:

in no case have states intervened when there were no vital interests at stake and/or where there were perceived to be high risks to the lives of intervening forces. This produces a pattern of intervention that is highly selective, frequently driven by considerations of national self-interest rather than humanitarian need. It also ensures that when intervention does take place it is widely viewed as morally hypocritical, a rhetorical instrument that rationalizes the projection of force by the powerful. Iraq is only the latest intervention where this long-standing critique can be strongly heard. (2006, p. 448)

In addition to this strong correlation between national interests and the exercise of purportedly 'humanitarian intervention', it is clear that when states do not have national interests at stake, the scale of human suffering has not convinced them to act altruistically. Catherine Lu notes: 'historically, the society of states has often acted like the drunken friends who desert the scene when violence breaks out' (2006, p. 10). The international inaction in the face of both the Armenian genocide in 1915 and the Rwandan genocide in 1994 seem to support this negative appraisal.

Thus the record of humanitarian intervention evidences two trends: first, the presence of a large degree of national interest whenever states have launched a supposedly humanitarian intervention; and second, a marked unwillingness amongst states to intervene when national interests are not at stake, regardless of the humanitarian suffering taking place. The following five chapters explore case studies in the post-Cold War era that have significantly influenced the debate on humanitarian intervention and provide qualitative insight into the contemporary difficulties posed by this issue.

Questions

- Is the debate regarding humanitarian intervention a function of the development of the modern state?
- To what extent, if any, has the dynamics of humanitarian intervention changed in the post-Cold War era?
- Can we identify any general trends in the history of humanitarian intervention?

Further reading

Arend, A. and Beck, R. (1993) *International Law and the Use of Force* (London: Routledge).
Bass, G. (2008) *Freedoms Battle: The Origins of Humanitarian Intervention* (New York: Vintage Books).
Bellamy, A. (2006) *Just Wars: From Cicero to Iraq* (London: Polity).
Brown, C. (2006) *Sovereignty, Rights and Justice: International Political Theory Today* (London: Polity).
Chesterman, S. (2002) *Just War or Just Peace?* (Oxford: Oxford University Press).

Danish Institute of International Affairs (1999) *Humanitarian Intervention: Legal and Political Aspects* (Copenhagen: Danish Institute of International Affairs).

International Commission on Intervention and State Sovereignty (2001) *The Responsibility to Protect: Research, Bibliography, Background* (Ottawa: International Development Research Centre), Chapters 4 and 5.

Simpson, G. (2004) *Great Powers and Outlaw States* (Cambridge: Cambridge University Press).

Weiss, T. (2007) *Humanitarian Intervention* (London: Polity), 2nd edn 2012 Chapter 2.

Wheeler, N. (2002) *Saving Strangers* (Oxford: Oxford University Press).

Chapter 10

Rwanda

The dreadful events that occurred in Rwanda in 1994 changed 'Rwanda', perhaps irrevocably, from the name of a state into a byword for slaughter and international inaction. The failure to act decisively in response to the Rwandan genocide is described by Paul Kennedy as 'the single worst decision the United Nations ever made' (2006, p. 103).

Hard as it may now be to believe, in the mid-1980s Rwanda was considered the 'Switzerland of Africa' (Hintjens, 1999, p. 244). Economic development was healthy and inter-ethnic relations, though far from being wholly harmonious, were not a source of major international concern. The descent into organized slaughter was swift, catalysed by the 'moral exclusion' of a category of people, allowing first their 'social death' and then their physical death (Uvin, 1999, p. 253). In response to the outbreak of depravity, the international community – particularly the UN and Western states – demonstrated a level of both inertia and apathy which continues to shroud their reputations.

I begin by charting the path to the genocide, particularly from 1990 onwards, and examine some explanations for the carnage. In the second section I assess the differing, though almost universally critical, perspectives on the international response, and I analyse whether more could have been done to either prevent or halt the genocide. In the final section I assess the impact Rwanda has had on the evolution of the humanitarian intervention debate, focusing on the proliferation of 'Never Again' commitments, calls for UN reform and the emergence of critical perspectives on the idea of international involvement in intra-state conflicts.

Nature of the crisis

While the disintegration of law and order in Rwanda was swift, and the speed of the genocide truly incredible, a number of historical factors – both internal and external – can be identified as having precipitated the violence in 1994. In this section I begin with a brief historical overview of the history of Rwanda in the 20th century and proceed to examine the main explanations for the genocide advanced since it occurred.

The evolution of the crisis

Present-day Rwanda was colonized 1898 – becoming part of German East Africa – although the indigenous social and political system largely remained. Following Germany's defeat in the First World War the territory, then named Rwanda-Urandi, was placed under Belgian control and administered from the Belgian Congo. The Belgians infamously based their rule on what they perceived as the existing ethnic hierarchy, thereby privileging the Tutsis over the majority Hutus (Destexhe, 1995, p. 38; Gourevitch, 1998, p. 55; Melvern, 2004, pp. 5–6).

The distinction between Tutsi and Hutu is highly contentious; while the genocide in 1994 is often portrayed as perpetrated by the Hutus against the Tutsis, and this was certainly the rallying cry of the aggressors, there is much to suggest that these distinctions are contrived 'state-enforced political identities' (Mamdani, 2001, p. 74). In 1933 the Belgians introduced ethnic identity cards which essentially froze the ethnicity of Rwandans and embedded ethnic difference in the political system (Gourevitch, 1998, p. 56). Prior to colonial administration the distinction between the Tutsis and Hutus was not deeply embedded: Tutsi and Hutu spoke, and still speak, the same language (Kinyarwanda), intermarriage was frequent and power alternated between the groups without necessarily causing ethnic conflict, although the cattle-owning Tutsis had traditionally been the political elite (Wheeler, 2002, p. 210). The Tutsis are often said to be physically distinct, especially in terms of their height, but mixed marriages have ensured that physical characteristics are largely indistinguishable, contrary to what many anthropologists think (Clapham, 1998, p. 197; Hintjens, 1999, p. 248). Tutsis and Hutus are, according to Alex de Waal, 'different strata of the same group differentiated by occupational and political status' (1994, p. 1). Regardless of whatever ambiguity surrounds 'Tutsi' and 'Hutu', these terms had become a feature of life in Rwanda since before independence in 1962 (Uvin, 1999, p. 255). Indeed, Peter Uvin argues that the idea prevalent amongst certain scholars that there is *no* difference between the two is an exaggeration and a product of a reaction against the extremist Hutu view which incited the slaughter in 1994 (Uvin, 2001, p. 77).

In 1959 Hutus rebelled against the Belgian-backed Tutsi administration and some 20,000 people were killed. In 1961 the Belgians left and the Tutsi regime was overthrown. A referendum was held in 1961 and a Hutu-dominated regime came to power under UN supervision, which lasted until 1962 when Rwanda formally became an independent state. In 1963 a Tutsi group launched a failed coup which resulted in widespread violence perpetrated by Hutus against the Tutsis. In 1973 General Juvenal Habyarimana, the minister for defence, led a coup which overthrew the regime of Gregoire Kayibanda and his Parmehutu Party. Habyarimana's supporters in the Mouvement Revolutionnaire National pour le Developpement (MNRD) were predominantly Hutu's from the north of the country who traditionally had less contact with the Tutsis than the Hutus in the south (Wheeler, 2002, p. 210). After President Habyarimana came to power discrimination in public office was practised through a quota system, especially in the army (Prunier, 1997, p. 49). Uvin agues, however, that the quota system 'served more to maintain the distinctions and allow for social control by the state than to actually discriminate' and that discrimination was not as pronounced in Rwandan civil society (1999, p. 258).

Following the overthrow of the government in 1961, thousands of Tutsis fled to Uganda where they formed militias. In 1987 Tutsi refugees in Uganda formed the Rwandan Patriotic Front (RPF) which, like its predecessor, the Rwandanese Alliance for National Unity, sought both to protect Tutsi refugees in Uganda and to return to Rwanda to take power. In 1986 the RPF helped Yoweri Museveni to overthrow Uganda's government and thereafter received material support and shelter from his regime.

On 1 October 1990 the RPF, with the support of Uganda, invaded northern Rwanda. France, Zaire and Belgium provided military support to Rwanda, which resulted in the invasion being a 'disaster' (Clapham, 1998, p. 200). While this initial military foray was unsuccessful it sparked a civil war which favoured the tactics of the RPF. The international community became involved in the situation, which, in June 1992, became engaged in extensive mediation efforts. The result was the Arusha Accords, proclaimed on 4 August 1993, which formally ended the civil war and established a new power-sharing political structure. The Accords granted a right of return to Tutsi exiles, provided equal representation for the RPF and MNRD, and reorganized the army so that representation was based on ethnic plurality. On 5 October 1993 the UN established the UN Assistance Mission for Rwanda (UNAMIR) which was to oversee the implementation of the Accords.

According to Wheeler two factors compelled President Habyarimana to seek some consolidation with the Tutsis. First, the civil war provoked by the 1990 invasion was a source of ongoing conflict and a drain on national resources. Second, President Habyarimana wanted to reform the country's political structures in line with the conditions of international aid donors. Wheeler argues that 'the peace process was doomed from the outset' as the Arusha Accords were unrealistic and unworkable. The Accords were described by some as 'a veritable coup d'etat for the RPF' (Clapham, 1998, p. 203). The Accords gave power to the smaller political parties at the expense of the extremists, though these groups had control over neither territory nor the armed forces and little popular support (Wheeler, 2002, pp. 212–14).

As soon as the Accords were signed, extremists within Habyarimana's regime, and even his own family, began killing Tutsis in an effort to scupper the peace process. Members of the Coalition pour la Defense de la Republique (CDR), established in 1992, and the *akuza* – a group of elites including Habyarimana's wife – had been deeply opposed to the peace process and were dismayed by the Arusha Accords. These groups began to organize militias such as the infamous *interhamwe* (those who stand together) and the *impuzamugambi* (the single-minded ones). These militias began as local football clubs and patriotic associations for the unemployed, but also as civil defence units established by the Rwandan government as a supplementary armed force (Melvern, 2004, pp. 20–4). Covert plans for genocide, which was referred to as the 'big job' (*akazi gakomeye*) or the 'special work' (*umuganda*), were made as the peace process took place (Hintjens, 1999, p. 268).

On 21 October 1993 the president of Burundi – Melchior Ndadaye – was killed in a military coup. As Ndadaye was a Hutu and his killers Tutsis, this strengthened the resolve of the CDR to keep the Tutsis from holding political office and reinforced the idea that the two communities could not share power. Following Ndadaye's death violence flared in Burundi and some 200,000 Hutu refugees fled to southern Rwanda. They brought tales of Tutsi oppression, causing widespread fear and panic, which pushed more people towards the Hutu extremists. Wheeler notes that by the time the Arusha Accords were finally signed there existed 'a chillingly effective organizational structure' which would later implement the genocide (2002, p. 212).

Rumours that massive violence was being planned were 'frequent', but Tutsis felt the possibility of coordinated genocide was 'unbelievable' (Hintjens, 1999, p. 270). The Carnegie Commission on Preventing Deadly Conflict (CCPDC) noted, however, that the group Africa Watch warned in 1993 that Hutu extremists had compiled lists of individuals to be targeted for retribution and that these were among the first victims the next year (CCPDC, 1997, p. 4). On 11 January 1994 Romeo Dallaire, force commander of UNAMIR, cabled the UN Department of Peacekeeping Operations (DPKO) to inform them that he had received intelligence suggesting the militias were planning to kill UN troops and aimed to exterminate 1,000 Tutsis every 20 minutes. Dallaire stated that he had been given the location of caches of weapons at sites where the massacres were to take place and requested permission to seize the weapons. The DPKO refused his request as staff felt this would exceed UNAMIR's mandate and potentially endanger UN troops. Kofi Annan, then head of DPKO, encouraged Dallaire to confront the Rwandan government with the intelligence, which Dallaire did; the Rwandan government, unsurprisingly, denied any knowledge of the plans and promised to investigate. The Security Council itself was not informed of Dallaire's warning when it met on 5 April. The Council passed Resolution 909 which commended 'the valuable contribution to peace being made in Rwanda by UNAMIR' and noted that the ceasefire had been respected.

On 6 April 1994 President Habyarimana and President Ntaryamira of Burundi, were killed when their plane was shot down. The perpetrators' identity is unknown although suspicions remain that Hutu extremists, rather than Tutsis, committed the attack. The killings began within hours; road blocks were set up across the country and identity cards were checked. This time-consuming process was superseded by murder on the basis of intelligence, suspicion and hearsay. The mass murder was coordinated by broadcasts from the radio station Radio Television Libre Mille Collines which encouraged the attackers and passed on intelligence as to where Tutsis were hiding. Moderate Hutus were also killed in their thousands in a horrific orgy of violence. Initially many Tutsis took refugee in churches and other buildings, from where they were able to fend off the poorly armed attackers. By 13 April, however, the Presidential Guard began arriving at these sites. They used grenades to flush out those hiding inside, and the militias killed those who fled with machetes and spiked clubs (Kuperman, 2001, pp. 15–16). Perhaps 250,000 were killed in the first two weeks, which equates to a figure of some 17,500 deaths per day (Kuperman, 2000a, p. 98). The death toll for the 100 days of bloodshed ranges from 500,000 to 1,000,000 depending on the methodology used. The Rwandan Ministry for Education conducted a survey which claimed some 1,364,000 had died, a figure described as 'probably too high' (Seybolt, 2007, pp. 70–1). In addition to the mass murder there were some 250,000–500,000 rapes (Weiss, 2007a, p. 62).

The genocide came to an end when the RPF began to overcome the government forces and establish control of Kirgali. The RPF were a more efficient military force and thus able to defeat the numerically superior government forces, who were more concerned with killing civilians than fighting the RPF (Seybolt, 2007, p. 71). On 22 June the French intervened in the south-west of the country, creating safe areas into which many thousands of the perpetrators of the genocide fled.

Explaining the genocide

The details of the atrocities committed provides us with a glimpse of the truly cruellest aspects of humanity's capacity for violence (see Box 10.1). Acts of coordinated mass violence such as this are not akin to murder committed in a fit of rage or psychopathic tendencies: rationale people chose to execute this slaughter and mobilized thousands to their cause, and thus, despite the egregious cruelty, it is possible to explain this seemingly irrational act.

While we may be able to explain the path to genocide, there is no single, simple explanation (Hintjens, 1999, p. 280). Uvin's review of the literature

on the endogenous causes of the genocide highlights three broad explana-
tory categories (2001, pp. 81–5). First is the suggestion that the violence
was caused by elite manipulation and the proliferation of racist ideology;
the *akuza* in particular are singled out as architects of the violence, driven
by a desire to maintain their privileged social and political positions. Uvin
suggests, however, that racism was widespread throughout Rwanda, albeit
not uniformly so, and thus the elites were 'both manipulative and manipulated' (ibid., p. 81). The second explanation relates to resource scarcity; the
burgeoning population created social tension as groups struggled to
survive. Indeed, Rwanda had one of Africa's highest population growth
rates and the highest population density in Africa for a predominantly rural
country. The third category identified by Uvin is the socio-psychological
features of the perpetrators. These explanations focus on the supposedly
obedient nature of the Rwandans and the resultant ability of the elites to
order the Hutu masses to commit genocide. Uvin is not convinced by this
explanation: 'at the same time that Rwandans are described as obedient and
docile; they are also described as distrustful, lying, and dissimulating –
features that contradict greatly the former' (ibid., p. 85).

A focus purely on endogenous causes is surely flawed and quite possibly
racist. The conflict was often portrayed as a function of 'ancient tribal
hatreds': indicatively John O'Shea of the NGO GOAL stated: 'two groups
are bent on destroying each other ... the dispute is ethnic ... There is out
and out hatred between the two groups' (Joras and Schetter, 2004, p. 320).

Box 10. 1   The horror

The next morning [1 May], at about 10 a.m., twenty-two soldiers returned
under the command of Lt. Ildephonse Hategekimana, head of the Ngoma
camp. After telling the displaced people that they would not be killed but
would be taken to prison, he called in the civilians to do the killing. A witness who was hidden heard the children crying and the women begging. He
heard the 'dull blows, followed by small cries', which he supposed were the
sounds of children being clubbed to death. Then, after an hour, silence.
There had been 476 people in the church, 302 of them children. Some victims were taken off to be killed in the nearby woods, a number of the women
raped ... It rained in the late morning, but when the rain ended in the early
afternoon, killers came to finish off the wounded children who were still
alive, lying on the grass. As they were clubbing them to death, a vehicle
belonging to the Ministry of Health appeared and several officials got out.
The killers chatted with them while continuing to club the children on the
ground. After the officials left, the killers pillaged the remaining rice stocks
of the church as payment for their 'work'.

Source: Des Forges (1999).

This 'ethnic hatred' explanation was encouraged by the perpetrators themselves, who 'portrayed the situation as one of uncontrollable spontaneous ethnic violence' (de Waal, 1994, p. 2). The extremists facilitated that strain of thinking in the international community, and the global media opposed intervention on the basis that this was an irrational conflict immune to external council (Melvern, 2004, p. 235). The idea of racial difference and ethnic enmity was certainly exploited by the killers, and indeed at times by the RPF, but this was no more than a highly effective myth (Hintjens, 1999, p. 251; Mueller, 2000, p. 42).

In fact, a number of external factors, as well as internal developments and trends, contributed to the explosion of violence. The basis of the Tutsi/Hutu distinction owed much to the colonial legacy which cemented this division. Additionally, while Rwanda was considered to be a positive economic model in the 1980s, it was heavily dependent on external aid and revenue from coffee. Receipts from coffee fell during 1986–7 from US$14 billion to US$5 billion, and thus Rwanda's debt increased as a result of external factors rather than domestic mismanagement (Hintjens, 1999, p. 256). In June 1990 the World Bank and the IMF forced Rwanda to implement structural adjustment packages which resulted in the currency being devalued by two-thirds. Farming incomes dropped sharply and budget restraints led to healthcare and food shortages. Rather than blame the international financial bodies, the Tutsis were portrayed as the cause of the decline in living standards.

Rwanda was but one of many African states which received support from Western countries during the Cold War despite its lack of democracy. This changed in the early 1990s when 'the international community suddenly rediscovered its attachment to democracy' (Uvin, 1999, p. 259). Aid was made conditional on democratization, which forced President Habyarimana to initiate domestic reforms (Collins, 2002, p. 160). This angered the Hutu elite and the army, who were opposed to any Tutsi involvement in government, and, in an effort to consolidate his constituency, Habyarimana responded to democratization 'by rallying the majority "faithful" against a purported common racial enemy, hoping in this way to prevent regional and class divisions from finding more open political expression' (Hintjens, 1999, p. 242). Despite the dubious way Habyarimana and his clique adapted to democracy, France maintained steadfast support for the regime (Kroslak, 2007, pp. 99–108). Gerard Prunier notes that France's 'blind commitment' to the Rwandan government had 'catastrophic consequences because as the situation radicalized the Rwandanese leadership kept believing that no matter what it did, French support would always be forthcoming' (1997, p. 108). French motivations for supporting Habyarimana against the RPF stemmed in part from a perception that Uganda and the United Kingdom were attempting to displace France's power base in Africa (Clapham, 1998, p. 199; Shawcross, 2001, p. 106).

Writing on the genocide in Rwanda is often, unsurprisingly, punctuated with moral outrage and highly charged superlatives. Mahmood Mamdani, however, writes of the 'three silences' which also characterize the writing on Rwandan genocide (2001, pp. 7–8). The first concerns the history of genocide, whereby many authors 'write as if the Rwandan genocide had no precedent ... For Africans it turns into a Rwandan oddity; and for non-Africans the aberration is Africa'. The second silence relates to the perpetrators of the genocide: Mamdani argues that there has been a tendency to ignore the role played by the masses who committed the killings and a preference for portraying the violence as 'exclusively a state project'. The third silence surrounds the portrayal of the genocide as a function of forces within Rwanda, which ignores the 'regional processes' which contributed to the carnage. Mamdani claims that the genocide was a 'natives' genocide': that is, an act committed by those who had previously been subjugated and victimized, and who saw their task as cleansing their land of a 'threatening alien presence' associated with the former colonial power. It was genocide committed by those who sought to affirm forcibly their power and even, paradoxically, their humanity (ibid., p. 14).

International response

The international reaction to the genocide has become the main focus of academic inquiry into events in Rwanda in 1994. The international community, in particular Western states and especially the US, have been strongly criticized for their inaction. In this section I initially provide an overview of the international response and then assess the claims that more could have been done to stop the massacre.

International reaction

On 7 April the prime minister of Rwanda, Ms Uwillingiyimana, a Hutu, and ten Belgian peacekeepers protecting her were murdered. The intention appears to have been to scare the international contingent in UNAMIR into leaving: the strategy worked. The Belgian government rapidly pulled out all its troops, stating in a letter to the UN Secretary General that UNAMIR was 'pointless' and 'powerless in the face of the worsening situation'. Belgian soldiers faced an 'unacceptable risk ... making continuation of the Belgian presence impossible' (UN Security Council, 1994). French troops flew into Kirgali to evacuate only foreign nationals, even leaving behind Rwandan staff in the French embassy.

UNAMIR's mandate, as per Resolution 872, was to monitor the cease-fire and the implementation of the Accords rather than engage in peace enforcement. Cognizant of this, Daillaire stated: 'the minute there is a significant ceasefire violation by either side ... my mandate does not exist here anymore' (Wheeler, 2002, p. 214). When the violence erupted and the UN troops themselves became targets, the UN Secretariat and DPKO appear to have decided to extricate UNAMIR before more UN troops were lost in what was claimed to be a civil war. Michael Barnett, a US diplomat at the UN at this time, states that while there was 'a brief discussion' about the possibility of UNAMIR intervening to halt the escalating violence, 'I was (and still am) unaware of a single member state who offered their troops for such an operation ... the Secretariat, who would be responsible for carrying out the mandate, was silent, and silence was widely interpreted as disapproval (1997, p. 559).

On 10 April, much to his dismay, Dallaire was told to prepare for withdrawal. According to Alison des Forges, the Hutus saw this as evidence that nothing would be done by the UN, and therefore the genocidal government would succeed at leading those who initially hesitated to take part in the genocide to take up arms (2000, p. 141). Dallaire and his small contingent were left to watch as the massacre unfolded. By 11 April Dallaire recalls his reaction to a cable from the UN in New York asking for more information: 'what more could I possibly tell them that I hadn't already described in horrific detail? The odour of death in the hot sun; the flies, maggots, rats and dogs that swarmed to feast on the dead' (Dallaire, 2004a, p. 289).

On 20 April 1994 UN Secretary General Boutros Boutros-Ghali outlined three options to the Security Council. The first was the deployment of thousands more troops under a Chapter VII mandate to force a ceasefire. The second involved scaling UNAMIR down to some 270 troops to engage in negotiations and assist the humanitarian relief operation. The third option was the complete withdrawal of UNAMIR. Wheeler argues that this proposal was based on an erroneous reading of the violence as the product of a 'tribal war'. He argues that portraying the situation as civil war rather than genocide enabled the United States, France and the UK to legitimize their decision not to intervene (2002, pp. 220–21). On 21 April, in what now appears an incredible move, the Security Council, on which ironically Rwanda then sat, voted to reduce UNAMIR to 270 troops. Wheeler argues that there was clearly no way UNAMIR could act effectively under its existing mandate, but this did not mean all UN troops had to be withdrawn; the alternative was 'a change of mandate and the deployment of an effective fighting force' (ibid., p. 222).

On 28 and 29 April the Security Council met to discuss the situation. Representatives from the Czech Republic and New Zealand urged the

Council to call the situation 'genocide' and initiate more robust action. The Secretary General also urged the Council to reconsider its troop pull-out. On 29 April the ICRC issued what Linda Melvern describes as 'the most strongly worded statement in its history', outlining the horror of the violence (2004, p. 225). The Security Council released a statement which quoted from the Genocide Convention but did not use the word 'genocide'. The Secretariat produced a plan to increase the UNAMIR force to 5,000 but according to Barnett this proposal was 'merely symbolic and highly impractical', as these troops would not be deployed for months and no one explained what their role would be (1997, p. 560).

On 17 May the Security Council passed Resolution 918 which referred to 'the killings of members of an ethnic group with the intention of destroying such a group in whole or in part'. This Resolution modestly altered UNAMIR's mandate and agreed to increase its number to 5,500 troops. According to Simon Chesterman, however, 'intense lobbying by the United States' ensured that the deployment would take place in two phases, with phase one comprising merely 150 unarmed observers and 800 Ghanaian soldiers deployed to secure the airport (2002, p. 145). Samantha Power (2001) argues that 'staying out of Rwanda was an explicit US policy objective', and she claims the US 'aggressively worked to block the subsequent authorization of UN reinforcements'. Resolution 925 on 8 June noted that 'acts of genocide have occurred in Rwanda' and issued a call for member states to 'respond promptly' to the Secretary General's request for resources. Logistically this phase II deployment could have taken up to three months to organize.

Then on 18 June France announced that it was willing to launch an intervention to establish a safe area in south-west Rwanda. This came as a significant relief to the US and the UK, who were pleased that an intervention was taking place without their involvement (Kroslak, 2007, p. 215). On 22 June the Council, somewhat reluctantly given the suspicions about France's motives (see the next section), passed Resolution 929 which sanctioned 'the establishment of a temporary operation under national command'. On the same day Operation Turquoise was launched and 2,500 French Foreign Legion troops entered Rwanda. According to Chesterman the main contribution of the French safe areas 'was to save the genocidaires from Tutsi-led retribution' (2002, p. 147), while Seybolt claims the Hutus sheltering in the safe areas 'contributed directly to two civil wars in Zaire in 1996 and 1998–2003 that killed more than 3 million people (mostly by disease) and destabilized the entire great lakes region' (2007, p. 76). On 22 July the US, with the support of the UK, launched Operation Support Hope to provide humanitarian assistance in and around Rwanda. Following the genocide tens of thousands of Hutus were killed in reprisal attacks (Uvin, 2001, p. 75).

Could more have been done?

Since the genocide members of the international community, academics and humanitarian NGOs have routinely stated that more could have been done to stop the genocide (see Box 10.2). Dallaire railed against 'inexcusable apathy by the sovereign states that made up the UN that is completely beyond comprehensible and moral acceptability' (Shawcross, 2001, p. 115). Prunier describes the international response as a 'mixture of realpolitik, humanitarian self-satisfaction, half-baked ideology, stale imperialism and economic blackmail' (1997, p. 341). Preventing 'another Rwanda' has become an oft-used rallying cry uttered to justify international interventions and engagements since. At the time, however, there were those who claimed that the violence was born from ingrained psychological tribal forces which could not be stopped (Des Forges, 1999). This perspective has lost appeal, and few now make these spurious claims.

What then is the basis for the claim that more could have been done? Key to this view is the fact that international actors were present in Rwanda prior to the outbreak of the genocide and should have noticed that plans were afoot. Wheeler notes that the CIA warned that 500,000 would die if the Arusha Accords failed and that France must have known that there was an appetite for genocide amongst the many Hutu soldiers French troops had trained (2002, p. 216). France launched Operation Amaryllis on 8 April to evacuate its staff, military officers and certain members of Habyarimana's inner circle, including his wife. The French troops deployed during this operation left on 14 April, and Daniela Kroslak notes that during this week they witnessed many atrocities and gathered extensive first-hand information on the true nature of the crisis (2007, p. 176). The evacuation of the French embassy was particularly swift, and French staff took care to shred all documents within the building. Kroslak argues: 'it is difficult not to wonder whether the French

---

Box 10.2   5,000 troops ... 500,000 lives?

The panel generally agreed that early military intervention – within two weeks of the initial violence – by a force of 5,000 could have made a significant difference in the level of violence in Rwanda and that there was a window of opportunity for the employment of this force during April 7–21, 1994. The group acknowledged that such a force would have had to be properly trained, equipped, and supported, and possess a mandate from the Security Council to enable it to use 'all means necessary' to protect vulnerable populations. In Rwanda in 1994, it is likely that 5,000 troops could have averted the slaughter of a half-million people.

Source: CCPDC (1997, p. 6).

government possessed information, owing to its close involvement, that justified such a reaction' (ibid., pp. 200–1).

Two days after the Arusha Accords were signed, Belgian intelligence warned that anger within the army was rife and violence was likely (Collins, 2002, p. 169). Timothy Docking argues that the US knew 'from the outset' that Hutus were planning genocide but the Somalia syndrome 'clearly contributed to the administration's failure to act' (2008, pp. 215–16), a view shared by Prunier (1997, p. 274). The UN 'Independent Inquiry into the Actions of the UN During the 1994 Genocide in Rwanda' noted that following the death of Habyaramana the US, Italy, France and Belgium moved swiftly to evacuate their personnel in what appears to have been anticipation of an upsurge of violence, yet these states did not share any intelligence with UNAMIR (UN, 1999, p. 47).

Many point specifically to the cable sent by Dallaire to the DPKO on 11 January which warned that mass killings were being planned. In the cable Dallaire (1994) noted that a 'top level' informant had passed on worrying information:

Principal aim of Interhamwe in the past was to protect Kigali from RPF. Since UNAMIR mandate he has been ordered to register all Tutsi in Kigali. He suspects it is for their extermination. Example he gave was that in 20 minutes his personnel could kill up to 1000 Tutsis.

This cable did not set alarm bells ringing in the DPKO, which refused Dallaire's request to seize weapons caches and did not pass this information to the Security Council. Dallaire claims the return cable from Kofi Annan 'caught me completely off guard', and he notes that 'I was beside myself with frustration' (2004a, p. 146). Kofi Annan has since expressed his regret at his decision, further supporting the idea that more could have been done at this juncture (BBC News, 2004). Had UNAMIR begun seizing weapons it would have required more troops and they would likely have acted as a deterrent (Wheeler, 2002, p. 218). Wheeler cautions, however, that, even if the Security Council had been informed of Dallaire's cable, 'it is not at all certain that this would have encouraged them to send extra troops' (ibid., p. 222).

The reluctance to deploy more troops to Rwanda stemmed from the legacy of the deployment in Somalia and the UN's own unwillingness to endanger another of its operations. A speculative cable from Dallaire, which today seems eerily prescient but at the time was perhaps one of many warnings dispatched to the DPKO, was unlikely to convince the UN Security Council to alter radically UNAMIR's mandate and increase its troop numbers. Alan Kuperman notes that Dallaire's cable only identified 135 weapons, whereas some 20,000 rifles and 500,000 machetes were eventually used (2000a, p. 113). Dallaire (1994) also warned in his cable that the intelligence may have been a 'set-up'. Kuperman argues that Dallaire's expression of concern could only have strengthened the DPKO's caution. This is not a convincing argument, however. Had the cable been the only correspondence between Dallaire and the DPKO then it is plausible that those equivocal aspects of the cable highlighted by Kuperman may have convinced the DPKO to reject the request to seize the caches. In fact Dallaire recalls that, following Kofi Annan's response forbidding the seizure, he 'made phone call after phone call to New York' explaining the need to carry out the raids (2004a, p. 146).

When the killings began, the situation on the ground was confused and information passed to the Security Council by the Secretariat was sketchy. Because the members of the Council had little independent information on what was happening, they largely relied on the Secretariat. Human Rights Watch notes that 'the secretary-general's special representative, Roger Booh-Booh minimized both the extent and the organized nature of the slayings', and thus the Security Council was provided with faulty information (Des Forges, 1999). Additionally, because many journalists left the country, the massacres outside Kirgali were not witnessed, so by 11 April international reports suggested that the killings had stopped or at least slowed down considerably, despite the fact that in rural Rwanda the exact opposite was the case (Kuperman, 2000a, p. 102). Prunier notes that because of the 'technical impossibility of catching the killers in the act' there were no television images of the genocide, and this had a major impact because 'in contemporary Western society events not seen on a TV screen do not exist' (1997, p. 274).

Nonetheless, by the second week of the killings evidence was emerging, not least from UNAMIR's commander, that the violence was a systemic attempt to kill Tutsis. France in particular continued to claim that the violence was a civil war, and called for a ceasefire despite the mounting evidence indicating genocide (Kroslak, 2007, pp. 194–9). By late April, representatives of the Czech Republic, Spain, New Zealand and Argentina pressed for more information and looked beyond the Secretariat. The information they received convinced them that genocide was occurring, and they called for more robust action. If these countries of modest international standing and intelligence capability could independently determine that genocide was occurring, then it is surely logical to assume that the P5 could have also done so – or perhaps they did, and decided to ignore the information.

In 1998 President Clinton flew to Rwanda. Although he stayed only a matter of hours and did not leave the airport, his visit was heralded by some as atonement for the US actions in 1994. In his speech Clinton stated:

We did not act quickly enough after the killing began ... We did not immediately call these crimes by their rightful name: genocide ... It may seem strange to you here ... but all over the world there were people like me sitting in offices, day after day after day, who did not fully appreciate the depth and the speed with which you were being engulfed by this unimaginable terror. (*New York Times*, 1998)

Clinton thus suggested that his administration simply did not know how bad the situation was, the implication being that more would have been done had they known. Kuperman argues that an analysis of UN reports, the reports of leading human rights organizations and international media coverage, including the CIA's Foreign Broadcasting Information Service, indicates that President Clinton could not have known about the genocide until 20 April (2001, p. 24). In fact, classified documents obtained through a freedom of information request in the US reveal that the Clinton administration received daily briefings from the CIA. On 23 April a CIA briefing described the situation as genocide, although the Clinton administration refused to use the term publicly until 25 May, when it acknowledged that 'acts of genocide' were occurring. Des Forges described the documents as 'powerful proof that they knew' (Carroll, 2004), while Power (2001) claims that the documents 'reveal that the U.S. government knew enough about the genocide early on to save lives, but passed up countless opportunities to intervene'.

Aside from the question about how much was known, there is evidence that intervention after the killings began would not have been as effective as some have claimed. It has been often suggested that a force of 5,000 troops could have been deployed to stop the killings. Taylor Seybolt argues, however, that because the killings were carried out with 'lightning speed', early intervention would have saved some tens of thousands of victims but not the majority who died (2007, p. 71). Had Dallaire's request on 10 April for 5,000 troops been heeded and acted upon, Kuperman states, it would have taken ten days to deploy these troops. By 20 April, however, half the total number of deaths had already occurred (Kuperman, 2001, pp. 84–5). Thus, Kuperman states, 'although some lives could have been saved by intervention at any point during the genocide, even a large force deployed immediately upon recognizing the genocidal intent would have arrived too late to save even half of the ultimate victims' (ibid., p. 2). Of course 'even half of the ultimate victims' amounts to some 400,000 people, which clearly cannot be dismissed, although it seems clear that, once the carnage began, any intervention force would have arrived too late to save the hundreds of thousands killed in the immediate outbreak of violence. The only way the genocide could have been prevented, Kuperman argues, was if UNAMIR been reinforced several months before the outbreak of genocide (2000a, p. 116).

The lack of action taken by the international community has led to speculation that certain states, especially France, were causally involved and had a vested interest in the completion of the genocide (Collins, 2002, p. 159). Uvin rejects this, noting that 'there are no genius mad-men, collective hysteria, or hidden sinister international complots' (2001, p. 97). Nonetheless France's role is open to question. The French had a long standing relationship with the Habyarimana regime and were certainly supportive of efforts to defeat the RPF. As the genocide unfolded France acquiesced in the inaction, and despite its strong ties to the country, failed to take the lead in pushing for greater action or provide information on events on the ground. As the Rwandan government began to buckle under pressure from the RPF, France suddenly expressed its willingness to intervene in an effort, according to Wheeler, 'to demonstrate to Africa and the rest of the world that France was no paper tiger and that it could project power rapidly on the continent' (2002, p. 233). The French force deployed was not equipped for a humanitarian mission and acted more as a traditional blue line around the south-west of the state. Bruce Jones offers three explanations for French action, gained from confidential interviews he conducted with French governmental officials: first, to secure northern Zaire from refugee flows; second, to demonstrate French power to the Security Council; third, to downplay negative domestic criticism (1995, p. 231).

Criticism of the international response has been a dominant feature of analyses of the genocide. The Security Council, according to Dallaire, 'floundered in the face of mounting heaps of bodies growing daily' (Shawcross, 2001, p. 119). The International Panel of Eminent Personalities of the Organization of African Unity conducted a review which stated:

> There can be not an iota of doubt that the international community knew the following: that something terrible was underway in Rwanda, that serious plans were afoot for even more appalling deeds, that these went far beyond routine thuggery, and that the world never the less stood by and did nothing. That does not mean that the world knew that by 1992 or 1993, genocide was systematically being planned and organized. In fact it seems to us likely that hardly anyone could bring themselves to believe this was the case. (Uvin, 2001, p. 91)

With globalization, 24-hour media channels and, not least, a UN peacekeeping force on the ground, it seems incredible that carnage on this scale was somehow kept secret. Refugees who fled Rwanda and the many mutilated bodies that flowed down the River Nyabarongo into Lake Victoria and neighbouring Uganda and Kenya certainly constituted evidence that something horrendous was happening (Destexhe, 1995, p. 49). It is difficult not to conclude, therefore, that while it was not clear that the situation was as egregious as we now know it was, there was sufficient evidence to warrant a far more robust international response.

Impact on the debate

Books and articles on humanitarian intervention published since 1994 invariably mention the Rwandan genocide as the archetypal case where more could have been done and intervention was warranted. The following sections outline three broad aspects of the impact Rwanda has had on literature on humanitarian intervention since.

Never again!

The refrain 'never again' was uttered in the wake of the Holocaust and catalysed a raft of human rights legislation (see Chapter 5). The many atrocities committed during the Cold War, in particular the Cambodian massacres in the mid-1970s, undermined the perceived commitment of the international community to the 'never again' refrain, but the genocide in 1994 constituted a uniquely 'staggering indictment' of the 'never again' commitments (Jones, 1995, p. 247). While the 1948 Genocide Convention was signed as a means by which the international community could halt such atrocities, the impact of this treaty in 1994 was limited to forcing Western states, and the United States in particular, into contriving ever more imaginative ways to describe the killings without using the 'g word', often provoking ridicule in the process (see Frontline, 2004). As William Schabas notes, this reluctance stemmed from a perception that use of the term triggered an obligation to intervene (2000, p. 496).

During the crisis certain world leaders rejected the idea that the international community had an obligation to halt suffering on this scale. President Clinton stated that US troops could not be sent to every trouble spot where Americans were 'offended by human misery', while French President François Mitterrand claimed that 'the international community could not act as a global police force and send peacekeepers to all the places where people fight' (Wheeler, 2002, pp. 229, 235). Such public disavowals of an obligation to act were far less frequent when the scale of the slaughter was made public (Weiss, 2007a, p. 99).

In the wake of the genocide, 'never again' once more gained currency. The rights afforded to sovereign states were increasingly questioned (Jones, 1995, p. 226; Chatterjee and Scheid, 2003, p. 4). Rwanda was one of the 'immediate stimuli' for the ICISS report, *The Responsibility to Protect* (Weiss, 2007a, p. 88; see Chapter 6). Indeed, the report opens with the words, 'we want no more Rwandas' (ICISS, 2001a, p. xiii). During NATO's intervention in Kosovo UN Secretary General Kofi Annan (1999c) stated:

> To those for whom the greatest threat to the future of international order is the use of force in the absence of a Security Council mandate, one might ask – not in the context of Kosovo – but in the context of Rwanda: If, in those dark days and hours leading up to the genocide, a coalition of States had been prepared to act in defence of the Tutsi population, but did not receive prompt Council authorization, should such a coalition have stood aside and allowed the horror to unfold?

In October 2001 Tony Blair stated that if something akin to Rwanda happened again, 'we would have a moral duty to act' (Fisher, 2007, p. 102). In justifying intervening in Libya in 2011 US Secretary of State Hillary Clinton referred to the lessons of Rwanda when the US government 'failed'; other prominent members of the Obama administration, including Susan Rice and Samantha Power, who pushed for intervention in Libya, cited the inaction in 1994 as an ongoing influence on their foreign policy outlook (Harris, 2011).

The barbarity in Rwanda led to a rise in the currency of the 'new wars' thesis, whereby analysts 'stress[ed] the irrational and uncontrollable nature of modern conflicts, alleged to be driven by a dangerous internal dynamic' (Collins, 2002, p. 158). Mary Kaldor indicatively wrote about identity politics as the cause of these conflicts (1999, p. 8). Such conflicts demanded external intervention, which global civil society could help to bring about by pressuring recalcitrant governments to take action (see Chapter 3. Indeed, Wheeler argues that the eventual French intervention was a product of domestic pressure within France for action, generated by media and NGO reports. Had global civil society mobilized more effectively, he argues, the Security Council might have been shamed into action (Wheeler, 2002, pp. 236–41).

Catherine Lu argues that had the idea of 'sovereignty as responsibility' been touted prior to 1994, the international community would have been legitimately entitled, if not required, to jam the radio stations that helped to coordinate the genocide (2006, p. 121). Similarly following the adoption of the idea of a 'responsibility to protect' in the 2005 World Summit 'Outcome Document', the then UK foreign secretary, Jack Straw, claimed that had this provision existed in 1994 thousands of lives could have been saved (Wheeler, 2005, p. 96).

Yet, while Rwanda sparked great outrage at the immorality of sovereign inviolability, the lack of intervention in 1994 had nothing to do with sovereignty: Wheeler notes that 'the principle of sovereignty was never raised ... no state tried to defend the UN's stance of non-intervention on the grounds that genocide fell within Rwanda's domestic jurisdiction' (2006, p. 36). The intervention in Kosovo in 1999 was routinely justified as atonement for Rwanda, yet the crisis in Darfur in 2003 had more obvious parallels with the situation in Rwanda, and a similar record of inaction has been the defining feature of the international response. There is some doubt, therefore, as to whether the outpouring of moral outrage and commitments to act evident since 1994 has had any real impact on the record of humanitarian intervention since. In the context of the conflict in Darfur Steve Crawshaw of Human Rights Watch highlighted the hypocrisy:

> There was much editorial soul-searching in April [2004] over the failures to chronicle the Rwandan genocide that had taken place 10 years earlier. That soul-searching was, however, accompanied by an almost complete disregard for the crimes against humanity that were being committed in Darfur at the very same time ... Even when the UN Secretary-General, Kofi Annan, used his Rwanda anniversary speech on April 7 to address the subject, few newspapers took much notice. A colleague noted: 'The international media don't seem to send reporters to cover genocides. They cover genocide anniversaries'. (Crawshaw, 2004)

The need for UN reform

Whenever a humanitarian crisis erupts people look to the UN for a solution. As the UN has no standing army and is dependent on the will of its member states to act, especially the P5, inaction in the face of tragedy is often not a function of a deficiency within the UN despite the criticism it invariably endures. The case of Rwanda in 1994 is different: the UN itself, particularly the DPKO and the Secretariat, were culpable of pronounced failings. On 31 May 1994 the Secretary General, Boutros Boutros-Ghali, lamented:

> We must all recognise that ... we have failed in our response to the agony of Rwanda, and thus have acquiesced in the continued loss of human life. Our readiness and capacity for action has been demonstrated to be inadequate at best, and deplorable at worst, owing to the absence of the collective political will. (Holzgrefe, 2005, p. 17)

The UN Independent Inquiry into the Actions of the UN During the 1994 Genocide in Rwanda found:

> The failure by the UN to prevent and subsequently to stop the geno-
> cide in Rwanda was a failure by the UN system as a whole. The funda-
> mental failure was the lack of resources and political commitment
> devoted to developments in Rwanda and to the UN presence there ...
> although UNAMIR suffered from a chronic lack of resources and
> political priority, it must also be said that serious mistakes were made
> with those resources which were at the disposal of the UN. (UN, 1999,
> p. 3)

Michael Barnett argues that the UN Secretariat, and particularly the
DPKO, failed in its task, which undermined the response of the Security
Council. The Secretariat 'thoroughly violated its professional obligations
and ethical duties' by suppressing critical information and providing the
Security Council with briefings which suggested that the violence was
simply a continuation of the civil war (Barnett, 2002, p. 174). Des Forges
(1999), the author of Human Rights Watch's 1999 review of the genocide, strongly criticized the UN for 'having failed to provide adequate
information and guidance to members of the Security Council'.
Additionally, according to Barnett, UN Secretary General Boutros
Boutros-Ghali 'emanated indecision to the point of paralysis, if not
complacency' (1997, p. 559).

The reluctance to act on the information provided to the DPKO by the
force commander of UNAMIR was a product of a fear among UN officials that a poorly executed mission would 'fatally harm the legitimacy of
the whole organization', and yet the failure to act had precisely this effect
(Cronin and Hurd, 2008, p. 11). Barnett argues that the UN calculated
that it had more to lose by taking action and being associated with
another failure than it did by not taking action and allowing the genocide
in Rwanda to occur (1997, pp. 561–2). Geoffrey Robertson went so far
as to accuse the UN of 'assisting with genocide' and being 'complicit in a
crime against humanity' (2002, p. 73).

This led to calls for reform of the UN and specifically initiatives to
increase the UN's early warning capacity (Jones, 1995, p. 232; Barnett,
2003, p. 175). Additionally the UN policy of neutrality in its peacekeeping operations was questioned: if, as ostensibly was the case in Rwanda,
there was an obvious aggressor, what was the point of maintaining a
non-partisan approach? According to Clapham, 'to remain "neutral", in
the way that a UN force was bound to do, was to be condemned, as eventually happened, to impotence' (1998, p. 206).

Despite the provisions of the Genocide Convention, the UN failed to
respond to the most aggressive act of genocide since the Holocaust, and
the utility of the Convention itself was questioned (Klinghoffer, 1998, p.
105). In 2001 Kofin Annan (2001) described the Genocide Convention

as a 'dead letter'. The lack of a military response derived in no small part from the fact that the UN lacked the capacity to launch an intervention without the support of the Security Council and the will of member states to supply troops. Calls for intervention made by states with modest military capacity in 1994 were, therefore, essentially calls for states with the necessary military capacity to take action (Wheeler, 2002, p. 227). This paradox is succinctly captured by Barnett, who notes caustically that 'the international community seemed willing to fight down to the last U.S. citizen' (1997, p. 572). Even if smaller states such as New Zealand and the Czech Republic had been willing to volunteer troops, as indeed Ghana and Senegal eventually were, these states lacked the capacity actually to deploy their troops, and were reliant on major states to provide the finances and logistical support. Thus, in light of this failing, radical reforms were proposed involving a standing UN army or rapid reaction force (Johansen, 2006). No concrete steps have been taken to implement these proposals, although in the wake of the crisis in Darfur (see Chapter 13) such proposals have regained some currency (Weiss, 2009, p. 180; Pattison, 2010, p. 229; Hehir, 2012).

Critiquing intervention

The genocide in Rwanda also led to a questioning of the very efficacy of both peacekeeping and humanitarian intervention. While, as already noted, many lamented the international community's 'failure to act' and the UN's inadequate preventative capacity (Evans, 2008, p. 79), others argued that the lesson of Rwanda was actually that international intervention, in the form of peacekeeping, mediation or military intervention, often had deleterious consequences (Kuperman, 2001, pp. 109–10).

Uvin notes that following the genocide scholars, policy makers and journalists engaged in 'collective self-flagellation'. In addition to lamenting their own, and the international community's, failure to act, they cried out for action to strengthen the capability of the international community to intervene before and during humanitarian crises. He argues, however, that there has been little public criticism of this position, although it 'may well be incorrect' (Uvin, 2001, p. 89). Anne Orford notes that Rwanda has become emblematic of the 'need for early action', yet she argues that 'surprisingly little attention has been paid to the presence and activity of international institutions and agencies ... prior to the outbreak of violence' (2003, p. 85). The idea that the genocide occurred because of a lack of international involvement is thus questioned, with certain authors arguing that international involvement was in fact pronounced and, most damningly, a causal factor in the eventual slaughter. The fact that the genocide was sparked by a number of external factors, such as the legacy of colonial rule, the structural adjustment programmes of the World Bank and the IMF, the pressure put upon Habyarimana in the early 1990s to democratize and the externally brokered Arusha Accords, suggested to some that international intervention was part of the problem, and thus calls for greater international involvement were counter-intuitive (Collins, 2002; Williams, 2005, p. 113).

The genocide was blamed by many observers on the unwillingness of the international community to get involved in Africa. Clapham argues, however, that 'this claim can scarcely be made in the case of the Rwandan conflict, where the international community, led by regional states and the Organisation of African Unity, took an active role in attempting to negotiate a solution from a very early stage' (1998, p. 200). James Mayall notes that 'in many ways the pre-genocide Rwanda peace process was exemplary' (2006, p. 136), while Wheeler argues:

> It has become an accepted truism to claim that preventative diplomacy is always better than a belated intervention when things start to go wrong. However, the lesson of the Arusha process is that outside intervention aimed at averting a civil war can have unintended consequences that produce human wrongs on an unimaginable scale. (2002, p. 214)

Jones similarly points to the fact that for at least three years prior to the genocide the international community was deeply involved in Rwanda: 'the ultimately catastrophic failure of those efforts should give pause for thought to those who believe that the appropriate response to Rwanda is to fashion an intrusive international regime of preventive intervention' (1995, p. 226).

There thus began to emerge a view that 'the liberal bias in peacemaking (in Rwanda) ... not only fails to alleviate human insecurity or promote emancipation but may even help create the conditions for further violence' (Bellamy, 2005c, p. 32). Thus preventive diplomacy, as clearly practised in Rwanda from 1990–4, is not universally heralded as a necessity (Clapham, 1998, pp. 203–4). The eventual French intervention, as previously noted, had mixed, if not in fact ultimately negative, results, and thus served to further tarnish the image of international intervention. While few argued that a policy of non-intervention should be maintained in the face of genocide, some concluded that it was perhaps best to stay out of intra-state conflicts as such disputes, like the American Civil War, can only be resolved by the parties themselves and probably through the defeat of one side by the other (Luttwak, 1999).

Conclusion

Speaking at a conference to mark the ten-year anniversary of the genocide, Dallaire claimed:

> I still believe that if an organisation decided to wipe out the 320 mountain gorillas [in Rwanda] there would be still more of a reaction by the international community to curtail or to stop that than there would be still today in attempting to protect thousands of human beings being slaughtered in the same country. (BBC News, 2004)

The international reaction to the crisis in Syria in 2012 is cited by some as evidence that, as Dallaire suggests, little has changed since 1994 despite the general acceptance that more should have been done.

Hindsight, of course, provides crystal clarity. It seems obvious today that the genocide was years in the planning and immediately obvious from 6 April 1994 onwards. Uvin, however, cautions that 'predicting an actual genocide was much more difficult than usually suggested' (2001, p. 90). Hitler infamously, though arguably accurately, remarked that no one remembered the Armenians despite their wholesale slaughter at the hands of the Turks in 1915. International reaction to the Turkish actions was minimal, and the event was soon consigned to the dark recesses of history. Unlike the Armenian genocide, however, the Rwandan genocide took place during the post-Cold War era of unprecedented global communication, when international cooperation against oppression was ostensibly more practicable. Thanks to the new globalized media we now know the gruesome details of what happened in 1994, and Rwanda will not, therefore, suffer the same fate as Armenia. This is surely cold comfort, however, for the 800,000 victims of the slaughter and the many more who continue to live with the scars.

Rwanda shattered any tentative conviction that the post-Cold War era had catalysed an attitudinal sea-change amongst Western states. The inaction seemed evidence that narrowly conceived national interests continued to dominate. Wheeler claims that President Clinton 'squandered a golden opportunity to make the case that the moral obligation to protect human rights in Rwanda was in conformity with an enlightened view of US national interests' (2002, p. 240). Whether Rwanda altered the view of states concerning their national interests is a matter of some contention, although, lamentably, the evidence against this view is compelling.

Questions

- What do you consider to have been the primary causes of the genocide in Rwanda?
- Could more have been done to prevent or halt the genocide?
- What lessons does the genocide in Rwanda have for the international community?
- To what extent does Rwanda demonstrate the dangers inherent in international intervention in intra-state conflicts?

Further reading

Barnett, M. (2002) *Eyewitness to Genocide: The UN and Rwanda* (Ithaca, NY: Cornell University Press).

Dallaire, R. (2004) *Shake Hands with the Devil: The Failure of Humanity in Rwanda* (London: Arrow).

Des Forges, A. (1999) *Leave None to Tell the Story: Genocide in Rwanda*, Human Rights Watch. Available at: www.hrw.org/legacy/reports/1999/rwanda/index.htm#TopOfPage.

Gourevitch, P. (1998) *We Wish to Inform You that Tomorrow we will be Killed with Our Families* (London: Picador).

Klinghoffer, J. (1998) *The International Dimension of Genocide in Rwanda* (Basingstoke and New York: Palgrave Macmillan).

Kroslak, D. (2007) *The Role of France in the Rwandan Genocide* (London: Hurst).

Kuperman, A. (2001) *The Limits of Humanitarian Intervention: Genocide in Rwanda* (Washington, DC: Brookings Institution Press).

Mamdani, M. (2001) *When Victims Become Killers: Colonialism, Nativism and the Genocide in Rwanda* (Princeton, NJ: Princeton University Press).

Melvern, L. (2004) *Conspiracy to Murder: The Rwandan Genocide* (London: Verso).

UN (1999) 'Report of the Independent Inquiry into the Actions of the UN During the 1994 Genocide in Rwanda', S/1999/1257, 15 December. Available at: www.un.org/News/dh/latest/rwanda.htm.

Uvin, P. (1998) *Aiding Violence: The Development Enterprise in Rwanda* (West Hartford, CT: Kumarian Press).

Wheeler, N. (2002) *Saving Strangers* (Oxford: Oxford University Press).

Chapter 11

Kosovo

NATO's intervention in Kosovo in 1999 constitutes one of the defining moments in post-Cold War IR; the significance of the campaign is described by Nicholas Wheeler as 'immense' (2002, p. 242). The fusion of many major IR themes generated great interest in the intervention, its origins and possible repercussions, and a subsequent plethora of academic investigations. NATO's intervention in Kosovo constitutes a decisive juncture in the history of humanitarian intervention with which all serious scholars of this issue must engage.

Significant disagreements exist over NATO's 'true' motivation, the nature of the conflict between the Serbs and the Kosovar Albanians, and the diplomacy that led to the launch of Operation Allied Force. In this chapter I engage with these questions but seek to address in greater detail those aspects of the campaign that had implications beyond Kosovo and which influenced the trajectory of the debate on humanitarian intervention.

I initially provide an overview of the crisis in Kosovo, highlighting those factors that led to the crisis in 1998–9. In the second section I assess the diplomatic role played by the international community in the ten years before the initiation of the air-strikes and the nature of the intervention itself. In the final section I analyse the impact Operation Allied Force had on the debate about humanitarian intervention and the differing perspectives on its merits.

Nature of the crisis

The history of the conflict in Kosovo is arguably as divisive an issue as NATO's intervention. Much of the violence in the Balkans in the 1990s was attributed to 'ancient ethnic hatreds', thereby suggesting the different ethnic groups were irreconcilably driven by past grievances (Kaplan, 1993). While in Kosovo 'history is war by other means' (Judah, 2000, p. 1), it is an exaggeration to attribute the violent implosion of the Socialist Federal Republic of Yugoslavia (SFRY) exclusively to historical legacies. According to Mark Mazower, a 'less jaundiced' understanding requires us to situate the Balkans in a broader European context which highlights that events there have been driven by 'more sweeping narratives of the development of European identity and civilisation' (2003, pp. 14–15). The crisis in Kosovo in 1999 did have deep historical roots, but as the IICK asserted 'the latest round of violence cannot be explained merely by reference to this history' (2000, p. 33).

A number of events in the early 1980s – the death of Tito in 1980, the global economic crisis and ongoing dissatisfaction with the provisions of the 1974 constitution – led to tensions among SFRY's constituent republics (Serbia, Croatia, Bosnia, Macedonia, Montenegro and Slovenia). In 1981, Albanian students at the University of Pristina protested at their poor facilities, and within weeks this had developed into a pro-independence rally. The Kosovo Serbs were shocked that the ethnic Albanians, who had seemingly benefited so much from the 1974 constitution, would protest so fiercely. The police launched a crackdown and the Kosovo Communist Party was purged. Nonetheless, many Serbs still felt that Albanians dominated the political system in Kosovo, and many left the province with (often unsubstantiated) tales of oppression, Albanian-inspired ethnic violence and the widespread rape of Serbian women (Mertus, 1999). The new post-Tito political climate was more tolerant of the public airing of grievances, although nationalism was still officially condemned as counter-revolutionary. In 1986 the Memorandum of the Serbian Academy of Sciences and Arts was published outlining the plight of the Serbs in Kosovo. There then began a spiral of allegations and counter-allegations proffered by the Serbs and the Albanians in Kosovo. The public disagreements soon embroiled other nations, and the issue of Kosovo became a catalyst for the emergence of nationalism throughout the SFRY in the mid-1980s (Horton, 1992; Pesic, 1996, pp. 33–4).

In 1989 Slobodan Milosevic, the then President of Serbia, repealed Kosovo's autonomy within Serbia. Previously Kosovo, like the northern province Vojvodina, was an autonomous province within Serbia, enjoying significant political independence. In response the majority of the members of the Kosovo Assembly met and declared independence for Kosovo. The change in Kosovo's legal status in 1989 and Belgrade's implementation of certain discriminatory laws between 1989 and 1991 are widely acknowledged as the starting points of the phase in Kosovo's history that culminated in NATO's intervention. The changes in 1989 are portrayed by supporters of NATO's later intervention as indicative of Milosevic's long-held bias against the Kosovar Albanians (Gow, 2003), while those who opposed NATO's intervention either downplay the significance of 1989 or suggest that the lack of Western action at the time shows how little the West really cared about the Kosovar Albanians, thereby contradicting the concern voiced over their plight ten years later (Jatras, 2000, p. 23).

From 1990 to 1995, in stark contrast to the violence elsewhere in the Balkans, an uneasy peace existed in Kosovo. The Kosovo Albanian majority operated a 'phantom state' whereby schools, hospitals and taxes were administered by the unrecognized local regime, while Serbs continued to adhere to rule from Belgrade. In 1995 the Dayton Peace Accords were signed primarily to end the conflict in Bosnia. The lack of any provision relating to Kosovo in the Accords is widely regarded as having inflamed the Kosovar Albanians (Hedges, 1999, p. 31). Dayton was 'an extraordinary trauma for the Kosovar Albanians', who were dismayed that their policy of peaceful civil resistance had been ignored (Judah, 2000, p. 124). The Accords are regarded by some as having sounded the death knell for the pacifist politics pursued by the largest Kosovo Albanian party, the Democratic League of Kosovo, led by Ibrahim Rugova, as the Kosovo Liberation Army (KLA) exploited the widespread dissatisfaction and began to step up its armed campaign (see Box 11.1). As Carl Hodge states, 'in effect Dayton told autonomists in Kosovo that the metal in Kosovo was not hot enough to bring about political change. The KLA decided to make it glow' (2000, p. 26). There followed an escalating cycle of retaliatory violence between the KLA and FRY's police and military, resulting in thousands of deaths, hundreds of thousands of internally displaced persons and thousands more refugees leaving Kosovo for neighbouring Albanian and Macedonia. The KLA adopted a strategy of provoking Belgrade into

---

Box 11.1   The rise of the KLA

In January 1982 the Gërvalla brothers established the Popular Movement for the Republic of Kosovo (LPRK). In 1993 the LPRK split into two factions, the Popular Movement for Kosovo (LPK) and the National Movement for the Liberation of Kosovo (LKCK). Those in the LKCK were Marxist-Leninists who sought to provoke a mass uprising. The LPK, the forerunners of the KLA, were committed to guerrilla tactics and were not ideologically homogeneous (Hedges, 1999, p. 58). In May 1993 the KLA claimed their first victims when two Serb policemen were shot in Glogovác. The KLA were a fringe group throughout much of the 1990s, and by 1997 their membership, mainly comprising families and local tribes, was about 150. In 1997 a 'Ponzi' pyramid scheme collapsed in Albania and the country descended into chaos. The KLA poured across the border and looted the abandoned army barracks. The KLA was soon well armed and financed but their numbers, though on the increase, remained small. By late 1997, the cycle of reprisal killings between the KLA and the Serb authorities was gaining momentum and, exploiting the high levels of disenchantment with peaceful politics, the Serbian crackdown and the 70 per cent unemployment rate in Kosovo, the KLA grew exponentially in size.

launching excessive counter-attacks in order to generate domestic support and, more importantly, force the international community to condemn the Milosevic regime and ultimately intervene on the side of the Kosovar Albanians (Gow, 2003, p. 256; Kuperman, 2006).

By autumn 1998 Kosovo was at the top of the international agenda, with Security Council Resolution 1199 describing the situation as a threat to peace and stability in the region and empowering the Council to act under Chapter VII of the UN Charter. The number of deaths in the year prior to NATO's intervention is estimated at 500, with some 400,000 people displaced (Wheeler, 2002, p. 269). The death toll is low compared with say Rwanda, but it was routinely stated at the time that without international action Milosevic would increase his oppression of the Kosovo Albanians and ultimately the death toll would rise drastically. The situation was often said to be analogous to that of the early stages of the war in Bosnia, and the eventual carnage in 1995 was proffered as the likely consequences of inaction in Kosovo (Hehir, 2006). The true scale of the suffering in the region was a source of debate; according to Gordon Bardos 'there was no humanitarian crisis in Kosovo in 1997, or in 1998, or in 1999 in any conventionally understood sense of the term' (2003, p. 57), whereas Timothy Garton-Ash claims that 'anyone who was in Kosovo, as I was, in the winter of 1998–9 could see that there was a humanitarian disaster' (2000, p. 2).

International response

The international response to Kosovo culminated in the 1999 military intervention. International engagement with the region was not always this direct, however. The following sections outline the various phases of international engagement.

1989–98: distracted superpowers

The crisis in Kosovo had been brewing since at least 1981, and many observers and fact-finding groups had warned that the situation was liable to explode. According to the IICK:

> From the 1980s onwards, Kosovo exhibited all the signs of a catastrophe waiting to happen ... the failure to respond adequately at an early stage of the evolution of the conflict created difficulties in later stages. At each stage of the conflict, the diplomatic options narrowed. (2000, 62)

While the break-up of SFRY was unquestionably a cause of great international concern, Kosovo was sidelined by the more violent conflicts between Serbia, Croatia and Bosnia. Before March 1998 the response of the international community to the situation in Kosovo was limited and reactive (Gow, 1994; Bellamy, 2002, p. 37). A number of NGOs had reported on the situation in the region, but official international political engagement was extremely limited and a number of opportunities for constructive engagement were missed (IICK, 2000, p. 51).

Given that Kosovo's explosive potentiality was so widely discussed, it is paradoxical that it didn't receive the attention its reputation should have commanded. On Christmas Eve 1992 the outgoing Bush administration issued the so-called 'Christmas warning'. Lawrence Eagleburger, acting US Secretary of State, sent a cable to the US chargé d'affaires in Belgrade with the instruction that the contents be read to Milosevic in person. The message stated: 'in the event of conflict in Kosovo caused by Serbian action, the US will be prepared to employ military force against Serbians in Kosovo and Serbia proper'. This warning was endorsed by the Clinton administration. As the situation in Kosovo degenerated, especially after 1995, this commitment increasingly became an embarrassment as inaction prevailed (IICK, 2000, p. 344; Bellamy, 2002, p. 50). Whereas from 1993 to 1999 in Macedonia a coordinated international conflict prevention mission was largely successful, Kosovo was ignored. Marc Weller writes of the 'schizophrenic' nature of the international response which acknowledged Kosovo's explosive potentiality but acted according to 'a hope that the situation would go away if ignored for a sufficiently long time' (1999, p. 33).

Alex Bellamy suggests three reasons why Kosovo was so marginalized in the various international diplomatic processes (2002, pp. 24–6). First, prior to 1998 there was not an alarming level of violence in Kosovo. While allegations of oppression were made by NGOs such as Amnesty, Save the Children and Oxfam, and particularly by Tadeusz Mazowiecki, the UN special rapporteur on human rights in the former Yugoslavia, it seems that the only statistics that would prompt an international response were those relating to deaths, and these did not become significant until 1998 (Daalder and O'Hanlon, 2000, p. 9). The second reason was that it was felt that to engage with the secessionists in Kosovo would have sparked a similar cry for secession from the Serbs in Croatia and Bosnia and further destabilize the region. The final reason is that those seeking independence were not in control of the territory they sought independence for. Had the Kosovars been in positions of political, judicial and military power in Kosovo, as the Croats and Slovenes were, then the international community may have countenanced the separation.

October 1998–March 1999: diplomatic failure

By mid-1998 the number of internally displaced persons and refugees fleeing to Albania and Macedonia ensured that Kosovo could no longer be ignored. According to the World Refugee Survey, Kosovo ranked in the top five globally for the number of refugees and internally displaced people, with the total figure an estimated 300,000. The credibility of the West, and NATO in particular, diminished as the conflict escalated without resolution. The more NATO threatened action and yet failed subsequently to do anything, the more the Milosevic regime appears to have concluded that nothing would ever happen (Weller, 1999, p. 398; Bellamy, 2002, p. 124).

A settlement was negotiated in October 1998 but failed to hold in large part because the chief US negotiator, Richard Holbrooke, gave personal assurances that the KLA would comply with the agreement, assurances later described by the IICK as 'ill founded' (2000, p. 149). The KLA did not abide by the agreement, and by the end of the year the cycle of retaliatory violence resumed. On 15 January 1999 Serb forces moved into the town of Racak in central Kosovo. The following day, media from around the world broadcast images of 45 dead ethnic Albanians, all purported to be civilians. International opinion turned sharply against Milosevic and the momentum in favour of more robust international involvement grew.

At the end of January the Contact Group (the United States, the United Kingdom, France, Russia, Germany and Italy) summoned all relevant parties to attend negotiations at Rambouillet, France, on 6 February. The next day NATO issued a statement threatening to use force against any party which did not attend and to any group which was the cause of a breakdown in the forthcoming negotiations. According to Weller, this 'remarkable' summons involved NATO 'acting as it were as the enforcement agent of the Security Council, albeit a self-appointed one'. Weller describes the NATO threat as 'entirely unprecedented in post UN Charter history and somewhat reminiscent of an exercise of Great Power diplomacy in the classical balance of power system of the post Napoleonic Concert of Europe' (1999, p. 397). NATO's threat did not merely suggest that the parties had to attend Rambouillet, it stipulated that they must reach an agreement there, based on a plan drawn up by the Contact Group. Indeed, Holbrooke described Rambouillet as 'a very legitimate attempt to bring the parties together to force them to agree' (Frontline, 2000).

Ultimately the Rambouillet negotiations broke down when the representatives from FRY rejected an agreement which the Kosovar Albanian delegation signed. Whether the negotiations were conducted fairly is a matter of some controversy. Some argue that the NATO powers contrived a situation whereby FRY would be cast as spoiler, thereby clearing the way for a bombing campaign. The provisions of Appendix B(8) (see Box 11.2) in particular have been cited as consciously unpalatable to Belgrade (Hagen, 1999, p. 59; Gowan, 2000, p. 8). Rambouillet is variously described as 'Albright's charade to get a bombing campaign', 'a textbook example of how not to practice diplomacy' and as having constituted

---

Box 11.2   The Rambouillet Accords

Appendix B(8): NATO personnel shall enjoy, together with their vehicles, vessels, aircraft, and equipment, free and unrestricted passage and unimpeded access throughout the FRY including associated airspace and territorial waters. This shall include, but not be limited to, the right of bivouac, maneuver, billet, and utilization of any areas or facilities as required for support, training, and operations.

'an inherently unstable' agreement (Jatras, 2000, p. 24; Layne, 2000, p. 15; Bandow, 2000, p. 33). Noam Chomsky argues that there was in fact no 'failure' at Rambouillet, but rather what happened 'was the rationally chosen course that led to a predictable victory for the values that mattered, with the fate of the populations as an incidental concern' (1999, p. 108).

The counter-perspective suggests that, while certain mistakes were made, Rambouillet was a genuine attempt to broker an agreement. Bellamy, while outlining a number of Western diplomatic errors during the negotiations, ultimately suggests that the Yugoslavs had a 'lack of interest in the diplomatic process' and that 'Milosevic had already decided that he would test NATO's resolve and go to war' (2002, pp. 147, 150). Although he describes Rambouillet as 'more a shambles then a grand design', Weller concludes that it was 'a heroic failure' given the earnest attempts made to reconcile the parties (1999, p. 392). He dismisses the argument that the contentious provisions of Appendix B were responsible for the Serb unwillingness to sign as 'conspiracy theories' (ibid., p. 397). The IICK detailed many of the flaws in both the deal proposed at Rambouillet and the manner in which the negotiations were pursued, particularly in relation to NATO's intransigence on the issue of Appendix B. While they argued that compromising on this aspect of the deal was 'an obvious negotiating opening that might have broken the impasse', they ultimately concluded: 'the minimum goals of the Kosovar Albanians and of Belgrade were irreconcilable' (IICK, 2000, pp. 157, 161). Either way the breakdown of the negotiations led directly to the initiation of NATO's air strikes.

24 March 1999–10 June 1999: intervention

On 24 March NATO began air-strikes against FRY. Support for the strikes was strong among the NATO states with the exception of Greece. Within the Security Council both China and Russia strongly opposed NATO's actions, as did India. The Russian foreign minister claimed the bombing constituted 'a strike against Russia' (Bellamy, 2002, p. 166). Additionally many of the West's tradition allies, such as Japan, Indonesia and South

Korea, far from being supportive of NATO, were 'mute in their response' (ibid., p. 167). The provisions of the Uniting for Peace resolution (see p. 104) which enables the General Assembly to act when the Security Council is unable to reach agreement on what action to take, were, according to Nigel White, 'conveniently forgotten in the case of the Kosovo crisis' (2000, p. 41). Indeed, prior to NATO's intervention it was suggested to the UK Foreign Office that NATO could use the Uniting for Peace provision, but this was rejected because officials felt it was highly unlikely that two-thirds of the General Assembly would vote in favour of NATO's actions (Chesterman, 2003, p. 57).

The international response to NATO's action was thus mixed if not negative. Critics of this assertion point to Russia's failed attempt to have Operation Allied Force condemned by the Security Council and to the support afforded to the operation by the Organisation for Islamic Conference (OIC) (Caplan, 2000: 24). While the 12–3 Security Council vote against Russia's draft resolution appears conclusive, Wheeler has noted that the result was less emphatic than it appears. He points to the fact that five of the 12 who voted against the resolution were members of NATO and only three of the remaining seven spoke in support of the intervention (2002, p. 291). Additionally, White notes that 'lack of condemnation by the Security Council cannot be seen as an authorization to use force' (2000, p. 33). The OIC's support for the intervention was largely the consequence of an expression of solidarity with Kosovo's predominantly Muslim population rather than support for the idea of humanitarian intervention per se. Indeed, 50 of the 57 members of the OIC were among the 133 states in the G-77 that voted twice in the wake of the intervention to condemn unconditionally the notion of unilateral humanitarian intervention.

Military advice stated categorically that the campaign would not be a short one (Clark, 2001, p. 185). This advice appears to have been ignored by NATO's political hierarchy, who continued to claim that Milosevic would quickly capitulate. The day the air strikes began, US Secretary of State Madeleine Albright stated: 'I don't see this as a long term operation. I think that this is something … that is achievable within a relatively short period of time' (Daalder and O'Hanlon, 2000, p. 91). However, Albright later stated that when President Clinton said to her on 25 March, 'This is not going to be over quickly', she replied, 'I feel the same way. Nobody should ever think that we had gone into this without our eyes wide open' (Sciolino and Bronner, 1999, p. 3). Similarly, two weeks into the campaign she proclaimed, 'We never expected this to be over quickly' (Layne, 2000, p. 11). The campaign itself lasted 78 days, resulting in 10,000 deaths, including those Kosovars killed by Yugoslav forces. NATO flew 38,400 sorties and dropped 26,614 air munitions. The US flew over 60 per cent of all sorties and carried out over 80 per cent of all strike sorties.

In his televised address on the first day of bombing President Clinton stated: 'I do not intend to put our troops in Kosovo to fight a war' (*New York Times*, 1999, p. 15). This categorical pledge is seen by many as an error as it let the FRY army know that they would not have to plan for a NATO ground intervention. To avoid Serbian anti-aircraft fire NATO planes flew above 15,000 feet, and this had three major consequences for the campaign. First, this made the targeting of FRY infantry, tanks and police units much more difficult. These components of the FRY military were most responsible for the ground operation within Kosovo yet they escaped the bombing relatively unharmed. Second, targeting from such a height depended on clement weather conditions, and when there was cloud cover the air strikes had to be halted, prolonging the campaign and negating the impact on the FRY military. Third, bombing from these heights increased the instances of 'collateral damage'. The IICK estimates that NATO bombs killed 495 civilians while HRW puts the figure at 527 (IICK, 2000, p. 94). Certain targets were harder to identify, and this resulted in strikes against civilian convoys and trains and the widespread bombing of decoy targets.

The enduring images of the NATO intervention are of Kosovar refugees huddling in makeshift camps in Macedonia. The unity of resolve among NATO members held in large part because of this refugee flow, and Ivo Daalder and Michael O'Hanlon speculate that, had Milosevic's forces not embarked upon this course of action, 'NATO could have lost the war' (2000, p. 6). NATO's resolve was severely tested at times, particularly early on in the campaign. After the first night the Italian Communist Party threatened to pull out of the coalition government, while 98 per cent of the population in Greece opposed the initiation of the military campaign (ibid., p. 167).

The activities of certain elements of the FRY military and police forces were used as a central justification for the bombing. According to the IICK over 90 per cent of the Kosovar population was displaced during Operation Allied Force (2000, p. 90). Advocates of NATO's intervention argue that it was necessary, because of the actions of FRY after the intervention began, and claim that Milosevic always planned to 'cleanse' Kosovo of its Albanian population (Robertson, 2002, p. 441). In defence of this argument certain observers have claimed the existence of 'Operation Horseshoe' – a military plan to forcibly expel the Kosovo Albanians, allegedly uncovered by Bulgarian intelligence and passed on to the German army prior to Operation Allied Force. While some doubt exists as to the authenticity of this plan (Chomsky, 1999, pp. 35–6; Judah, 2000, pp. 240–1), even if it is accepted that it was real, this begs the question posed by Bellamy:; 'if Operation Horseshoe was known about, why was so little done to prepare the UNHCR and other agencies to receive refugees in Albania and Macedonia?' (2002, p. 165).

NATO's intervention unquestionably led to a dramatic increase in ethnic cleansing, with Misha Glenny accusing NATO of having 'contributed to a flood of biblical proportions' (1999, p. 658). Despite numerous warnings, and the predictions of senior military figures like General Clark, few preparations were made for the refugee crises that erupted. In a 6 March meeting, Madeleine Albright had asked General Clark, 'if we commence the strikes will the Serbs attack the population?'. He replied, 'almost certainly' (Clark, 2001, p. 173). Yet General Clark later noted that 'one of the most obvious features of the conflict was the West's lack of preparedness when the conflict actually began' (ibid., p. 423).

This lack of preparedness was strongly criticized by human rights organizations, and particularly by Macedonia, which felt the brunt of the refugee exodus. A UN High Commissioner for Refugees (UNHCR) report following the campaign noted that 'UNHCR received no advance warning from any government or other source', and asserted that prior to Operation Allied Force NATO governments had in fact been urging the organization to prepare for the implementation of the Rambouillet Accords (Judah, 2000, p. 240). The longer the campaign went on without halting the ethnic cleanings, the more NATO's strategy and capacity were called into question. Defeating the FRY military and stemming the tide of refugees thus became a matter of enormous political importance for NATO's member states and the very credibility of the organization itself (see Box 11.3).

The termination of the NATO air strikes came on 10 June, when the FRY army and NATO signed the Military Technical Agreement. Though heralded in some quarters as a capitulation by Milosevic, the provisions of the peace plan were considerably less draconian than those presented at Rambouillet, leading Simon Chesterman to ask, 'why were the terms presented to Serbia at Rambouillet more onerous than those offered after a 78 day bombing campaign?' (2003, p. 54). Significantly Appendix B had been removed from the Military Technical Agreement and the deployment of NATO was no longer a *sine qua non*. The IICK noted that 'the final agree-

---

Box 11.3   NATO credibility?

What Milosevic never really understood was this wasn't a conflict strictly about Kosovo. It wasn't even a conflict ultimately about ethnic cleansing. It was a battle about the future of NATO, about the credibility of the United States as a force in world affairs. And the longer it went on the more clearly the nations of the West could see those issues.

Source: General Clark (quoted in Prokopijevic, 2004, p. 187).

ment did contain some gains from the FRY point of view' (2000, p. 96), and Security Council Resolution 1244 which endorsed this agreement recognized FRY's territorial integrity and Belgrade's jurisdiction over Kosovo. Of course, all FRY military had to leave Kosovo, and they have not returned.

Impact on the debate

Operation Allied Force catalysed intense international debate about the merits of NATO's intervention and also about the broader issue of humanitarian intervention. Opinion was sharply divided on a number of key issues, and the intervention propelled the issue of humanitarian intervention to the top of the international political agenda.

A war fought for values

While many humanitarian NGOs, such as Amnesty International and HRW, were critical of the manner in which Operation Allied Force was executed (see pp. 238–40), the intervention was favourably received by many global civil society activists and those keen to enable the enforcement of human rights. NATO's action was seen to 'represent the wave of the future' (Fuller, 1999, p. 12) and many heralded the dawn of a new age of human rights. Geoffrey Robertson described Operation Allied Force as 'the first war waged for ethical principles alone', and but one of many 'hopeful signs that we are indeed entering the third age of the human rights revolution: the era of enforcement' (2002, pp. 451, 387).

The intervention, supporters argued, highlighted the changed attitudes of Western states and the power of global civil society to influence foreign policy. Constituting 'the first war of humanitarian intervention ever carried out by the Western military powers' (Coll, 2001, p. 128) the extensive humanitarian rationale espoused by the intervening states – such as Tony Blair's statement that this was a war fought for 'values' (Chatterjee and Scheid, 2003, p. 7) – suggested that the pressure exerted by proponents of human security had effected change. Bellamy argues that the intervention pointed to 'a heightened degree of liberal institutionalism in global politics' and illustrated the 'extent to which international values and interests have begun to come together during the 1990s' (2002, pp. 211–14). Wheeler and Dunne highlighted the UK's particularly important role in pushing for the intervention and hailed the Blair government as a 'norm entrepreneur' (1998, p. 177). Operation Allied Force thus was held to illustrate the capacity of the human rights movement and global civil society to compel Western states to alter their priorities from narrow national interests towards a universal concern with human security (Thomas and Tow, 2002, p. 178).

This apparent new concern with morality, and specifically human rights, amongst the West was correctly deemed of major significance. Traditionally, states had demonstrated a pronounced unwillingness to act in defence of others where there were no national interests involved. The attitudinal sea-change ostensibly highlighted by Operation Allied Force created the prospect of greater humanitarian activism, increased coercive enforcement of human rights norms and the development of Western foreign policy based on universal values rather than national interests. In the wake of Operation Allied Force, therefore, significant optimism prevailed, amongst those eager to prioritize human security, that Western states were finally prepared to act on their humanitarian commitments and forge a new international system based on human rights. HRW (2000) described the 1999 interventions in Kosovo and East Timor as indicative of a new era for human rights in which Western states would use their military to come to the aid of victims of atrocities.

'The new military humanism'

Those opposed to the intervention argued that Kosovo highlighted a disturbing trend towards greater Western interventionism and the unwarranted expansion of Western interests. The moral arguments were considered either entirely hypocritical or foolhardy. This perspective is manifest in (broadly) two forms: a left-wing and a realist critique.

Left-wing critics argued that NATO's action was inspired by the desire to proliferate capitalism and project power into Eastern Europe. The argument that NATO was compelled by moral concern was deemed implausible given the West's history of oppression (Chomsky, 1999, p. 74). The edited collection *Masters of the Universe* presented the intervention as a purely self-interested exercise in great power domination with humanitarianism serving as a consumer friendly veneer: Operation Allied Force was 'all about US global hegemony' (Wood, 2000, p. 190). Diana Johnstone similarly argued that NATO, far from being driven by a sense of moral duty, was motivated 'quite simply by the desire to demonstrate NATO's new mission in time for its fiftieth anniversary' (2000, p. 8). This new mission constituted an effort by American liberals and European social democrats to maintain the illusion that they were determined to pursue social justice. Maya Chadda asserted that the real motive behind the intervention was 'to establish hegemonic influence enabling [NATO] to structure interstate relations in the region and be able to punish and reward states that deny the contour of political/ideological order advantageous to the hegemonic state' (2003, p. 321). David Chandler argued that

Operation Allied Force constituted an escalation of an already prevalent Western disposition towards legitimizing greater influence in international affairs through the discourse of human rights and the establishment of a compliant international community subordinate to Western cultural and political values (2002, p. 17). NATO's action was thus seen by many on the left as the precursor to greater Western expansionism and an attempt to subvert the existing norms in international relations.

Many realists argued that the intervention set a dangerous precedent which would destabilize the international system. Stanley Kober argued that NATO's illegal action would anger other countries, lead to the rapid degradation of international law and culminate with the world 'primed for major conflict' (2000, p. 117). Douglas Bandow suggested that the intervention 'deepened European dependence on America for defence of European interests that have little relevance to America' and 'put US military personnel at risk without any serious, let alone vital, US interest at stake' (2000, p. 31). Michael Mandelbaum (1999) argued that the intervention severely strained relations with Russia and China and also destabilized the wider Balkans.

Realists are inherently sceptical of, if not actively hostile to, the influence of morality in international relations, and the idea of rejecting formal legal authority in favour of moral authority is deemed undesirable. As explored in Chapter 7, the question 'who decides?' is of paramount importance; international law comprises a hierarchical structure which provides an answer to this question, whereas morality is, by definition, subjective and devoid of formal authoritative structure. Thus the move to moral authority seemingly signalled by NATO's intervention disrupted the existing authoritative structure with potentially destabilizing effects.

So while the left-wing and realist critiques shared a scepticism about the moral imperative cited by NATO, and both viewed the intervention as a strategy of expansion, they differed in their views on this expansionism, with the left seeing it as capitalist oppression and the realists decrying unsustainable over-extension.

International law after Kosovo

The dominant rationale advanced by NATO in 1999 was the moral imperative to aid the Kosovar Albanians (Guicherd, 1999, p. 19). However, certain NATO states also advanced a legal justification in tandem with the more prominent humanitarian argument. The three NATO states on the Security Council argued that their actions were consistent with Security Council Resolutions 1160, 1199 and 1203. While these resolutions did empower the Security Council to act under Chapter VII, there is no obvious provision in any of the three that could be said to constitute a trigger for collective, let alone unilateral, military intervention. The then UK defence minister George Robertson stated: 'we are in no doubt that NATO is acting within international law. Our legal justification rests upon the accepted principle that force may be used in extreme circumstances to avert a humanitarian catastrophe' (Holbrook, 2002, p. 141). This principle permitting the use of force in extreme circumstances to prevent a humanitarian crisis was certainly not 'accepted', as the legal debate which followed testified. The UK House of Commons Foreign Affairs Select Committee concluded that NATO's military action was 'of dubious legality in the current state of international law' (House of Commons, 2000, para. 1138) – and this is the dominant view, although NATO still officially maintains that its action was in accordance with international law (Hehir, 2008b, 2009a).

While NATO did not gain Security Council approval for its actions, the intervention was justified by its supporters on the grounds that positive law, and especially the Security Council veto, had to be subverted by the moral need to intervene. Jane Stromseth (2005) argued that the intervention demonstrated that deviation from international law could be legitimate in 'exceptional circumstances'. The majority of the supporters of the intervention did not rejoice in the fact that the UN was ignored but rather used this case to highlight the ostensibly anachronistic nature of existing international law. Many turned to natural or moral law in preference to positive law as a means by which to justify this 'illegal' action.

The controversy surrounding the legality of NATO's actions thus led to increased speculation about the key tenets of international law and its very utility. David Armstrong and Theo Farrell note that Kosovo revelled in the tension between law and legitimacy more starkly than even the later intervention in Iraq (2005, p. 13). The legality of NATO's actions, and unilateral humanitarian intervention more generally, became a subject of intense debate amongst scholars of IR and international law. As was discussed in detail in Chapter 5, the majority view was that international law did not permit humanitarian intervention of the kind prosecuted by NATO, although perhaps it should and one day might (Ambos, 1999; Cassese, 1999; Simma, 1999). This debate catalysed a comprehensive review of the existing tenets of international law and especially the process of customary law formation (Hehir, 2009b).

The debate reignited the issue of authority and legitimacy in international relations (see pp. 146–52). The Security Council may well have formal legal authority but many felt it lacked legitimacy. The refusal of China and Russia to support measures to forcibly halt the oppression of the Kosovo Albanians was deemed to be indicative of both states' general reluctance to look beyond narrow national interests when deliberating at the Security Council (Bellamy, 2002, p. 212). If authority is distinguishable from power by the perceived legitimacy of the formally authoritative actor (Hurrell, 2005, p. 16) then the Security Council, by virtue of China and Russia's membership, had lost its legitimacy, although it retained its formal legal authority. Remarkably similar arguments were made in 2012 in the context of the response to the situation in Syria (see Chapter 14).

The IICK found that Operation Allied Force was 'illegal but legitimate', and noted that this disjuncture required action (2000, p. 10), a view later supported by ICISS (2001a, p. 3). Thus, many argued that, rather than viewing Operation Allied Force as indicative of NATO's disregard for legal norms, it should be seen as the catalyst for much-needed amendments to international law and the UN Charter in particular (Simma, 1999, p. 6; Guicherd, 1999, p. 20). The call for reform also came from critics of NATO's intervention, who argued that the existing provisions governing the use of force for human protection were inadequate and widely perceived as such, and therefore constituted a potential pretext for unilateral action. States could justify bypassing the UN by pointing to its anachronistic provisions, thereby potentially legitimizing any illegal use of force and undermining the very basis of international law (Hehir, 2008a, pp. 121–30).

Finally, more broadly, the legal controversy led many to question the utility of international law. Certain observers argued that, given the veto powers of the P5 and the attitudes of both China and Russia, acting without Security Council authorization was inevitable and often just (Daalder and O'Hanlon, 2000, p. 218). Bellamy posed the question: 'why ... should undemocratic states with poor human rights records prevent a group of democratic states from protecting people in foreign countries?' (2002, p. 212). It was claimed that, as both Russia and China so obviously remained wedded to narrow geopolitical worldviews and retained a stranglehold over international law, the utility of law was diminished. International law was, therefore, deemed by some as subordinate to morality and natural law, and they argued that certain ostensibly more ethically advanced states should not be bound by provisions that enable genocide and human rights violations (Linklater, 2000; Cooper, 2002; Robertson, 2002; Nardin, 2003).

Conversely critics of the invasion argued that NATO's actions graphically highlighted the West's, and especially the US's, disregard for international law (Chomsky, 1999, p. 150; Bowring, 2008, pp. 49–54). The flouting of international law was further evidence, some argued, of the West's determination to disregard all legal constraints in its quest for global dominance. The intervention illustrated the extent to which the US acts as 'an all powerful Monarch' in an international system 'where the justice system becomes subordinated to personal whims and self-interests' (Thomas, 2003, p. 171). The manner in which the intervention was prosecuted showed 'a disturbing disregard for the principles of humanitarianism that should guide any such action' (Hayden, 2003, p. 276).

In light of the legal controversy generated by the intervention, Kofi Annan called for new thinking on the issue. In response the Canadian Government established ICISS, which released its report – *The Responsibility to Protect* – in December 2001. The report outlined a means by which the terms of the debate surrounding humanitarian intervention could be altered to put the onus on the host state's responsibilities rather than the legal right of the intervening states (see Chapter 6). Bellamy argues that, while the debate regarding NATO's intervention was divisive, it did highlight an emerging global consensus over the responsibility states have towards their citizens. The 'widespread acknowledgement of sovereign responsibility that accompanied the Kosovo war provided a catalyst for new thinking about the use of armed force for humanitarian purposes' and led directly to the incorporation of the idea of a 'responsibility to protect' in the 2005 World Summit 'Outcome Document' (Bellamy, 2009b, p. 164).

Force protection and international humanitarian law

NATO's tactics, particularly its decision to bomb from 15,000 feet, drew criticism from many human rights organizations which argued that this was a contradictory, if not counter-productive, means of protecting human life. With the commencement of military action NATO's main priority appeared to be the safety of its own soldiers rather than the Kosovar Albanians. Despite the rhetoric of the politicians advocating air strikes, the military were clear about their objectives and did not attempt to portray the campaign as anything other than a targeted military strike. While Tony Blair said that the objective was 'to avert a humanitarian catastrophe' (Bellamy, 2002, p. 157), General Clark suggested that the goal was not humanitarian:

> [Operation Allied Force] was not designed as a means of blocking Serb ethnic cleansing. It was not designed as a means of waging war against the Serb and MUP forces in Kosovo. Not in any way. There was never any intent to do that. That was not the idea. (Chomsky, 1999, p. 36)

According to Michael Ignatieff, NATO 'talked the language of ultimate commitment and practiced the warfare of minimal risk' (2000, p. 111). Flying at high altitudes meant that NATO was largely unable to prevent the Yugoslav forces on the ground from attacking the KLA and the civilian population, and thus NATO's tactics had the effect of 'exporting virtually all the risk of harm or death to non-combatants' (Lucas, 2003, p. 79).

General Clark admitted during the campaign that 'air power alone cannot stop paramilitary action' (Wheeler, 2002, p. 270).

At the initiation of the air strikes General Clark outlined three 'Measures of Merit' that would determine the prosecution of the campaign and the analysis of its success or failure. They were: first, not to lose aircraft; second, to 'impact the Yugoslavian military and police activities on the ground as rapidly and as effectively as possible'; and third, to 'protect our ground forces' (Clark, 2001, p. 185). As is clear, two of the three measures directly related to the safety of NATO personnel. The second measure was conditional on accommodating the other two, and its realization was, as such, dependent on NATO's assessment of the risk involved. As Bellamy notes, 'interesting omissions were the protection of the Kosovar Albanian victims ... the wholesale ethnic cleansing and mass murder of Kosovar Albanians did not alter Clark's understanding of success or failure' (2002, p. 160). As the war progressed it became clear that NATO was prepared to do very little that would impact on the Yugoslav activities on the ground because of the dangers involved. Ground troops were ruled out by President Clinton from the beginning, and the strategy employed remained bombing from the safe distance of 15,000 feet.

The majority of bombs dropped were aimed at non-military infrastructure, and thus the aim of the campaign appeared to be to intimidate the population and make living conditions as difficult for them as possible so as to compel them to pressure Milosevic to concede (Coll, 2001, p. 144; Shue 2003, p. 99). During the campaign Kenneth Roth, executive director of HRW, wrote: 'we are concerned that NATO bombed the civilian infrastructure not because it was making a significant contribution to the Yugoslav military effort but because its destruction would squeeze Serb civilians to put pressure on Milosevic to withdraw from Kosovo' (2000).

NATO General Mike Jackson was open about the strategy, stating that 'just focusing on fielded forces is not enough ... The people have got to get the point that their lights are turned off, their bridges are blocked so they can't get to work' (Hayden, 2003, p. 264). This strategy of intentionally increasing hardship amongst civilians is certainly both illegal and contrary to the Just War tradition.

The US Defense Department admitted dropping over 1,100 cluster bomb canisters with 220,000 'bomblets' over Kosovo, while the UK dropped approximately 500 bombs, each with 147 'bomblets' (ibid., p. 262). HRW (2001), describing cluster bombs as 'grave violations of humanitarian law', estimates that up to 150 civilians were killed in Kosovo by these devices, and notes that the Red Cross found that more than 150 people died in the 12 months *after* Operation Allied Force because unexploded cluster bombs detonated. Amnesty International's (2000) assessment of NATO's campaign concluded, 'civilian deaths could have been significantly reduced if NATO forces had fully adhered to the laws of war ... NATO did not always meet its legal obligations in selecting targets and in choosing means and methods of attack'. In March 2000 NATO admitted that it had dropped 31,000 rounds of depleted uranium throughout Kosovo. A report issued by the Balkan Task Force, established by the United Nations in 1999 to assess the environmental impact of the air strikes, noted that NATO had not supplied it with sufficient information about the nature of these devices (Sulyok, 2003, p. 154).

Thus, the methods employed led to a debate about the morality of 'bombing for humanity' (Brown, 2000, McCoubrey, 2000, Miller, 2000a; Young, 2000). IICK argued that NATO's priorities somewhat undermined the mission they sought to achieve (2000, p. 181). NATO's overall record was described by IICK, however, as 'unprecedented to the extent that it avoided civilian damage through the accuracy of its targeting' (ibid.). This strategy of bombing designed to ensure zero casualties led Ignatieff to coin the phrase 'virtual war'. Ignatieff worried that the manner in which the campaign was prosecuted could inure Western citizens and political leaders to the consequences of military action. He warned that 'if war becomes virtual and without risk, democratic electorates may be more willing to fight especially if the cause is justified in the language of human rights and even democracy itself' (2000, pp. 179–80).

The concern regarding a future of 'virtual war' was somewhat negated by the interventions in Afghanistan and Iraq, where ground forces were deployed and heavy losses endured. The 2011 intervention in Libya, however, was prosecuted with a very similar determination to avoid putting NATO soldiers at risk (see Chapter 14). The Just War tradition contends that the use of force is just only when the provisions of both *jus ad bellum* and *jus in bello* are met, and many argued that Operation Allied Force failed in terms of the latter. Of course, as dealt with in Chapter 8, it is perhaps to be expected that states will deploy their troops in a way that minimizes their exposure to risk and this is arguably likely to be more pronounced if the use of force is carried out in defence of others (Miller, 2000a). Whether this concern undermines the very idea of bombing for humanity is, therefore, an ongoing matter of debate. Additionally, certain observers hold that it is not valid to preclude an intervention from being considered humanitarian if we discern an element of self-interest on the part of the intervening forces (Brown, 2001, p. 23; Wheeler, 2002, p. 38; Weiss, 2007a, p. 7).

Conclusion

Many cases in the 1990s catalysed intense debate about humanitarian intervention, and Kosovo constituted the high water mark of this discussion. While the intervention sparked intense controversy and was criticized on a number of grounds, the support for Operation Allied Force was unprecedented, and it constitutes the most widely acclaimed act of military humanitarian intervention in the contemporary era. In light of the widespread international outcry at the attempt to portray the invasion of Iraq in 2003 as an act of humanitarian intervention (see Chapter 12), Kosovo has increasingly come to be used as an example of a 'genuine' humanitarian intervention by those eager to counter the claim that such action is always hypocritical and a function of geopolitics.

Interest in this issue remains enormous, and Kosovo's place in the history of humanitarian intervention is surely secure. The details of the conflict between the Serbs and Kosovo Albanians will doubtless remain contested, and Kosovo's declaration of independence in February 2008 renewed the controversy surrounding the relationship between these two polarized groups. Milosevic's indictment for crimes against humanity in the midst of NATO's campaign and subsequent trial at The Hague, cut short by his death in 2006, constituted a new, if highly controversial, departure for international law. The ICISS report commissioned in the wake of Operation Allied Force continues to generate debate, and the role of international law, seemingly exposed as limited by NATO's actions, remains a seminal political issue.

It is perhaps to be regretted, though it is not surprising, that the enormous interest in humanitarian intervention generated by Operation Allied Force has not resulted in a resolution of the penumbra that is humanitarian intervention. The primary sources of dissonance exposed by Operation Allied Force remain despite the many efforts since to generate consensus.

Questions

- To what extent did the lack of violence in Kosovo from 1989–95 impact on international engagement with the issue? What are the implications of this?
- Did NATO's tactics during Operation Allied Force fundamentally undermine the humanitarian credentials of its intervention?
- Did Operation Allied Force constitute evidence of the West's new moral dispensation?
- How convincing are the critiques of Operation Allied Force?

Further reading

On the history of the crisis in Kosovo

Glenny, M. (1999) *The Balkans, 1804–1999* (London: Grant).
Judah, T. (2000) *Kosovo, War and Revenge* (New Haven and London: Yale University Press).
Malcolm, N. (1998) *Kosovo: A Short History* (London: Papermac).
Mazower, M. (2003) *The Balkans* (London: Phoenix).
Mertus, J. (1999) *Kosovo: How Myths and Truths Started a War* (London: University of California Press).

Positive perspectives on Operation Allied Force

Bellamy, A. (2002) *Kosovo and International Society* (Basingstoke and New York: Palgrave Macmillan).
Daalder, I. and O'Hanlon, M. (2000) *Winning Ugly* (Washington, DC: Brookings Institution Press).
Gow, J. (2003) *The Serbian Project and its Adversaries: A Strategy of War Crimes* (Montreal: McGill-Queen's University Press).
Robertson, G. (2002) *Crimes Against Humanity: The Struggle for Global Justice* (London: Penguin).
Weller, M. (1999) *The Crisis in Kosovo 1989–1999: International Documents and Analysis* (Cambridge: Documents and Analysis Publishing).

Critical perspectives on Operation Allied Force

Ali, T. (ed.) (2000) *Masters of the Universe? NATO's Balkan Crusade* (London: Verso).
Carpenter, T.G. (ed.) (2000) *NATO's Empty Victory* (Washington, DC: Cato Institute).
Chandler, D. (2002) *From Kosovo to Kabul: Human Rights and International Intervention* (London: Pluto).
Chomsky, N. (1999) *The New Military Humanism: Lessons from Kosovo* (London: Pluto).
Hammond, P. and Herman, E. (eds) (2000) *Degraded Capability: The Media and the Kosovo Crisis* (London: Pluto).
Johnstone, D. (2002) *Fools' Crusade: Yugoslavia, NATO and Western Delusions* (London: Pluto).
Thomas, R. (ed.) (2003) *Yugoslavia Unraveled: Sovereignty, Self Determination, Intervention* (Oxford: Lexington).

On the legacy of Operation Allied Force

Booth, K. (ed.) (2000) *The Kosovo Tragedy: The Human Rights Dimension* (London: Routledge).
Bowring, B. (2008) *The Degradation of the International Legal Order?: The*

Rehabilitation of Law and the Possibility of Politics (Oxon: Routledge-Cavendish).

Chesterman, S. (2002) *Just War or Just Peace?* (Oxford: Oxford University Press).

Hehir, A. (2008) *Humanitarian Intervention after Kosovo: Iraq, Darfur and the Record of Global Civil Society* (Basingstoke and New York: Palgrave Macmillan).

Hehir, A. (ed.) (2010) *Kosovo, Intervention and Statebuilding* (London, Routledge).

Jokic, A. (ed.) (2004) *Lessons of Kosovo: The Dangers of Humanitarian Intervention* (Toronto: Broadview Press).

Weiss, T. (2007) *Humanitarian Intervention* (London: Polity), 2nd edn 2012.

Wheeler, N. (2002) *Saving Strangers* (Oxford: Oxford University Press).

Chapter 12

Iraq

The invasion and occupation of Iraq generated unprecedented controversy and caused a deep division within the international community. After the invasion the US was cast as a global pariah, in stark contrast to the international solidarity shown after 11 September 2001 (Singh, 2006, p. 14). In his resignation speech to the United Kingdom House of Commons former Foreign Secretary Robin Cook stated:

> Only a year ago, we and the United States were part of a coalition against terrorism that was wider and more diverse than I would ever have imagined possible. History will be astonished at the diplomatic miscalculations that led so quickly to the disintegration of that powerful coalition. (BBC News, 2003)

Indeed, by 2006 a poll found that 69 per cent of British respondents believed US policies since 2001 had made the world less safe, 75 per cent considered President Bush a threat to world peace and 71 per cent stated that the war in Iraq was unjustified (Glover, 2006).

Had the US-led coalition justified their actions solely on the basis of the threat posed by Saddam Hussein's regime, then Operation Iraqi Freedom would have little importance for the humanitarian intervention debate. The fact is, however, that, in tandem with the security rationale, a robust humanitarian justification was proffered, particularly when weapons of mass destruction (WMD) failed to materialize. As a consequence the invasion of Iraq, Fernando Tesón notes, 'reignited the passionate humanitarian intervention debate' (2005b, p. 1).

This chapter begins with an overview of the international policy towards Iraq prior to the 11 September 2001 attacks. The subsequent section outlines the key events in the 2002–3 period, demonstrating how Iraq rapidly became the target of ever more bellicose threats from the US and the UK and consequently became the paramount international political issue. In the final section I analyse the impact of Operation Iraqi Freedom, highlighting those aspects of the contentious debate on the intervention which have influenced the contemporary debate on humanitarian intervention.

Nature of the crisis

Iraq is often referred to as the 'cradle of civilization' in reference to the fact that the Sumerian culture established there in the late 6th millennium BC exported mathematics, writing, law and philosophy across the region and the wider world. Iraq's strategic location has been much coveted and its history is characterized by invasion and occupation. From 1831 to 1918 the region was part of the Ottoman Empire, and following the dissolution of the Empire in 1918 the League of Nations granted the territory to the UK as a mandate. In 1932 the UK approved Iraq's independence, recognizing the Hashemite King Faisal as head of state. In 1941 the UK invaded Iraq again, amidst fears that the government would cut off oil supplies to the Allies. The occupation lasted until 1948 when the Hashemite monarchy was restored. The monarchy was overthrown in 1958 by a military coup and in 1968 the pan-Arab socialist Ba'ath Party assumed power.

According to Toby Dodge, even before Iraq gained independence in 1932 politics there has been dominated by 'the deployment of extreme levels of organized violence by the state to dominate and shape society'. Dodge argues that the state, throughout the various changes in leadership, has functioned on the basis of bribery and oil revenues which have enabled the state to 'increase its autonomy from society' (2003, p. 169). The ruling elite, and in particular the Ba'athist regime, were thus able to act independently of their people and maintain power through oppression and externally generated wealth. The Ba'ath Party often brutally suppressed opposition and played on ethnic prejudices; fearful of the Shia community's support for the Iranian regime, the Ba'athists largely privileged the Sunni community and consistently opposed the Kurdish community's calls for greater autonomy and independence.

The ideologically driven Ba'athist movement, which had parties in other states in the region, attempted to impose itself on the wider Middle East in the late 1970s, particularly when Saddam Hussein assumed power in 1978. Hussein sought to assume the position of leader of the Arab world, and undertook a highly confrontational foreign policy particularly towards Iran and Israel. Given the US's extreme hostility towards the Iranian regime of Ayatollah Khomeini, during the 1980s Saddam and the Ba'athist regime were 'the toasts of much of Washington' (Malone, 2006, p. 7). In September 1980 Iraq invaded Iran, sparking a war that would last until 1988 and claim over 500,000 lives.

The 'muted international outcry' in response to Iraq's invasion and conduct of the war appears to have emboldened Saddam (Sutterlin, 2003, p. 105). The UN's response to Iraq's attacks, according to David Malone, 'doubtless contributed to Saddam Hussein's contempt for the UN with fateful consequences ten years later' (2006, p. 22). In August 1990 Iraq invaded Kuwait, claiming it was historically part of Iraq. Based on the reaction to his invasion of Iran, Saddam had concluded 'that the Security Council would ... again take no early action' (Sutterlin, 2003, p. 17). Gorbachev's *perestroika* reforms in the Soviet Union and the greatly improved relations between East and West, however, meant that the Security Council was far less polarized and hence paralysed in 1990 than it had been ten years earlier. In November 1990 the Security Council passed Resolution 678 demanding that Iraq withdraw from Kuwait or be forced to do so. Following the expiry of the deadline for withdrawal, the US led a coalition, mandated by the UN, against Iraq in Kuwait on 17 January 1991 which pushed the Iraqi army out. Combat operations officially ended on 6 April.

During the Gulf War in 1991 the US Government encouraged the Iraqis to 'take measures into their own hands' and overthrow Saddam Hussein. When the Kurds and the Shiites did rise up against the regime, however, 'the USA stood idly by' (Crawford, 2006, p. 36). As the suppression of the Kurds in particular grew more extreme and international media reports more frequent, momentum in favour of action increased and ultimately prevailed. Resolution 688, passed by the Security Council on 5 April 1991, mandated the deployment of UN troops to Northern Iraq and also provided for no-fly zones over northern and later southern Iraq. Apart from earlier resolutions on Rhodesia and South Africa, Resolution 688 was the first time the Security Council had described a humanitarian crisis as a threat to international peace and stability. The initial reaction of the Soviet Union – soon to be replaced by the Russian Federation – and China to Resolution 688 stressed the territorial integrity and sovereignty of Iraq. Malone notes, however, that throughout the 1990s 688 was used by the US, the UK and to a lesser extent France as a pretext for attacking Iraq, and Russia and China largely acquiesced (2006, p. 88).

Following the invasion of Kuwait, Iraq was the subject of what came to be a highly controversial sanctions regime. The sanctions were exploited by Saddam, and the impact was borne by the civilian population, especially children. Air strikes against Iraq were conducted by the US and the UK throughout the 1990s, allegedly in retaliation for breaches of international law. In August 1998 the US Congress passed the Iraqi Liberation Act calling for regime change in Iraq.

The election of George W. Bush in 2000 led to a more belligerent US policy towards Iraq. The Bush Administration included a number of neo-conservatives who had long called for the overthrow of Saddam and had been vocal critics of President George H. W. Bush's decision in 1991 not to invade Iraq following the liberation of Kuwait. In 1991 President Bush had defended his decision, warning that the occupation of Iraq would 'turn the whole Arab world against us ... [and] plunge that part of the world into even greater instability (Ryan, 2007, p. 131). Such caution was, however, routinely dismissed by the neoconservative group 'Project for a New American Century', which called for action against Iraq throughout the 1990s.

Malone suggests four reasons why the neoconservatives were 'itching to take on Iraq' (2006, p. 188). First, many harboured an inherent appetite for military action, believing that the US military was a tool to be used regularly. Second, they were conscious of the threat posed to oil reserves in the Middle East by Saddam's unpredictable and patently aggressive regime. Third, many felt that Saddam was an active sponsor of terrorist groups and could only be prevented from doing so by decisive military force. Fourth, neoconservativism is based on a vision of universal morality, proactive international engagement and the validity of the democratic peace theory, and hence the overthrow of tyranny is a fundamental goal.

Following the 11 September 2001 attacks the influence of this group appears to have increased dramatically, and while the clear links between al-Qaeda and Afghanistan led to an initial focus on the Taliban, attention soon shifted to Saddam Hussein's Iraq.

International response

By 2002 the US and the UK had dramatically increased their warnings about the dangers posed by Iraq, and the world was consumed by the debate about its alleged stockpile of WMDs.

The Bush doctrine and Iraq

The 2002 US National Security Strategy (NSS) outlined the Bush administration's post-11 September worldview and constituted a coherent expression of what has become known as 'the Bush doctrine'. According to Jean-Marc Coicaud, the NSS was 'based on and expresses a rather dark vision of the world' and constituted 'a significant depreciation of international rules, treaties and security partnerships as they had previously been conceived' (2006, pp. 427–8). The NSS refers to pre-emptive force, the dangers of failed states and rogue regimes, and the apocalyptic threat posed by global terrorism. In January 2002 President Bush identified Iraq as part of an 'Axis of Evil' – along with Iran and North Korea – and accused it of sponsoring terrorism and stockpiling WMDs. Throughout 2002 the US and UK increasingly accused Iraq of violating the terms of Security Council Resolution 678 and of supporting international terrorism. The leaders of the key states calling for an intervention in 2002–3 each outlined the moral imperative of acting to halt Saddam Hussein's tyranny.

In a speech to the UN in late 2002, President Bush outlined a litany of humanitarian abuses being committed in Iraq and warned of the 'horrors concealed from the world by the apparatus of a totalitarian state' (Bush, 2002). On 17 March 2003 Bush, in addition to highlighting the threat posed by Iraq's arsenal of WMDs, emphasized the humanitarian aspect of the looming intervention:

> We will tear down the apparatus of terror and we will help you to build a new Iraq that is prosperous and free. In a free Iraq, there will be no more wars of aggression against your neighbors, no more poison factories, no more executions of dissidents, no more torture chambers and rape rooms. The tyrant will soon be gone. The day of your liberation is near. (White House, 2003a)

Prior to the invasion John Howard, Prime Minister of Australia, stated: 'the end of Saddam Hussein's regime would provide an opportunity to lessen the suffering of the Iraqi people' and warned of 'the enormous humanitarian cost ... to the people of Iraq, of Saddam Hussein remaining in charge'. Howard described in explicit detail the abuses carried out by Iraq, such as the mutilation of children and the systematic amputation of tongues, and noted that 'the removal of Saddam Hussein's regime would produce a better life and less suffering for the people of Iraq than its continuation (Howard, 2003). Tony Blair stated: 'riding the world of Saddam will be an act of humanity. It is leaving him there that is in truth inhumane' (Hinsliff, 2003).

The US and the UK demanded that Iraq allow weapons inspectors unfettered access, and on 8 November 2002 the Security Council passed Resolution 1441 which asserted: 'Iraq's non-compliance with Council resolutions and proliferation of weapons of mass destruction and long-range missiles poses a threat to international peace and security'. The Council agreed to give Iraq one last chance to comply with its disarmament obligations. Thereafter the world eagerly awaited the reports of the UN Monitoring, Verification and Inspection Commission (UNMOVIC), which set about trying to verify Saddam's claims that he had destroyed his arsenal of chemical weapons.

From December 2002 to February 2003 Hans Blix, the head of UNMOVIC, reported his team's findings, noting that Iraqi compliance with the inspections was often lacking and that more time would be required to search the country and verify the regimes claims. Following a 7 March report by Blix, where he again noted Iraq's often uncooperative stance, but also stated that there was no evidence of WMDs, the US determined that Iraq was in material breach of Resolution 1441 and hence more robust measures were required. There then began a frantic round of diplomacy whereby the UK in particular attempted to secure a second UN Security Council resolution sanctioning military action. France, China and Russia all refused to support such a resolution, and the matter was never put to a vote. On 19 March the US-led 'Coalition of the Willing' launched Operation Iraqi Freedom.

Operation Iraqi Freedom

The military campaign against Iraq was relatively short and hugely successful. After the rout of the Iraqi army the intervening coalition briefly appeared militarily and morally victorious, as Iraqis clamoured to dismantle the iconography of the old regime. On 1 May 2003 President Bush declared 'mission accomplished' aboard the USS *Abraham Lincoln*. The scale of the ensuing insurgency and the exposé of the enormous intelligence failure regarding the non-existent WMDs and the lack of any link between Hussein and al-Qaeda quickly undermined support for the invasion.

It soon became clear that the intervening coalition had grossly underestimated the scale of the task involved in stabilizing Iraq and suppressing the insurgency. Soon after he declared major combat operations to be over, President Bush was asked about the escalating insurgent attacks. He responded, 'Bring 'em on' (Malone, 2006, p. 204). Insufficient troops were deployed to post-invasion Iraq largely as a result of a mistaken belief that the coalition would be greeted as liberators. US Vice President Dick Cheney stated in September 2002, 'after liberation the streets in Basra and Baghdad are sure to erupt in joy in the same way the throngs in Kabul greeted the Americans' (Herring and Rangwala, 2006, p. 11).

Eric Herring and Glen Rangwala note that the State Department and the Pentagon both outlined competing strategies for the invasion and post-conflict reconstruction of Iraq. The Bush administration came down on the side of the Pentagon, whose strategy involved 'a high degree of trust in the assurances of supportive exiled groups' (ibid., p. 12). Ahmad Chalabi of the Iraqi National Congress was central to the Pentagon's planning, and it was he who claimed that the regime had WMDs, that US forces would be welcomed as liberators, and that his organization would be able to provide security after the invasion. Each claim proved false.

A litany of excessive violence ostensibly aimed at routing insurgents, such as the destruction of Fallujah and the systematic human rights violations perpetrated by the coalition troops (in particular the prisoner abuse scandal in Abu Ghraib), soon undermined what little goodwill existed amongst the Iraqi population (Ryan, 2007, p. 130). Malone argues that the fierce insurgency which erupted after the invasion 'should have occasioned little surprise' as the sanctions regime had produced a 'ruralized, radicalized, increasingly undereducated, unemployed mass of young men with hatred of the West in their hearts' (2006, p. 136). Certain policies implemented by the US Administration in Baghdad exacerbated the problem. The policy of de-Ba'athification, whereby some 30,000 individuals purportedly linked to the previous regime were fired, had disastrous results, creating an enormous administrative black hole resulting in severe breakdown in the country's infrastructure, power supply and internal economy (Herring and Rangwala, 2006, p. 73). Additionally the decision to disband the Iraqi army had the effect of 'instantly creating some 500,000 unemployed, highly trained, armed enemies of occupation, most of them Sunni' (Malone, 2006, p. 203). Despite an enormous public relations campaign, the US-led coalition failed to project an image of benign liberators: a poll conducted among Iraqis as early as September 2003 found only 5 per cent of respondents believed the invasion to have been motivated by a desire to help the Iraqi people, while nearly half said the motivation was Iraq's oil (Tyner, 2006, p. 107).

Most destructive to the coalition's cause was the realization that the stockpile of WMDs did not exist and that Iraq did not constitute the threat alleged prior to the invasion. According to Hans Blix (2004), Iraq was 'not an imminent or even a remote threat to the US or to Iraq's neighbors'. In July 2004 the US Senate Intelligence Committee confirmed that many of the claims made by the Bush administration were 'either substantially or completely wrong' (Malone, 2006, p. 235).

Lies?

It has since been alleged that the intervening coalition, particularly the Bush Administration, manipulated intelligence to support their determination to go to war. Richard Clark, chief counter-terrorism adviser on the US National Security Council, noted that immediately after the 11 September attacks President Bush 'wanted me to come back with a report that said "Iraq did this"' (ibid., p. 187). Within months of al-Qaeda's attacks the Bush administration began to contradict many of its own earlier declarations which suggested Saddam's military capability had been crippled by the sanctions regime (see Box 12.1). In February 2001 Colin Powell had praised the effectiveness of the sanctions regime in containing Saddam's military capability, declaring 'he has not developed any significant capability with respect to weapons of mass destruction'. Only 18 months later Condoleezza Rice warned, 'we don't want the smoking gun to be a mushroom cloud' (Gardner, 2007, pp. 16, 19).

By July 2002 the UK government was convinced that the US was committed to invading Iraq regardless of what the weapons inspectors found. Jack Straw, then UK Foreign Secretary, stated that, following a meeting with US officials, 'it seemed clear that Bush had made up his mind

---

Box 12.1   'WMDs? It's a slam dunk!'

In a December 2002 Oval Office meeting, the President had sought the firmest commitment from [George] Tenet that the DCI [Director of Central Intelligence for the CIA] would stand behind the WMD intelligence. 'George, how confident are you?' Rising from one of the couches, Tenet, an avid Georgetown fan, threw his arms in the air, 'Don't worry, it's a slam dunk!'

Source: Gardner (2007, p. 23).

There is no doubt that Saddam Hussein now has weapons of mass destruction. There is no doubt he is amassing them against our friends, against our allies, against us ... Many of us are convinced that Saddam will acquire nuclear weapons fairly soon.

Source: Dick Cheney, 26 August 2002 (quoted in White House, 2002b).

Intelligence gathered by this and other governments leaves no doubt that the Iraq regime continues to possess and conceal some of the most lethal weapons ever devised.

Source: George Bush, 17 March 2003 (quoted in White House, 2003a).

---

to take military action, even if the timing was not yet decided' (Malone, 2006, p. 191). According to Paul Wolfowitz, then US Deputy Secretary of Defense, 'the truth is that for reasons that have a lot to do with US government bureaucracy we settled on the one issue that everyone could agree on, which was weapons of mass destruction as the core reason' (Cortright, 2006, p. 89). The Bush Administration thus appears to have chosen to focus primarily on WMDs because this offered the greatest potential for garnering support, rather than because it was an accurate assessment of Iraq's military capability. According to Malone, 'in retrospect the fear of WMD seems to have been instrumentalized to sell a decision to go to war that had already been made in Washington' (2006, p. 212).

By the end of 2008 the number of civilian deaths in Iraq was at least 100,000, over 4,000 coalition troops had been killed, while some 4.4 million Iraqis remained displaced (HRW, 2008, p. 478). The International Crisis Group's (2008) assessment of Iraq five years after the invasion was bleak: 'Iraq has plunged into a crisis of governance, with a popularly elected but weak government, unremitting insurgency, growing sectarian strife and rule by militia'.

Impact on the debate

The invasion of Iraq has proved to be a hugely divisive issue, one that will doubtless continue to incite passions for decades. Regardless of how well Iraq functions in the coming years, questions will always remain about the decision to intervene and the humanitarian claims made by the US-led coalition.

The abuse of humanitarian intervention

Operation Iraqi Freedom is considered by many to have dealt a significant blow to the status of humanitarian intervention. As Alex Bellamy notes:

> rightly or wrongly, a large majority of the world's states believe that the coalition abused humanitarian justifications to suit their own purposes. This will set back attempts to galvanize a global consensus on the necessity of action when basic human rights are violated on a massive scale. (2006b, p. 221)

The humanitarian intent advanced by the US-led coalition both before and particularly after the invasion has been deemed evidence of the extent to which claims of a 'humanitarian intervention' are invariably cynical.

The primary rationale advanced for the intervention was the security threat posed by Saddam's regime: that is, his alleged stockpile of WMDs, links to al-Qaeda and attempts to import uranium from Niger. A robust humanitarian rationale was additionally proffered, however. President Bush stated that one of the US's key goals of the invasion was 'to free the Iraqi people' (White House, 2003b), and the name of the military operation – 'Iraqi Freedom' – attests to the emphasis sought for this humanitarian aspect of the intervention. Bellamy notes that when it became clear that the Security Council was not going to sanction the invasion, the rationale for the intervention increasingly focused on the humanitarian justifications. Bellamy therefore concludes: 'it appears that humanitarian justifications were abused to justify a war that could not be justified by either positive international law or reasons of the state' (2004, p. 145).

Nicholas Wheeler and Justin Morris suggest that Blair's moral instincts, more than his security concerns, pushed him to support the invasion, and that he assented to the security arguments because he knew a humanitarian intervention would have been illegal. Both security *and* humanitarian considerations, they argue, were crucial to Blair, but legitimating the war could only be done by reliance on the Security Council, and hence the argument that Iraq was in breach of successive UN resolutions (2006, p. 454).

When the WMDs were not found and the links to al-Qaeda lost credibility, renewed emphasis was placed on the moral aspect of the intervention which, it was claimed, meant that, even though the security-oriented rationale proved largely false, the invasion was still justifiable on humanitarian grounds. Tony Blair stated:

> I can apologise for the information that turned out to be wrong, but I can't, sincerely at least, apologise for removing Saddam. The world is a better place with Saddam in prison not in power ... success for us in Iraq is not success for America or Britain or even Iraq itself but for the values and way of life that democracy represents. (2004b)

As the credibility of the security rationale eroded, Blair declared in a key speech to his constituency party, 'we surely have a responsibility to act when a nation's people are subjected to a regime such as Saddam's' (2004a). This speech drew parallels between Kosovo and Operation Iraqi Freedom, and Blair emphatically reiterated his belief in the 'Doctrine of the International Community' speech he made during the intervention in Kosovo (see Chapter 11).

Bush similarly focused more on the humanitarian side of the invasion as the reality of Saddam's military capability came to light. In April 2004 Bush spoke of 'America's commitment to freedom in Iraq' and claimed that a 'free Iraq will confirm to a watching world that America's word, once given, can be relied upon, even in the toughest times (White House, 2004a). Richard Melanson argues that the heightened emphasis placed on the humanitarian aspect of the intervention initially worked, as the American public seemed willing to forgive the WMD 'mistakes' because the invasion seemed to have brought such rich humanitarian benefits (2007, p. 59). This was a short-lived view as the revelations of extensive atrocities perpetrated by coalition forces, the rising death toll of coalition troops and the obvious resistance amongst the citizens of Iraq to the 'liberators' clearly undermined the purported 'humanitarian' inclinations and effects.

Tesón, however, argues that the invasion 'was morally justified as humanitarian intervention' (2005b, p. 2). He distinguishes between intention and motive: intention relates to 'the willed act and the consequences of the willed act', whereas motive 'is a further goal that one wishes to accomplish with the intended act' (ibid., p. 5). Thus Tesón argues that it is entirely appropriate to criticize the governments for erring or lying about the WMDs, and yet also to praise the act of intervention which brought an end to a reign of terror (ibid., p. 6). Additionally, he argues that it is simply wrong to argue that the intervening coalition was not significantly motivated by humanitarian aims: 'the removal of Hussein was central in the minds of political leaders throughout the whole exercise' and part of the US-led drive to promote international democracy and liberalism as a means to achieving international peace (ibid., p. 10). Terry Nardin, writing in response to Tesón's article, argues that, even if the collation was significantly motivated by the desire to overthrow Saddam Hussein, regime change of this type does not necessarily constitute humanitarian intervention: it is not the character of a regime but its crimes that determine whether humanitarian intervention is warranted (2005, p. 21). Additionally, Nardin challenges Tesón's endorsement of the US-led global democratization project. This radical challenge to the status quo posed by the US and its allies is justified on the basis that the overthrow of tyranny worldwide will be good not just for those suffering directly at the hands of tyrants but also for the global community. Tesón's endorsement of action 'in the name of humanity', Nardin argues, is 'a contribution to the literature of empire' and not related to the accepted understanding of humanitarian intervention (Nardin, 2005, p. 25).

The 'true' motives of the intervening coalition are difficult to discern and will doubtless be a source of controversy for some time. Less subjective is the situation in Iraq prior to the intervention. As Bellamy notes, 'the problem of viewing Iraq as a humanitarian intervention is not so much the interveners' motives as the difficulty of arguing that humanitarian conditions in early 2003 were so bad as to warrant unauthorised intervention' (2006b, p. 220). Material conditions within Iraq were certainly extremely poor, but this was arguably a function of the sanctions regime. While Saddam's regime certainly had a record of extreme brutality, in 2002–3 there was no sudden upsurge in oppression. The time of greatest humanitarian need was arguably during the Al-Anfal campaign against the Kurds between 1986 and 1989, when some 100–200,000 Kurds were killed, including more than 3,000 when chemical weapons were used against the citizens of Halabja. At this time, however, Iraq was fighting Iran, and hence in the US's favour, and the international reaction was limited (Hiltermann, 2007). Gareth Evans notes the irony that after the 2003 invasion Iraq *did* become a humanitarian catastrophe (2008, p. 71).

The humanitarian rationale used to justify the invasion of Iraq 'broke the Kosovo liberal intervention consensus' (Clark, 2003) and burst the bubble of optimism that had been tentatively building after Kosovo, East Timor and to some extent Afghanistan. The seemingly cynical misuse of humanitarian rhetoric undermined the arguments of those who believed a new moral dispensation had evolved amongst Western states and confirmed the worst fears of the many states in the developing world who viewed NATO's intervention in Kosovo in 1999 with alarm. The acrimony caused by the invasion created a 'poisonous' atmosphere within the General Assembly, which had definite implications for attempts to forge consensus on new rules governing the use of force and the 2005 World Summit in particular (Weiss, 2007a, p. 125).

The role of international law

The invasion of Iraq polarized the international community on a number of issues, not least its legality. Many argued that the intervening coalition had not only broken international law, they had in fact conducted 'a multiple assault on the foundations and rules of the existing UN-centred world order' (Thakur and Sidhu, 2006, pp. 3–4).

The cause of much of the dissonance at the Security Council in 2002–3 centred, to a large extent, on the relevance of Resolution 678 and the meaning of the term 'serious consequences' as used in Resolution 1441. The US and the UK noted that Resolution 678 in 1990 authorized the use of all necessary measures to restore international peace in the region and was the basis for the use of force to expel Iraq from Kuwait. Resolution 687 was linked to 678, and obliged Iraq to disarm certain weapons and cease the production and development of these weapons. Provided Iraq complied with 687, the threat contained within 678 was suspended. Resolution 1441, however, ostensibly reactivated 678 as it found Iraq to have failed to comply with 687. Resolution 1441 noted that Iraq had failed to comply with its disarmament obligations as per Resolution 687 and stated 'the Council has repeatedly warned Iraq that it will face serious consequences as a result of its continued violations of its obligations'. Lord Goldsmith, the UK Attorney General, outlined this position in his legal advice to the UK government:

> Authority to use force against Iraq exists from the combined effect of resolutions 678, 687 and 1441. All of these resolutions were adopted under Chapter VII of the UN Charter which allows the use of force for the express purpose of restoring international peace and security ... all that resolution 1441 requires is reporting to and discussion by the Security Council of Iraq's failures, but not an express further decision to authorise force. (Number 10, 2003)

Ruth Wedgewood (2003) described Resolution 687 as 'the mother of all resolutions, setting out the requirements for post-Gulf-war Iraq. This 1991 resolution requires, in perpetuity, that Iraq give up its weapons of mass destruction and permit verification'. Wedgewood later argued: 'there is nothing in the text of resolution 678 that limits its duration or suggests expiry' and she maintained that 1441 did not rescind 678 but gave Saddam Hussein one last opportunity to comply with its provisions. Hussein was found to have breached 678 by the weapons inspectors, and thus the threat inherent in 678 could be acted on. Following the overthrow of Hussein's regime, Wedgewood notes that the Iraq Survey Group *did* find evidence that Iraq had developed a 'clandestine network of laboratories and facilities' for the production of biological weapons (ibid., p. 422). Blair also maintained that the post-invasion inspections demonstrated 'that Iraq was indeed in breach of UN Resolution 1441' (Blair, 2004b).

Of course this is not a universally endorsed view. Kofi Annan described the war as illegal (Kreiger, 2006, p. 386), while Richard Falk noted that it is always possible to find some lawyer to contrive a legal defence for any action, although this does not constitute an objective or accurate legal appraisal (2005a, p. 48). In a letter to *The Guardian* newspaper, 19 experts on international law wrote: 'there is no justification under international law for the use of military force against Iraq' (*Guardian*, 2003). Similarly David Kreiger claimed that the argument that Resolution 678 provided a legal justification 'is basically ... sophistry in relation to the 2003 attack' (2006, p. 385). It has additionally been seen as curious that the US, and especially the UK, would expend so much time and energy seeking to secure another Security Council resolution before launching their invasion if ultimately these same states later maintained that another resolution was unnecessary. As noted by former UK Foreign Secretary Robin Cook in his resignation speech on the eve of the invasion, 'the very intensity of those attempts [to secure a second resolution] underlines how important it was to succeed. Now that those attempts have failed, we cannot pretend that getting a second resolution was of no importance' (BBC News, 2003). Prior to the invasion President Bush asked, 'will the UN serve the purpose of its founding, or will it be irrelevant?' (Malone, 2006, p. 192). Failure on the part of the Security Council to support the US was therefore portrayed, somewhat ironically, as a dereliction of duty and a blow to the UN-centred system of international law.

The invasion was seen by some as part of a broader post-Cold War trend in Western policy towards international law. According to Nigel White:

> In many ways the Iraq crisis of 2003 was the culmination of a decade of pressure by the US and UK directed at changing the legal framework governing the use of force contained in the UN Charter, in a concerted effort to widen both exceptions to the ban on the threat or use of force. (2004, p. 660)

The intervention in Kosovo – itself of questionable legality – was cited by certain supporters of the invasion of Iraq, who pointed out that Operation Allied Force had also been 'illegal but legitimate'. Ann-Marie Slaughter (2003) made the comparison, noting 'the Bush administration has started on a course that could be called "illegal but legitimate" a course that could end up, paradoxically, winning UN approval for a military campaign in Iraq'. Clearly, it would be an exaggeration to claim that Operation Iraqi Freedom was a consequence of Operation Allied Force, although the continuities between the two interventions are strong. Opponents of the invasion of Iraq argued that NATO's actions in 1999 contributed to the erosion of the status of the UN and international law (Orford, 2003, p. 5). This loss of faith in international law and the attendant acceptance that the UN was not the world's only legitimate authority was a central aspect of the pro-invasion perspective in 2003, although many supporters of the NATO action in 1999 rejected this claim and were the most vociferous opponents of the invasion of Iraq (Clark, 2003).

While the intervening coalition did proffer a robust legal justification, this was rejected by the majority of observers. In tandem with the legal rationale, many of those supportive of the invasion expressed a desire to change the rules governing the use of force, thereby suggesting in effect that, while the invasion may not have been strictly legal, international law, and the UN system itself, had to change to meet the demands of the modern era. James Gow argued that the invasion 'was neither a breach of international law, nor the end of the UN' but rather 'an important incident in the continuing evolution of international affairs, and particularly with regard to the laws governing the use of force' (2005, p. 122). Similarly Tony Blair stated:

> It may well be that under international law as presently constituted, a regime can systematically brutalise and oppress its people and there is nothing anyone can do, when dialogue, diplomacy and even sanctions fail, unless it comes within the definition of a humanitarian catastrophe (though the 300,000 remains in mass graves already found in Iraq might be thought by some to be something of a catastrophe). This may be the law, but should it be? (2004b)

Wheeler and Morris argue that Blair felt he had to frame his justifications for the use of force in the more traditional language of Chapter VII rather than humanitarianism, and they note 'the attempts he has made since the war both to justify Iraq as a humanitarian intervention and to change international law so that armed intervention would be permissible against tyrants such as Saddam' (2006, p. 454).

Others argued that the rejection of international law was born less from conviction and more from expediency. According to Michael Byers, the UN system has functioned relatively well given the constraints it faces, and can only continue to function and increase its effectiveness if the most powerful states adhere to its most important provisions. He notes, however, that since 2001 the US has demonstrated 'contempt' for international law (Byers,

2005a, p. 67). Falk claimed after the invasion that the UN had been relegated to the role of 'a debating society' (2005a, p. 42), while Malone similarly lamented: 'above all, the UN was the loser, not in terms of compromise to its principles, but in perceptions of its effectiveness and centrality' (2006, p. 247). Yet, the fact that the Security Council 'stood up to the US' and refused to support the invasion is heralded by some as evidence of the UN's vitality. Ian Hurd argues that 'far from undermining the Council the spectacular diplomatic confrontations and failures pre- and post-war enhanced the Council by reinforcing its basis of legitimization' (2007, p. 190). In this respect the UN faced a dilemma: to support the invasion could have been read either as the maintenance of the principle that Security Council authorization for the use of force was an accepted principle of international law, or as the capitulation of the P5 in response to US bullying. Conversely the refusal to endorse the invasion has been cast as both the death knell of the organization and the affirmation of its continued utility.

The utility of the Just War criteria

NATO's intervention in Kosovo appeared to signify a new dispensation on the part of certain liberal democracies to act to preserve basic human rights even if this action was not strictly legal (see Chapter 11). While extensive human rights legislation had been codified since the Second World War, the enforcement of this legislation was heavily dependent on states voluntarily abiding by the new codes or, failing this, coercive action by the Security Council. The record in both respects, however, had been quite poor: states evidently felt able to assent to human rights legislation without actually adhering to it, while the Security Council remains paralysed by politically motivated decision making. NATO's intervention suggested that Western states were prepared to fill this enforcement vacuum and act, in effect, as the guardians of universal human rights.

So as to retain some framework of constraint and appraisal for 'illegal but legitimate' action, many looked to the tenets of the Just War theory (see Chapter 2). The DIIA proffered a list of criteria specifically drawing on the Just War theory, noting that 'such a list could be used to justify one's own interventions and to criticise those of others'. They suggest that, equipped with this criteria, 'the international community ... may choose on a case by case basis not to condemn if the intervention is truly humanitarian and morally justifiable' (DIIA, 1999, pp. 104–5). States that claimed to be acting in the interests of humanity could therefore be tested on their adherence to the Just War theory, thereby ensuring that in the absence of positive law some framework of constraint could be maintained. Mark Evans described Operation Iraqi Freedom 'as a laboratory in which the [Just War] theory may be put to the most exacting tests' (2005b, p. 71).

Determining the legality of an act, though not without the potential for genuine dispute, is largely a matter of facts. The morality of an action, however, is clearly much more subjective. Thus, many argued that a fundamental proviso for any state wishing to appeal to the 'moral' or 'natural' law was that this state be democratic (Shaw, 1994, pp. 180–1). Democratic states, it was argued, were inherently less likely to make false claims; and, if false claims were made, they were easier to expose given the openness and accountability of these regimes. Additionally, democratic states were considered more likely to act in accordance with the Just War tradition's tenets given their inherent desire to win broad domestic and foreign support (Wheeler, 1997b, p. 22).

The invasion of Iraq dealt a blow to this conception in two key respects. First, there is evidence that the intervening coalition falsified intelligence and knowingly contrived a bogus legal argument prior to the intervention, and thus effectively lied to both their domestic public and the international community; some have even supported the idea of prosecuting Bush and Blair for the crime of aggression (Monbiot, 2012). Second, it seems that while many utilized the Just War tradition as a means by which to critique the invasion, the effectiveness of this critique has been minimal.

One of the main reasons that the debate about the invasion of Iraq proved so divisive was the allegation that the intervening coalition was creative with the truth if not complicit in massive international deception. Both the legal defence and the claims that Iraq possessed WMD are alleged by many to have been fabricated. In January 2003 the UK Attorney General Lord Goldsmith advised the Foreign Office on the legality of an invasion of Iraq, and while he did not unequivocally state that such action would be legal or illegal, he certainly did not advise that it would be legal. His advice on 17 March 2003, however, was that action would be legal under Resolution 1441. This new more definite legal advice has been portrayed as dubious, and, according to Philippe Sands QC, the Attorney General was pressured by legal advisors from the US to fabricate a legal justification for the invasion (2006, p. 196). This is an allegation the Attorney General has strongly refuted (see Box 12.2).

There is clearly no doubt that the allegation regarding Iraq's WMD have proved to have been greatly exaggerated. This could of course have been the function of faulty intelligence rather than a nefarious plot, and Prime Minister Blair has since apologized for 'the intelligence which turned out to have been wrong' (2004b). Others have suggested that the intelligence was not mistaken but rather falsified (Bellamy, 2004, p. 145; Malone, 2006, p. 212). At a meeting of key UK ministers and intelligence chiefs on 23 July 2002, Sir Richard Dearlove, the chief of MI6, stated that 'the intelligence and the facts were being fixed around policy' (Sands, 2006, p. 184). The UK government warned in a dossier in September 2002 – the now infamous

> ### Box 12.2   Operation Iraqi Freedom as legal
>
> I stand by my conclusion that military action was lawful. That was a judg-
> ment I had to reach. I reached it and I stand by it ... And I want to reject the
> suggestions that I was leant on, or that this somehow was not my genuine
> opinion. These suggestions that this was not genuinely my view – these are
> fantasies and they need to be seen as such ... I would not have hesitated to
> give negative advice if that had been my conclusion.
>
> *Source*: Lord Goldsmith, UK Attorney General, 26 May 2005 (quoted in Rengger,
> 2005, p. 145).

'dodgy dossier' – that 'the Iraqi military are able to deploy these weapons
[of mass destruction] within 45 minutes of a decision to do so' (HM
Government, 2002, p. 17). This claim was later retracted when it was
proven to lack any factual basis. The extent to which 'evidence' about
Iraq's arsenal, links to al-Qaeda and attempts to import uranium from
Niger began to surface with increasing frequency in 2002 is seen by many
as suspicious when viewed in the context of the evident desire on the part
of a number of officials within the UK and the US to attack Iraq. It seems
clear that the least favourable evidence about Iraq was proffered as definitive with little substantive critical appraisal. Thus, given the increased
evidence that both the legal and security rationale for the invasion were
knowingly false, the idea of allowing Western democracies exceptional
powers of intervention has lost some of its attraction.

Additionally, even leaving aside the suspicions regarding the coalition's
claims, it is clear that, even amongst supporters of the idea of an international responsibility to protect, there was disagreement over whether the
situation in Iraq warranted military intervention. Michael Ignatieff argued
prior to the invasion that Iraq was a definite threat to international peace
and security, and also a persistent violator of human rights. Iraq was thus
indicative of those situations 'when war is the only real remedy for regimes
that live by terror' (Ignatieff, 2003). Evans, conversely, argues that while
the human rights situation in Iraq prior to the invasion in 2003 was a cause
for concern, it was 'not much worse than a score or two of other countries'
and certainly not a situation that demanded coercive military intervention
(2008, p. 71).

The effectiveness of the Just War tradition as a means by which the
actions of states can be constrained is premised on the receptiveness of
states to critical council (Bellamy, 2004, p. 134). 'Normative pressure' was
indeed exercised prior to, during and after the invasion of Iraq, although
the effectiveness of this pressure appears to have been limited. The coalition that invaded Iraq did make a case for it having adhered to the criteria,

though, and perhaps more damningly, it was not significantly influenced by the rejection of the veracity of its humanitarian claims. If the humanitarian justifications for the invasion were prompted by a desire to present a sectional intervention as an act of altruism, then, as evidenced by the now routine rejection of these claims, this strategy failed. The fact that the case for intervention was rejected but intervention occurred anyway, however, potentially suggests that the power of the Just War tradition to constrain the actions of states is limited (Hehir, 2012, p. 127).

The invasion of Iraq also suggests that massive domestic pressure can be resisted by Western democracies. The scale of the opposition to the invasion was unprecedented: on 15 February 2003 up to one million people marched in each of London, Rome and Madrid in what David Cortright described as 'the largest-scale single day of anti-war protest in human history' (2006, p. 75). Patrick Tyler (2003) wrote that the demonstrations highlighted that the US now faced a 'rival superpower' – world public opinion – and that 'politicians and leaders are unlikely to ignore it'. Yet the global demonstrations were ignored when the US led the invasion of Iraq. This highlights, at the very least, a breakdown in communication between the government and the public within these democracies. At worst it suggests that governments – even democratic ones – determined to pursue what they believe to be a necessary foreign policy will do so regardless of whether there is support for this policy within their domestic constituency. Cortright, however, rejects this negative diagnosis, arguing that the anti-war movement exerted 'considerable international influence'. He suggests that 'the strength of worldwide anti-war sentiment prevented the Bush administration from gaining UN support for its planned invasion and forced the administration to abandon efforts to win UN endorsement' (2006, p. 75). While it is difficult to determine definitively exactly why France, Russia and China refused to support the US and the UK, it is hard to believe that government officials in Moscow and Beijing in particular were influenced in their deliberations by anti-war demonstrations in Western cities.

Taylor Seybolt writes, with respect to the claim that the invasion was a humanitarian intervention: 'human rights organizations ... forced the US administration of President George W. Bush to back away from the claim when they exposed its absurdity' (2007, p. 2). Thus while the US may have claimed to have adhered to moral guidelines, objective observers were able to use these guidelines to expose the US's many failings. Thomas Weiss employs the Just War tradition's criteria as a means by which the invasion can be critiqued and argues that this framework bolstered the anti-war case (2007a, pp. 126–7). Indeed, as noted in Chapter 2, the utility of the Just War theory is not necessarily evident in its capacity to prevent spurious 'just wars' or 'humanitarian interventions'. Rather it is a means by which the morality of a particular conflict can be assessed and judged (Rengger, 2002). In the same way that states may appeal to international law to justify an act and be judged according to the tenets of positive law, states may assert that their actions adhere to the principles of the Just War tradition, and in doing so they must accept critical judgement on this basis. A finding that a supposedly 'just war' failed to meet the Just War criteria cannot, many argue, be deemed a failing of the tradition.

Conclusion

In his now infamous 'mission accomplished' speech aboard the USS *Abraham Lincoln* on 1 May 2003, President Bush stated: 'in the Battle of Iraq, the US and our allies have prevailed. And now our coalition is engaged in securing and reconstructing that country' (White House, 2003b). The 'securing and reconstructing' of Iraq proved more costly and bloody than President Bush and indeed many others could have imagined. According to Vittorio Parsi, a vociferous supporter of US foreign policy, after the invasion Iraq became 'a never ending nightmare' (2006, p. 79).

The invasion of Iraq proved to be the most divisive issue of the post-Cold War era, plunging the UN into a crisis of confidence and deeply dividing the international community. Old fissures between Russia and the West have re-emerged while relations between the Islamic world and the West have plummeted. On the day of the invasion UN Secretary General Kofi Annan stated: 'we must all feel that this is a sad day for the UN and the international community' (Malone, 2006, p. 204).

The fact that the coalition portrayed their intervention as motivated to a significant extent by a desire to aid suffering Iraqis has significantly undermined the status of 'humanitarian intervention'. The term was so tarnished by association with Iraq that it appeared unlikely that any consensus on this emotive issue would be reached in the near future; the intervention in Libya in 2011, however, reinvigorated the pro-interventionists (see Chapter 14).

Clearly the invasion was not motivated primarily by humanitarian intent, and the intervening coalition did not justify their invasion solely on this basis. As the security rationale evaporated, however, 'the human rights argument was the only one left with a shred of credibility and was embraced accordingly' (Evans, 2008, p. 70). By this stage, however, the coalition had arguably lost all credibility given the exposé of the WMD debacle and the other clearly false – though not necessarily contrived – threats posed by Saddam's regime. Had the post-invasion insurgency not occurred, and the coalition had been greeted – as indeed they expected to be – as liberators, then perhaps the invasion of Iraq might well have left a more positive legacy for the humanitarian intervention debate (O'Driscoll, 2008, p. 117). Indeed, perhaps as the years go by and Iraq stabilizes, such a conclusion could yet be reached. As Wheeler and Morris note:

> If Iraq evolves in the next few years into a tolerant rights-respecting society, then this will provide support to those who seek to represent the Iraq war as a justifiable humanitarian intervention ... The final conclusions that one should draw from this complex balancing act are yet to be determined. (2006, pp. 450–1)

'Iraq' much like 'Vietnam' is destined to be utilized by critics of humanitarian intervention and US foreign policy for the foreseeable future, as indeed it was throughout 2011 and 2012 with respects to the crises in the Arab World. What exactly we mean by 'Iraq' is liable to change, however, and it is not inconceivable that someday it may well be a by-word for success; as the consequences of the invasion are evolving, so is history's judgement.

Questions

- How convincing are the legal arguments put forward by the coalition that invaded Iraq in 2003?
- Has the invasion of Iraq demonstrated the weaknesses of international law and the impotence of the UN?
- To what extent were the humanitarian justifications offered for the invasion convincing?
- Has the invasion of Iraq irrevocably tarnished the status of humanitarian intervention?

Further reading

Blair, T. (2004b) 'Speech to the Labour Party Conference', 28 September. Available at:http://news.bbc.co.uk/1/hi/uk_politics/3697434.stm (accessed 13 December 2012).

Buckley, M. and Singh, R. (eds) (2006) *The Bush Doctrine and the War on Terrorism* (London: Routledge).

Dodge, T. (2003) *Inventing Iraq: The Failure of Nation-Building and a History Denied* (New York: Colombia University Press).

Dumbrell, J. and Ryan, D. (eds) (2007) *Vietnam in Iraq* (London: Routledge).

Heazle, M. and Islam, I. (2006) *Beyond the Iraq War: The Promises, Pitfalls and Perils of External Interventionism* (Cheltenham: Edward Elgar).

Herring, E. and Rangwala, G. (2006) *Iraq in Fragments: The Occupation and its Legacy* (London: Hurst).

Malone, D. (2006) *The International Struggle Over Iraq: Politics in the UN Security Council 1980–2005* (Oxford: Oxford University Press).

O'Driscoll, C. (2008) *Renegotiation of the Just War Tradition and the Right to War in the Twenty-First Century* (Basingstoke: Palgrave Macmillan)

Parsi, V.E. (2006) *The Inevitable Alliance: Europe and the US Beyond Iraq* (Basingstoke and New York: Palgrave Macmillan).

Rogers, P. (2008) *Why We Are Losing the War on Terror* (London: Polity).

Thakur, R. and Sidhu, W.P.S. (eds) (2006) *The Iraq Crisis and World Order: Structural, Institutional and Normative Challenges* (New York: UN University Press).

Weiss, T. (2007) *Humanitarian Intervention* (London: Polity), 2nd edn 2012.

Chapter 13

Darfur

Many hoped at the end of the Cold War that the international community, and the US in particular, would engage more with Africa on issues such as human rights. Given that the Soviet threat no longer existed it was hoped that the US could begin to distance itself from those pro-Western dictators it had previously supported. In reality 'geostrategic imperatives of national interest continued to hold sway over suggestions to move toward new foreign policy approaches' (Docking, 2008, p. 208). Many have argued that the crisis in Darfur is evidence of this prioritization.

The situation in Darfur deteriorated rapidly in 2003 and by 2004 was arguably the worst humanitarian crisis in the world. The international community certainly did not ignore the issue: NGOs devoted enormous resources to publicizing the crisis and many Security Council resolutions were passed. Yet, the response to the crisis has been roundly criticized as ineffective and timid (Lu, 2006, p. 2). Many have argued that the situation demanded a humanitarian intervention as the Sudanese government was actively involved in the killings and displacement. Although UN troops have been deployed to Darfur they have had limited impact and have been deployed with the consent of the Sudanese government, despite the fact that the President, Omar al-Bashir, was accused by the Special Prosecutor of the ICC of having orchestrated genocide, war crimes and crimes against humanity (see Box 13.1: p. 276).

This chapter begins with an overview of the crisis in Darfur, highlighting those factors that led to the crisis in 2003. In the second section I assess the international reaction to the crisis and in particular the role played by the Security Council from 2003–8. In the final section I analyse the impact the crisis in Darfur has had on the debate about humanitarian intervention.

Nature of the crisis

The borders of post-independence Sudan owed more to the legacy of the British occupation (1899–1956) than to any demographic trends or topography. Indeed, Stuart Kaufman describes Sudan as 'one of the less sensible results of map-making by colonial powers in Africa' (2008, p. 208). Sudan

265

has rarely enjoyed national unity and since independence in 1956 there have been only 11 years of peace, with the northern and southern regions in a near perennial state of conflict (Straus, 2005). A civil war between the Islamic north – which has generally controlled the government in Khartoum – and the Christian/animist south erupted in 1983, claiming some 2 million lives, although the world largely ignored it (Fisher, 2007, p. 102). This broader conflict has been simmering in parallel throughout the course of the recent crisis in Darfur in western Sudan. The Comprehensive Peace Agreement signed in January 2005 formally ended the north–south war, and many have suggested that the Sudanese government used this agreement as a bargaining chip during the crisis in Darfur (Mayroz, 2008, p. 365). In 2011 South Sudan became an independent state, though border disputes with Sudan soon followed.

The roots of the conflict in Darfur can arguably be traced back hundreds of years, although it is clearly unfeasible to engage in such historical detail here (O'Reilly, 2004; de Waal, 2007b). Darfur is a region with a large number of different ethnic groups, although the vast majority are Islamic. The region is divided primarily between two groups: the 'Africans' whose livelihood is based around sedentary agriculture, and the 'Arabs' who are predominantly semi-nomadic livestock herders (Straus, 2005). The conflict in Darfur has regularly been portrayed as one between the Arab and African groups, although this conceptualization has been criticized as over-simplistic (de Waal, 2004; Hoile, 2005, pp. 93–111).

The UN High-Level Mission to Darfur in 2006 noted that administrative changes made by the Sudanese government in the 1970s eroded the system of tribal dispute settlement mechanisms (UN Human Rights Council, 2007, p. 11). This system had previously reduced conflict amongst the various groups competing for food, land and water in Darfur. When drought and desertification hit the region in the late 1970s competition for resources intensified, and without the old dispute settlement mechanisms groups lacked legitimate institutional means by which to channel their concerns and ultimately mediate conflicts. Alex de Waal argues that complex relationships amongst competing elites in Khartoum and local powers in the periphery, such as in Darfur, have resulted in a dysfunctional Sudanese leadership, largely incapable of negotiating effective peace agreements (2007c, pp. 23–4). Additionally the people of Darfur have traditionally felt disenfranchised from the national political system and the Khartoum regime, and, as tensions escalated, many began to form village defence groups and militias. In 2001 the Sudanese Liberation Army (SLA) and the Justice and Equality Movement (JEM) were formed from these local militias.

In February 2003 the SLA launched attacks against government military installations, and they were soon joined by JEM. While the rebel forces initially achieved some success, the central government launched a fierce counter-attack in April. The Sudanese Air Force was deployed and a large number of civilians were killed. The mobilization of the Janjaweed militia proved most destructive, however, and the violence perpetrated by this group has become the iconic image of the conflict's brutality. The Janjaweed – which roughly translates as 'evil men on horseback' – are far from a homogeneous organization, and it has been asserted that the term is a catch-all with little empirical quality (Hoile, 2005, pp. 112–25).

Many of the militias in Darfur acted in concert with the Sudanese government and received funding and logistical support from Khartoum. According to HRW (2007), 'government forces waged a systematic campaign of "ethnic cleansing" against the civilian population', noting further that 'Sudanese government forces and the Janjaweed militias burned and destroyed hundreds of villages, caused tens of thousands of civilian deaths, displaced millions of people, and raped and assaulted thousands of women and girls'. The sheer scale and barbarity of the violence soon generated international attention. Negotiations and ceasefires followed but none succeeded in stemming the violence. By April 2004 the counter-insurgency had killed 30,000 people, mostly civilians. This figure rose to 70,000 by September, by which time some 1.2 million people had fled their homes, with 200,000 entering Chad. By mid-2004 the World Health Organization estimated that between 240 and 440 people were dying every day, and Darfur was by this stage 'commonly described within the UN system and Western states as "the most serious humanitarian emergency in the world today"' (Williams and Bellamy, 2005, p. 30).

International response

The primary focus of academic inquiry into the crisis in Darfur has been on the response of the international community rather than the dynamics of the situation itself. In general, appraisals of this response have been negative, and many have drawn parallels between the response to Darfur and the reaction to the Rwandan genocide in 1994.

2003–5

The first Security Council resolution to mention the situation in Darfur was passed on 11 June 2004, 16 months after the conflict began. Resolution 1547 contained one sentence on Darfur: '[the Security Council] calls upon the parties to use their influence to bring an immediate halt to the fighting in the Darfur region'. The resolution did not blame any one of the 'parties' for the humanitarian crisis and contained no threats of further action. Resolution 1556, passed on 30 July 2004, went further, although again it lacked real substance. Resolution 1556 recognized the territorial integrity of Sudan and called on the Sudanese government to protect its civilians from the Janjaweed and 'establish credible security conditions for the protection of the civilian population'. The Security Council threatened further action if the government did not disarm the Janjaweed within 30 days. Given that there was widespread evidence that the government was actually working with, if not effectively employing, the militias, it was somewhat paradoxical to call on Khartoum to disarm, apprehend and bring to justice the Janjaweed.

In April 2004 the UNHCR blamed the government of Sudan for the crisis and stated: 'it is clear there is a reign of terror in Darfur ... [our] mission identified disturbing patterns of massive human rights violations in Darfur perpetrated by the Government of the Sudan and its proxy militia' (UNHCR, 2004, pp. 6, 3, 22). Additionally, even if the will existed within the government, disarming the militia within 30 days was a tall order, with de Waal (2004) describing it as 'frankly impossible'. None of the states that voted for Resolution 1556 asserted that the Security Council had a right or duty to intervene in Darfur, with the onus instead placed on the Sudanese government and, failing that, the AU. In June 2004 Russia, China and Pakistan noted at a meeting of the Security Council that they believed the government of Sudan should deal with the crisis, as the scale was insufficient to warrant external interference (Bellamy, 2006b, p. 223).

When the Security Council passed Resolution 1556 the US Ambassador to the UN, John Danforth, acknowledged that the resolution did not go as far as many wished and, noting the calls for a declaration of genocide, stated: 'it is important that we not become bogged down over words. It is essential that the Security Council act quickly, decisively and with unity. We need to fix this humanitarian problem now' (UN Security Council, 2004, p. 4). Danforth stated that the resolution guaranteed that Darfur would be on the Security Council's agenda 'for as long as it takes to ensure that the people of Darfur can live in peace' (ibid., p. 5). As with all other states supportive of the resolution, however, the US threatened only to impose further sanctions if the government of Sudan did not cooperate. Resolution 1556 did mandate the deployment of a contingent of AU troops – the African Union Mission in Darfur (AMIS) – in August 2004. AMIS was under-resourced and under-staffed, however, and it soon became clear that the AU was unable to deploy the 3,000 troops required. In December 2004 Kofi Annan stated that AMIS was 'not working' (Bellamy, 2006b, p. 224).

Security Council Resolution 1564 in September 2004 recognized that the Sudanese government had failed to honour Resolution 1556. This resolution did not impose any punitive measures, however, stating only that the Council 'shall consider taking additional measures' should Sudan's non-compliance continue. Humanitarian organizations had been hoping for a stronger resolution (Hoge, 2004). Resolution 1564 established the International Commission of Enquiry on Darfur (ICED), which, in January 2005, published its report which detailed a litany of extreme violence and widespread sexual cruelty. The report found that 'the Government of Sudan and the Janjaweed are responsible for serious violations of international human rights and humanitarian law amounting to crimes under international law' (2005, p. 3).

In September 2004 the Bush Administration accused the government of Sudan of genocide. This was not a universally endorsed view: the AU and reputable humanitarian organizations such as MSF disagreed (Assembly of the African Union, 2004, para. 2; MSF, 2005). Indeed, throughout 2004 the AU continued to assert that the situation in Darfur was improving, in contrast to the many UN reports stating precisely the opposite.

2005–8

Seven resolutions were passed by the Security Council in 2005, and, while each constituted strongly worded condemnations, none implemented significant punitive action. AMIS's mandate was extended and a 'panel of experts' was established to oversee and report on the crisis. Resolution 1593 in March 2005 referred the situation to the ICC (see Box 13.1). In April 2006 the Security Council agreed to impose targeted sanctions against four individuals. This constituted the most forceful action taken by the Council to that point; according to Thomas Weiss, 'the chasm between the magnitude of the suffering and the international response could hardly have been greater' (2007a, p. 55). Security Council Resolution 1706 in August 2006 finally authorized the deployment of 17,300 troops and 3,300 civilian police to replace the 7,000-strong AMIS contingent. Once again, however, this action was taken with the consent of the Sudanese Government.

The situation improved somewhat in late 2006, although conditions in the region remained extremely poor. A Report of the UN High-Level Mission in March 2007 advised that the steps taken by the international community in response to the crisis in Darfur 'have not proven adequate' (UN Human Rights Council, 2007, p. 22). According to HRW (2007):

As of September 2007, approximately 2.2 million displaced people live in camps in Darfur and more than 200,000 people have fled to neighbouring Chad, where they live in refugee camps. In addition to the people displaced by the conflict, at least 2 million additional people are considered 'conflict-affected' by the UN and many need some form of food assistance because the conflict has damaged the local economy, markets, and trade in Darfur.

Box 13.1   Sudan and the ICC

In April 2007 the ICC issued warrants for government minister Ahmad Harun and Janjaweed leader Ali Kushayb. The Sudanese Government is not a party to the Rome Statute and has consistently refused to cooperate with the ICC. Indeed, subsequent to the ICC's issuing a warrant Ahmad Harun was promoted to minister for humanitarian affairs. On 4 March 2009 Luis Moreno-Ocampo, the ICC prosecutor, issued an arrest warrant for the Sudanese President Omar al-Bashir for war crimes, crimes against humanity and genocide. On the 12 July 2010 the Pre-Trial Chamber of the ICC issued a second arrest warrant.

Estimates of the number of deaths range from 300,000 to 400,000 (SaveDarfur, 2007, p. 1). A report drafted by 15 humanitarian NGOs found that in the first ten months of 2008 some 290,000 people had been displaced – 40,000 in September alone – while some 4 million were in need of humanitarian assistance (Coalition of NGOs on Darfur, 2008, pp. 7–8). The UN special rapporteur on Sudan, Sima Samar, reported in September 2008 that 'violence and sexual abuse of women and children ... continue almost unabated throughout Darfur' (UN General Assembly, 2008, p. 12).

Impact on the debate

Three explanations have been frequently cited for the lack of military intervention (Mayroz, 2008, pp. 362–4). First, the sheer size of Sudan – then the largest state in Africa – and its infrastructural limitations, in particular the poor roads, railways and lack of modern air bases, made it logistically difficult to intervene. Second, it was feared that an intervention would disrupt aid supplies to those already suffering in Darfur. Third, it was claimed that such an intervention would be poorly received in the Arab world. Sending troops into Sudan would be seen as 'one more incursion of a Christian army into an Islamic land' (Rieff, 2006). Eyal Mayroz additionally suggests a fourth reason: 'the defensive campaign against external intervention carried out by the regime in Khartoum' (2008, p. 365). The Sudanese Government exploited the disunity within the Security Council and the AU and variously portrayed itself as the victim of Western aggression, as an honest broker eager to resolve an internal dispute and as an impoverished state in need of assistance. Mayroz argues that Sudan's repeated success in delaying, watering down and disrupting the implementation of many Security Council resolutions has set a precedent likely to undermine the Council's authority and credibility in dealing with future crises (2008,

p. 366). Whichever factor or combination thereof is responsible for the response to the crisis, Darfur has become synonymous with inaction and failure, much like Rwanda ten years earlier (see Chapter 10).

Back to Rwanda?

The nature and scale of the crisis in Darfur evoked memories of the genocide in Rwanda in 1994. The international community's seemingly wilful paralysis in the face of the death of some 800,000 people is arguably the most frequently decried episode in contemporary international politics. Following that genocide, 'never again' became a frequent refrain of political leaders, and the intervention in Kosovo five years later suggested that this commitment was finally being realized (see Chapter 11). Hugo Slim highlighted the legacy of Rwanda when he described Darfur as the 'test case by which to judge whether the international community has got any better at responding to genocide and crimes against humanity' (2004, p. 811).

In March 2004 the UN humanitarian coordinator in Khartoum, Mukesh Kapila, publicly drew parallels between the crisis in Darfur and the early stages of the genocide in Rwanda (ibid., p. 815). The coverage of the unfolding disaster in Darfur by the media, NGOs and UN fact-finding missions in 2003 surpassed that of the initial stage of the genocide in Rwanda, and the violence which followed was therefore not an unexpected eruption. Regarding the response to Darfur, Roméo Dallaire (2004b), force commander for the UN Assistance Mission in Rwanda in 1994, wrote:

> Although the early stages of the Darfur situation received more news coverage than the Rwanda genocide did, at some level the Western governments are still approaching it with the same lack of priority. In the end, it receives the same intuitive reaction: 'What's in it for us? Is it in our "national" interest?'

Dallaire described the reaction to Darfur bluntly as 'not nearly enough' (2004b). Instead, according to John Mueller, 'the international community, after ten years of mea culpa breast beating over its failure to intervene in Rwanda, responded with little more than huffing and puffing' (2005, pp. 122–3).

As noted in Chapter 10, in 1994 ever more creative ways to describe the carnage in Rwanda were employed in an effort to avoid using the term 'genocide' and somehow downplay the extent of the violence. In September 2004, however, US Secretary of State Colin Powell announced before the US Senate Foreign Relations Committee that 'genocide has been committed in Darfur and ... the Government of Sudan and the Jingaweit [*sic*] bear responsibility' (US Department of State, 2004). This constituted the first time that any state had officially accused another of genocide while it was allegedly occurring (Mayroz, 2008, p. 367). Yet Powell subsequently stated:

> no new action is dictated by this determination ... let us not be too preoccupied with this designation ... Call it civil war; call it ethnic cleansing; call it genocide; call it 'none of the above'. The reality is the same. There are people in Darfur who desperately need the help of the international community. (US Department of State, 2004)

President Bush endorsed Powell's view on 21 September (White House, 2004b). Powell's plea 'not be too preoccupied with this designation' was a clear attempt to distance the US from any obligation to intervene. The Clinton Administration had feared in 1994 that to describe the violence in Rwanda as 'genocide' would have obliged it to take action under the 1948 Genocide Convention. Evidently the legal advice received by the Bush Administration in 2004 was that using the term 'genocide' 'would not obligate the US to anything beyond – in the words of the Genocide Convention – calling "upon the competent organs of the UN to take such action"' (Mayroz, 2008, p. 367).

From a strict legal perspective the US administration was quite possibly correct that a finding of genocide only compelled it to refer the matter to the Security Council – which it did – rather than to take action. As Yoram Dinstein notes, the Genocide Convention does not contain any provision that triggers military action once the 'g-word' is used (2005, pp. 72–3). Yet articulating a legal defence for a seemingly ineffective response to what you acknowledge as being genocide certainly undermines the 'never again' declarations routinely made after 1994. As Weiss laments, 'if we recognize the existence of genocide and do nothing besides ask the ICC to split genocidal hairs, the 1948 Convention on the Prevention and Punishment of the Crime of Genocide is literally not worth the paper on which it is reproduced' (2007a, p. 54).

John Danforth, US Ambassador to the UN in 2004, stated, after he stepped down in 2005, that the finding of genocide was made for 'internal consumption within the US' and never intended as an act that would alter US policy (Mayroz, 2008, p. 371). David Hoile argues that the term was 'transparent political opportunism' designed to deflect public attention from Iraq during the 2004 US Presidential elections (2005, p. 95).

Scott Straus notes that the case of Darfur has 'made it clear that "genocide" is not a magic word that triggers intervention'. While the term provokes attention, and in the case of Darfur ensured the situation would be at the top of the international political agenda, the subsequent inaction 'showed that the Genocide Convention does not provide nearly the impetus that many thought it would'. He notes that previously, most notably in the case of Rwanda in 1994, governments avoided using the term genocide, yet the crisis in Darfur 'shows that the definitional dance may not have mattered' (Straus, 2005, p. 132). The parallels between Darfur and the Rwandan genocide, itself evocative of the Holocaust, were clear in terms of both the violence and the ineffective international response. According to Weiss, 'the collective yawn in the face of Darfur's disaster could be even more destructive of the fabric of international law than the 800,000 deaths in Rwanda' (2007a, p. 54). Kofi Annan's appraisal of the reaction to Darfur concluded that 'we were slow, hesitant, uncaring and we had learnt nothing from Rwanda' (Fisher, 2007, p. 103).

R2P RIP?

Following NATO's intervention in Kosovo in 1999 ICISS was established to find a means by which human rights and sovereignty could be reconciled and the efficacy of international responses to mass atrocities improved. ICISS's main argument was that states had the primary responsibility for the welfare of their people, and if they failed in this respect the responsibility transferred to the international community which could, if necessary, intervene militarily without the host state's consent. These provisions were endorsed by all the world's states in 2005 at the World Summit, albeit in a somewhat diluted form (Wheeler, 2005; Bellamy, 2006a).

The reaction of the international community to Darfur suggests that the latter responsibility – that of the international community to those suffering at the hands of oppressive or incompetent regimes – was not readily assumed. Clearly the Security Council was unwilling to take military action, and the legal wrangling and habitual calls for more information by the Council in the face of evident tragedy stands as an unedifying portrait of its effectiveness and the priorities of its members. The Security Council remained 'seized of the matter' since Resolution 1547 in June 2004 and passed many resolutions since criticizing the Khartoum government. Yet a consistent feature of Security Council action has been the expressed desire to operate in concert with the Sudanese Government. Indicatively, Resolution 1706 which finally authorized the deployment of a robust military force 'invites the consent of the Government of National Unity' and requests their involvement in the decision regarding the deployment of the new force. This therefore possibly constituted a regression from the proposals put forward by ICISS, which explicitly stated that consent was not required. The Khartoum government has been accused by reputable international humanitarian organizations and the UN itself of intentionally preserving conditions of poor sanitation and famine (Mayroz, 2008,

p. 361) and conducting 'genocide by attrition', leaving the non-Arab population 'in the throes of a slow, remorseless destruction' (Reeves, 2005). The expressed desire for an invitation from the very perpetrators of the crime which necessitated action, according to Weiss, 'mocks the values of the emerging R2P norm' (2007a, p. 58).

The ICISS report stated that the Security Council remained the primary international arbiter of when it was right to intervene and outlined its commitment to make the Council work better rather than to find alternatives to its authority. Nonetheless ICISS did state that it could not accept that failure by the Security Council to act must be the last port of call, and warned that it was unreasonable to expect that inaction by the Council in the face of mass atrocities to be tolerated by concerned states (2001a, pp. 53–5). This therefore appeared to allow for the possibility of 'illegal but legitimate' action, such as that ostensibly undertaken by NATO in 1999 in Kosovo, and clearly suggested that certain states were unwilling to tolerate the systematic violation of human rights by others. The scale of the tragedy in Darfur was, as many have suggested, of sufficient magnitude to warrant legitimately external intervention regardless of the Security Council's position or the views of the Sudanese Government, as the situation had clearly passed any 'just cause threshold' (Bellamy, 2006b, p. 223). Yet, as Slim states, 'whatever the right legal label, such extreme policies operated by the Sudanese government demanded a concerted, immediate and assertive international political and humanitarian response. No such response emerged' (2004, p. 815). The 'Somalia syndrome', derived from the US's bad experiences in Somalia in 1993 (see pp. 53–4), appears to have influenced the decision not to intervene in Darfur in 2004, as it had in Rwanda ten years earlier. This syndrome suggests that interventions in Africa are doomed to fail given the endemic ethnic hatreds and violent opposition towards external interference prevalent in the region. Additionally, as Weiss notes, the US was 'disinclined to commit significant political and military resources to human protection' (2007a, p. 119) given its enormous military commitments in Afghanistan and Iraq.

While the explanations for the response of the international community, and the West in particular, may be accurate, they do suggest that massive human rights violations in themselves are insufficient to compel states to intervene to protect suffering masses abroad. As with Rwanda in 1994, it seems that despite the scale of the 'genocide' in Darfur the costs of intervention were deemed too high and the benefits too low. This need not necessarily lead us to conclude that states are hypocritical or amoral; it suggests rather that any 'responsibility to protect' foreign citizens is very much secondary to national responsibilities and domestic exigencies. According to de Waal, the fixation with coercive action against the Sudanese Government and military intervention diverted attention from the only viable solution to the crisis, the deployment of UN peacekeepers and the simultaneous provision of emergency humanitarian aid. He dismissed R2P as 'a slogan', and argued that in light of the response to Darfur we must conclude 'RIP R2P' (2008). One consequence of the emergence of 'the responsibility to protect' doctrine not anticipated by either its proponents or critics was the extent to which this normative prescription actually facilitated inaction; and, as noted in Chapter 6, this use of R2P to justify inaction was a feature of the international response to Darfur (Bellamy, 2006a, p. 33).

While Darfur was been deemed by many to have crossed the threshold for military intervention, others have argued that this in itself is not sufficient grounds for launching such action. According to Gareth Evans there is a difference between a necessary and a sufficient condition for intervention: while the scale of the crisis in Darfur was certainly grave enough potentially to warrant military intervention, this is not the only factor to be considered when deciding whether or not to intervene militarily. According to Evans, 'a nonconsensual military intervention ... would almost certainly be disastrously counterproductive, in terms of its impact on current humanitarian relief operations and the very fragile north–south peace process' (2008, p. 61). In this situation the international community's response had to 'take other forms', in particular earlier and more robust deployment of UN and AU peacekeepers, and therefore the reaction to the crisis, though flawed on many levels, was not an 'R2P failure' (ibid.). Likewise Francis Deng, UN Special Advisor on the Prevention of Genocide, stated that 'it would complicate matters to intervene militarily' (2010, p. 87). De Waal similarly cautioned against the clamour for military intervention, noting that 'providing physical protection for Darfurians with international troops is not feasible' (2007a).

The argument that military intervention was impractical is rejected by Bellamy, who argued that it would have been possible to use air power and light infantry to protect those huddled in camps and ensure the safe passage of humanitarian aid (2006b, p. 225). Susan Rice (2005) – later US Ambassador to the UN under President Obama – also criticized the 'excuses' offered for the lack of what she believes was a duty to intervene, with or without the assent of Khartoum or the UN Security Council. Similarly a report by the US National Defense University found that a military intervention prosecuted in a certain way would have achieved success (see Box 13.2).

It is, of course, impossible to determine what effects a non-consensual military intervention would have had in 2003–4. Any such move would doubtless have been fiercely resisted by the Sudanese army and the various militias, and the impact of the intervention would have been dependent on the military tactics employed. Given the localized nature of the killings on the ground, and the tactics of the militias, one could reasonably argue that an intervention prosecuted exclusively from the air, in the style of Operation Allied Force, would have potentially caused an escalation in the terror tactics of the militias. A ground offensive, if sufficiently robust, might well have constituted the only viable means by which a military intervention could have had a positive humanitarian impact.

Many critics of R2P argued that it paved the way for increased Western interventionism based on subjective claims of humanitarian need (Chandler, 2004a). The crisis in Darfur has arguably shown that the age-old problem of 'inhumanitarian non-intervention' remains the norm. 'Overzealous military action for insufficient humanitarian reasons', notes Weiss in light of Darfur, 'certainly is no danger. Rather the real threat to international society comes from doing nothing while condoning massive suffering' (2007a, p. 52). Darfur shows that, even if agreement on the criteria justifying humanitarian intervention can be reached, disagreement over whether these criteria have been met is still possible, and this has implications for the effectiveness of R2P. Indeed Bellamy (2009a) argues that the disagreement over the merits of intervention in Darfur highlighted the need for those concerned about the utility of R2P to abandon the search for criteria for decision making about the use of force in favour of using the R2P framework to identify and neutralize potential moral hazards and highlight alternatives to coercive military intervention.

Box 13.2   Would military intervention have been effective?

An intervening combat force would have had little trouble stopping killings by the Janjaweed if it could have tracked and engaged them. The killers lack skill, strong motivation, and capabilities, and with decent intelligence it is not very difficult to distinguish them from their civilian targets ... On balance, it seems reasonable to expect that a fast, light, lethal, well-trained, and well-led African combat force, operating in distributed, interconnected, and collaborative fashion, could have been more forward deployed and dispersed to strategic points throughout Darfur, better able to obtain intelligence on Janjaweed movements and intentions, mobile enough to move quickly to areas of potential or ongoing killings, and stop or deter mass killing, provided the force could get deep into Darfur, receive ample intelligence, and be backed up by precision air-strikes if trapped, ambushed, or confronted by Sudanese military units. Western support would be indispensable; with it, decisive success would be feasible.

Source: Gompert et al. (2005, p. 26).

The limits of global civil society?

Many argued that NATO's intervention in Kosovo in 1999 demonstrated the power of global civil society and the so-called 'boomerang effect' (see p. 58). The Kosovo Albanians alerted the world to their plight by appealing to international human rights organizations and their overseas diaspora. Humanitarian NGOs publicized the situation and attracted increased media attention, which combined to create a momentum amongst domestic publics in the West for action against Milosevic's regime. NATO's eventual intervention, though certainly criticized by many global civil society activists for the manner in which it was executed, thus seemed to demonstrate the power of this new international actor. Clearly, if foreign policy was now, to some significant extent, an internationalized bottom-up process, then the nature of international relations would have changed markedly.

The conflict in Darfur since 2003 evidences a contrast between enormous international publicity of the crisis and timid and equivocal action on the part of the UN Security Council and Western states. The international media, NGOs and many UN reports consistently highlighted the suffering occurring in Darfur from 2003. Additionally, many, though by no means all, states acknowledged the extent of the violence, with the US going so far as to use the term 'genocide'. While, in contrast to China and Russia, Western states have vocally condemned the Sudanese government, the practical steps taken to stop the killings have been, from the perspective of respected international observers, a 'dismal failure' (Wheeler and Morris, 2006, p. 457).

MSF noted that 'the media attention and political involvement means that everyone knows about the conflict here, but in the last four years the situation has not improved. In fact, for most people things have got worse' (Huig, 2007). NGOs such as HRW, the International Crisis Group and Amnesty International regularly criticized the response of the international community and appealed for more direct engagement. Certain activists, frustrated with the UN's response, called on Western powers to take unilateral action. Indicatively John O'Shea, head of the charity GOAL, declared: 'the US as the superpower should take the action on its own ... There is nothing that the UN has done since day one that has saved the life of a single person in Darfur' (De Bréadún, 2004). The UN's capacity to act is of course dependent on the Security Council, which is itself reliant on its permanent members, including the US, and thus 'the UN' cannot reasonably be criticized for not taking military action as it does not have the independent capacity to do so. Appealing to Western states to extricate themselves from the restrictive embrace of the UN is of questionable utility given that the Western powers, and the US in particular, have maintained a very close adherence to the deliberations and rulings of the Security Council in contrast to their behaviour over Kosovo in 1999 and Iraq in 2003.

SaveDarfur, an NGO umbrella group comprising 114 different NGOs and some 48 regional groups, was to the fore in highlighting the issue of Darfur within the US. SaveDarfur's strategy is based on the fundamental assumptions behind the project of global civil society: 'we utilize media outreach, public education, targeted coalition building and grassroots mobilization to pressure policymakers and other decision-makers in the US and abroad to help the people of Darfur' (SaveDarfur, 2007). The group launched the 'Million Voices for Darfur' campaign in January 2006, and by the end of June it had collected 1 million signatures from people in the US urging the Bush Administration to support the deployment of a large military force to the region. On 30 April 2006 hundreds of thousands of people attended approximately 20 separate rallies across the US calling on President Bush to do more to stop the conflict in Darfur, and a second rally was held on 17 September.

The campaign to raise awareness was a success. According to SaveDarfur, 'just about everyone who's heard of Darfur believes that more should be done to help Darfur'. Yet despite the massive public outcry, SaveDarfur described its campaign as 'complex, grinding, and profoundly frustrating'. It credited the AU with taking a proactive approach, contrasting this with 'the rest of the international community [who] stood by and watched' (Meixner, 2007). This record does not complement the notion that sustained and widespread pressure will compel democratic states to act abroad. In this case, despite the widespread mobilization of domestic and global civil society in favour of robust military intervention, the US, and the West generally, have successfully resisted popular moral outrage. Three years after the killings began and the appeals for action were made, Weiss noted that the only country to respond unequivocally to the UN's calls for peacekeeping troops was the US, which 'categorically said "no"' (2007a, p. 55).

Clearly such a response, not just to the crisis itself but to the international campaign for action, challenges the assumptions that global civil society is a key actor in contemporary IR and that Western states are receptive to calls for intervention. Of course, the widely heralded interventions in Kosovo and East Timor in 1999 took place during the tenure of President Clinton, and thus the character of the US administration had changed by the time the crisis in Darfur began. Additionally, Darfur occurred after 11 September 2001, by which time the US and the wider Western world had adopted a foreign policy characterized by 'the prioritization of strategic concerns to the virtual exclusion of humanitarian ones' (Weiss, 2007a, p. 55). In this respect, the context in which the response to Darfur occurred differed greatly from that of Kosovo in 1999.

Nonetheless, while these differences perhaps explain why the responses to Kosovo and Darfur were so different, they do not alter the fact that the power of global civil society appeared to have waned.

In its defence global civil society has never claimed to have an irresistible impact on Western foreign policy, and it obviously has no independent military capacity. The movement is based on the assumption that crises abroad will be highlighted by NGOs, which will put pressure on governments to take action. This action need not necessarily take the form of military intervention, and therefore the lack of military intervention is not indicative of global civil society's failings. Mayroz (2008) argued that the US's response to the crisis in Darfur, though certainly not as robust as many would have wished, evidences a new willingness to act on the recommendations of global civil society and pressure the Sudanese government despite the fact that Sudan was an important ally in the war on terror. Additionally Adam Jones highlighted the actions of students in high schools and universities across the US who called for action and urged boycotts of companies linked to Sudan as a 'truly encouraging sign' that attitudes to foreign policy have changed thanks to global civil society (2008, p. 194). Thanks to the campaign waged by global civil society, public awareness was quite high, groups were effectively mobilized and Darfur became a key domestic political issue, even impacting on the 2004 US presidential elections. If the proponents of global civil society asserted that it would always force states to act and that this action would take the form of military intervention, then clearly the response to Darfur undermines these ideals. Global civil society did not, and does not, make these claims, however, and this must temper any appraisal of its capacity. Many humanitarian organizations cautioned against military intervention, and therefore the response to Darfur, though arguably ineffective, may well tally with that advocated by global civil society.

Conclusion

On 11 September 2006 Kofi Annan, by this stage 'at the end of his tether', posed three questions:

> Can we, in conscience, leave the people of Darfur to such a fate? Can the international community, having done not enough for the people of Rwanda in their time of need, just watch as this tragedy deepens? Having finally agreed just one year ago that there is a responsibility to protect, can we contemplate failing yet another test? (Weiss, 2007a, p. 57)

Weiss laments that each of these questions 'actually received affirmative responses' (ibid.). Perhaps the most disappointing if not disturbing aspect of the crisis in Darfur was that, while the situation received enormous international publicity and few states denied the scale of the tragedy, the response was certainly ineffective and arguably weak. According to Bellamy, 'the concern with Darfur is not so much that the US and UK have not intervened but that neither these states nor their allies seem to have accepted their duty to protect Darfurians' (2006b, p. 226). He further argued: 'states that invoked a broad right of intervention in the Kosovo and/or Iraq cases cannot avoid a duty to act in a case like Darfur without undermining future claims for a permissive right of intervention' (ibid.). Thus Darfur has seemingly exposed in tragic clarity the selective approach to humanitarian crises and the continuing dominance of national interests.

Whatever one's perspective on humanitarian intervention, the response to Darfur can only be seen in a negative light. Unquestionably millions of people have suffered terrible hardship, with thousands killed, raped, starved and many more displaced. Darfur shows that the international community of states, even after agreeing to the idea of a collective 'responsibility to protect' in 2005, has yet to find an effective means by which such humanitarian disasters can effectively be halted. Whether a humanitarian intervention would have been an effective solution is debatable, but clearly something more should have been done. Many imagined that the Rwandan genocide so shocked the conscience of humankind that no such atrocity would be permitted to take place again. As Weiss notes, however, while 'never again' was the mantra espoused post-Rwanda, the crisis in Darfur and the attendant international inaction means that '"here we go again" is closer to the truth' (2007a, p. 154).

Questions

- What does the use of the term 'genocide' in the context of Darfur tell us about the effectiveness of the Genocide Convention?
- What options were available to the Security Council that it did not take advantage of? Why do you think this was the case?
- Has the crisis in Darfur demonstrated the limitations of global civil society?
- Kofi Annan claims that Darfur demonstrates that 'we had learnt nothing from Rwanda'. Do you agree?

Further reading

On the history of the crisis in Darfur

Daly, M.W. (2007) *Darfur's Sorrow: A History of Destruction and Genocide* (New York: Cambridge University Press).
De Waal, A. (2006) *Darfur: A Short History of a Long War* (New York: Zed).
O'Fahey, R.S. (2008) *The Darfur Sultanate: A History* (London: Hurst).
Prunier, G. (2005) *Darfur: The Ambiguous Genocide* (Ithaca, NY: Cornell University Press).

On the international response to the crisis

Chedle, D. and Prendergast, J. (2007) *Not on our Watch: The Mission to End Genocide in Darfur and Beyond* (Meath: Maverick House).
De Waal, A. (ed.) (2007) *War in Darfur and the Search for Peace* (Cambridge: Global Equity Initiative, Harvard University).
Hoile, D. (2005) *Darfur in Perspective* (London: European-Sudanese Public Affairs Council).
International Commission of Enquiry on Darfur (2005) 'Report of the International Commission of Inquiry on Darfur to the UN Secretary-General', 25 January. Available at: www.un.org/news/dh/sudan/com_inq_darfur.pdf.
Mamdani, M. (2009) *Saviours and Survivors: Darfur, Politics, and the War on Terror* (London: Pantheon).
Weiss, T. (2007) *Humanitarian Intervention* (London: Polity), 2nd edn 2012.

Chapter 14

Libya and the Arab Spring

The Arab Spring began in innocuous, if horrific, fashion on 17 December 2010. Mohamed Bouazizi, a 26-year-old street vendor, had his fruit-cart confiscated by municipal police in Sidi Bouzid, Tunisia. After an unsuccessful appeal for the return of his cart, Bouazizi doused himself in petrol and set himself alight while standing outside the governor's office. Few could have envisaged the profound repercussions of his actions; indeed, Gregory Gause noted that 'the vast majority of academic specialists on the Arab World were as surprised as everyone else by the upheavals' (Gause, 2011, p. 81).

Following the protests which subsequently erupted across the Middle East, humanitarian intervention has again dominated international politics. Though, at the time of writing, the Arab Spring has lasted just over two years, its duration has encompassed a dizzying oscillation in the perceived efficacy of R2P and attitudes towards humanitarian intervention more generally. The optimism which abounded after NATO's intervention in Libya in March 2011 was soon replaced with despair at the lamentable response to the escalating violence in Syria. The crises in Egypt, Bahrain and Yemen also raised myriad questions about contemporary attitudes towards human rights, the pervasive influence of geopolitics and the role of the UN. While the slogan *Ash-sha'b yurīd isqāṭ an-nizām* ('the people want to bring down the regime') has rung out loudly across the region, the international response has been noticeably inconsistent and could be summarized as 'it depends which regime you want to bring down'. While events in the Middle East continue to evolve, two things are clear: first, that humanitarian intervention remains a pertinent and emotive issue; second, that there is still much that needs to be done to improve the international community's response to intra-state crises.

The Arab Spring involves a number of cases which are relevant to many of the issues and debates explored in earlier chapters of this book, but this chapter focuses in particular on NATO's intervention in Libya. For many this constituted the archetypal example of laudable humanitarian intervention and irrefutable evidence that R2P has real influence (Evans, 2011; Daalder and Stavridis, 2012). This positive appraisal was not universally held of course, and many questioned both the wisdom of the intervention and the wider claims made about its novelty and implications

(Chesterman, 2011a; Walzer, 2011; Kuperman, 2013; de Waal, 2013). Perspectives on the motives behind, and the legitimacy of, the intervention have been shaped by the international response to other uprisings in the Middle East – hence additional cases (Syria and Bahrain in particular) will also be discussed.

This chapter begins with an overview of the events which led to the conflict between Colonel Gaddafi and the rebel Transitional National Council (TNC), situating these more in the context of the Arab Spring than the minutia of Libyan history. I then outline the international response and look at two regional actors – the Arab League and the AU – who played an unusually central role in shaping this response. In the final section I assess the various appraisals – critical and exhortatory – of the intervention and organize these thematically with a view to understanding the contours of future debates.

Nature of the crisis

Libya's history is one of near constant external intervention and it has been variously ruled by the Greeks, Romans, Ottomans, Italians, French and British. Indeed, its history during the 20th century alone has been described as 'an extraordinary odyssey' (Vandewalle, 2006, p. 1). Like many African states Libya owes its present shape to imperial machinations and astronomical configurations; it is very obviously an artificial construct with straight lines constituting its borders with Egypt, Sudan, Chad and Niger (Herbst, 1989). Libya is the third largest country in Africa but has a population of only 6.5 million, largely concentrated along the Mediterranean on the Northern coast; some 90 per cent of the country is desert.

In 1912 Italy wrested control of the area from the Ottoman Empire calling their new acquisition – comprising the three regions Cyrenaica, Tripolitania and Fezzan – 'Italian North Africa'. While de facto Italian rule was limited, especially in the Fezzan province, the colony's coastline – known as Italy's 'fourth shore' – was of great strategic importance (Vandewalle, 2006, p. 3). In 1934 Italy officially changed the name of the colony to 'Libya' and for much of the 1930s it violently repressed local resistance led by the Emir of Cyrenaica, Idris al-Mahdi as-Senussi, the future King of Libya.

During World War II Italy lost control of the territory to Britain (which administered Cyrenaica and Tripolitania) and France (which administered Fezzan). On Christmas Eve 1951 the 'United Kingdom of Libya' declared independence with the support of the UK, France and the General Assembly. Though now officially a united and independent state, east/west divisions within Libya proved resilient: transport links between Bengazi in the east and Tripoli in the west had always been poor while the tribes in the east have often tended to identify with their brethren in Egypt more than their co-nationals in the west (International Crisis Group, 2011a, p. 17). King Idris's largely pro-Western rule lasted until 1 September 1969 when a coup led by the 27-year-old Colonel Mu'ammer Gaddafi ushered in a new regime.

Libya under Gaddafi

In its review of the 2011 crisis in Libya, the UN Human Rights Council noted that 'it is not possible to understand the violence which occurred in Libya during the course of 2011 … without understanding first how profoundly damaged Libyan society has been over the last 40 years' (2012, p. 36). This damage can be attributed to the idiosyncratic rule and aberrant personality of Colonel Gaddafi, the self-proclaimed 'Brother Leader' of Libya for 42 years.

Soon after the overthrow of the monarchy by the 'Free Officers' Gaddafi assumed control. He quickly moved to sever Libya's ties with the West and take power from the business elite by nationalizing the banks and seizing holdings in the oil sector owned by foreign companies. He also abolished the parliament, outlawed opposition groups and imprisoned large numbers of intellectuals and activists considered a threat to his rule. Gaddafi's profound restructuring of Libya derived from his ideological belief in forging the 'Jamahiriya' (meaning the 'state of the masses'). To this end, in 1977 Gaddafi changed Libya's official name to 'The Great Socialist People's Libyan Arab Jamahiriya'. This unique mix of Arab nationalism, socialism and sharia law was outlined in great detail in Gaddafi's 'Green Book' which claimed to propound a 'Third Universal Theory' as an alternative to capitalism and communism. Despite the implications of the title 'state of the masses', the new regime was, even for the region, unusually dictatorial and 'a personal creation largely dependent on [Gaddafi's] role' (The International Crisis Group, 2011a, p. i). The new political system was based on a hierarchical structure comprising 'people's congresses' whereby (in theory) the will of the people was expressed directly without the need for political parties and fed upwards through the political system to ensure the government received, and acted upon, the people's demands.

In practice, this system enabled Gaddafi to exercise unrivalled and unaccountable power across all sectors of Libya's society and economy. Though obviously the locus of power, after 1977 Gaddafi held no formal position: his title 'Brother Leader' or 'Leader of the Revolution' was not recognized in the political system, allowing him to portray himself as above politics and, indeed, the people's champion against incompetent and/or corrupt governments (Vandewalle, 2006, p. 100).

Gaddafi's foreign policy proved highly controversial, regionally and internationally. His attempts to portray himself variously as the 'African King of Kings' and the 'Iman of the Muslims' often met with both hostility and derision (Bellamy and Williams, 2011, p. 842). He aligned himself with figures such as Fidel Castro, Yasser Arafat and Gamal Nasser and supported 'anti-colonial' movements worldwide, including the Polisario in Morocco, the IRA in Northern Ireland and various groups in Latin America. The US accused Gaddafi of supporting global terrorism and, beginning in 1981, periodically attacked Libyan planes and ships in the Gulf of Sidra. In retaliation, on 5 April 1986 Libyan agents planted a bomb in a Berlin nightclub frequented by US soldiers which killed three and injured over 200. Ten days later the US bombed Tripoli and Benghazi. On 21 December 1988, Pan Am flight 103 from London to New York exploded over Lockerbie, Scotland, killing all 259 passengers and crew – the majority of whom were American – and 11 people on the ground. In 1989 Libya was widely accused of planting a bomb on the French UTA plane which exploded over Niger killing all 171 people on board. In response the Security Council imposed a series of economic sanctions. In 1991 a UK-led investigation into the Lockerbie bombing issued indictments against two Libyans, Abdelbaset al-Megrahi and Lamin Khalifah Fhimah. Gaddafi agreed to hand over the suspects in 1999 and in January 2001 Fhimah was acquitted but al-Megrahi was found guilty.

Libya's relationship with the West improved greatly following the 2003 invasion of Iraq which appears to have convinced Gaddafi to temper his belligerent stance. Gaddafi's new policies were regularly cited by advocates of the 'war on terror' as examples of the benefits derived from Bush's confrontational foreign policy. According to David Frum and Richard Perle, 'Qaddafi's surrender is precisely the result that the robust polices of the Bush administration is calculated to achieve' (2004, p. 260). While the fate of Saddam Hussein certainly appears to have frightened Gaddafi, the US and EU also offered his regime a series of financial inducements to move in from the cold (Malone, 2006, p.170). In a letter to the Security Council in August 2003 Libya accepted responsibility for the Lockerbie bombing and three months later Gaddafi announced he was ceasing his chemical weapons programme. In 2004 Gaddafi toured Europe and by 2005 normal diplomatic relations had been restored. Abdelbaset al-Megrahi was released on compassionate grounds in August 2009 and his return to Libya was portrayed as a great personal victory for Gaddafi.

Ash-sha'b yurīd isqāṭ an-niẓām

Karen Dalacoura cautions against seeing recent events in the Arab World as overly interconnected. She argues that this stems from a historic trend –

the myth of 'Arabism' – whereby these peoples are perceived as almost homogeneous. The tumultuous events of 2011, she claims, have some generic catalysts but ultimately stem from 'profoundly different causes [and] contexts' (Dalacoura, 2012, p. 63). Others, however, view the events as indicative of the pervasive influence of 'pan-Arabism' which explains how the turmoil spread so quickly (Gause, 2011). While civil society in the Arab World had often been depicted as weak and the prospects for democracy slim (Stephan and Robertson, 2003; Yom, 2005), the perceived strength of many regimes derived from a superficial understanding of society in these states and the 'Orientalist' notion that these people were predisposed to authoritarianism (Santini, 2011). This was facilitated in part by the extent to which the West interacted with these states on an elite level, dealing primarily, and at times exclusively, with regimes, thereby ignoring the people, civil society and ultimately the underlying societal discontent. Jo Becker of HRW, for example, notes that protests had taken place in Bengazi for almost four years prior to the 2011 uprisings. The demonstrators sought information about the massacre of some 1,200 prisoners at the Abu Salim prison in Tripoli in 1996, but their efforts 'went unnoticed by most of the world' (Becker, 2011).

The West supported a number of undemocratic regimes in the Middle East during the Cold War, and after the 11 September 2001 attacks the EU and the US arguably again prioritized security over democratization and human rights (Blakeley, 2009). Many regimes in the Middle East exploited the new disposition, enabling them to align with the West in the 'war on terror' whilst perpetuating domestic oppression (Hollis, 2012, p. 93). This was particularly the case with respect to Libya which came to play a key role in the war on terror as a site of 'extraordinary rendition' (Amnesty International, 2012; Cobain, 2012). According to a report by Amnesty International in 2010:

> Libya's reintegration into the international community has not been accompanied by significant reforms or long-lasting improvements in the domestic human rights situation. The slow pace of domestic reform contrasts sharply with Libya's increased visibility on the international scene and prompts fears that members of the EU and the USA ... are turning a blind eye to the human rights situation in order to further national interests. (2010, p. 9)

This did not go unnoticed amongst the people on the ground. Indeed, following the invasion of Iraq, Western support for democracy in the region was viewed with suspicion, if not hostility: the West's policies were increasingly seen as naked realpolitik with the continued support afforded to Israel despite the plight of the Palestinians, ostensibly evidence of a broader selective adherence to human rights and liberty (Hollis, 2012, pp. 85–6).

While rising oil prices had increased the wealth of many of the regimes in the Middle East, by 2011, Dalacoura notes, ordinary people were increasingly frustrated at their 'relative depravation' which stemmed from 'a combination of persistently high-unemployment ... rampant corruption, internal regional and social inequalities' (2012, p. 67). Paradoxically, the West's political and economic support for oppressive regimes had helped to create this volatility by facilitating the widening of both the financial gap between rich and poor and the governance gulf between rulers and ruled; according to Hollis, 'EU policies did help to trigger the Arab revolts, but by default rather than design' (2012, p. 93). Many on the ground, it seems, concluded that change would have to come from within.

In response to the popular protests which erupted in the wake of Mohamed Bouazizi's self-immolation, Tunisian President Zine el-Abidine Ben Ali mobilized his forces. The crack-down failed, however, when on 10 January the army declared it would no longer oppose the protestors and on 14 January Ben Ali fled to Saudi Arabia. This inspired protestors elsewhere, especially in Egypt where, on 25 January some 20,000 people took to the streets. While President Mubarak attempted to appease the protestors by forming a new government, replacing figures in the General Intelligence Service and announcing he would not stand for re-election, his regime fell on 11 February and the army assumed power.

Unsurprisingly events in Egypt influenced Libyans in the east of the country owing to their strong tribal ties. On 15 February mass demonstrations took place in Bengazi which soon spread throughout the rest of the country. By the 22nd protests had occurred in Tripoli. The speed with which the protests spread was striking, though in retrospect understandable: according to the International Crisis Group decades of repression, corruption and economic malaise had led to a situation where Libya was 'a large pressure cooker ready to explode' (2011a, p. 2). The 15 February protests precipitated this explosion and mobilized the disenchanted masses. In the wake of Libya's 'coming in from the cold' the economy had improved greatly but the benefits were largely concentrated in the hands of the elites (International Crisis Group, 2011a, p. 2; Hollis, 2012, p. 85).

While initially Gaddafi sought to align himself with the protestors, claiming he shared their frustration with the government's incompetence, he soon changed strategy when the nature of the rebellion became clear. Gaddafi then declared the protestors variously to be members of al-Qaeda, agents of the UK, France and the US and, most bizarrely, under the influence of hallucinogenic drugs and/or alcohol. The crisis thus quickly became a life-or-death struggle as, owing to the peculiarity of the regime in Libya, there were no independent internal actors capable of resolving the grievances and avoiding massive violence. In Morocco and Jordan the government initiated reforms to appease the protestors, while in Tunisia and Egypt the army aligned with the protestors against the regime on behalf of the state. Unlike Tunisia and Egypt where the state and the regime were separate (albeit relatively so) in Libya there was no such distinction and thus the conflict between the rebels and Gaddafi was more zero-sum in nature (The International Crisis Group, 2011a, p. ii).

Distrustful of the army, Gaddafi had created a series of brigades comprising members of his own tribe and mercenaries under the command of his sons. Violent clashes soon erupted throughout Libya but particularly in the east where rebels claimed to control the cities of Bengazi and Misrata. After four days hundreds were dead; HRW (2011b) claimed approximately 230 people had been killed, while Franco Frattini, the Foreign Minister of Italy, suggested the figure was closer to 1,000 (Fahim and Kirkpatrick, 2011). On 24 February the International Federation for Human Rights (2011) issued a statement claiming that 'Gaddafi is implementing a strategy of scorched earth. It is reasonable to fear that he has ... decided to largely eliminate, wherever he still can, Libyan citizens who stood up against his regime and, furthermore, to systematically and indiscriminately repress civilians'. While the rebels achieved some successes in the initial engagements, by the end of February Gaddafi's forces were in the ascendancy. On 16 March, as his forces closed in on Bengazi, Gaddafi warned: 'we are coming tonight ... We will find you in your closets ... We will show no mercy' (Heneghan, 2011).

International response

The Middle East and North Africa are areas of great geostrategic importance not least because of their huge reservoirs of oil. Prior to the Arab Spring the region constituted a complex tapestry of alliances, both regional and international, and a series of tenuous interlinked stalemates, such as between Israel and its neighbours Egypt and Jordan (Smith, 2011, p. 64). Disturbances in any of these states, therefore, whatever the normative agenda of the demonstrators, constituted a potential threat to regional order and international security. Indeed, in response to the early stages of the Arab Spring a senior Israeli official was quoted as saying, 'when some people in the West see what's happening in Egypt they see Europe 1989. We see Tehran 1979' (ibid., p. 62). This is indicative of the long-held fear that popular uprisings, and indeed democratization, in this region would usher in fundamentalist regimes opposed to both Israel and the West (Mueller, 1999: Kaplan, 2001; Eubank and Weinberg, 2001, p. 160). The election of Hamas in Palestine in 2006 was cited as evidence in support of this preference for authoritarianism (Hehir, 2007, p. 326). Unsurprisingly, therefore, the international response to events in 2011 was influenced by the fear that change would precipitate insecurity. While the demonstrators championed democracy and human rights, these laudable aims were often insufficient in themselves to convince democratic states to support immediately their cause. The influence of geopolitics is dealt with in more detail later in the chapter; the focus here is on the response to Libya, but it is important to note that this rapid and emphatic response was, in many respects, comparatively unique.

The Arab League and the African Union

Prior to the Arab Spring neither the Arab League nor the AU were considered key international actors. In the wake of the uprisings, and especially in the intervention in Libya, this perception has changed, especially with respect to the former. The support of the Arab League, the OIC, the Gulf Cooperation Council (GCC) and the AU – albeit less emphatically – for action against Libya was a crucial factor in the ultimate decision to intervene, though, as explored later in the chapter, these organizations have demonstrated a markedly selective approach to human rights protection (Williams, 2011).

Traditionally these organizations have confined their statements on such issues to endorsements of sovereign inviolability and vague calls for restraint. This had led many to dismiss the 'developing world' as one of recalcitrant purveyors of anachronistic values (Cooper, 2002; Evans, 2006). While there is no doubt but that the developing world has often voiced concerns about humanitarian intervention, some have argued that this has more to do with a concern for procedural legality and an opposition to *unilateral* intervention rather than a principled hostility to forcible human rights protection (Bellamy, 2009c, p. 38; Weiss, 2011, p. 5; Hehir 2012, p. 198). Indeed, Article 4(h) of the AU's Constitutive Act expressly legitimizes external interference by the AU and has been advanced as the most obvious manifestation of a move towards 'non-indifference' (Williams 2007; ICRtoP, 2012b).

On 22 February the OIC (2011) described the violence against protestors as 'a humanitarian disaster incompatible with Islamic and human values'. Later that day the Arab League took the unusual step of suspending Libya, only the second time in its history that it had taken such action (the first being the suspension of Egypt in 1979 in protest at the Egypt–Israel Peace Treaty). The following day the AU's Peace and Security Council declared that it 'strongly condemns the indiscriminate and excessive use of force and lethal weapons against peaceful protestors'. On 10 March the AU issued a communiqué which again condemned the violence

Box 14.1   Arab League Statement, 12 March 2011

[The Council of the Arab League decides:]

1 To call on the Security Council to bear its responsibilities towards the deteriorating situation in Libya, and to take the necessary measures to impose immediately a no-fly zone on Libyan military aviation, and to establish safe areas in places exposed to shelling as a precautionary measure that allows the protection of the Libyan people and foreign nationals residing in Libya, while respecting the sovereignty and territorial integrity of neighbouring States.

2 To cooperate and communicate with the Transitional National Council of Libya and to provide the Libyan people with urgent and continuing support as well as the necessary protection from the serious violations and grave crimes committed by the Libyan authorities, which have consequently lost their legitimacy.

and further recognized 'the legitimacy of the aspirations of the Libyan people for democracy, political reform, justice, peace and security'. The communiqué also expressed, however, the AU's 'rejection of any foreign military intervention'. It was the Arab League's statement on 12 March, however, that had arguably the greatest impact (see Box 14.1). In an unusually unequivocal statement the League declared that Libya's authorities had 'lost their legitimacy' and called on the Security Council to impose a no-fly zone and cooperate with the TNC (League of Arab States, 2011). US Secretary of State Hillary Clinton (2011) described the Arab League's statement as precipitating a 'sea-change' in attitudes at the Security Council.

The Security Council acts

As the violence in Libya escalated a number of UN bodies issued condemnatory statements. The UN Special Adviser on the Prevention of Genocide and the Special Adviser on the Responsibility to Protect issued a joint statement on 22 February which condemned 'systemic attacks against civilian populations by military forces, mercenaries and aircraft' (UN Press Release, 2011). On the same day the UN High Commissioner for Human Rights echoed this statement, warning that the attacks 'may amount to crimes against humanity' (Bellamy, 2011, p. 2). The UN Human Rights Council convened a special session on the situation in Libya on 25 February at which they condemned violence and called for Libya to be suspended. The formal suspension, the first of its kind, was unanimously endorsed by the General Assembly on 1 March; in response UN Secretary

General Ban Ki-moon stated: 'the winds of change are sweeping across the Middle East' (General Assembly, 2011).

The Security Council passed Resolution 1970 on 26 February 2011 which invoked the Council's Chapter VII powers. The resolution referred the situation to the ICC and imposed an arms embargo, travel ban and asset freeze against the Libyan authorities. The resolution warned that the Council would 'review the appropriateness of the measures contained in this resolution, including the strengthening ... as may be needed'. Considering the first significant protests had begun only 11 days earlier, and China and Russia's usual antipathy to such measures, this resolution was a surprisingly robust display of unity and resolve (Weiss, 2011).

Nonetheless, despite continued condemnation from UN bodies, NGOs, regional organizations and the ICC officially launching an investigation into the situation on 3 March, the violence continued to escalate. Fears grew that Resolution 1970 had been exposed as bluster; but on 17 March the Security Council passed Resolution 1973 which sanctioned the imposition of a no-fly zone over Libya. The Resolution condemned 'the gross and systematic violation of human rights ... committed by the Libyan authorities' and warned that these acts may 'amount to crimes against humanity'. The Security Council sanctioned 'a ban on all flights in the airspace of the Libyan Arab Jamahiriya' and authorized states to 'take all necessary measures ... to protect civilians and civilian populated areas under threat of attack'. The Resolution also included an injunction to all states to deny permission to any aircraft registered in Libya to take off from, land in or overfly their territory. The Resolution was passed with ten in favour and five abstentions (China, Russia, Germany, Brazil and India). Gaddafi described the action as 'terrorism' (Golovnina, 2011).

Operation Unified Protector

The military action against Libya which began on the 19 March was initially led by the US, France and the UK and comprised four officially separate, though coordinated, national operations. On 24 March NATO agreed to lead the operation – thereafter called Operation Unified Protector – despite the concerns of prominent members such as Germany and Poland. On 4 April Barack Obama withdrew US forces from direct combat, though the US continued to play a central role in the mission (Barry, 2011, p. 5). This was rather misguidedly described as 'leading from behind' by one of President Obama's aides and has come to be used as a pejorative term deployed by critics of Obama's foreign policy more generally (Chesterman, 2011a, p. 5). Nonetheless the US's role was crucial: it provided 75 per cent of the intelligence, surveillance, reconnaissance data and refuelling planes used (Daalder and Stavridis, 2012). A number of non-NATO members – Sweden, Jordan, Qatar, Morocco and the UAE – also took part in the operation.

NATO's mission had three official aims: police the arms embargo, patrol the no-fly zone, and protect civilians (ibid.). While the first two were achieved without major difficulty the third proved more onerous. The rebels soon proved unable to hold their gains let alone defeat Gaddafi's forces, and there is little doubt that they would have been resoundingly defeated had NATO not provided massive military support (Barry, 2011, p. 9). This necessitated, however, creatively interpreting the mandate provided in Resolution 1973. As with the intervention in Kosovo in 1999 (see Chapter 11) NATO's tactics evolved from an initial focus on the regime's military bases and heavy weapons to a more expansive approach which necessitated portraying a wide array of Libyan infrastructure as implicated in attacks on the civilian population. This angered many states, with China, Russia and South Africa particularly damning the strategy employed (Barry, 2011, p. 6). Additionally, the increasing determination to remove Gaddafi from power was legitimized as consistent with the need to 'protect civilians' as per Resolution 1973; but this divided international opinion. Indeed, within days of the mission commencing NATO member state governments were calling for Gaddafi to step down (Western and Goldstein, 2011, p. 49). As the International Crisis Group noted, 'the leading Western governments supporting NATO's campaign make no secret of the fact that their goal is regime change' (2011a, p. i). The European Union, indeed, had stated on 11 March that it believed Gaddafi must be replaced. During the Security Council discussions on Resolution 1973 regime change was, however, expressly ruled and cited by China as a *sine qua non* for it abstaining on, rather than vetoing, the resolution (Buckley, 2012, p. 86).

While in retrospect the intervention appears to have been swift and successful, at times the mission appeared to be faltering. By the end of May, in fact, it seemed that the rebel-held cities of Misrata and Jebel Nafusa would fall, prompting France unilaterally to air-drop weapons to the rebels (Barry, 2011, p. 7). In April the AU issued a statement calling for an end to the campaign, noting that 'there is no military solution to the crisis in Libya' (AU, 2011, p. 11); and by June the International Crisis Group was calling for 'an immediate ceasefire' to facilitate negotiations (2011a, p. ii). On 26 April the AU called for an end to NATO's bombing campaign and rejected the calls for Gaddafi to step down, warning that 'it should be left to Libyans to choose their leaders and international actors should refrain from taking positions or making pronouncements that can only complicate the search for a solution' (AU, 2011, p. 12). NATO's campaign suffered from a lack of resources. Whereas military planners had hoped to fly 300 sorties a day they could manage only about 150. To ensure success, NATO stretched the terms of Resolution 1973 beyond breaking point. By August this, combined with defections from Gaddafi's regime, and arms illegally smuggled to rebels from the UAE, Qatar and France, turned the tide (Smith, 2011, p. 75). Operation Unified Protector officially ended on 31 October, 222 days after it had started. Colonel Gaddafi was dead and a Transitional National Council was in power.

In total NATO flew 26,000 sorties – an average of 120 per day – and the operation cost significantly less than previous interventions in the Balkans, Iraq and Afghanistan. Nonetheless some did wonder at the value of the military expenditure (Valentino, 2011) and the damage done to NATO's credibility due to the obvious internal divisions and unwillingness of many members to take part in the mission (Clarke, 2011b). At the conclusion of the operation, NATO Secretary General Anders Fogh Rasmussen stated: 'when the United Nations took the historic decision to protect you [the Libyan people], NATO answered the call. We launched our operation faster than ever before ... We were effective, flexible and precise' (NATO, 2011). The head of Libya's Transitional National Council, Mustafa Abdul Jalil, praised NATO at the operation's conclusion, stating: 'the operations of NATO were successful. The strikes were so accurate that civilians were not harmed' (ibid.). A report by the Human Rights Council's commission of enquiry, however, investigated 20 NATO airstrikes and found that 60 civilians were killed and 55 injured. In one airstrike alone, on Majer on 8 August 2011, NATO bombs killed 34 civilians and injured 38 (Human Rights Council, 2012, p. 17). The Commission also noted that NATO had provided 'a lack of sufficient information' for a number of strikes impeding the work of the Commission (ibid., p. 18). Nonetheless, the Commission's overall findings read: 'NATO conducted a highly precise campaign with a demonstrable determination to avoid civilian casualties. For the most part they succeeded' (ibid., p. 22).

Impact on the debate

The intervention in Libya was heralded by many in the West as both laudable and the dawn of a new era of human rights enforcement. The intervention was certainly far less contentious than the previous Western intervention in the region – the 2003 invasion of Iraq – and undeniably constituted a remarkably swift response which contrasted sharply with the widely criticized reaction to recent crises in Darfur, Sri Lanka and the Democratic Republic of Congo. Of course, international reaction was not unanimously positive and the sub-sections below outline the major sources of contestation.

Interests or humanitarianism?

According to the International Crisis Group, the Western media 'from the outset presented a very one-sided view of the logic of events'. In particular, they claim that the media chose to 'ignore evidence that the protest movement exhibited a violent aspect from very early on' (2011a, p. 4). This suggests that the image presented by Western states of helpless victims fighting cruel tyranny in Libya over-simplified and distorted the reality on the ground. Gaddafi was certainly not the only besieged leader to use force against his people during the Arab Spring. Why he alone incurred a NATO intervention is the subject of much debate.

There has been a persistent suspicion that Europe's primary interests in the Arab World are twofold: to stem the flow of migrants (Hollis, 2012, p. 84) and to secure access to the region's vast oilfields (Rutledge, 2005, pp. 21–37). These concerns, many argue, have shaped the West's response to the Arab Spring and explain the often cautious support afforded to the pro-democracy protestors and the manifestly inconsistent treatment of relatively similar situations (Crocker, 2011). It has, additionally, not gone unnoticed that the US and Europe have supplied oppressive regimes in the Middle East with arms for decades, even during the Arab Spring. In February 2011 UK Prime Minister David Cameron spoke to protestors in Tahrir Square, in Cairo, about his regret that his country had supplied Mubarak's regime with arms for decades. Yet, the delegation which travelled with him to Egypt and later Oman, Qatar and Kuwait included representatives from eight defence and aerospace companies seeking new clients (Smith, 2011, p. 84). A 2012 report by the House of Commons Foreign Affairs Committee (2012, p. 42) criticized the presence of these arms dealers as having 'squandered' an opportunity to repair damage to the UK's, and the West's, credibility amongst the protestors who were already dismayed by the West's decades-long military support for oppressive regimes across the region. A report by Amnesty International in 2011 condemned arms sales to the Middle East, highlighting the trade between NATO states and regimes in Bahrain, Egypt, Libya, Syria and Yemen. The report noted that Belgium, France, Germany, Italy, Spain and the UK had been supplying arms to Gaddafi since 2005 (Amnesty, 2011). Russia and China also continued to supply arms to certain oppressive regimes, including Libya and Syria, while violence was being perpetrated (Barnard, 2011; Branigan, 2011; Amnesty, 2011).

While Tunisia's geopolitical importance has always been relatively minor, it has been claimed that the West's initial desire was to preserve order and protect the regime. It is alleged that France offered Tunisia's President Ben-Ali military support just before his regime fell (Halim, 2011). Similarly, the protestors in Egypt found that their democratic agenda and humanitarian appeals failed to guarantee them Western support. While Mubarak's regime was obviously undemocratic and corrupt, he was widely seen as key to stability in the region, owing in large part to his willingness to recognize and maintain peaceful relations with Israel (Smith, 2011, p. 11). Western support for the protestors arguably only became vociferous and unequivocal once preserving the old regime was obviously no longer tenable.

The response of the West to the situation in Bahrain, however, arguably highlights the inconsistency more graphically. Of Bahrain's population, 80 per cent are Shia Muslims who have traditionally felt unfairly treated by the Sunni monarchy. At a major protest rally held on 14 February government forces fired on the crowds. This mobilized protestors and a series of further rallies were held all of which met with violence from the police and military. As the government struggled to contain the situation and disperse protestors from their rallying point at the Pearl Roundabout in the capital Manama, the GCC sent troops into Bahrain on 14 March. The arrival of these troops, largely from Saudi Arabia and the UAE, enabled the government to declare and enforce a state of emergency. What followed was described by the International Crisis Group as a 'campaign of retribution':

> Before the crackdown [on 14 March] Bahraini security forces were accused of using excessive force, beating, torturing and in some cases killing peaceful demonstrators. Following the GCC troop's arrival, these security forces came down on protestors and opposition groups even harder. (International Crisis Group, 2011b, p. 4)

Despite this, the ICG note that Western states, the US in particular, criticized the violence 'relatively mildly' and 'threw its weight behind the Crown Prince's efforts to jump-start a substantive reform effort'. This was a consequence, they note, of the US's desire to appease the Saudi royal family who considered the continuation of the monarchy in Bahrain an 'existential issue' (2011b, p. 21).

The response to the situation in Libya, however, was far from equivocal, with the West and the Arab League emphatically aligning with the protestors almost immediately. While Gaddafi had been contained to some degree after 2003 he was still widely viewed as a dangerously unpredictable leader. Additionally, Gaddafi's tenure had none of the geostrategic attributes of Mubarak or the Bahrain Royal family and thus his removal was considerably more palatable (Clarke, 2011a; Smith, 2011, p. 77). Had Gaddafi continued his campaign of violence it would undoubtedly have led to destabilizing refugee flows into Egypt and across the Mediterranean into Europe. There was also, of course, the not insignificant fact that Libya is the world's tenth largest oil producer. As the historian Dirk Vandewalle noted, 'the two central features in the development of Libya after its independence in 1951 have been oil, and the revenues its sales generated' (2006, p. 2). Gaddafi's belligerent foreign policy was funded by Libya's oil; removing Gaddafi and facilitating the ascension of a regime favourably disposed to the West would remove a threat and ensure the highly prized reliable supply of Libyan oil (Ali, 2011). This conspiratorial position was disputed by others, however, who argued that Gaddafi's ability to preserve order in Libya and his new conciliatory posture meant, on a purely materialistic calculation, that it was more attractive to keep him in power than support a disparate alliance of unknown, and possibly fundamentalist, groups. Testifying before the UK Foreign Affairs Committee Alistair Burt, UK Undersecretary of State for the Middle East and North Africa, dismissed the charge of inconsistency over the response to Libya and Bahrain, stating that 'each of these countries is different. How do I explain inconsistency? Exactly that way: each place is different' (House of Commons Foreign Affairs Committee, 2012, ev 41).

It is also clear that the West's – particularly the US's – decision to act was heavily influenced by the Arab League's support for military action. While the Arab League stated in its 12 March statement that its motivation stemmed from humanitarian concern, Alex Bellamy and Paul Williams offered three alternative, and less altruistic, explanations. First, they note that not all League members attended the meeting on 12 March and thus the pro-US GCC faction exercised a disproportionate influence on the statement issued; second, Gaddafi's pariah status within the region, particularly amongst influential heads of state such as the Saudi royal family, facilitated the call for action; third, 'some regional governments may have calculated that turning the international spotlight on Libya would divert attention from their own troubles' (Bellamy and Williams, 2011, p. 842). Likewise, it has been claimed that Saudi Arabian officials admitted they supported Western air strikes against Libya in exchange for the US's silence over events in Bahrain (Blomfield, 2011). The Arab Spring has certainly witnessed a new activism on the part of Saudi Arabia, often exercised through Oman and Qatar, states it heavily influences. While Saudi Arabia, itself a repressive and undemocratic state, has pursued a seeming quixotic approach to human rights and democracy, its policy has been consistent if judged by a different standard: the country has supported protestors where the aim was to overthrow Shia regimes – such as Assad in Syria – but it has supported Sunni regimes against popular uprisings, as in Egypt and Bahrain.

By definition it is very difficult to determine the 'real' motivation behind a state's decision to intervene. It is certainly unlikely than any state will take action for one reason alone, and few supporters of humanitarian intervention demand such parsimony. Indeed, President Obama admitted that the intervention was undertaken 'because our *interests* and values are at stake'. Later in the same speech he stated that 'America has an important strategic interest in preventing Qaddafi from overrunning those who oppose him' (White House, 2011). As explored in detail in Chapter 8, many argue that even if we can conclusively prove that action – such as the intervention in Libya – was a product of more than just concern for human rights and democracy, this does not mean the intervention cannot be deemed humanitarian.

'The Responsibility to Protect has arrived'

R2P, as discussed at length in Chapter 6, has been championed as a way to improve the international community's response to intra-state crises. The intervention in Libya was described as 'a textbook case of the R2P norm working exactly as it was supposed to' (Evans, 2011) and 'a triumph ... for R2P' (Thakur, 2011). The ICRtoP declared that the intervention 'reflects a historic embrace of the RtoP principles' (ICRtoP, 2011a), while Ban Ki-moon declared triumphantly that 'by now it should be clear to all that the Responsibility to Protect has arrived' (2011c). Thus, the triumphalism which greeted the Libyan intervention was not limited to Libya: the decision to act was seen by many as evidence that a profound change had occurred at the Security Council, specifically amongst the P5. The intervention, Bellamy and Williams have argued, signified that the Security Council was now motivated by 'a new politics of protection' (2011, p. 826), while Ban Ki-moon declared that Resolution 1973 'affirms, clearly and unequivocally, the international community's determination to fulfil its responsibility to protect civilians from violence perpetrated upon them by their own government' (2011a).

Others, however, have challenged the idea that R2P was a key causal factor in the Security Council's decision. As detailed in Chapters 5 and 6, the Security Council has always had the power to undertake action of the type mandated against Libya under Chapter VII of the Charter (Stahn, 2007; Reinhold, 2010). Nonetheless, while these powers have long existed they have not always been used, and thus if it can be proved that R2P has created a momentum which pushes the P5 to utilize its pre-existing powers then this would be significant. Yet, while Resolution 1973 certainly coheres with the spirit of Pillar III of R2P it is noteworthy that there is no mention of this subsidiary international responsibility in either Resolution 1970 or 1973. The term 'responsibility to protect' appears once in Resolution 1970 – 'the Security Council ... Recalling the Libyan authorities' responsibility to protect its population' – while Resolution 1973 includes the sentence 'reiterating the responsibility of the Libyan authorities to protect the Libyan population'. In both cases the 'responsibility to protect' cited is that of the host state. There is no mention of the international community's 'responsibility to protect' or of the action having been a function of, or even informed by, this responsibility.

During the debate at the Security Council on draft Resolution 1973 held on 17 March there were markedly few references to R2P. The ten states who voted in favour of the Resolution justified the intervention as necessary to prevent a humanitarian tragedy, not that they felt duty-bound to do so because of the existence of R2P. Of these states only Colombia, the US, France and the UK identified a legitimate authoritative basis for the action to supplement the humanitarian/moral justification; all cited Chapter VII, or Resolution 1970 adopted under Chapter VII. The French and Colombian representatives both declared that Libya had failed in its responsibility to protect its own people and South Africa stated that by passing Resolution 1973 the Security Council had 'acted responsibly to protect and save the lives of countless civilians' (UNSC, 2011, pp. 3, 7, 10). There was, however, no mention during the meeting of the external dimension of R2P constituting a basis – legal or normative – for the action taken.

President Obama's televised speech to the nation on 28 March justifying the intervention made no mention of R2P (White House, 2011). UK Prime Minister David Cameron, likewise, did not refer to R2P in his statement the day the air strikes began or during his address to the London Conference on Libya ten days later (Cameron, 2011a, 2011b). An article jointly written by President Obama, Prime Minister Cameron and French President Nicolas Sarkozy also failed to mention R2P (Obama et al., 2011). Two explanations for R2P's relative absence are possible: first, though the action was motivated by R2P the key leaders didn't want to acknowledge this lest it create a precedent for future action. This would be in keeping with the Security Council's determination to include a reference to the 'exceptional' nature of the action sanctioned in all Chapter VII resolutions passed in the 1990s. Second, the action was motivated by R2P, but because the term is unpopular with many states it was not used lest it erode support (Welsh, 2011, p. 1).

Resolution 1973 was certainly not the first time that the Security Council had justified a Chapter VII Resolution on the basis of humanitarian need as some claimed (Adams, 2011). Resolution 794 on Somalia in December 1992 cited 'the magnitude of the human tragedy ... the deterioration of the humanitarian situation' as its rationale. During the course of the debate on Resolution 794 a number of states argued that the Security Council had a responsibility to save lives; Russia, in fact, declared that the action was being taken because of the existence of 'obligations to put an end to the human tragedy in that country' (UNSC, 1992, p. 27). Russia's avowal of an 'obligation' was, as Wheeler notes, seen as 'groundbreaking' (2002, p. 185). In 1999, two years before the publication of *The*

Responsibility to Protect, the Security Council passed Resolution 1265 which advanced an expansive summation of the Council's understanding of the responsibilities of states to adhere to international humanitarian law and its remit to act in cases where states fail to meet this responsibility. States, including the P5, have, therefore, affirmed 'moral responsibilities' and even obligations prior to the emergence of R2P. The problem, of course, is that these declarations did not lead to a more consistent response to intra-state crises.

Additionally, while many proclaimed the passing of Resolution 1973 as a moment when the international community displayed an unprecedented collective determination to halt a mass atrocity (Western and Goldstein, 2011; Daalder and Stavridis, 2012), others were more pessimistic. Bruce Jones, pointing to the fact that the five states which abstained on Resolution 1973 are key international actors, worried that this highlighted the lack of a shared understanding of international security and 'a shared sense of responsibility' which 'bodes ill for our collective ability to manage the mounting security challenges of our time' (2012, p. 52). The reasons why the P5 supported intervention also appear to suggest a minimal role for R2P: while the UK and France supported military action from an early stage, the US, Russia and China were more reticent. The Arab League's 12 March call for action was a key factor in the US's decision to support military action and Russia and China's abstention. Indeed, according to Bellamy and Williams, Resolution 1973 was 'unthinkable without the Arab League's resolution' (2011, p. 843), while Evans described the Arab League's support as 'absolutely crucial' in convincing Russia and China to abstain (2011). The fact that Resolution 1973 was passed because of the Arab League's support must give us pause for thought: if the situation in Libya was as ominous as the intervening coalition repeatedly stated once 1973 was passed, why would the support from the Arab League be a *sine qua non* given that the humanitarian situation on the ground would have been the same whatever the League said? Additionally, predicating international action to protect human rights on the support of the Arab League is troubling given that 19 of the 22 members of the League are authoritarian regimes (Economist Intelligence Unit, 2010; Freedom House, 2011).

Some have argued that the decision by China and Russia to abstain was a wholly cynical ploy to help the West blunder into another costly quagmire. Michael Walzer (2011) suggested they 'abstained on the final Security Council vote, perhaps because they can't imagine an outcome that better suits their interests in the Middle East and Africa'. The fact that representatives of Gaddafi's regime seeking to purchase arms travelled to China during NATO's intervention led some to wonder aloud about China's intentions and humanitarian credentials (Barnard, 2011; Branigan, 2011).

Many who heralded the intervention as evidence of R2P's efficacy did, however, acknowledge the influence exerted by other factors (Evans, 2011; Thakur, 2011). Bellamy described the intervention as the result of a 'confluence of factors' which he accepted 'is unlikely to be often repeated' (2011, p. 4). Indeed, only five weeks after sanctioning military action against Libya the Security Council failed to agree on a statement condemning the violence in Syria due to China and Russia's opposition. The situation deteriorated and a draft resolution was put to the Council on 4 October. The draft resolution was far less robust than 1973, yet China and Russia both exercised their veto in an unusually emphatic rejection. Ban Ki-moon decried the P5 for having failed to abide by their responsibility, and the decision was denounced by the ICRtoP as 'a failure of the Security Council's responsibility to protect the Syrian population' (Ki-moon, 2011c; ICRtoP, 2011b). On 4 February 2012 a second draft resolution was put to the Security Council and again China and Russia both used their veto. At the time of writing the violence continues.

The claims made by Ban Ki-moon in the wake of the intervention against Libya that 'R2P has arrived' and that the Security Council acted out of a collective 'determination to fulfil its responsibility to protect civilians from violence perpetrated upon them by their own government' seem less convincing in light of the Security Council's response to Syria. In this case the propitious confluence of factors which enabled Resolution 1973 did not occur. Given that R2P has not altered the decision-making process, or powers, of the Security Council, it is debatable whether the new era proclaimed by some in the wake of Resolution 1973 is imminent if action is so obviously predicated on the – all too rare – confluence of P5 interests and human suffering (Buchanan and Keohane, 2011, p. 51; Hehir, 2012, p. 211).

Never again?

The operations in both Afghanistan and Iraq very obviously tempered enthusiasm for military interventions and many wondered whether these had rendered such operations a thing of the past. The intervention in Libya, therefore, came as a surprising relief to many advocates of intervention who welcomed it as not just laudable in itself but the dawn of 'a more humane world' (Axworthy, 2011). The 'official' NATO view, perhaps unsurprisingly, was that this was 'a model intervention' and indicative of its continued importance and future role (Daalder and Stavridis, 2012, p. 2). While the intervention was, in many respects, 'an unprecedented moment' (Williams, 2011, p. 249), whether it has precedential qualities is obviously a key question going forward.

It is debatable whether NATO will ever conduct a similar operation in the future. Assessing the mission on operational grounds, Michael Clarke highlighted the internal divisions which surfaced and warned that 'the strain that this curious little war has already put on the forces of the most capable European allies ... is a poor omen for the future; it may come to look like a tipping point in the transatlantic evolution of NATO' (Clarke, 2011b). In addition to the political problems, the mission exposed NATO's insufficient resources; remarkably, European states ran out of ammunition in the early phases of the operation (Smith, 2011, p. 77). At points, in fact, some feared that the end of NATO, and US hegemony, was nigh (Daalder and Stavridis, 2012, p. 3). A gloomy appraisal has implications far beyond the future of NATO itself: if its capacity to act has been diminished by the intervention, then obviously the prospects of it launching military operations declines, with obviously ominous implications for the future of humanitarian intervention.

The manner in which NATO conducted the operation has additionally meant, according to some, that non-NATO states will never again sanction the imposition of a no-fly zone. NATO, it is argued, exceeded the terms of Resolution 1973 particularly with respect to their goal of 'regime change' and thus diminished the prospects of future collective action (Falk, 2011). This 'abuse' of the authorization granted by the Security Council appeared to confirm the fear voiced during the negotiations on 1973 that Western states could not be trusted with a restrictive mandate (Milne, 2011; Bellamy and Williams, 2011, p. 843). Indeed, within days of the military action the Secretary General of the Arab League criticized NATO for exceeding its mandate (Bellamy and Williams, 2011, p. 845), while various African leaders and AU officials openly decried the abuse of the mandate and illegitimate 'mission creep' (AllAfrica, 2011).

Michael Schmitt challenges this view, however, arguing that the mandate contained in Resolution 1973 is significantly different from previous no-fly zone authorizations. He notes 'that which most sharply distinguishes [Resolution 1973] ... lies in the fact that it contemporaneously authorizes military action beyond the maintenance of a no-fly zone to protect civilians and civilian "populated areas"' (2011, p. 56). This instruction to 'protect civilians and civilian populated areas' necessitated more than just policing the skies. While Schmitt's defence of the legality of the campaign may be accurate, there is no denying that the tactics employed have created an antipathy amongst states for agreeing to similar mandates in future (Barry, 2011, p. 12).

Beyond these factors, it has been suggested that the Libya operation constituted a unique, never-to-be-repeated constellation of factors. From an operational perspective Libya proved a uniquely favourable target for a number of reasons, including: its close proximity to NATO bases across the Mediterranean; the Libyan army's inability to attack NATO's command networks, communication links or homelands; and the regime's 'ham-fisted' propaganda campaign (ibid., p. 11). Additionally, Gaddafi was, according to Clarke, 'a weak and crazy opponent' (2011b); with the exception of President Mugabe of Zimbabwe and President Museveni of Uganda, few regional leaders supported Gaddafi, who constituted a uniquely unpopular leader whose overthrow few lamented. Not only did Gaddafi lack regional support, the major powers had little interest in preserving his rule, thus, unlike the Russian support for Assad in Syria, Gaddafi had no 'friends' on the Security Council willing to veto action. Had the Security Council been divided it appears highly unlikely that President Obama would have supported unilateral intervention and thus Gaddafi could have continued his campaign against the rebels unhindered.

The viability of prevention

Gaddafi's relationship with Libya was far more symbiotic than that of Ben Ali in Tunisia and Mubarak in Egypt where there was a separation between the leader and the state/army. This extended to Gaddafi's entire family and circle of appointees; hence Saif Gaddafi's vow that 'we will keep fighting until the last man, or even the last woman is left standing' can be seen as more than just posturing: Gaddafi and his cabal had little choice but to try to crush the protestors (International Crisis Group, 2011a, p. 4). Additionally, few foreign states were enthusiastic about receiving an exiled Gaddafi, so the option of stepping down and leaving, as both Ben Ali and President Saleh of Yemen did, was arguably not available.

Gaddafi's speech on 16 March, in which he promised to slaughter all those who opposed him as his troops marched towards Bengazi, appeared to signal that preventative diplomacy was no longer an option (see Box 14.2). Such emphatic declarations of murderous intent are rare and given his track record, believing he was implacable, was understandable (Chesterman, 2011a).

While the dominant narrative suggests a mass atrocity was looming and the intervention prevented it, Alan Kuperman argues that there is no evidence to support this. Rather, he suggests that Gaddafi had employed a strategy of 'narrowly targeting the armed rebels' (Kuperman, 2011). Gaddafi had not perpetrated a mass slaughter in Zawiya, Misurata or Ajdabiya, cities he had retaken from the rebels prior to his march on Bengazi and thus, Kuperman argues, there is no basis for the dire predictions that Bengazi would have been razed. The best way to prevent massive loss of life was thus to refrain from using force against Gaddafi (Kuperman, 2013). In (sharp) contrast a report by the Human Rights Council outlines a litany of excessive force, murder, torture and rape perpetrated by Gaddafi's forces, including prior to the 16 March speech when some 200 protestors were killed during clashes on 20–21 February in Tripoli alone (2012, p. 7).

> **Box 14.2 The moment of truth has come': Gaddafi's 16 March speech**
>
> They are finished, they are wiped out. From tomorrow you will only find our people. You all go out and cleanse the city of Benghazi ... We will track them down, and search for them, alley by alley, road by road, the Libyan people all of them together will be crawling out. Massive waves of people will be crawling out to rescue the people of Benghazi, who are calling out for help, asking us to rescue them ... And I, Muammar Gaddafi, I will die for my people. With Allah's help. No more fear, no more hesitation, we are no longer reluctant. The moment of truth has come ... we did not initiate this violence, they started it. Of course, these words will have an impact on the traitors and infidels. Tonight they will panic and they will collapse. You are capable of doing it. You are capable of achieving this. Let's set our women and daughters free from those traitors. God is great.
>
> *Source*: Tomasky (2011).

On 10 March the AU announced the establishment of an Ad Hoc High Level Committee charged with finding a diplomatic solution to the crisis. The commencement of NATO's bombing campaign obviously made this task significantly more difficult and the AU was critical of the manner in which its diplomatic path was sidelined and in the intransigence of the TNC, especially their insistence that Gaddafi stand down (AU, 2011).

Libya is interesting, however, in terms of a different aspect of the debate on prevention. Since 2005, in an effort to reframe R2P, many of its supporters have stressed its preventative potential (Bellamy, 2009a, p. 3). This has dismayed certain vocal advocates of the idea (Weiss, 2007a, p. 104) and the value of R2P's avowal of prevention has been questioned by others (Hehir, 2012, p. 87). Regardless of one's views on the efficacy of prevention, it is by definition based on an assumption that conflicts can be identified as looming while still in their infancy, hence the widely quoted cliché 'nipping conflicts in the bud'.

The crisis in Libya, however, erupted to the great surprise of most; indeed the Arab Spring as a whole was not predicted by even Middle East specialists (Gause, 2011). Societal discontent is not unusual in a dictatorship but the unease of the Libyan people had certainly not reached noteworthy proportions until February 2011. As Bellamy notes:

> None of the world's various risk-assessment frameworks viewed the country as posing any sort of threat of mass atrocities. Neither was a conflict widely anticipated. For example, CrisisWatch, the early-warning arm of the International Crisis Group, did not even mention Libya

in its report of February 2011, and did not issue a 'conflict risk alert' until after the conflict had actually erupted. (2011, p. 4).

The Minorities at Risk Coalition, indeed, listed 68 states as being 'at risk' though it did not include Libya (Bellamy and Williams, 2011, p. 838). A report by UNICEF in 2010 noted that Libya had experienced a 'buoyant' growth rate, high per capita income, high literacy rates and high life expectancy and ranked the country 55 out of 182 states (International Crisis Group, 2011a, p. 2). Internationally Libya continued its rehabilitation into late 2010; in May of that year it was elected uncontested to the UN Human Rights Council and in October the EU and Libya agreed a deal on migration cooperation, to the dismay of human rights organizations (HRW, 2011a, p. 567). A review of Gaddafi's 40-year reign in late 2009, by UK journalist Ian Black, concluded by saying:

> many things are going his way; Western oil companies and investors are flocking to Tripoli, domestic repression has eased somewhat, and even tourism is developing ... Gaddafi stills turns heads everywhere he goes, even sharing a photo call with Barack Obama at the G8 Summit in Italy. Shortly after the 40th anniversary celebrations he will address the United Nations in New York as Chair of the African Union. The handsome young Colonel has come a long way. (Black, 2009)

Just over two years later Gaddafi – deposed and facing prosecution at the ICC – was dragged from a drainage pipe as he desperately sheltered from NATO bombs, beaten by a mob and shot dead. For days people queued to have their picture taken with his corpse, displayed unceremoniously on the floor of an industrial freezer. Few, if any, foresaw his demise until the protests had erupted. Thus, while prevention has long been vaunted as preferable to intervention once hostilities have begun, the compelling logic of this assertion belies the fact that prevention requires a degree of forewarning that is very often unavailable (Huttenbach, 2008, p. 472). Thus, the sudden eruption of violence in Libya demonstrates that, while preventative measures, such as early warning frameworks, should not be ignored, they are not likely to identify all future atrocities. Crafting improved ways to *respond* to crises, therefore, still has great merit.

Conclusion

When asked about the significance of the 1789 French Revolution, the Chinese Communist leader Zhou Enlai is reported to have said: 'it is too soon to say'. While this story is likely to be apocryphal, it has served commentators well in their reflections on a variety of tumultuous events in the modern era. It is certainly apposite with respects to the Arab Spring. The dust has not yet settled on the region and events throughout 2010–12 have followed a remarkably mercurial path. In many cases elation at the break with the past has been quickly replaced by fear of the future. Indeed, as Smith notes, 'the term "Arab Spring" has stuck. If the events of 2011 were being named now, however, something less optimistic might be chosen' (2011, p. 86).

NATO's intervention in Libya was remarkable for the support it was afforded within the Security Council, across the Middle East and the rest of the world. Few could have predicted such unanimity behind Western military action in the wake of the acrimonious invasion of Iraq. This led to wildly optimistic assessments of the future which were quickly dispelled as the situation in Syria deteriorated and the Security Council dithered. The 'humanitarian intervention' in Libya thus increasingly appears as an aberration. No other state caught in the maelstrom of the Arab Spring has been subjected to coercive outside intervention; while in Tunisia and Egypt domestic forces proved too strong for the rulers, protestors in Bahrain and especially Syria have fared much worse. The fact that the Libyan intervention fits the pattern of inconsistency discussed throughout this book does not mean, however, that it cannot be regarded as a humanitarian intervention. It is quite possible to herald Operation Unified Protector as just, while lamenting non-intervention elsewhere. So long as the US and Europe 'seem intent on preserving relations with some of their key regional authoritarian allies' (Santini, 2011) a consistent response to the ongoing crises will likely remain elusive. It must be remembered too that China and Russia are emerging as major powers and this will have a bearing on the future of humanitarian intervention (Hehir and Murray, 2012). As Alexandar Konovalov, President of the Institute of Strategic Analysis in Moscow notes, 'a new Middle East is taking shape and Russia is not indifferent to how it emerges' (Buckley, 2012, p. 82). Predictions about the precedential qualities of the Libyan intervention must be tempered, therefore, by the realization – evident throughout the Arab Spring – that democratic states are not immune to realpolitik and that profound shifts in the global distribution of power, away from the West, are underway.

Questions

- Was the intervention in Libya necessary?
- What does the passing of Resolution 1973 tell us about decision making at the Security Council?
- Do you think R2P influenced the decision to intervene in Libya?
- What do the different international responses to the uprisings in Libya, Bahrain and Syria tell us about contemporary attitudes to human rights protection?
- To what extent does the response to the situation in Syria after the intervention in Libya influence our appraisal of the latter?

Further reading

In 2011 *Ethics and International Affairs* published a special issue (25/3) on the intervention in Libya, which comprises an excellent collection of reflective analyses. For an in-depth overview of Gaddafi's reign see Dirk Vandewalle (2006) *A History of Modern Libya* (Cambridge: Cambridge University Press). A very comprehensive overview of events before and during the intervention in Libya is provided in Ben Smith (2011) 'The Arab Uprisings', House of Commons Library, Research Paper 11/73, 11 November, available at: http://www.parliament.uk/briefing-papers/RP11-73 (accessed 13 December 2012).

Barry, B. (2011) 'Libya's Lessons', *Survival*, 53/5, 5–14.

Bellamy, A. and Williams, P. (2011) 'The New Politics of Protection? Cote d'Ivoire, Libya and the Responsibility to Protect', *International Affairs*, 82/7, 825–50.

Dalacoura, K. (2012) 'The 2011 Uprisings in the Arab Middle East', *International Affairs*, 88/1, 63–79.

Gause, G. (2011) 'Why Middle East Studies Missed the Arab Spring', *Foreign Affairs*, 90/4, 81–90.

Hehir, A. and Murray, R. (eds) (2013) *Libya, the Responsibility to Protect and the Future of Humanitarian Intervention* (Basingstoke: Palgrave Macmillan).

Hollis, R. (2012) 'No Friend of Democratization: Europe's Role in the "Arab Spring"', *International Affairs*, 88/1, 81–94.

House of Commons Foreign Affairs Committee (2012) 'British Foreign Policy and the Arab Spring', 3 July. Available at: www.parliament.uk/business/committees/committees-a-z/commons-select/foreign-affairs-committee/inquiries1/parliament-2010/british-foreign-policy-and-the-arab-spring/

International Crisis Group (2011) 'Popular Protests in the Middle East and North Africa: Making Sense of Libya', Middle East/North Africa Report 107, 6 June. Available at: www.crisisgroup.org/en/regions/middle-east-north-africa/north-africa/libya/107-popular-protest-in-north-africa-and-the-middle-east-v-making-sense-of-libya.aspx .

Western, J. and Goldstein, J. (2011) 'Humanitarian Intervention Comes of Age' *Foreign Affairs*, 90/6, 48–59.

Conclusion: The Future of Humanitarian Intervention?

At the time of writing Syria dominates the international political agenda, with the conflict proving as intractable as it is bloody. Over 20,000 people have died since the conflict began in March 2011 and images of the suffering have been broadcast across the globe on a daily basis. In August 2012 Kofi Annan stepped down as UN-Arab League Envoy to Syria after less than six months in the post. In his resignation speech he decried the Syrian government's 'intransigence' and the 'escalating military campaign' waged by the rebels. He also, however, chastised the Security Council for its 'disunity' and their preoccupation with 'finger-pointing and name-calling' (Annan, 2012). China and Russia have twice vetoed resolutions at the Security Council aimed at increasing the pressure on Assad's regime. Annan's successor, Lakhdar Brahimi, began his tenure with less than stirring words; admitting that he was 'scared' he stated that brokering a peace deal was 'nearly impossible' (BBC, 2012b).

For those interested in the issues raised in this book, the international response to Syria and the Arab Spring more generally is compelling. The unforeseen eruption of intra-state conflicts across the region has certainly provided researchers with enough material to last many years; we can surely expect a flood of academic publications akin to the deluge post-Kosovo. While this is a boon for academics weary of writing about Kosovo, Darfur and Iraq these events are, ultimately, a damning indictment of the present international system; any assessment of 'human progress' must be tempered, not just by the barbarity within Syria, but as much by the obfuscation without. The various theories, legal debates and moral complexities discussed throughout this book at times obscure the terrible nature of the issues under discussion. I hope anyone inspired by the previous chapters will do more than treat this topic as an abstract curiosity and, mindful of the human suffering inherent in this issue, seek to effect change; it is perhaps too much to imagine that humanity's propensity to inflict violence will be eliminated anytime soon, but it is surely possible to contrive a means by with orchestrated mass murder is at least halted.

Unlike some issues in IR, humanitarian intervention is an aspect of international politics that generates intense popular concern, as evidenced by the general outrage at the violence in Syria. The question of how, or indeed whether, to 'save strangers' interrogates humanity's moral calculus and necessarily provokes emotive reactions. A scepticism towards, and even a rejection of, humanitarian intervention does not necessarily constitute an immoral or even amoral outlook; genuine concerns remain about the effects that such action has, with many arguing that humanitarian intervention does more harm then good. As Alan Kuperman rightly notes, 'no policy of humanitarian military intervention should be implemented without a sober consideration of its unintended consequences' (2000a, p. 118).

This final chapter highlights potential future trajectories for the status of humanitarian intervention and the arguments for and against each. Security Council use of Chapter VII since the 1990s has meant that we can now affirm with at least some confidence that the Council has the power to sanction humanitarian intervention, even if the basis for this competency is somewhat ambiguous (DIIA, 1999, p. 62; Chesterman, 2002, p. 48). The focus in this chapter, therefore, is on the status of unilateral humanitarian intervention: that is, intervention not explicitly sanctioned by the Security Council.

As the contentious debate about humanitarian intervention has raged, certain academics and policy makers have advanced prescriptions in an effort to resolve the dispute. In the following sections I assess the pros and cons of three such approaches, beginning with the argument for the maintenance of the status quo, then the perspective in favour of legal and political reform, and finally, most radically and controversially, the argument that the current foundational norms and practices of international law are no longer apposite and should be disregarded.

In defence of the status quo

Despite the fact that the current status of humanitarian intervention is clearly problematic, many support the maintenance of the status quo. Advocates of this perspective argue that any change in favour of humanitarian intervention would necessarily undermine the principle of sovereign inviolability and negatively impact on international peace and stability.

As the tenets of sovereignty constitute a bulwark, albeit a normative one, against great-power interference in the affairs of smaller states, the principle of non-intervention, it is argued, is a norm that should be maintained (Ayoob, 2002, pp. 82–3; Bickerton et al., 2006). Sovereignty has acted as an ordering principle in international relations, and diminishing its provisions, even for ostensibly altruistic reasons, would have a destabilizing effect on the international system, as states would subjectively judge each other's moral rectitude, leading to a proliferation of interventions and wars (Holbrook, 2002, p. 148; Gibbs, 2009, p. 222; Cunliffe, 2011). Since 1945 the principle of non-intervention has, it is claimed, been responsible for a reduction in inter-state wars, and this progressive trend will be jeopardized if sovereignty is diluted (Reus-Smit, 2005, pp. 72–5; O'Connell, 2011). Therefore, a new law regarding humanitarian intervention may have positive effects on the willingness of states to adhere to international human rights legislation but would certainly lead to more wars between states, the negative consequences of which would outweigh any related positives (Jackson, 2000, pp. 291–2; Pape, 2012).

It is argued that moves to facilitate humanitarian intervention, far from protecting the weak from the strong, will actually further empower the existing international hierarchy, which will abuse this new doctrine (Whitman, 2005, p. 266; Amin, 2008; Mamdani, 2009). Adherents to this view are inherently sceptical of the willingness of states to act morally and fear that any increase in the scope of legitimate intervention would be abused (McCormack, 2010, p. 120; Chomsky, 2011). Many point to the inaction in the face of the genocide in Rwanda to support their claim that interests must be involved when states intervene, and thus that humanitarian intervention is illusory (Burke, 2004, pp. 77–8; Whitman, 2005, pp. 261–3).

Clearly, therefore, one school of thought on the need to maintain the status quo derives its conviction from an inherent suspicion of humanitarian intervention; to paraphrase Robert Cox, intervention is always for someone and some purpose (see Chapter 4). Not all adherents to the idea of maintaining the status quo, however, base their prescriptions on this view. Many agree that changing international law to accommodate humanitarian intervention would have negative effects, though they do not discount the possibility that a genuine humanitarian intervention may well have positive consequences. Certain writers have argued, therefore, that the current tenets of international law should be maintained but that humanitarian interventions, though always illegal, should be tolerated provided they are judged to have been genuinely humanitarian.

In contrast to those who are inherently critical of humanitarian intervention, proponents of the 'mitigation' perspective seek to enable interventions with positive humanitarian consequences without adversely affecting the status of sovereignty as the foundation of the international system (Wheeler, 2002, p. 129). Simon Chesterman argues that 'in the event of an intervention alleged to be on humanitarian grounds, the better view is that such an intervention is illegal but that the international community may, in extreme circumstances, tolerate the delict' (2002, pp. 231–2). Rather than excluding the possibility that humanitarian intervention could ever be justified, or contriving a new legal doctrine of intervention, this perspective advocates maintaining the present illegality of such action but suggests that judgements should be made on a case-by-case basis. If a particular act is deemed to have had a positive humanitarian outcome, it could be deemed illegal but judged leniently (Byers and Chesterman, 2003, pp. 198–203; Stromseth, 2005, pp. 243–4; Rengger, 2005, pp. 159–61). Thomas Franck argues that this idea of mitigation has precedents in the national legal systems of most countries. He cites those cases where illegal acts have undeniably been committed and yet, though a guilty verdict is returned, the judge takes account of the circumstances and motivations behind the act and the punishment is mitigated accordingly: 'law does not thrive when its implementation produces *reductio ad absurdum*: when it grossly offends most person's common moral sense of what is right' (Franck, 2005, p. 212). Humanitarian intervention could therefore conceivably be excused as an extraordinary remedy to a great wrong (Simma, 1999, p. 22).

While this idea of mitigation is certainly attractive, proponents are somewhat vague about who the jury would be and how exactly their opinion could be gauged (Byers and Chesterman, 2003, pp. 198–203; Falk, 2005a, p. 48). Additionally how sanctions might be imposed against those states that fail to have their plea of mitigation accepted is problematic: the Security Council certainly has the power to impose sanctions but requires the assent of the P5 to do so. Therefore, the rejection of a state's claim of mitigation could very well have no adverse consequences for that state if it is convinced that a member of the P5 will block any censure. Additionally, while the idea of not creating a potentially destabilizing precedent is proffered as a means to close the floodgates to intervention, there is no way to guarantee that instances when mitigation is granted will not be cited in the future. A number of NATO states, particularly Germany, expressly stated in 1999 that they did not want Operation Allied Force to become a precedent, yet it has been cited since, most notoriously by Russia during its 2008 intervention in Georgia. Without clear guidelines about what constitutes a legitimate humanitarian intervention, determining when mitigation should be afforded is inherently subjective. Formally codifying the basis for legitimate humanitarian intervention is a solution to this particular concern, but this necessarily involves initiating legal change which constitutes a change to the status quo.

The need for legal reform

In the wake of NATO's intervention in Kosovo in 1999, a number of major international commissions argued that legal change to the status of humanitarian intervention is a pressing requirement (IICK, 2000, p. 186; ICISS, 2001a, p. 3). As the Security Council constitutes the only viable means by which humanitarian intervention can legally be sanctioned, and because the Council is so obviously partisan, it was suggested that reform of the international legal and political system is a necessity (Simma, 1999, p. 6; Guicherd, 1999, p. 20; Weiss, 2009, p. 1). As Cherif Bassiouni notes, the efficacy of, and support for, a legal system is, to a significant extent, a function of its capacity to adhere to 'predictable and consistent outcomes' (2009, p. 37). At present, there is a very obvious lack of predictability with respects to the official international response to intra-state crises which is thus potentially corrosive. As Koskenniemi writes, 'the point of law is to give rise to standards that are no longer merely "proposed" or "useful" or "good", and which therefore can be deviated from if one happens to share a deviating notion of what in fact is useful and good (2006, p. 69). The 'deviation' Koskenniemi here warns about can be seen to manifest, in the specific case of humanitarian intervention, with respect to the discretionary powers of the P5 which by definition facilitates political selectivity that is destructive of the original law.

There are many aspects of international law that require reform, but humanitarian intervention is presented as uniquely important by virtue of 'the degree to which international society is affected morally and practically by humanitarian catastrophe' (Hurrell, 2005, p. 30). Unlike the status quo/mitigation perspective, advocates of legal reform are uncomfortable with a legal system that criminalizes legitimate action. As Paul Christopher states, 'surely in those cases where we find our legal and moral rules at odds, we should endeavor to reconcile these differences' (2004, p. 248). Clearer rules would serve to remove the subjectivity currently inherent in the legality of humanitarian intervention, as detailed in Chapter 5, and enable more consistent and regulated action in defence of the oppressed.

The idea of reforming the existing system was a recurrent theme during ICISS's consultations prior to the publication of *The Responsibility to Protect*. In Latin America, 'suggestions were made for a modification of the UN Security Council and creation of a tribunal or other body within the General Assembly to make pronouncements upon the gravity of human rights abuses and the related necessity or otherwise of an intervention' (ICISS, 2001b, p. 372). In Egypt participants believed 'the mechanisms and procedures of the intervention process must be subject to objective international regulation' but that the Security Council was not sufficiently objective (ibid., pp. 375–6). To ensure intervention was 'objective, nonselective and free from double standards' the participants called for reform of the Security Council's powers: 'it was suggested that an international body of eminent persons be created to make recommendations to the President of the Security Council or to the Secretary General as to when collective intervention might be required' (ibid., p. 377). At the consultations held in India there were calls for 'an international independent body established outside the UN in order to make sure that standards and conditions are met by interveners' (ibid., p. 389). These calls from the developing world for the regulation of humanitarian intervention by an international body is further evidence of a general willingness to countenance intervention in certain circumstances but also a deep concern as to the existing mechanisms for so doing, especially regarding the powers vested in the Security Council.

Within academia differing perspectives exist regarding precisely what this legal reform should involve. Proposals suggested thus far include: a new treaty of unilateral humanitarian intervention (Burton, 1996); the creation of a new military force exclusively at the disposal of the United Nations (Johansen, 2006; Pattison, 2010, p. 229); the establishment of new international bodies empowered to deploy troops when situations deteriorate to certain levels (Woodhouse and Ramsbotham, 2005, p. 152; Buchanan and Keohane, 2011; Hehir, 2012, p. 228); and reforming the membership and powers of the Security Council (UN High-Level Panel on Threats, Challenges and Change, 2004, pp. 77–83; Chesterman, 2011b). Changing the law to permit unilateral humanitarian intervention is clearly the proposal that most directly addresses the dilemma posed by humanitarian intervention, and it is, perhaps unsurprisingly, also the most controversial.

A rationale for advocating reform of the existing political/legal structure is that this structure currently prevents genuine humanitarian interventions from taking place. This premise is rejected by those who argue that the reason interventions do not take place has little to do with the legal prescriptions against such action and much more to do with the lack of will for such action (Chesterman, 2002, p. 54). Reform, therefore, is a solution to a problem which does not exist. Additionally, many are concerned that permitting unilateral intervention 'would encourage more frequent resort to the practice in less compelling circumstances than at present by creating an additional doctrinal basis for justifying the use of force' (Stromseth, 2005, p. 257). Advocates of new rules have countered that this concern lacks credibility given that it assumes that international law is currently free from potential abuse, which is patently not the case (Chopra and Weiss, 1992). Additionally Michael Burton notes:

> while no legal norm is entirely free from potential abuse ... the use of codified criteria will diminish rather than exacerbate the problem of pre-textual interventions. A codified rule of intervention is less prone to abuse than is the current 'sublegal' status accorded unilateral humanitarian intervention. (1996, p. 422)

The concern expressed by those who support the status quo lest reform undermine sovereignty is potentially assuaged if reform is initiated with the consent of the international community of states. Indeed, as Hedley Bull, one of the most vocal proponents of the principle of sovereignty, stated, 'the idea of sovereign rights existing apart from the rules laid down by international society itself and enjoyed without qualification has to be rejected in principle' (1984a, pp. 11–12). The status of sovereignty at any given time should therefore reflect the general will of states, and changes in this status can occur if the international community agrees that these changes are required. Amendments to the law governing humanitarian intervention, derived from an inclusive process and with the assent of all states, would potentially constitute a diminution of the status of sovereignty but would be based on general agreement rather than the initiative of a powerful elite (Burton, 1996, pp. 233–6).

Beyond current international law

Reforming international law is notoriously difficult: the lack of enthusiasm and subsequent action that greeted the publication in 2004 of the recommendations of the UN High-Level Panel on Threats, Challenges and Change, and the negligible reforms implemented at the 2005 World Summit, are indicative of the difficulties inherent in achieving international consensus (Weiss, 2007a, p. 112; Evans, 2008, p. 47; Chesterman, 2011b). This difficulty is particularly pronounced when it comes to issues as sensitive as intervention and sovereignty.

Frustrated by the often glacial pace of reform and not least the developing world's seemingly intransigent adherence to ostensibly anachronistic legal doctrine, many have argued that the necessary reforms cannot be achieved through consensus. The opposition voiced by states to changes to the status of sovereignty, and the willingness of China and Russia to veto any substantial reform in the status of humanitarian intervention, are portrayed as self-interested spoiling by illiberal governments that reflect neither the wishes of their own citizens or world opinion (Reisman, 2000, pp. 13–15; Pattison, 2007, pp. 307–8). It is argued, therefore, that change must be forced through by those 'enlightened states' that embody progressive moral rectitude (Glennon, 1999, p. 2).

Geoffrey Robertson has argued that 'the struggle for global justice' is a struggle against sovereignty. He suggests that a state's right to sovereignty must be conditioned on its record, and in this respect 'the reality is that states are not equal' (2002, p. 372). Increased intervention is championed by those who believe the West has a duty to engage in 'a new kind of imperialism, one acceptable to a world of human rights and cosmopolitan values' (Cooper, 2002). A new legal asymmetry between Western states and 'old fashioned kinds of states outside the post-modern continent of

Europe [and America]' is legitimized on the basis that the West is a positive trail blazing force in international affairs (ibid.). It is argued that as long as international law lags behind the evolution of moral values and facilitates the perpetuation of human suffering, it is legitimate to bypass its tenets.

This strain of thought has led to the idea of assigning unique powers to democracies. Democracies would be granted special dispensation to act when morally necessary for the good of humankind (Elshtain, 2003b; Daalder and Lindsay, 2007). A new right of humanitarian intervention would, therefore, be created, but this right would be conditional on the democratic credentials of the intervening state and subject to the judgement of other ostensibly 'morally reliable' actors, namely liberal democracies (Buchanan and Keohane, 2004; Ikenberry and Slaughter, 2006, pp. 25–6). The fear that a new right of intervention reserved for a select few constitutes a regression is rejected; intervention would still be constrained by the normative pressure exercised by other democracies which would ensure that the new privilege was not abused (Glennon, 1999; Reisman, 2000, pp. 16–17; Gow, 2005, pp. 13–14, 123). This idea was espoused during the 2008 US presidential elections by Republican nominee Senator John McCain, who spoke of his belief in the need to create a 'league of democracies' (McCain, 2007).

It is claimed that the rationale for creating a new conditional right of unilateral humanitarian intervention is further enhanced by the additional assertion that the use of force by liberal democracies will necessarily benefit the world through the spread of liberal values and the expansion of the community of democratic states. The spread of democracy is good not only for the people within these newly liberated states but also for the global community, due to the fact that democracies do not go to war with other democracies, so the zone of peace will expand. Hence democratic interventionism will bring positive benefits to the oppressed who are saved, to the global community which will enjoy a reduction in warfare, and to the intervening state itself which benefits from increased global stability and security (Gow, 2005; Slaughter, 2011a).

As noted in Chapter 5, the evolution of international law and the increased preference for codification as the source of international law since 1945 have been driven to a large extent by a perceived need to create a more egalitarian international regime, though the extent of this democratization of international law should not be exaggerated (Simpson, 2004; Orford, 2011). The rehierarchization of the international sphere into liberal and illiberal states clearly challenges this trajectory and is therefore considered by some to constitute regression rather than progress (Reus-Smit, 2005; Douzinas, 2009).

More generally, the presumption that democratic states are uniquely reliable actors in international relations is contested (Alvarez, 2001;

Cunliffe, 2011; Hehir, 2012, p. 127). This presumption has undeniably been tarnished by the Bush Administration's foreign policy. Prior to becoming US secretary of state, Condoleezza Rice argued that 'America's pursuit of the national interest will create conditions that promote freedom, markets and peace ... American values are universal' (2000, p. 47), while President G. W. Bush continually stressed the need for the US to assume unilaterally a leadership role in defending civilization and spreading democratic values. Proponents of the view that international law must be superseded by a new normative framework would certainly recoil at an association with Bush's more bellicose statements, such as 'I don't care what the international lawyers say; we are going to kick some ass' (Coicaud, 2006, p. 426). The record of the Bush administration in terms of defending freedom, spreading liberal values and increasing international security was mixed to say the least. Moves to alter unilaterally the rules governing the use of force and the status of sovereignty in the wake of the invasion of Iraq understandably fermented tensions in international relations, as the so-called unenlightened states resisted such moves (Falk, 2004, p. 41).

In the contemporary era there is less appetite for a new legal order based on unilateral US/Western leadership; the election of Barack Obama in 2008 led many to hope that a new era of multilateralism would begin, which, in certain respects has come to pass. The intervention in Libya in 2011 certainly constituted a uniquely inclusive military action with support (albeit of varying intensity) from the Security Council, the Arab League, the AU, NATO, the EU and the OIC; the contrast with the international division which greeted the invasion of Iraq is obvious. Yet, Obama's prodigious use of unmanned drones and his inability/unwillingness to close the detention centre at Guantanamo Bay and ratify the ICC statute have tempered the optimism. Beyond just the different character of the Obama administration the rise of China and Russia must also be recognized as compelling a change in US foreign policy (Hehir and Murray, 2013). As these two states grow in power, and others such as Brazil, German, India, Turkey and South Africa also increase their international activism, the international system is arguably moving towards a new era of multipolarity; this can only have an effect on the future of humanitarian intervention. Indeed, as much as the intervention in Libya constituted a moment of unique international unity, the manner in which NATO interpreted Resolution 1973 has created significant disquiet and arguably turned many off the idea of authorizing no-fly zones, let alone full-scale military interventions. The debate about unilateral intervention could well, therefore, re-emerge in the coming years.

Conclusion

The prescriptions assessed in this chapter constitute three potential scenarios for the future status of humanitarian intervention. As is clear, none is without contention and each holds the potential to contribute to, rather than reduce, instability and violence. Over the course of the next decade it will be interesting to see which – if indeed any – achieves ascendancy. While international politics often appears to be characterized by division and acrimony, especially over humanitarian intervention, there are grounds for some optimism. ICISS reported that its global consultations on humanitarian intervention demonstrated, 'even in states where there was the strongest opposition to infringements on sovereignty, there was a general acceptance that there must be limited exceptions to the non-intervention rule for certain kinds of emergencies' (2001a, p. 31). Research carried out by the Institute for Global Policy found little opposition to the principle of humanitarian intervention in the developing world, though they reported significant concerns as to the authorization of such action (Institute for Global Policy, 2009, pp. 7–8). This suggests that there isn't widespread opposition to the principle of the international community having *some* role in upholding universally agreed human rights domestically, so long as there is openness, consistency and accountability. The support of the GCC, the OIC and the Arab League for the Security Council-mandated military action against Libya in March 2011, of course, provided a more contemporary and emphatic example of this willingness to countenance external intervention (Bellamy, 2011, p. 1). This was definitive evidence that sovereign inviolability is not a sacrosanct principle in the developing world (Weiss, 2011, p. 5). Of course, as discussed in Chapter 14, the response to Bahrain must temper positive assessments of the response to Libya.

Over the past 25 years views on humanitarian intervention have fluctuated widely; from being portrayed generally as either inconceivable or highly dangerous during the Cold War, to being touted as a global panacea in the 1990s, to once again being deemed misplaced, and indeed dangerous, utopianism in the wake of 11 September 2001. The intervention in Libya briefly led to a surge in optimism but the failure to respond to the crisis in Syria once again tempered expectations. One constant during this period has been that at any given time somewhere in the world people have been systematically persecuted by their own state and they have cried out to the nebulous 'international community' for help. While some lucky souls have indeed been rescued, many, many more have not. During the bloody 20th century far more people were killed at the hands of their own government than by foreign forces, and instances of intra-state violence have continued to degrade international relations in the new millennium.

Violence has been a perennial feature of human history. We can think not only of the organized violence of the industrialized state or the mechanized slaughter of the Holocaust. Evidence from the pre-modern world suggests that humanity has always found a rationale for the use of force. The eminent historian Ronald Wright has pointed to troubling evidence that our disposition to violence may well be a genetic function of our ancestral evolution, and specifically the struggle between our ancestors the Cro-Magnons and the Neanderthals:

> If it turns out that the Neanderthals disappeared because they were an evolutionary dead end, we can merely shrug and blame natural selection for their fate. But if they were in fact a variant or race of modern man, then we must admit to ourselves that their death may have been the first genocide. Or, worse, not the first – merely the first of which evidence survives. It may follow from this that we are descended from a million years of ruthless victories, genetically predisposed by the sins of our fathers to do likewise again and again. (2006, p. 25)

Wright's thesis highlights that, despite the often self-congratulatory talk of 'progress', contemporary civilization faces a number of challenges which bear striking similarities to those our ancestors confronted, and if anything we appear to be failing to meet them more spectacularly than ever before. Indeed, despite the enormous changes that have occurred in the last 200 years in both domestic and international politics, it is sobering that the dilemma posed by humanitarian intervention remains unresolved.

The concepts 'human rights' and 'humanitarian intervention' are certainly (relatively) new, but debates about the morality of war and the more vexed question of coming to the aid of the suffering certainly are not. There is no reason to suspect that in the future these debates, central to the issue of humanitarian intervention, will somehow resolve themselves, or that some international accord will emerge with such normative or legal force that intra-state violence will cease. It is safe to say, therefore, that intra-state atrocities will occur periodically, and thus the issue of humanitarian intervention will continue to exercise the minds of academics, complicate the agenda of international statesmen and women and outrage the moral sensibilities of the general public.

One of our most exalted human characteristics is our capacity for empathy and perennial predisposition towards the avowal of, if not always the adherence to, moral norms. Yet, we have failed to find a way to resolve these traits with our preferred unit of political order, the state. The emergence of the state as the dominant unit of currency in IR has facilitated some of the worst atrocities in human history. Unless we conclude that, on this basis, the state has lost its utility we must find some way to accommodate the state with human rights. The significance of the relationship between sovereignty and human rights is immense, and, as Chris Brown notes, 'has plenty of life left in it as a focus for study' (2006, p. 4). Humanitarian intervention is interesting, depressing and hugely important. I hope this book has stimulated interest in this subject and that it will serve as the basis for much-needed further research.

Bibliography

Adams, S. (2011) 'R2P and the Libya Mission', *Los Angeles Times*, 28 September 2011, [online] http://globalr2p.org/media/pdf/R2P_and_the_Libya_mission_Simon_Adams.pdf accessed 28 November 2011 (accessed 2 September 2012).

Ali, T. (ed.) (2000) *Masters of the Universe? NATO's Balkan Crusade* (London: Verso).

Ali, T. (2011) 'Who Will Reshape the Arab World?' *The Guardian*, 29 April, [online] http://www.guardian.co.uk/commentisfree/2011/apr/29/arab-politics-democracy-intervention (accessed 12 September 2012).

AllAfrica (2011) 'Libya: Ambiguities Over the Interpretation of UN Resolutions 1973 Causing Global Consternation', 23 March. [online] http://allafrica.com/stories/201103230883.html (accessed 12 September 2012).

Alvarez, J. (2001) 'Do Liberal States Behave Better? A Critique of Slaughter's Liberal Theory', *European Journal of International Law*, 12:2, 183–246.

Ambos, K. (1999) 'Comment – NATO, the UN and the Use of Force: Legal Aspects', *European Journal of International Law*, 10:1, 1–22.

Amin, S. (2008) *The World We Wish To See* (New York, NY: Monthly Review Press).

Amnesty International (2000) 'NATO/Federal Republic of Yugoslavia: "Collateral Damage" or Unlawful Killings?' [online] http://www.amnesty.org/en/library/info/EUR70/018/2000 (accessed 25 September 2012).

Amnesty International (2010) *'Libya of Tomorrow': What Hope for Human Rights?* (London: Amnesty International Publications).

Amnesty International (2011) 'Arms Trade to Middle East and North Africa Shows Failure of Export Controls', 19th October. [online] http://www.amnesty.org/en/news-and-updates/report/arms-trade-middle-east-and-north-africa-shows-failure-export-controls-2011-1 (accessed 2 May 2012).

Amnesty International (2012) 'Libyan Rendition Case Shows it's Time for UK to Come Clean', April 18. [online] http://www.amnesty.org/en/news/libyan-rendition-case-shows-it-s-time-uk-come-clean-2012-04-18 (accessed 2 May 2012).

Anderson, B. (1991) *Imagined Communities: Reflections on the Origins and Spread of Nationalism* (London: Verso).

Anderson, M. S. (1998) *The Origins of the Modern European State System, 1494–1618* (London: Longmans).

Anheier, H., Glasius, M. and Kaldor, M. (2001) 'Introducing Global Civil Society', in H. Anheier, M. Glasius and M. Kaldor (eds), *Global Civil Society 2001* (Oxford: Oxford University Press).

Annan, K. (1999a) *The Question of Intervention* (New York: United Nations University Press).

Annan, K. (1999b) 'Two Concepts of Sovereignty', *Economist*, 18 September, 49–50.

Annan, K. (1999c) 'Secretary-General Presents his Annual Report to General Assembly', UN document SG/SM/7136-GA/9596, 20 September [online] http://www.un.org/News/Press/docs/1999/19990920.sgsm7136.html (accessed 2 May 2009).

Annan, K. (2000) 'Annex 1: Opening Remarks', in J. Sherman (rapporteur), *Humanitarian Action: A Symposium Summary*, International Peace Academy, International Policy Conference, 20 November [online] http://www.ciaonet.org/wps/shj04/ (accessed 2 May 2009).

Annan, K. (2001) 'Message Honouring Raphael Lemkin', Press Release SG/SM/7842, 13 June. [online] http://www.un.org/News/Press/docs/2001/sgsm7842.doc.htm [accessed November 2012].

Annan, K. (2005a) *In Larger Freedom: Towards Development, Security and Human Rights for All*, UN document A/59/2005, 21 March [online] http://www.un.org/largerfreedom/ (accessed 2 May 2012).

Annan, K. (2005b) 'In Larger Freedom: Decision Time at the UN', *Foreign Affairs*, 84:3, 63–70.

Annan, K. (2012) 'Press Conference by Kofi Annan Joint Special Envoy for Syria', 2 August. [online], http://www.unog.ch/unog/website/news_media.nsf/%28httpNewsByYear_en%29/

9483586914CF2E3FC1257A4E00589EE7?OpenDocument&cntxt=FA0FE&cookielang=en (accessed 13 September 2012).

Anscombe, G. (1981) 'The Justice of the Present War Examined', *Ethics Religion and Politics* (Blackwell: Oxford).

Arbour, L. (2008) 'The Responsibility to Protect as a Duty of Care in International Law and Practice', *Review of International Studies*, 34:3, 445–8

Archibugi, D. (2003) 'Cosmopolitical Democracy', in D. Archibugi (ed.), *Debating Cosmopolitics* (London: Verso).

Arend, A. and Beck, R. (1993) *International Law and the Use of Force* (London: Routledge).

Armstrong, D. and Farrell, T. (2005) 'Introduction: Force and Legitimacy in World Politics', in D. Armstrong and T. Farrell (eds), *Force and Legitimacy in World Politics* (Cambridge: Cambridge University Press).

Armstrong, D., Farrell, T. and Lambert, H. (2007) *International Law and International Relations* (Cambridge: Cambridge University Press).

Armstrong, D., Farrell, T. and Maiguashca, B. (eds) (2005) *Force and Legitimacy in World Politics* (Cambridge: Cambridge University Press).

Assembly of the African Union (2004) 'Decision on Darfur', Third Ordinary Session, 6–8 July, Addis Ababa, Ethiopia [online] www.iss.co.za/AF/profiles/Sudan/darfur/audecjul04.pdf (accessed 25 September 2012).

AU (African Union) (2011) 'Report of the Chairperson of the Commission on the Activities of the AU High Level Ad Hoc Committee on the Situation in Libya', PSC/PR/2(CCLXXV), 26 April. [online] http://www.peaceau.org/uploads/275reportonlibyaeng.pdf (accessed 12 September 2012).

Axworthy, L. (2011) 'In Libya, We Move Toward a More Humane World', *Globe and Mail*, 23 August.

Ayoob, M. (2002) 'Humanitarian Intervention and State Sovereignty', *International Journal of Human Rights*, 6:1, 81–102.

Bain, W. (2003a) *Between Anarchy and Society* (Oxford: Oxford University Press).

Bain, W. (2003b) 'The Political Theory of Trusteeship and the Twilight of International Equality', *International Relations*, 17:1, 59–77.

Bain, W. (ed.) (2006) *The Empire of Security and the Safety of the Peoples* (London: Routledge).

Bain, W. (2007) 'In Praise of Folly: International Administration and the Corruption of Humanity', in A. Hehir and N. Robinson (eds), *State-Building: Theory and Practice* (London: Routledge).

Bain, W. (2010) 'Responsibility and Obligation in the "Responsibility to Protect"', *Review of International Studies*, 36, 25–46.

Bainton, R. (1986) *Christian Attitudes Towards War and Peace* (Nashville, TN: Abingdon Press).

Bandow, D. (1999) 'Europe's Welfare Queens', Cato Institute, 30 March [online] http://www.cato.org/pub_display.php?pub_id=5502 (accessed 2 May 2009).

Bandow, D. (2000) 'NATO's Hypocritical Humanitarianism', in T. G. Carpenter (ed.), *NATO's Empty Victory* (Washington DC: Cato Institute).

Bardos, G. (2003) 'International Policy in Southeast Europe: A Diagnosis', in R. Thomas (ed.), *Yugoslavia Unraveled: Sovereignty, Self Determination, Intervention* (Oxford: Lexington).

Barnard, A. (2011) 'China Sought to Sell Arms to Qaddafi, Documents Suggest', *The New York Times*, 4 September 2011, [online] http://www.nytimes.com/2011/09/05/world/africa/05libya.html?_r=2&pagewanted=1&hp (accessed 2 September 2012).

Barnett, M. (1997) 'The UN Security Council, Indifference, and Genocide in Rwanda', *Cultural Anthropology*, 12:4, 551–78.

Barnett, M. (2002) *Eyewitness to Genocide: The United Nations and Rwanda* (Ithaca, NY: Cornell University Press).

Barnett, M. (2003) 'Bureaucratizing the Duty to Aid: The United Nations and the Rwandan Genocide', in A. Lang (ed.), *Just Intervention* (Washington DC: Georgetown University Press).

Barnett, M. (2010) *The International Humanitarian Order* (London: Routledge)

Barry, B. (2011) 'Libya's Lessons', *Survival*, 53:5, 5–14.

Bass, Gary (2008) *Freedoms Battle: The Origins of Humanitarian Intervention* (New York: Vintage Books).

Bassiouni, C. (2009) 'Advancing the Responsibility to Protect Through International Criminal Justice', in R.H. Cooper and J.V. Kohler (eds.) *Responsibility to Protect: The Global Moral Compact for the 21st Century* (Basingstoke and New York: Palgrave Macmillan).

Baylis, J. and Smith, S. (eds) (2007) *The Globalization of World Politics* (Oxford: Oxford University Press).

BBC News (2003) 'Cook's Resignation Speech', 18 March [online] http://news.bbc.co.uk/1/hi/2859431.stm (accessed 25 September 2012).

BBC News (2004) 'UN Chief's Rwanda Genocide Regret', 26 March [online] http://news.bbc.co.uk/2/hi/africa/3573229.stm (accessed 25 September 2012).

BBC News (2012a) 'UN Envoy Brahimi Says Syria Mission 'Nearly Impossible', 3 September [online] http://www.bbc.co.uk/news/world-middle-east-19460919 (accessed 13 September 2012).

BBC News (2012b) 'Syria Envoy Lakhdar Brahimi Warns of "staggering" Crisis', 4 September [online] http://www.bbc.co.uk/news/world-middle-east-19484240 (accessed 13 September 2012).

Becker, J. (2011) 'Events of Two years Ago Sparked Current Uprisings in Libya', *Global Post*, 11 March [online] http://www.hrw.org/news/2011/03/11/ events-2-years-ago-sparked-current-uprising-libya (accessed 1 August 2012).

Beetham, D. (1991) *The Legitimisation of Power* (Basingstoke and New York: Palgrave Macmillan).

Beitz, C. (1992) 'Cosmopolitanism and Sovereignty', *Ethics*, 103, 48–75.

Bellamy, A. (2002) *Kosovo and International Society* (Basingstoke and New York: Palgrave Macmillan).

Bellamy, A. (2003) 'Humanitarian Intervention and the Three Traditions', *Global Society*, 17:1, 3–20l.

Bellamy, A. (2004) 'Ethics and Intervention; The "Humanitarian Exception" and the problem of Abuse in the Case of Iraq', *Journal of Peace Research*, 41:2, 131–47.

Bellamy, A. (2005a) 'Responsibility to Protect or Trojan Horse? The Crisis in Darfur and Humanitarian Intervention after Iraq', *Ethics and International Affairs*, 19:2, 31–54.

Bellamy, A. (2005b) 'Introduction'. in A. Bellamy (ed.), *International Society and its Critics* (Oxford: Oxford University Press).

Bellamy, A. (2005c) 'The "Next Stage" in Peace Operations Theory', in P. Williams and A. Bellamy (eds), *Peace Operations and the Global Order* (Oxon: Routledge).

Bellamy, A. (2006a) 'Whither the Responsibility to Protect? Humanitarian Intervention and the 2005 World Summit', *Ethics and International Affairs*, 20:2, 143–69.

Bellamy, A. (2006b) *Just Wars: From Cicero to Iraq* (London: Polity).

Bellamy, A. (2009a) *Responsibility to Protect* (London: Polity).

Bellamy, A. (2009b) 'The Responsibility to Protect and the Problem of Military Intervention', *International Affairs*, 84:4, 615–39.

Bellamy, A. (2009c) 'Kosovo and the Advent of Sovereignty as Responsibility', *Journal of Intervention and Statebuilding*, 3:2, 163–84.

Bellamy, A. (2011) 'Libya and the Responsibility to Protect: The Exception and the Norm', *Ethics and International Affairs*, 25:3, pp. 1–7, [online], http://www.carnegiecouncil.org/resources/journal/index.html (accessed 13 December 2012).

Bellamy, A. and Wheeler, N (2010) 'Humanitarian Intervention in International Society', in J. Baylis and S. Smith (eds), *The Globalization of World Politics*, 2nd edn (Oxford: Oxford University Press).

Bellamy, A. and Williams, P. (2011) 'The New Politics of Protection? Cote d'Ivoire, Libya and the Responsibility to Protect', *International Affairs*, 82:7, 825–50.

Bellamy, A. and Williams, P. (2012) 'On the Limits of Moral Hazard: The Responsibility to Protect, Armed Conflict and Mass Atrocities', *European Journal of International Relations*, 18:3, 539–571.

Belloni, R. (2006) 'The Tragedy of Darfur and the Limits of the "Responsibility to Protect"', *Ethnopolitics*, 5:4, 327–46.

Benin (2009) 'Statement by the Permanent Representative of Benin to the UN', General Assembly, A/63/PV.100, 28 July.

Bennett, W. (2000) 'Morality Character and American Foreign Policy', in I. Kristol and R. Kagan (eds), *Present Dangers* (San Francisco: Encounter).

Berdal, M. (2003) 'The UN Security Council: Ineffective but Indispensable', *Survival*, 45/2, 7–30.

Berman, F. (2007) 'Moral Versus Legal Legitimacy', in C. Reed and D. Ryall (eds), *The Price of Peace* (Cambridge: Cambridge University Press).

Bickerton, C., Cunliffe, P. and Gourevitch, A. (eds) (2006) *Politics without Sovereignty: A Critique of Contemporary International Relations* (London: Routledge).

Black, Ian (2009) 'Libya under Muammar Gaddafi' *The Guardian*, 31 August, [online] http://www.guardian.co.uk/world/audioslideshow/2009/aug/31/libya-gaddafi (accessed 3 August 2012).

Blair, T. (1999) 'Doctrine of the International Community', Speech at the Economic Club, Chicago, 24 April [online] http://www.pbs.org/newshour/bb/international/jan-june99/blair_doctrine4-23.html (accessed 27 September 2012).

Blair, T. (2004a) 'Full Text: Tony Blair's Speech', *Guardian*, 5 March [online] http://www.guardian.co.uk/politics/2004/mar/05/iraq.iraq (accessed 27 September 2012).

Blair, T. (2004b) 'Speech to the Labour Party Conference', 28 September [online] http://www.labour.org.uk/ac2004news?ux_news_id=ac04tb (accessed 2 May 2009).

Blakeley, R. (2009) *State Terrorism and Neoliberalism* (London: Routledge).

Blix, H. (2004) 'The Importance of Inspections', Carnegie Endowment for International Peace, Proliferation Brief 7, No. 11 [online] http://carnegieendowment.org/2004/07/26/importance-of-inspections/4lbn (accessed 27 September 2012).

Blomfield, A. (2011) 'Bahrain Hardliners to Put Shia MPs on Trial', *The Telegraph*, 30 March 2011, [online] http://www.telegraph.co.uk/news/worldnews/middleeast/bahrain/8416953/Bahrain-hardliners-to-put-Shia-MPs-on-trial.html (accessed 2 September 2012).

Bloom, W. (1990) *Personal Identity, National Identity and International Relations* (Cambridge: Cambridge University Press).

Bolton, J. (2005) 'Letter to President Ping', 30 August [online] http://www.responsibilityto protect.org/index.php/government_statements/554?theme=alt1 (accessed 27 September 2012).

Booth, K. (ed.) (2000) *The Kosovo Tragedy: The Human Rights Dimension* (London: Routledge).

Booth, K. (2001) 'Three Tyrannies', in T. Dunne and N. Wheeler (eds), *Human Rights in Global Politics* (Cambridge: Cambridge University Press).

Bosco, D. (2009) *Five to Rule Them All* (Oxford: Oxford University Press)

Boucher, D. (1998) *Political Theories of International Relations* (Oxford: Oxford University Press).

Boucher, D. and Kelly, P. (2003) *Political Thinkers: From Socrates to the Present*, (Oxford: Oxford University Press).

Bourantonis, D. (2007) *The History and Politics of Security Council Reform* (London: Routledge).

Boutros-Ghali, B. (1992) 'An Agenda for Peace', Report of the Secretary-General, UN document A/47/277-S/24111), 17 June [online] http://www.un.org/docs/SG/agpeace.html (accessed 27 September 2012).

Bowring, B. (2008) *The Degradation of the International Legal Order? The Rehabilitation of Law and the Possibility of Politics* (Oxford: Routledge-Cavendish).

Boyle, J. (2006) 'Traditional Just War Theory and Humanitarian Intervention', in T. Nardin and M. Williams (eds), *Humanitarian Intervention: NOMOS XLVII* (New York: New York University Press).

Branigan, T. (2011) 'Chinese Arms Companies "Offered to Sell Weapons to Gaddafi Regime"', *The Guardian*, 5 September, [online] http://www.guardian.co.uk/world/2011/sep/05/chinese-arms-companies-weapons-gaddafi-regime (accessed 2 September 2012).

Brazil (2011) 'Responsibility While Protecting', A/66/551-S/2011/701, 11 November. [online] http://www.globalr2p.org/resources/RwP.php (accessed 24 September 2012).

Brichambaut, M. P. de (2000) 'The Role of the UN Security Council in the International Legal System', in M. Byers (ed.), *The Role of Law in International Politics* (Oxford: Oxford University Press).

Briggs, H. (1945) 'Power Politics and International Organization', *American Journal of International Law*, 39, 4, 664–79.

Brown, C. (1992) *International Relations Theory: New Normative Approaches* (Hemel Hempstead: Harvester Wheatsheaf).

Brown, C. (2000) 'A Qualified Defense of the Use of Force for Humanitarian Reasons', in K. Booth (ed.), *The Kosovo Tragedy: The Human Rights Dimension* (London: Routledge).

Brown, C. (2001) 'Ethics Interests, and Foreign Policy', in K. E. Smith and M. Light (eds), *Ethics and Foreign Policy* (Cambridge: Cambridge University Press).

Brown, C. (2002) 'Marxism and International Ethics', in T. Nardin and D. Mapel (eds), *Traditions of International Ethics* (Cambridge: Cambridge University Press).

Brown, C. (2006) *Sovereignty, Rights and Justice: International Political Theory Today* (London: Polity).

Brown, C. and Ainley, K. (2005) *Understanding International Relations* (Basingstoke and New York: Palgrave Macmillan).

Brown, C., Nardin, T. and Rengger, N. (eds) (2002) *International Relations in Political Thought* (Cambridge: Cambridge University Press).

Brownlie, I. (1973) 'Thoughts on Kind-Hearted Gunmen', in R. B. Lillich (ed.), *Humanitarian Intervention and the United Nations* (Charlottesville, VA: University Press of Virginia).

Brownlie, I. (1974) 'Humanitarian Intervention', in J. Moore (ed.), *Law and Civil War in the Modern World* (Baltimore, MD: Johns Hopkins University Press).

Buchanan, A. and Keohane, R. O. (2004) 'The Preventive Use of Force: A Cosmopolitan Institutional Proposal', *Ethics and International Affairs*, 18:1, 1–22.

Buchanan, A. and Keohane, R. (2011) 'Precommitment Regimes for Intervention: Supplementing the Security Council', *Ethics and International Affairs*, 25:1, 41–63.

Buckley, C. A. (2012) 'Learning from Libya, Acting in Syria', *Journal of Strategic Security*, 5:2, 81–104.

Buckley, M. and Singh, R. (eds) (2006) *The Bush Doctrine and the War on Terrorism* (London, Routledge).

Bull, H. (1984a) *Justice in International Relations: Hagey Lectures*, (Ontario: University Publications Distribution Service).

Bull, H. (1984b) 'Conclusion', in H. Bull (ed.), *Intervention in World Politics* (Oxford: Oxford University Press).

Bull, H. (2002) *The Anarchical Society: A Study of Order in World Politics* (Basingstoke: Palgrave Macmillan and New York: Columbia University Press).

Burchill, S. (2005) 'Liberalism', in S. Burchill, R. Devetak, A. Linklater, M. Paterson, C. Reus-Smit and J. True (eds), *Theories of International Relations* (Basingstoke and New York: Palgrave Macmillan).

Burchill, S., Devetak, R., Linklater, A., Paterson, M., Reus-Smit, C. and True, J. (2005) *Theories of International Relations* (Basingstoke and New York: Palgrave Macmillan).

Burchill, S. and Linklater, A. (2005) 'Introduction', in S. Burchill, R. Devetak, A. Linklater, M. Paterson, C. Reus-Smit and J. True (eds), *Theories of International Relations* (Basingstoke and New York: Palgrave Macmillan).

Burke, A. (2004) 'Just War or Ethical Peace? Moral Discourses of Strategic Violence after 9/11', *International Affairs*, 80:2, 329–53.

Burton, M. (1996) 'Legalising the Sublegal', *Georgetown Law Journal*, 85, 417–54.

Bush, G. (2002) 'Transcript: Bush's Speech to the UN on Iraq', *New York Times*, 12 September.

Buzan, B. (1991) *People, States and Fear: An Agenda for International Security Studies in the Post-Cold War Era* (London: Harvester Wheatsheaf).

Byers, M. (ed.) (2001) *The Role of International Law in International Politics* (Oxford: Oxford University Press).

Byers, M. (2005a) 'Not Yet Havoc: Geopolitical Change and the International Rules on Military Force', in D. Armstrong, T. Farrell and B. Maiguashca (eds), *Force and Legitimacy in World Politics* (Cambridge: Cambridge University Press).

Byers, M. (2005b) 'High Ground Lost on UN's Responsibility to Protect', *Winnipeg Free Press*, 18 September.

Byers, M. and Chesterman, S. (2003) 'Changing the Rules About Rules?' in J. Holzgrefe and R. Keohane (eds), *Humanitarian Intervention: Ethical, Legal and Political Dilemmas* (Cambridge: Cambridge University Press).

Callinicos, A. (2000) 'The Ideology of Humanitarian Intervention', in T. Ali (ed.), *Masters of the Universe? NATO's Balkan Crusade* (London: Verso).

Cameron, D. (2011a) 'Prime Minister's Statement on Libya', 19 March, [online] http://www.number10.gov.uk/news/prime-ministers-statement-on-libya-2/ (accessed 2 September 2012).

Cameron, D. (2011b) 'Prime Minister David Cameron Opening Remarks at the London Conference on Libya', 29 March, [online] http://www.number10. gov.uk/news/pms-speech-at-london-conference-on-libya/ (accessed 2 September 2012).

Camilleri, J. A. and Falk, J. (1992) *The End of Sovereignty* (London: Elgar).

Campbell, D. (1994) 'The Deterritorialization of Responsibility: Levinas, Derrida, and Ethics After the End of Philosophy', *Alternatives*, 19:4, 455–84.

Campbell, D. (1998a) *National Deconstruction: Violence, Identity and Justice in Bosnia* (Minneapolis, MN: University of Minnesota Press).

Campbell, D. (1998b) 'Why Fight: Humanitarianism, Principles, and Post-structuralism', *Millennium*, 27:3, 497–521.

Canning, J. (2003) 'Aquinas', in D. Boucher and P. Kelly (eds), *Political Thinkers: From Socrates to the Present* (Oxford: Oxford University Press).

Capital and Class (2003) 'Editorial Comment on the War in Iraq', *Capital and Class*, 22 June.

Caplan, R. (2000) 'Humanitarian Intervention: Which Way Forward?' *Ethics and International Affairs*, 14, 23–38.

Carr, E. H. (2001) *The Twenty Years Crisis* (Basingstoke: Palgrave Macmillan).

Carroll, R. (2004) 'US Chose to Ignore Rwandan Genocide', *Guardian*, 31 March.

Carpenter, T.G. (ed.) (2000) *NATO's Empty Victory* (Washington, DC: Cato Institute).

Cassese, A. (1999) '*Ex iniuria ius oritur*: Are we Moving Towards International Legitimisation of Forcible Humanitarian Countermeasures in the World Community?', *European Journal of International Law*, 10:1, 23–30.

Cassese, A. (2005) *International Law* (Oxford: Oxford University Press).

CCPDC (Carnegie Commission on Preventing Deadly Conflict) (1997) 'Preventing Deadly Conflict: Final Report with Executive Summary', December [online] http://www.wilson center.org/subsites/ccpdc/pubs/rept97/finfr.htm (accessed 2 May 2009).

Chadda, M. (2003) 'Intervention in Ethnic and Civil Wars', in R. Thomas (ed.), *Yugoslavia Unraveled: Sovereignty, Self Determination, Intervention* (Oxford: Lexington).

Chalk, F., Dallaire, R., Matthews, K., Barqueiro, C. and Doyle, S. (2010) *Mobilizing the Will to Intervene: Leadership to Prevent Mass Atrocities* (Montreal: McGill University Press).

Chandler, D. (2000a) 'International Justice', *New Left Review*, 6, Nov/Dec, 55–66.

Chandler, D. (2000b) *Bosnia: Faking Democracy after Dayton* (London: Pluto).

Chandler, D. (2002) *From Kosovo to Kabul* (London: Pluto).

Chandler, D. (2004a) 'The Responsibility to Protect? Imposing the "Liberal Peace"', *International Peacekeeping*, 11:1, 59–81.

Chandler, D. (2004b) *Constructing Global Civil Society: Morality and Power in International Relations* (Basingstoke and New York: Palgrave Macmillan).

Chandler, D. (2009) 'Unravelling the Paradox of "The Responsibility to Protect"', *Irish Studies in International Affairs*, 20, 27–39.

Chatterjee, D. and Scheid, D. (2003) 'Introduction', in D. Chatterjee and D. Scheid (eds), *Ethics and Foreign Intervention* (Cambridge: Cambridge University Press).

Chavez, H. (2005) Speech Given by President Hugo Chavez at 60th UN General Assembly, New York, 15 September [online] http://www.embavenez-us.org/news.php?nid=1745 (accessed 15 September 2012).

Chedle, D. and Prendergast, J. (2007) *Not on our Watch: The Mission to End Genocide in Darfur and Beyond* (Meath: Maverick House).

Chesterman, S. (2002) *Just War or Just Peace?* (Oxford: Oxford University Press).

Chesterman, S. (2003) 'Hard Cases Make Bad Law' in A. Lang, (ed.) *Just Intervention* (Washington DC, Georgetown University Press).

Chesterman, S. (2006) 'Humanitarian Intervention and Afghanistan', in J. Welsh (ed.), *Humanitarian Intervention and International Relations* (Oxford: Oxford University Press).

Chesterman, S. (2011a) '"Leading from Behind": The Responsibility to Protect, the Obama Doctrine, and Humanitarian Intervention after Libya', *Ethics and International Affairs*, 25/3, 1–7. [online], http://www.carnegiecouncil.org/resources/journal/index.html (accessed 11 September 2011).

Chesterman, S. (2011b) 'The Outlook for UN Reform', New York University School of Law, Public Law & Legal Theory research Paper Series, Working Paper No. 11-55, August. [online] http://ssrn.com/abstract=1885229 (accessed 12 September 2012).

Chesterman, S. and Byers, M. (1999) 'Has US Power Destroyed the UN?' *London Review of Books*, 29 April, 21.

Chesterman, S., Franck, T. and Malone, D. (2008) *Law and Practice of the United Nations* (Oxford: Oxford University Press).

Chomsky, N. (1999) *The New Military Humanism: Lessons from Kosovo* (London: Pluto).

Chomsky, N. (2011) 'The Skeleton in the Closet: The Responsibility in History', in P. Cunliffe (ed.) *Critical Perspectives on the Responsibility to Protect* (London: Routledge).

Chopra, J. and Weiss, T. (1992) 'Sovereignty is No Longer Sacrosanct', *Ethics and International Affairs*, 6, 95–117.

Christopher, P. (2004) *The Ethics of War and Peace* (Upper Saddle River, NJ: Prentice Hall).

Clapham, C. (1998) 'Rwanda: The Perils of Peacemaking', *Journal of Peace Research*, 35:2, 193–210.

Clapham, C. (1999) 'Sovereignty and the Third World State', *Political Studies*, 47:3, 522–37.

Clark, D. (2003) 'Iraq Has Wrecked Our Case for Humanitarian Wars', *Guardian*, 12 August, 20.

Clark, I. (2005) *Legitimacy in International Society* (Oxford: Oxford University Press).

Clark, W. (2001) *Waging Modern War* (Oxford: Public Affairs).

Clarke, M. (2011a) 'Un-strategic Victory in Libya', RUSI Commentary, 1 June [online] http://www.rusi.org/analysis/commentary/ref:C4DE4F24B36A54/ (accessed 2 September 2012)

Clarke, M. (2011b) 'Curious Victory for NATO in Libya', RUSI Commentary, 24 August, [online] http://www.rusi.org/analysis/commentary/ref:C4DE4F2 4B36A54/ (accessed 2 September 2012).

Clinton, H. (2011) 'There's "No Way" United States Will Take Unilateral Action in Libya', CBS News, 16 March, [online] http://www.cbsnews.com/8301-503544_162-20043991-503544.html (accessed 2 September 2012).

CNN (2012) 'Syrian Civil War Marks Grim Record' CNN, 27 September [online] http://edition.cnn.com/2012/09/26/world/meast/syria-civil-war/index.html (accessed 19 October 2012).

Coalition of NGOs on Darfur (2008) 'Rhetoric vs. Reality: The Situation in Darfur' [online] http://www.hrw.org/sites/default/files/related_material/darfur1208.pdf (accessed 2 May 2009).

Coates, A. J. (1997) *The Ethics of War* (Manchester: Manchester University Press).

Coates, A. J. (2006) 'Humanitarian Intervention: A Conflict of Traditions', in T. Nardin and M. Williams (eds), *Humanitarian Intervention: NOMOS XLVII* (New York: New York University Press).

Cobain, I. (2012) 'Special Report Rendition Ordeal that Raises New Questions About Secret Trials', *The Guardian*, 8 April.

Cockayne, J. and Samii, C. (2006) 'Structural and Normative Challenges', in R. Thakur and W. P. S. Sidhu (eds), *The Iraq Crisis and World Order: Structural, Institutional and Normative Challenges* (New York: United Nations University Press).

Cohen, J. (2004) 'Whose Sovereignty? Empire Versus International Law', *Ethics and International Affairs*, 18:3, 1–24.

Cohen, M. (1984) 'Moral Skepticism and International Relations', *Philosophy and Public Affairs*, 13:4, 299–346.

Cohen, R. (2011) 'Score One for Interventionism', *The New York Times*, 29 August, [online] http://www.nytimes.com/2011/08/30/opinion/30iht-edcohen30.html (accessed 2 September 2012).

Coicaud, J. M. (2006) 'Iraq and the Social Logic of International Security', in R. Thakur and W. P. S. Sidhu (eds), *The Iraq Crisis and World Order: Structural, Institutional and Normative Challenges* (New York: United Nations University Press).

Coicaud, J. M. and Wheeler, N. (2008) 'Introduction: The Changing Ethics of Power Beyond Borders', in J. M. Coicaud and N. Wheeler (eds), *National Interests and International Solidarity* (New York: United Nations University Press).

Coleman, W. and Wayland, S. (2006) 'The Origins of Global Civil Society and Nonterritorial Governance', *Global Governance*, 12, 242–5.

Coll, A. (2001) 'Kosovo and the Moral Burdens of Power', in A. Bacevich and E. Cohen (eds), *War Over Kosovo* (New York: Columbia University Press).

Collins, B. (2002) 'New Wars and Old Wars? The Lessons of Rwanda', in D. Chandler (ed.), *Rethinking Human Rights* (Basingstoke and New York: Palgrave Macmillan).

Connelly, J. and Carrick, D. (2011) 'Ethical and Legal Reasoning about War in a Time of Terror' in A. Hehir, N. Kuhrt and A. Mumford (eds.) *International Law, Security and Ethics* (London: Routledge).

Considine, S. C. and Sonner, H. (2009) 'Interview between author and Sapna Chhatpar Considine, Project Manager, International Coalition for the Responsibility to Protect and Heather Sonner, International Secretariat of the Institute for Global Policy', Tuesday, 18 August, New York.

Convention on the Rights and Duties of States (1933) *Convention signed at Montevideo December 26, 1933* [online] http://avalon.law.yale.edu/20th_century/intam03.asp (accessed 1 February 2009).

Cook, M. (2003) '"Immaculate War": Constraints on Humanitarian Intervention', in A. Lang (ed.), *Just Intervention* (Washington DC: Georgetown University Press).

Cooper, R. (2002) 'The New Liberal Imperialism', *Observer*, 7 April.

Cooper, R. (2004) *The Breaking of Nations* (London: Atlantic).

Cortright, D. (2006) 'The World Says No: The Global Movement Against War', in R. Thakur and W. P. S. Sidhu (eds), *The Iraq Crisis and World Order: Structural, Institutional and Normative Challenges* (New York: United Nations University Press).

Cox, R. (1981) 'Social Forces, States and World Orders', *Millennium*, 10:2, 127–55.

Cox, R. (1986) 'Social Forces, States and World Orders', in R. Keohane (ed.), *Neorealism and its Critics* (New York: Colombia University Press).

Cox, R. (1996) *Approaches to World Order* (Cambridge: Cambridge University Press).

Crawford, J. and Olleson, S. (2006) 'The Nature and Forms of International Responsibility', in M. Evans (ed.), *International Law* (Oxford: Oxford University Press).

Crawford, T. (2006) 'Moral Hazard, Intervention and Internal War', in T. Crawford and A. Kuperman (eds), *Gambling on Humanitarian Intervention* (London: Routledge).

Crawshaw, S. (2004) 'Genocide? What Genocide', *The Financial Times*, 21 August.

Crocker, C. (2011) 'The Arab Spring', United States Institute for Peace, 25 April [online] http://www.usip.org/publications/the-arab-spring (accessed 2 September 2012).

Cronin, B (2008) 'International Consensus and the Changing Legal Authority of the UN Security Council', in B. Cronin and I. Hurd (eds), *The UN Security Council and the Politics of International Authority* (London: Routledge).

Cronin, B. and Hurd, I. (2008) *The UN Security Council and the Politics of International Authority* (London: Routledge).

Cuéllar, J.P. de (1991) 'Report of the Secretary-General on the Work of the Organization', UN Document A/46/1, 13 September

Cunliffe, P. (2011) 'A Dangerous Duty: Power, Paternalism and the Global "Duty of Care"', in P. Cunliffe (ed.) *Critical Perspectives on the Responsibility to Protect* (London: Routledge).

Daalder, I. and O'Hanlon, M. (2000) *Winning Ugly* (Washington DC: Brookings Institution Press).

Daalder, I. and Lindsay, J. (2007) 'Democracies of the World Unite', *The American Interest*, January/February, Available online http://www.the-american-interest.com/article.cfm?piece=220 (accessed 14 September 2012).

Daalder, I. and Stavridis, J. (2012) 'NATO'S Victory in Libya', *Foreign Affairs*, 91:2, 2–7.

Dalacoura, K. (2012) 'The 2011 Uprisings in the Arab Middle East', *International Affairs*, 88:1, 63–79.

Dallaire, R. (1994) 'Request for Protection of Informant: 11 January', PBS Frontline – "The Triumph of Evil" [online] http://www.pbs.org/wgbh/pages/frontline/shows/evil/warning/cable.html (accessed 2 May 2009).

Dallaire, R. (2004a) *Shake Hands with the Devil: The Failure of Humanity in Rwanda* (London: Arrow).

Dallaire, R. (2004b) 'Looking at Darfur, Seeing Rwanda', *New York Times*, 4 October.

Dallmayr, F. (2003) 'Cosmopolitanism: Moral and Political', *Political Theory*, 31:3, 421–42.

Daly, M. W. (2007) *Darfur's Sorrow: A History of Destruction and Genocide* (New York: Cambridge University Press).

Danish Institute of International Affairs (1999) *Humanitarian Intervention: Legal and Political Aspects* (Copenhagen: Danish Institute of International Affairs).

De Bréadún, D. (2004) 'A Defiant Bush Defends Iraq Strategy Before the UN', *Irish Times*, 22 September, 11.

De Waal, A. (1994) 'Genocide in Rwanda', *Anthropology Today*, 10:3, 1–2.

De Waal, A. (2004) 'Darfur's Deep Grievances Defy All Hopes for a Fast Solution', *Observer*, 25 July.

De Waal, A. (2006) *Darfur: A Short History of a Long War* (New York: Zed).

De Waal, A. (ed.) (2007) *War in Darfur and the Search for Peace* (Cambridge: Global Equity Initiative, Harvard University).

De Waal, A. (2007a) 'No Such Thing as Humanitarian Intervention', *Harvard International Review*, 21 March [online] http://www.harvardir.org/articles/1482/3/ (accessed 2 May 2011).

De Waal, A. (ed.) (2007b) *War in Darfur and the Search for Peace* (Cambridge, MA: Harvard University Press).

De Waal, A. (2007c) 'Sudan: The Turbulent State', in A. de Waal (ed.), *War in Darfur and the Search for Peace* (Cambridge: Global Equity Initiative, Harvard University).

De Waal, A. (2008) 'Why Darfur Intervention is a Mistake', BBC World News, 21 May [online] http://news.bbc.co.uk/2/hi/africa/7411087.stm (accessed 2 May 2012).

De Waal, A. (2013) '"My Fears, Alas, Were Not Unfounded:" Africa's Responses to the Libya Conflict', in A. Hehir and R.W. Murray (eds.), *Libya, the Responsibility to Protect and the Future of Humanitarian Intervention* (Basingstoke and New York: Palgrave Macmillan).

Deane, H. (1963) *The Political and Social Ideas of St Augustine* (New York: Colombia University Press).

Deng, F. (2010) 'JISB Interview: The Responsibility to Protect', *Journal of Intervention and Statebuilding*, 4, 1, 83–9.

Deng, F. M., Kimaro, S., Lyons, T., Rothchild, D. and Zartman, I. W. (1996) *Sovereignty and Responsibility: Conflict Management in Africa* (Washington, DC: Brookings Institution).

Der Derian, J. and Shapiro, M. J. (eds) (1989) *International/Intertextual Relations: Postmodern Readings of World Politics* (Lexington, KY: Lexington Books).

Des Forges, A. (1999) *Leave None to Tell the Story: Genocide in Rwanda*, Human Rights Watch [online] http://www.hrw.org/legacy/reports/1999/rwanda/index.htm#TopOfPage (accessed 27 September 2012).

Des Forges, A. (2000) 'Shame – Rationalizing Western Apathy on Rwanda: Alas we Knew', *Foreign Affairs*, 79:3, 141–2.

Destexhe, A. (1995) *Rwanda and Genocide in the Twentieth Century* (London: Pluto).

Devetak, R. (2009) 'Post-structuralism' in S. Burchill, A. Linklater, R. Devetak, J. Donnelly, T. Nardin, M. Paterson, C. Reus-Smit and J. True, *Theories of International Relations* (Basingstoke and New York: Palgrave Macmillan).

DIIA (Danish Institute of International Affairs) (1999) *Humanitarian Intervention: Legal and Political Aspects* (Copenhagen: Danish Institute of International Affairs).

Dinstein, Y. (2005) *War, Aggression and Self-Defence* (Cambridge: Cambridge University Press).

Dixon, M. (2007) *Textbook on International Law* (Oxford: Oxford University Press).

Docking, T. (2008) 'US Foreign Policy Towards Africa', in J. M. Coicaud and N. Wheeler (eds), *National Interests and International Solidarity* (New York: United Nations University Press).

Dodge, T. (2003) *Inventing Iraq: The Failure of Nation-Building and a History Denied* (New York: Colombia University Press).

Donaldson, T. (2002) 'Kant's Global Rationalism', in T. Nardin and D. R. Mapel (eds.) *Traditions of International Ethics* (Cambridge: Cambridge University Press).

Donnelly, J. (1989) *Universal Human Rights in Theory and Practice* (Ithaca, NY: Cornell University Press).

Donnelly, J. (2002) 'Twentieth Century Realism', in T. Nardin and D. Mapel (eds), *Traditions of International Ethics* (Cambridge: Cambridge University Press).

Douzinas, C. (2000) *The End of Human Rights* (Oxford: Oxford University Press).

Douzinas, C. (2009) 'Speaking Law: On Bare Theological and Cosmopolitan Sovereignty', in A. Orford (ed.) *International Law and its Others* (Cambridge: Cambridge University Press).

Doyle, M. (1986) 'Liberalism and World Politics', *American Political Science Review*, 80:4, 1151–69.

Dryzek, J. and Dunleavy, P. (2009) *Theories of the Democratic State* (Basingstoke and New York: Palgrave Macmillan).

Duffield, M. (2005) 'Getting Barbarians to Fight Savages: Development, Security and the Colonial Present', *Conflict, Security and Development*, 5:2, 141–59.

Duffield, M. (2006) *Global Governance and the New Wars: The Merging of Development and Security* (London: Zed).

Duffield, M. and Waddell, N. (2006) 'Securing Humans in a Dangerous World', *International Politics*, 43:1, 1–23.

Dumbrell, J. and Ryan, D. (2007) 'Introduction', in J. Dumbrell and D. Ryan (eds), *Vietnam in Iraq* (London: Routledge).

Dunleavy, P. and O'Leary, B. (1987) *Theories of the State* (London: Macmillan).

Dunne, T. (1998) *Inventing International Society* (Basingstoke: Palgrave Macmillan).

Dunne, T. Kurki, M. and Smith, S. (2007) *International Relations Theories: Discipline and Diversity* (Oxford: Oxford University Press).

Economist Intelligence Unit (2010) 'Democracy Index 2010: Democracies in Retreat', [online] http://graphics.eiu.com/PDF/Democracy_Index_2010_ web.pdf (accessed 2 September 2012).

Edkins, J. (2000) *Whose Hunger? Concepts of Famine, Practices of Aid* (Minneapolis, MN: University of Minneapolis Press).

Edkins, J. (2003) 'Humanitarianism, Humanity, Human', *Journal of Human Rights*, 2:2, 253–8.

Edkins, J. (2005a) *Poststructuralism and International Relations: Bringing the Political Back In* (Boulder, CO: Lynne Rienner).

Edkins, J. (2005b) 'Ethics and Practices of Engagement: Intellectuals as Experts', *International Relations*, 19:1, 64–9.

Edkins, J. and Pin-Fat, V. (1998) 'The Subject of the Political', in J. Edkins, N. Persram and V. Pin-Fat (eds), *Sovereignty and Subjectivity* (Boulder, CO: Lynne Rienner).

Elshtain, J. B. (ed.) (1992) *Just War Theory* (New York: New York University Press).

Elshtain, J. B. (2003a) 'St Augustine', in D. Boucher and P. Kelly (eds), *Political Thinkers: From Socrates to the Present* (Oxford: Oxford University Press).

Elshtain, J. B. (2003b) 'International Justice as Equal Regard and the Use of Force', *Ethics and International Affairs*, 17:2, 63–75.

Eubank, W.L. and Weinberg, L.B. (2001) 'Terrorism and Democracy: Perpetrators and Victims', *Terrorism and Political Violence*, 13:1, 155–64.

Evans, G. (2006) 'The Responsibility to Protect: Unfinished Business', *Issues and Instruments*, 17 July, [online] http://www.gevans.org/opeds/oped73.html (accessed 2 September 2012).

Evans, G. (2008) *The Responsibility to Protect: Ending Mass Atrocity Crimes Once and For All* (Washington DC: Brookings Institution Press).

Evans, G. (2011) 'The RtoP Balance Sheet after Libya', September 2, [online] http://www.gevans.org/speeches/speech448%20interview%20RtoP.html (accessed 28 November 2011).

Evans, G. (2012) 'Statement by Co-Chair of the Global Centre for the Responsibility to Protect on "Responsibility While Protecting"', Informal General Assembly Discussion, 21 February [online] at, http://www.globalr2p.org/media/pdf/GarethEvansStatementResponsibility WhileProtecting.pdf (accessed 17 September 2012).

Evans, M. (2005a) 'Moral Theory and the Idea of a Just War' in M. Evans (ed.) *Just War Theory: A Reappraisal* (Edinburgh: Edinburgh University Press).

Evans, M. (2005b) 'In Defence of Just War Theory' in M. Evans (ed.) *Just War Theory: A Reappraisal* (Edinburgh: Edinburgh University Press).

Fahim, K. and Kirkpatrick, D. (2011) 'Qaddafi Massing Forces in Tripoli as Rebellion Spreads', *New York Times*, 23 February.

Fake, S. and Funk, K. (2009) 'R2P: Disciplining the Mice, Freeing the Lions', *Foreign Policy in Focus*, 23 March [online], http://www.fpif.org/fpiftxt/5984 (accessed March 2011).

Falk, R. (1995) *On Humane Governance* (Cambridge: Polity).

Falk, R. (2004) 'Humanitarian Intervention After Kosovo', in A. Jokic (ed.), *Lessons of Kosovo: The Dangers of Humanitarian Intervention* (Toronto: Broadview Press).

Falk, R. (2005a) 'Legality and Legitimacy: The Quest for Principled Flexibility and Restraint', in D. Armstrong, T. Farrell and B. Maiguashca (eds), *Force and Legitimacy in World Politics* (Cambridge: Cambridge University Press).

Falk, R. (2005b) '(Re)Imagining the Governance of Globalization', in A. Bellamy (ed.), *International Society and its Critics* (Oxford: Oxford University Press).

Falk, R. (2011) 'Preliminary Libyan Scorecard: Acting Beyond the UN Mandate', *Foreign policy Journal*, 8 September [online] http://www.foreignpolicyjournal.com/2011/09/08/preliminary-libyan-scorecard-acting-beyond-the-u-n-mandate/ (accessed 28 November 2011).

Farer, T. (2003) 'The Ethics of Intervention in Self Determination Struggles', in D. Chatterjee and D. Scheid (eds.), *Ethics and Foreign Intervention* (Cambridge: Cambridge University Press).

Feinstein, L. (2007) 'Beyond Words: Building Will and Capacity to Prevent More Darfurs', *The Washington Post*, 26 January.

Feinsten, L. and De Bruin, E (2009) 'Beyond Words: US Policy and the Responsibility to Protect', in R. H. Cooper and J.V. Kohler (eds.) *Responsibility to Protect: The Global Moral Compact for the 21st Century* (Basingstoke and New York: Palgrave Macmillan).

Finnemore, M. and Sikkink, K. (1998) 'International Norm Dynamics and Political Change', *International Organization*, 52:4, 887–917.

Finnis, J. (1998) *Aquinas: Moral, Political and Legal Theory* (Oxford: Oxford University Press).

Fisher, D. (2007) 'Humanitarian Intervention', in C. Reed and D. Ryall (eds), *The Price of Peace* (Cambridge: Cambridge University Press).

Fisher, D. (2011) *Morality and War* (Oxford: Oxford University Press).

Fitzmaurice, M. (2006) 'The Practical Working of the Law of Treaties', in M. Evans (ed.), *International Law* (Oxford: Oxford University Press).

Focarelli, C. (2008) 'The Responsibility to Protect Doctrine and Humanitarian Intervention: Too Many Ambiguities for a Working Doctrine', *Journal of Conflict and Security Law*, 13:2, 191–213.

Foucault, M. (1980) 'Truth and Power', in M. Foucault and C. Gordon (eds), *Power/Knowledge: Selected Interviews and Other Writings 1972–1977* (London: Longman).

Foucault, M. (1991) *Discipline and Punish* (London: Penguin).

Fox, F. (2002) 'Conditioning the Right to Humanitarian Aid? Human Rights and the "New Humanitarians"', in D. Chandler (ed.), *Rethinking Human Rights: Critical Approaches to International Politics* (Basingstoke: Palgrave Macmillan).

Franck, T. (1999) 'Lessons of Kosovo', *American Journal of International Law*, 93:4, October, 857–60.

Franck, T. (2005) 'Interpretation and Change in the Law of Humanitarian Intervention', in J. L. Holzgrefe and R. O. Keohane (eds), *Humanitarian Intervention: Ethical, Legal and Political Dilemmas* (Cambridge: Cambridge University Press).

Franck, T. and Rodley, N. (1973) 'After Bangladesh: The Law of Humanitarian Intervention by Military Force', *American Journal of International Law*, 67, 275–305.

Freedman, L. (2005) 'The Age of Liberal Wars', in, D. Armstrong, T. Farrell and B. Maiguashca (eds), *Force and Legitimacy in World Politics* (Cambridge: Cambridge University Press).

Freedom House (2011) 'Combined Average Ratings – Independent Countries', [online] http://www.freedomhouse.org/uploads/fiw11/CombinedAverage Ratings(Independent Countries)FIW2011.pdf (accessed 2 September 2012).

Frontline (2000) 'War in Europe Interview with Richard Holbrooke' [online] www.pbs.org/wgbh/pages/frontline/shows/kosovo/interviews/holbrooke.html (accessed 2 November 2011).

Frontline (2004) 'Ghosts of Rwanda – Transcript' [online] http://www.pbs.org/wgbh/pages/frontline/shows/ghosts/etc/script.html (accessed 2 November 2011).

Frost, M. (2001) 'The Ethics of Humanitarian Intervention', in K. E. Smith and M. Light (eds), *Ethics and Foreign Policy* (Cambridge: Cambridge University Press).

Frum, D. and Perle, R. (2004) *An End to Evil* (New York: Random House).

Fukuyama, F. (1992) *The End of History and the Last Man* (New York: Avon).

Fukuyama, F. (2006) 'Nation-building and the Failure of International Memory', in F. Fukuyama (ed.), *Nation-Building: Beyond Afghanistan and Iraq* (New York: Johns Hopkins University Press).

Fuller, G. (1999) 'Two, Three, Many Kosovars', *New Perspectives Quarterly*, 16, 4.

Gardner, J. (2007) 'The Final Chapter?' in J. Dumbrell and D. Ryan (eds), *Vietnam in Iraq* (London: Routledge).

Garton-Ash, T. (2000) 'The War We Almost Lost', *Guardian*, 4 September.

Gause, G. (2011) 'Why Middle East Studies Missed the Arab Spring', *Foreign Affairs*, 90:4, 81–90.

Gazzini, T. (2005) *The Changing Rules on the Use of Force in International Law* (Manchester: Manchester University Press).

Gellner, E. (1994) *The Conditions of Liberty* (London: Hamish Hamilton).

General Assembly (2011) 'General Assembly Suspends Libya from Human Rights Council', GA/11050, 1 March, [online] http://www.un.org/News/Press/docs//2011/ga11050.doc.htm (accessed 2 September 2012).

Gibbs, D.N. (2009) *First Do No Harm: Humanitarian Intervention and the Destruction of Yugoslavia* (Nashville: Vanderbilt University Press).

Glanville, L. (2011) 'Darfur and the Responsibilities of Sovereignty', *International Journal of Human Rights*, 15:3, 462–80.

Glanville, L. (2012) 'The Responsibility to Protect Beyond Borders', *Human Rights Law Review*, 12:1, 1–32.

Glennon, M. (1999) 'The New Interventionism', *Foreign Affairs*, 78:3, 2–7.

Glenny, M. (1999) *The Balkans, 1804–1999* (London: Granta Books).

Global Centre for R2P (2009) 'Implementing the Responsibility to Protect. The 2009 General Assembly Debate: An Assessment', GCR2P Report, August. [online], http://globalr2p.org/media/pdf/GCR2P_General_Assembly_Debate_Assessment.pdf (accessed 3 August 2012).

Glover, J. (2006) 'British believe Bush is more dangerous than Kim Jong-il', *Guardian*, 3 November.

Golovnina, M. (2011) 'Western Powers Strike Libya: Arab League has its doubts', Reuters, 20 March, [online] http://www.reuters.com/article/2011/03/20/us-libya-idUSTRE7270JP2011 0320?pageNumber=1 (accessed 28 November 2011).

Gompert, D. C., Richardson, C., Kugler, R. L. and Bernath, C. H. (2005) 'Learning from Darfur: Building a Net-Capable African Force to Stop Mass Killing', Centre for Technology and National Security Policy, National Defense University [online] http://www.dtic.mil/cgi-bin/GetTRDoc?AD=ADA450148 (accessed 26 September 2012).

Gourevitch, P. (1998) *We Wish to Inform You that Tomorrow We Will be Killed with Our Families* (London: Picador).

Gow, J. (1994) 'Nervous Bunnies: The International Community and the Yugoslav War of Dissolution, the Politics of Military Intervention in a Time of Change', in L. Freedman (ed.), *Military Intervention in European Conflicts* (Oxford: Blackwell).

Gow, J. (1997) *Triumph of the Lack of Will: International Diplomacy and the Yugoslav War* (New York: Colombia University Press).

Gow, J. (2000) 'A Revolution In International Affairs?' *Security Dialogue*, 31:3, 293–306.

Gow, J. (2003) *The Serbian Project and its Adversaries* (Montreal: McGill-Queens University Press).

Gow, J. (2005) *Defending the West* (Cambridge: Polity).

Gow, J. (2011) 'Principles of Pre-emption: A Commentary on Issues and Scenarios for Self-defence in the 21st Century', in A. Hehir, N, Kurht and A. Mumford (eds.) *International Law, Security and Ethics* (London: Routledge).

Gowan, P. (2000) 'The Euro-Atlantic Origins of NATO's Attack on Yugoslavia', in T. Ali (ed.), *Masters of the Universe?* (London: Verso).

Gowan, P. (2003) 'The New Liberal Cosmopolitanism', in D. Archibugi (ed.), *Debating Cosmopolitics* (London: Verso).

Gowlland-Debbas, V. (2000) 'Functions of the United Nations Security Council in the International Legal System', in M. Byers (ed.), *The Role of International Law in International Politics* (Oxford: Oxford University Press).

Graubart, J. (2008) 'NGOs and the Security Council', in B. Cronin and I. Hurd (eds), *The UN Security Council and the Politics of International Authority* (London: Routledge).

Gray, C. (2001) 'No Good Deed Shall Go Unpunished', in K. Booth (ed.), *The Kosovo Tragedy* (London: Frank Cass).

Green, L. (1988) *The Authority of the State* (Oxford: Clarendon).

Greenwood, C. (1993) 'Is There a Right of Humanitarian Intervention?' *World Today*, 49:2, 34–40.

Griffins, M. (2007) *International Relations Theory for the 21st Century* (London: Routledge).

Group of 77 (G-77) (2000) 'Declaration of the South Summit', Havana, Cuba, 10–14 April, article 54 [online] http://www.g77.org/summit/Declaration_ G77Summit.htm (accessed 6 June 2012).

Guardian, The (2003) 'War would be illegal', letter, *Guardian*, 7 March.

Guicherd, C. (1999) 'International Law and the War in Kosovo', *Survival*, 41:2, 19–34.

Hagen, W. (1999) 'The Balkans Lethal Nationalisms', *Foreign Affairs*, 78/4, 52–64.

Halim, S. (2011) 'The Arab Wall Begins to Fall: The Impossible Happened', *Le Monde Diplomatique*, February. [online] http://mondediplo.com/2011/02/ 01impossible (accessed August 3 2012).

Hamburg, D. (2008) *Preventing Genocide* (Boulder CO: Paradigm).

Hammond, P. (2002) 'Moral Combat', in D. Chandler (ed.), *Rethinking Human Rights* (Basingstoke and New York: Palgrave Macmillan).

Hammond, P. and Herman, E. (eds) (2000) *Degraded Capability: The Media and the Kosovo Crisis* (London: Pluto).

Harris, E. (2011) 'Clinton Cites Bosnia, Rwanda in Rationale for Libya Intervention', ABC News, 27 March.

Harrison, G. (2004) *The World Bank in Africa: The Construction of Governance States* (London: Routledge).

Hashmi, S.H. (2003) 'Is there an Islamic Ethic of Humanitarian Intervention?', in A. Lang, (ed.) *Just Intervention* (Washington D.C., Georgetown University Press).

Hayden, P. (2005) *Cosmopolitan Global Politics* (Aldershot: Ashgate).

Hayden, R. (2003) 'Biased Justice', in R. Thomas (ed.), *Yugoslavia Unraveled: Sovereignty, Self Determination, Intervention* (Oxford: Lexington).

Heazle, M. and Islam, I. (2006) *Beyond the Iraq War: The Promises, Pitfalls and Perils of External Interventionism* (Cheltenham: Edward Elgar).

Hedges, C. (1999) 'Kosovo's Next Masters', *Foreign Affairs*, 78:3, 24–42.

Hehir, A. (2006) 'The Impact of Analogical Reasoning on US Foreign Policy Towards Kosovo', *Journal of Peace Research*, 43:1, 67–81.

Hehir, A. (2007) 'The Myth of the Failed State and the War on Terror', *Journal of Intervention and Statebuilding*, 1:3, 307–332.

Hehir, A. (2008a) *Humanitarian Intervention after Kosovo: Iraq, Darfur and the Record of Global Civil Society* (Basingstoke and New York: Palgrave Macmillan).

Hehir, A. (2008b) 'Interview with Jamie Shea: NATO's Role in Statebuilding', *Journal of Intervention and Statebuilding*, 2:2, 227–41.

Hehir, A. (2008c) 'The Changing Conception of Self-Defense', in I. Wilson and J. Forest (eds), *Defence Politics: International and Comparative Perspectives* (London: Routledge).

Hehir, A. (2009a) 'Interview with Lord Robertson', *Journal of Intervention and Statebuilding*, 3:2, 259–75.

Hehir, A. (2009b) 'NATO's Humanitarian Intervention in Kosovo: Precedent or Aberration?' *Journal of Human Rights*, 8:3, 1–20.

Hehir, A. (ed.) (2010) *Kosovo, Intervention and Statebuilding* (London, Routledge).

Hehir, A. (2010a) 'The Responsibility to Protect: Sound and Fury Signifying Nothing?', *International Relations*, 24, 2, 218–239.

Hehir, A. (2010b) 'Microcosm, Guinea Pig, or *Sui Generis*? Assessing International Engagement with Kosovo' in A. Hehir (ed.) *Kosovo, Intervention and Statebuilding* (London: Routledge).

Hehir, A. (2011a) 'The Responsibility to Protect in International Political Discourse: Encouraging Statement of Intent or Illusory Platitudes?', *International Journal of Human Rights*, 15/8, 1329–46.

Hehir, A. (2011b) 'The Special Adviser on the Prevention of Genocide: Adding Value to the UN's Mechanisms for Preventing Intra-state Crises?', *Journal of Genocide Research*, 13,3, 271–86.

Hehir, A. (2012) *The Responsibility to Protect: Rhetoric, Reality and the Future of Humanitarian Intervention* (Basingstoke: Palgrave Macmillan).

Hehir, A. and Murray, R.W. (2012) 'Intervention in the Emerging Multipolar System: Why R2P will Miss the Unipolar Moment', *Journal of Intervention and Statebuilding*, 6: 4, 387–406.

Hehir, A. and Robinson, N. (eds) (2007) *State-building: Theory and Practice* (London: Routledge).

Heinbecker, P. (2011) 'Plenty of Credit to go Around in Gadhafi's Fall', *Montreal Gazette*, August 23, [online] http://www.montrealgazette.com/news/Plenty+credit+around+Gadha fi+fall/5291961/story.html (accessed 2 September 2012).

Heinze, E. (2009) *Waging Humanitarian War: The Ethics, Law, and Politics of Humanitarian Intervention* (Albany, NY: State University of New York Press).

Held, D. (1995) *Democracy and the Global Order* (London: Polity).

Held, D. (2004) *A Globalizing World?* (London: Routledge).

Held, D. (2005) 'Globalization: The Dangers and the Answers', in D. Held (ed.), *Debating Globalization* (London: Polity).

Heller, T. and Sofaer, A. (2001) 'Sovereignty: The Practitioners' Perspective', in S. Krasner (ed.), *Problematic Sovereignty: Contested Rules and Political Possibilities* (New York: Colombia University Press).

Hendrickson, D. (1997) 'In Defense of Realism: A Commentary on Just and Unjust Wars', *Ethics and International Affairs*, 11, 19–55.

Henkin, L. (1990) 'Compliance with International Law in an Inter-State System', *Academie de droit international, Recueil des cours 1989* (Dordrecht: Martinus Nijhoff).

Heneghan, T. (2011) 'Gaddafi Tells Rebel City, Benghazi, "We Will Show No Mercy"',

Huffington Post, March 17, [online] http://www.huffingtonpost.com/2011/03/17/gaddafi-benghazi-libya-news_n_837245.html (accessed 13 December 2012).

Henry Jackson Society (2011) 'The Responsibility to Protect: Roundtable with Jared Genser, Thor Halvorssen, and Serena Sharm'. 11 November, London.

Hensel, H. (2004) 'Introduction', in H. Hensel (ed.), *Sovereignty and the Global Community* (Aldershot: Ashgate).

Herbst, J. (1989) 'The Creation and Maintenance of National Boundaries in Africa', *International Organization*, 43:4, 673–92.

Herring, E. and Rangwala, G. (2006) *Iraq in Fragments: The Occupation and its Legacy* (London: Hurst).

Herz, J. (1957) 'Rise and Demise of the Territorial State', *World Politics*, 9:4, 473–93.

Heuser, B. (1997) 'Sovereignty, Self-Determination and Security', in S. Hashmi (ed.), *State Sovereignty: Change and Persistence in International Relations* (Pennsylvania PA: Pennsylvania State University Press).

Hilpold, P. (2001) 'Humanitarian Intervention: Is There a Need for a Legal Reappraisal?' *European Journal of International Law*, 12:3, 437–67.

Hiltermann, J. (2007) *A Poisonous Affair: America, Iraq and the Gassings of Halabja* (Cambridge: Cambridge University Press).

Hinsliff, G. (2003) 'Blair Stakes His Political Future on Beating Iraq', *Observer*, 16 February.

Hintjens, H. M. (1999) 'Explaining the 1994 Genocide in Rwanda', *Journal of Modern African Studies*, 37:2, 241–86.

HM Government (2002) 'Iraq's Weapons of Mass Destruction: The Assessment of the British Government', September [online] http://www.archive2.official-documents.co.uk/document/reps/iraq/cover.htm (accessed 25 September 2012).

Hobbes, T. (1968 [1651]) *Leviathan*, ed. C. B. Macpherson (London: Penguin).

Hobson, J. (2000) *The State and International Relations* (Cambridge: Cambridge University Press).

Hodge, C. (2000) 'Casual War: NATO's Intervention in Kosovo', *Ethics and International Affairs*, 14, 39–54.

Hoffman, F. (2009) 'Human Rights, the Self and the Other' in A. Orford (ed.) *International Law and its Others* (Cambridge: Cambridge University Press).

Hoffmann, S. (2003) 'Intervention: Should It Go On? Can It Go On?' in D. Chatterjee and D. Scheid (eds), *Ethics and Foreign Intervention* (Cambridge: Cambridge University Press).

Hoge, W. (2004) 'U.N. Council Threatens to Punish Sudan Over Militia Killings', *New York Times*, 31 July.

Hoile, D. (2005) *Darfur in Perspective* (London: European-Sudanese Public Affairs Council).

Holbrook, J. (2002) 'Humanitarian Intervention', in D. Chandler (ed.), *Rethinking Human Rights* (Basingstoke and New York: Palgrave Macmillan).

Hollis, M. and Smith, S. (1991) *Explaining and Understanding International Relations* (Oxford: Clarendon Press).

Hollis, R. (2012) 'No Friend of Democratization: Europe's Role in the "Arab Spring"', *International Affairs*, 88:1, 81–94.

Holmes, R. (1992) 'Can War be Morally Justified?' in J. B. Elshtain (ed.), *Just War Theory* (Oxford: Blackwell).

Holmes, R. L. (1989) *On War and Morality* (Princeton, NJ: Princeton University Press).

Holzgrefe, J. L. (2005) 'The Humanitarian Intervention Debate', in J. L. Holzgrefe and R. Keohane (eds), *Humanitarian Intervention: Ethical, Legal and Political Dilemmas* (Cambridge: Cambridge University Press).

Horton, J. (1992) 'The National Question', in J. Allcock, J. Horton and M. Milivojevic (eds), *Yugoslavia in Transition* (Oxford: Berg).

House of Commons (2000) *Foreign Affairs – Fourth Report*, No. HC 28-1 of 7 June 2000, [online] www.publications.parliament.uk/pa/cm199900/cmselect/cmfaff/28/2802.htm (accessed 12 June 2007).

House of Commons Foreign Affairs Committee (2012) 'British Foreign Policy and the Arab Spring', 3 July. Available at, http://www.parliament.uk/business/committees/committees-a-z/commons-select/foreign-affairs-committee/inquiries1/parliament-2010/british-foreign-policy-and-the-arab-spring/ (accessed 2 November 2012).

Howard, J. (2003) 'Transcript of the Prime Minister's Address to the National Press Club', 14 March [online] http://www.pm.gov.au/media/Speech/2003/speech74.cfm (accessed 4 October 2007).

Howard, M. (2000) *The Invention of Peace* (London: Profile).

HRW (Human Rights Watch) (2000) 'Introduction', *World Report 2000* [online] http://www.hrw.org/legacy/wr2k/ (accessed 27 September 2012).

HRW (Human Rights Watch) (2001) 'Cluster Bombs in Afghanistan: A Human Rights Watch Backrounder', October [online] http://www.hrw.org/backgrounder/arms/cluster-bck1031.pdf (accessed 2 November 2010).

HRW (Human Rights Watch) (2007) 'Human Rights News: Crisis in Darfur', 18 September [online] http://www.hrw.org/english/docs/2004/05/05/darfur8536. htm (accessed 8 October 2007).

HRW (Human Rights Watch) (2008) *2008 World Report* [online] http://www.hrw.org/sites/default/files/reports/wr2k8_web.pdf (accessed 2 November 2012).

HRW (Human Rights Watch) (2011a) World Report 2011. [online] http://www.hrw.org/sites/default/files/reports/wr2011.pdf (accessed August 4 2012).

HRW (Human Rights Watch) (2011b) 'Libya: Government Should Demand End to Unlawful Killing', February 20. [online] http://www.hrw.org/en/news/ 2011/02/20/libya-governments-should-demand-end-unlawful-killings (accessed August 4 2012).

Huig, A. (2007) 'Darfur has Become an Even Greater Challenge for Humanitarian Action', Médecins Sans Frontières, 26 October [online] http://www.msf.org.uk/articledetail.aspx?fId=Darfur_has_become_an_even_greater_challenge_for_humanitarian_action (accessed 4 June 2009).

Human Rights Council (2012) 'Report of the International Commission of Inquiry on Libya', A/HRC/19/68, 2 March.

Hurd, I. (2007) *After Anarchy: Legitimacy and Power in the United Nations Security Council* (Princeton, NJ: Princeton University Press).

Hurd, I. (2008) 'Theories and Tests of International Authority', in B. Cronin and I. Hurd (eds), *The UN Security Council and the Politics of International Authority* (London: Routledge).

Hurd, I. (2011) 'Is Humanitarian Intervention Legal?', *Ethics and International Affairs*, 25:3, 293–313.

Hurrell, A. (2005) 'Legitimacy and the Use of Force: Can the Circle be Squared?' in D. Armstrong, T. Farrell and B. Maiguashca (eds), *Force and Legitimacy in World Politics* (Cambridge: Cambridge University Press).

Hutchings, K. (1999) *International Political Theory* (London: Sage).

Huttenbach, H.R. (2008) 'From the Editors: Genocide Prevention: Sound Policy or Pursuit of a Mirage?', *Journal of Genocide Research*, 10: 4, pp. 471–3.

ICED (International Commission of Enquiry on Darfur) (2005) 'Report of the International Commission of Inquiry on Darfur to the United Nations Secretary-General', 25 January [online] http://www.un.org/news/dh/sudan/com_inq_darfur.pdf (accessed 21 December 2008).

ICISS (International Commission on Intervention and State Sovereignty) (2001a) *The Responsibility to Protect* (Ottawa: International Development Research Centre).

ICISS (International Commission on Intervention and State Sovereignty) (2001b) *The Responsibility to Protect: Research, Bibliography, Background* (Ottawa: International Development Research Centre).

ICRtoP (The International Coalition for the Responsibility to Protect) (2009) 'Report on the General Assembly Plenary Debate on the Responsibility to Protect', 15 September. [online] http://www.responsibilitytoprotect.org/ ICRtoP%20Report-General_Assembly_Debate_on_the_Responsibility_to_Protect%20FINAL%209_22_09.pdf (accessed 12 September 2012).

ICRtoP (The International Coalition for the Responsibility to Protect) (2011a), 'FAQs on Impact of Action in Libya on the Responsibility to Protect', 6 May, [online] http://www.responsibilitytoprotect.org/index.php/component/content/ article/35-r2pcs-topics/3436-icrtop-2-page-faq-on-the-impact-of-action-in-libya-on-rtop (accessed 28 November 2011).

ICRtoP (The International Coalition for the Responsibility to Protect) (2011b), 'UN Security Council fails to uphold its Responsibility to Protect in Syria', 7 October 2011, [online] http://www.responsibilitytoprotect.org/index.php/ component/content/article/136-latest-news/3688-un-security-council-fails-to-uphold-its-responsibility-to-protect-in-syria (accessed 28 November 2011)

ICRtoP (The International Coalition for the Responsibility to Protect) (2012a) 'Special Adviser on the Responsibility to Protect: Background to the Position'. [online] http://www.

responsibilitytoprotect.org/index.php/edward-luck-special-adviser-with-a-focus-on-the-responsibility-to-protect (accessed September 2012).

ICRtoP (The International Coalition for the Responsibility to Protect) (2012b) 'Africa', [online] http://www.responsibilitytoprotect.org/index.php/africa (accessed 2 September 2012).

ICTY (International Criminal Tribunal for the Former Yugoslavia) (1996) *Prosecutor v Tadic*, Judgement, ICTY Case No. IT-94-1-AR72 (Jurisdiction), Appeals Chamber, 1995, 35 ILM 35.

Ignatieff, M. (2000) *Virtual War: Kosovo and Beyond* (New York: Picador).

Ignatieff, M. (2003) 'The American Empire: The Burden', *New York Times Magazine*, 5 January.

IICK (Independent International Commission on Kosovo) (2000) *Kosovo Report* (Oxford: Oxford University Press).

Ikenberry, J. and Slaughter, A. M. (2006) 'Forging A World of Liberty under Law: U.S. National Security in the 21st Century', *Princeton Project Papers*, 27 September.

Institute for Global Policy (2009) 'Global Consultative Roundtables on the Responsibility to Protect', [online] http://www.responsibilitytoprotect.org/index.php/africa (accessed 3 December 2011).

International Crisis Group (2008) *Iraq Country Report* [online] http://www.crisis-group.org/home/index.cfm?id=2436andl=1 (accessed 21 December 2008).

International Crisis Group (2011a) 'Popular Protests in the Middle East and North Africa: Making Sense of Libya', Middle East/North Africa Report 107, 6 June.

International Crisis Group (2011b) 'Popular Protests in the Middle East and North Africa: Bahrain's Rocky Road to Reform, Middle East/North Africa Report 111, 28 July.

International Federation for Human Rights (2011) 'Libya: Strategy of scorched earth, desire for widespread and systematic elimination', 24 February. [online] http://www.fidh.org/Libya-Strategy-of-scorched-earth (accessed 1 August 2012).

Jackson, R. (1996) *Quasi-States: Sovereignty, International Relations and the Third World* (Cambridge: Cambridge University Press).

Jackson, R. (2000) *The Global Covenant: Human Conduct in a World of States* (Oxford: Oxford University Press).

Jackson, R. (2006) 'The Safety of the People is the Supreme Law: Beyond Hobbes but not as far as Kant', in W. Bain (ed.), *The Empire of Security and the Safety of the People* (London: Routledge).

Jackson, R. (2007) *Sovereignty: Evolution of an Idea* (London: Polity).

Jackson, R. and Sørensen, G. (2003) *Introduction to International Relations* (Oxford: Oxford University Press).

James, A. (1986) *Sovereign Statehood* (London, Allen & Unwin).

Janzekovic, J. (2006) *The Use of Force in Humanitarian Intervention: Morality and Practicalities* (Aldershot: Ashgate).

Jatras, J. (2000) 'NATO's Myths and Bogus Justifications for Intervention', in T. G. Carpenter (ed.), *NATO's Empty Victory* (Washington DC: Cato Institute).

Jentleson, B.W. (2009) 'The Dilemma of Political Will' in S. Totten and P.R. Bartop (eds.) *The Genocide Studies Reader* (London: Routledge).

Job, B. (2006) 'International Peace and Security and State Sovereignty: Contesting Norms and Norm Entrepreneurs', in R. Thakur and W. P. S. Sidhu (eds), *The Iraq Crisis and World Order: Structural, Institutional and Normative Challenges* (New York: United Nations University Press).

Johansen, R. (ed.) (2006) *A United Nations Emergency Peace Service to Prevent Crimes Against Humanity* (New York: World Federalist Movement).

Johnson, J. T. (1987) *The Quest for Peace: Three Moral Traditions in Western Cultural History* (Princeton, NJ: Princeton University Press).

Johnston, J. T. (2005) 'Just War, as it was and is', *First Things*, 149, 14–24.

Johnstone, D. (2000) 'NATO and the New World Order', in P. Hammond and E. Herman (eds), *Degraded Capability: The Media and the Kosovo Crisis* (London: Pluto).

Johnstone, D. (2002) *Fools' Crusade: Yugoslavia, NATO and Western Delusions* (London: Pluto).

Johnstone, I. (2011) 'Managing Consent in Contemporary Peacekeeping Operations', *International Peacekeeping*, 18:2, 168–82.

Jokic, A. (ed.) (2004) *Lessons of Kosovo: The Dangers of Humanitarian Intervention* (Toronto: Broadview Press).

Jones, A. (2008) 'Genocide and Mass Killing', in P. Williams (ed.), *Security Studies: An Introduction* (London: Routledge).

Jones, B. D. (1995) '"Intervention without Borders": Humanitarian Intervention in Rwanda 1990–94', *Millennium*, 24:2, 225–49.

Jones, B. D. (2012) 'Libya and the Responsibility of Power' *Survival*, 53:3, 51–60.

Jones, T. (2011) 'Who Killed the Right to Self-defence?', in A. Hehir, N, Kurht and A. Mumford (eds.) *International Law, Security and Ethics* (London: Routledge).

Joras, U. and Schetter, C. (2004) 'Hidden Ties: Similarities Between Research and Policy Approaches to Ethnic Conflicts', in A. Wimmer, R. Goldstone, D. Horowitz, U. Joras and C. Schetter (eds), *Facing Ethnic Conflicts: Towards a New Realism* (Oxford: Rowman & Littlefield).

Joyner, D. H. (2002) 'The Kosovo Intervention: Legal Analysis and a more Persuasive Paradigm', *European Journal of International Law*, 13:3, 597–619.

Judah, T. (2000) *Kosovo: War and Revenge* (New Haven, CT: Yale University Press).

Kaldor, M. (1999) *New and Old Wars* (London: Polity).

Kaldor, M. (2003) *Global Civil Society: An Answer to War* (London: Polity).

Kaldor, M. (2005) 'What is Human Security?', in D. Held (ed.), *Debating Globalization* (London: Polity).

Kaplan, R. (1993) *Balkan Ghosts: A Journey Through History* (New York: St Martin's Press).

Kaplan, R. (2001) 'Don't Try to Impose Our Values', *Wall Street Journal*, 10 October.

Kaplan, R. (2003) *Warrior Politics: Why Leadership Demands a Pagan Ethos* (New York: Random House).

Kaufman, S. (2008) 'Ethnic Conflict' in P. Williams (ed.), *Security Studies: An Introduction* (London: Routledge).

Kaul, I. (1995) 'Peace Needs no Weapons', *Ecumenical Review*, 47:3, 313–19.

Keane, J. (2003) *Global Civil Society?* (Cambridge: Cambridge University Press).

Keck, M. and Sikkink, K. (1998) *Activists Beyond Borders: Advocacy Networks in International Politics* (Ithaca, NY: Cornell University Press).

Kedourie, E. (1971) *Nationalism* (London: Hutching University Library).

Keen, D. (2001) 'War and Peace: What's the Difference?', *International Peacekeeping*, 7:4, 1–22.

Kelsen, H. (1972) *Peace Through Law* (Cambridge MA: Harvard University Press)

Kennan, G. (1985) 'Morality and Foreign Policy', *Foreign Affairs*, 64:2, 205–18.

Kennedy, D. (2005) *The Dark Sides of Virtue: Reassessing International Humanitarianism* (Princeton, NJ: Princeton University Press).

Kennedy, D. (2009) 'Reassessing International Humanitarianism: The Dark Sides', in A. Orford (ed.) *International Law and its Others* (Cambridge: Cambridge University Press), 131–55.

Kennedy, P. (1987) *The Rise and Fall of the Great Powers* (New York: Random House).

Kennedy, P. (2006) *The Parliament of Man: The Past, Present and Future of the United Nations* (New York: Random House).

Keohane, R. and Nye, J. (1977) *Power and Interdependence: World Politics in Transition* (Boston, MA: Little, Brown).

Khong, Y. F. (1992) *Analogies At War* (Princeton, NJ: Princeton University Press).

Ki-moon, B. (2009a) 'Implementing the Responsibility to Protect: Report of the Secretary-General', A/63/677, 12 January. [online] http://globalr2p. org/pdf/SGR2PEng.pdf (accessed 13 September 2012).

Ki-moon, B. (2009b) 'Secretary-General, Moved by Statements of Member States, is Eager to Move Forward', UN Department of Public Information, 14 September. [online] http://www.un.org/News/Press/docs/2009/sgsm12452.doc. htm (accessed 12 September 2012).

Ki-moon, B. (2011a) 'Statement by the Secretary-General on Libya', 17 March, [online] http://www.responsibilitytoprotect.org/index.php/crises/190-crisis-in-libya/3269-ban-says-historic-resolution-was-clearly-the-international-community-fulfilling-of-its-responsibility-to-protect (accessed 28 June 2011).

Ki-moon, B. (2011b) 'The Role of Regional and Sub-regional Arrangements in Implementing the Responsibility to Protect', 27 June, [online] http://www.responsibilitytoprotect.org/RtoP%20Info%20Note%20and%20Programme%20-%20SG%20Report%20-%206%206%20July%202011.pdf (accessed 7 November 2012).

Ki-moon, B. (2011c) 'Remarks at Breakfast Roundtable with Foreign Ministers on "The Responsibility to Protect: Responding to Imminent Threats of Mass Atrocities"', UN News

Centre, 23 September, [online] http://www.un.org/apps/news/infocus/sgspeeches/
search_full.asp?statID=1325 (accessed 28 November 2011).

Kinloch-Pichat, S. (2004) *A UN Legion: Between Utopia and Reality* (London: Routledge).

Kinsella, H. (2005) 'Discourses of Difference: Civilians, Combatants, and Compliance with the
Laws of War', in D. Armstrong and T. Farrell (eds), *Force and Legitimacy in World Politics*
(Cambridge: Cambridge University Press).

Kissinger, H. (1992) 'Humanitarian Intervention has its Hazards', *International Herald
Tribune*, 14 December.

Klein, B. S. (1994) *Strategic Studies and World Order* (Cambridge: Cambridge University
Press).

Klinghoffer, J. (1998) *The International Dimension of Genocide in Rwanda* (Basingstoke and
New York: Palgrave Macmillan).

Kober, S. (2000) 'Setting Dangerous International Precedents', in T. G. Carpenter (ed.),
NATO's Empty Victory (Washington DC: Cato Institute).

Koskenniemi, M. (2001) *The Gentle Civilizer of Nations* (Cambridge: Cambridge University
Press).

Koskenniemi, M. (2006) 'What is International Law For?' in M. Evans (ed.) *International Law*
(Oxford: Oxford University Press).

Kouchner, B. (1999) 'The Right to Intervention: Codified in Kosovo', *New Perspectives
Quarterly*, 16, Summer, 4.

Krasner, S. (1999) *Sovereignty: Organized Hypocrisy* (Princeton, NJ: Princeton University
Press).

Krasno, J. and Das, M. (2008) 'The Uniting for Peace Resolution and other ways of
Circumventing the Authority of the Security Council', in B. Cronin and I. Hurd (eds), *The
UN Security Council and the Politics of International Authority* (London: Routledge).

Kratochwil, F. (1995) 'Sovereignty as Dominium', in G. Lyons and M. Mastanduno (eds),
Beyond Westphalia: State Sovereignty and International Intervention (Baltimore: Johns
Hopkins University Press).

Kreiger, D. (2006) 'The War in Iraq as Illegal and Illegitimate', in R. Thakur and W. P. S. Sidhu
(eds), *The Iraq Crisis and World Order: Structural, Institutional and Normative Challenges*
(New York: United Nations University Press).

Kristol, W. and Brooks, D. (1997) 'What Ails Conservatism', *Wall Street Journal*, 15
September.

Kroslak, D. (2007) *The Role of France in the Rwandan Genocide* (London: Hurst).

Krygier, M. (1986) 'Law as Tradition', *Law and Philosophy*, 5, 237–62.

Küng, H. (1991) *Global Responsibility* (New York: Crossroad).

Kum, J. (1990) 'African Interstate Conflict: A Perceptual Approach', *Journal of Peace Research*,
27:4, 445–60.

Kuperman, A. (2000a) 'Rwanda in Retrospect', *Foreign Affairs*, 79:1, 94–118.

Kuperman, A. (2000b) 'Shame – Rationalizing Western Apathy on Rwanda: Kuperman
Replies', *Foreign Affairs*, 79:3, 142–4.

Kuperman, A. (2001) *The Limits of Humanitarian Intervention: Genocide in Rwanda*
(Washington, DC: Brookings Institution Press).

Kuperman, A. (2003) 'Transnational Causes of Genocide', in R. Thomas (ed.), *Yugoslavia
Unraveled: Sovereignty, Self Determination, Intervention* (Oxford: Lexington).

Kuperman, A. (2006) 'Suicidal Rebellions and the Moral Hazard of Humanitarian
Intervention', in T. Crawford and A. Kuperman (eds), *Gambling on Humanitarian
Intervention* (London: Routledge).

Kuperman, A. (2011) 'False Pretence for War in Libya?', *Boston Globe*, April 14.

Kuperman, A. (2013) 'NATO Intervention in Libya: A Humanitarian Success?", in A. Hehir
and R.W. Murray (eds.), *Libya, the Responsibility to Protect and the Future of
Humanitarian Intervention* (Basingstoke and New York: Palgrave Macmillan).

Landman, T. (2005) *Studying Human Rights* (London: Routledge).

Lang, A. (2003) 'Humanitarian Intervention: Definition and Debates', in A. Lang (ed.), *Just
Intervention* (Washington DC: Georgetown University Press).

Langille, P. (2002) 'Bridging the Commitment-Capacity Gap' (New York: The Centre for UN
Reform Education, New York).

Laughland, J. (2002) 'Human Rights and the Rule of Law: Achieving Universal Justice?' in D.
Chandler (ed.), *Rethinking Human Rights* (Basingstoke and New York: Palgrave
Macmillan).

Lauterpacht, H. (1952) 'The Problem of the Revision of the Law of War', *British Yearbook of International Law*, 29.

Layne, C. (1993) 'The Unipolar Illusion: Why new Great Powers Will Rise', *International Security*, 17:4, 5–51.

Layne, C. (1994) 'Kant or Cant: The Myth of the Democratic Peace', *International Security*, 19:2, 5–49.

Layne, C. (2000) 'Miscalculations and Blunders Lead to War', in T. G. Carpenter (ed.), *NATO's Empty Victory* (Washington, DC: Cato Institute).

League of Arab States (2011) 'The Implications of the Current Events in Libya and the Arab Position', 12 March, [online] http://responsibilitytoprotect.org/Arab%20League%20Ministerial%20level%20statement%2012%20march%202011%20-%20english(1).pdf (accessed 2 September 2012).

Lenin, V. I. (1964) *Collected Works* (Moscow: Progress).

Levy, J. (1989) 'Domestic Politics and War', in R. Rotberg and T. Rabb (eds). *The Origin and Prevention of Major Wars* (Cambridge: Cambridge University Press).

Levy, M. A., Young, O. R. and Zürn, M. (1995) 'The Study of International Regimes', *European Journal of International Relations*, 1:3, 267–330.

Lillich, R. (1967) 'Forcible Self-Help by States to Protect Human Rights', *Iowa Law Review*, 53, 290–314.

Linklater, A. (1998) *The Transformation of Political Community* (Oxford: Polity).

Linklater, A. (2000) 'The Good International Citizen and the Crisis in Kosovo', in A. Schnabel and R. Thakur (eds), *Kosovo and the Challenge of Humanitarian Intervention* (New York: United Nations University Press).

Linklater, A. (2005) 'The English School', in S. Burchill, R. Devetak A. Linklater, M. Paterson, C. Reus-Smit and J. True (eds), *Theories of International Relations* (Basingstoke: Palgrave Macmillan).

Linklater, A. (2006) 'The Achievements of Critical Theory', in S. Smith, K. Booth and M. Zalewski (eds), *International Theory: Positivism and Beyond* (Cambridge: Cambridge University Press).

Lu, C. (2006) *Just and Unjust Interventions in World Politics: Public and Private* (Basingstoke and New York: Palgrave Macmillan).

Lucas, G. R. (2003) 'From *jus ad bellum* to *jus ad pacem*: Re-thinking Just-war Criteria for the Use of Military Force for Humanitarian Ends', in D. K. Chatterjee and D. E. Scheid (eds), *Ethics and Foreign Intervention* (Cambridge: Cambridge University Press).

Luck, E. (2010) 'The Responsibility to Protect: Growing Pains or Early Promise?', *Ethics and International Affairs*, 24/4, September. [online] http://www. carnegiecouncil.org/resources/journal/24_4/response/001.html (accessed 30 June 2011).

Lund, M. (2004) 'Operationalizing the Lessons from Recent Experience in Field-Level Conflict Prevention Strategies', in A. Wimmer, R. Goldstone, D. Horowitz, U. Joras and C. Schetter (eds.) (2004) *Facing Ethnic Conflicts: Towards a New Realism* (Oxford: Rowman and Littlefield).

Luttwak, E. (1999) 'Give War a Chance', *Foreign Affairs*, 78:4, 36–44.

Lyons, G. and Mastanduno, M. (1995) 'Introduction', in G. Lyons and M. Mastanduno (eds), *Beyond Westphalia: State Sovereignty and International Intervention* (Baltimore: Johns Hopkins University Press).

Macfarlane, N., Thielking, C. and Weiss, T. (2004) 'The Responsibility to Protect: Is Anyone Interested in Humanitarian Intervention?', *Third World Quarterly*, 25:5, 977–92.

Malanczuk, P. (2006) *Akehurst's Modern Introduction to International Law* (London: Routledge).

Malcolm, N. (1998) *Kosovo: A Short History* (London: Papermac).

Malcolm, N. (2002) *Aspects of Hobbes* (Oxford: Oxford University Press).

Malmvig, H. (2001) 'The Reproduction of Sovereignties: Between Man and State During Practices of Intervention', *Cooperation and Conflict*, 36:3, 251–72.

Malone, D. (2006) *The International Struggle Over Iraq: Politics in the UN Security Council 1980–2005* (Oxford: Oxford University Press).

Mamdani, M. (2009) *Saviors and Survivors: Darfur, Politics, and the War on Terror* (London: Pantheon).

Mamdani, M. (2001) *When Victims Become Killers: Colonialism, Nativism and the Genocide in Rwanda* (Princeton, NJ: Princeton University Press).

Mandel, M. (2003) 'Illegal Wars, Collateral Damage and International Criminal Law', in R.

Thomas (ed.), *Yugoslavia Unraveled: Sovereignty, Self Determination, Intervention* (Oxford: Lexington).

Mandelbaum, M. (1999) 'A Perfect Failure; NATO's War Against Yugoslavia', *Foreign Affairs*, 78:5, 2–8.

Marx, K. (2006 [1867]) *Capital: Critique of Political Economy, III*, trans. D. Fernbach (London: Penguin).

Mayall, J. (2006) 'Humanitarian Intervention and International Society: Lessons From Africa', in J. Welsh (ed.), *Humanitarian Intervention and International Relations* (Oxford: Oxford University Press).

Mayroz, E. (2008) 'Ever Again? The United States, Genocide Suppression, and the Crisis in Darfur', *Journal of Genocide Research*, 10:3, 359–88.

Mazower, M. (2003) *The Balkans* (London: Phoenix).

McCain, J. (2007) 'An Enduring Peace Built on Freedom', *Foreign Affairs*, 86:6, 19–34.

McCormack, T. (2010) *Critique, Security and Power: The political limits to emancipatory approaches* (London: Routledge).

McCoubrey, H. (2000) 'International Humanitarian Law and the Kosovo Crisis', in K. Booth (ed.), *The Kosovo Tragedy: The Human Rights Dimension* (London: Routledge).

McMahan, J. (2005) 'Just Cause for War', *Ethics and International Affairs* 19:3, 1–21.

Mearsheimer, J. (1990) 'Back to the Future', *International Security*, 15:4, 5–56.

Mearsheimer, J. (1994) 'The False Promise of International Institutions', *International Security*, 19:3, 5–49.

Meixner, A. (2007) 'Darfur: A Problem Worth Solving', SaveDarfur, 1 November [online] http://www.savedarfur.org/blog/entries/darfur_a_problem_worth_solving/ (accessed 2 November 2007).

Melanson, R. (2007) 'Unraveling the Domestic Foreign Policy Consensus', in J. Dumbrell and D. Ryan (eds), *Vietnam in Iraq* (London: Routledge).

Melvern, L. (2004) *Conspiracy to Murder: The Rwandan Genocide* (London: Verso).

Mertus, J. (1999) *Kosovo: How Myths and Truths Started A War* (London: University of California Press).

Meyer, S. (2009) 'In Our Interest: The Responsibility to Protect', in R.H. Cooper and J.V. Kohler (eds.) *Responsibility to Protect: The Global Moral Compact for the 21st Century* (Basingstoke and New York: Palgrave Macmillan).

Miller, D. (2007) *National Responsibility and Global Justice* (Oxford: Oxford University Press).

Miller, R. (2000a) 'Humanitarian Intervention Altruism, and the Limits of Casuistry' *Journal of Religious Ethics*, 28:1, 3–35.

Miller, R. (2000b) 'Respectable Oppressors, Hypocritical Liberators: Morality, Intervention and Reality', in D. Chatterjee and D. Scheid (eds), *Ethics and Foreign Intervention* (Cambridge: Cambridge University Press).

Milne, S. (2011) There's nothing moral about NATO's intervention in Libya', *The Guardian*, March 23, [online] http://www.guardian.co.uk/commentisfree/2011/mar/23/nothing-moral-nato-intervention-libya (accessed 2 September 2012)

Molloy, S. (2006) *The Hidden History of Realism* (Basingstoke and New York: Palgrave Macmillan).

Monbiot, G. (2012) 'We're One Crucial Step Closer to Seeing Tony Blair at the Hague', *The Guardian*, 3 September.

Morgenthau, H. J. (1951) *In Defense of the National Interest: A Critical Examination of American Foreign Policy* (New York: Alfred Knopf).

Morgenthau, H. J. (1954) *Politics Among Nations: The Struggle for Power and Peace* (New York: Alfred Knopf).

Moxon-Browne, E. (1998) 'A Future for Peacekeeping?', in E. Moxon-Browne (ed.), *A Future for Peacekeeping?* (New York: St Martin's Press).

MSF (Médecins Sans Frontières) (2005) 'MSF Condemns Violence in Darfur', 8 April [online] http://www.msf.org/msfinternational/invoke.cfm?component=articleandobjectid=2260FE2B-E018-0C72-09DACE85BB3176F8andmethod=full_html (accessed 2 November 2007).

MSF (Médecins Sans Frontières) (2008) 'About Us: What is Doctors Without Borders/Médecins Sans Frontières?' [online] http://www.doctorswithoutborders.org/aboutus/ (accessed 2 November 2007).

Mueller, J. (1999) *Capitalism, Democracy and Ralph's Pretty Good Grocery* (Princeton, NJ: Princeton University Press).

Mueller, J. (2000) 'The Banality of "Ethnic War"' *International Security*, 25:1, 42–70.

Mueller, J. (2005) 'Force, Legitimacy, Success, and Iraq', in D. Armstrong, T. Farrell and B. Maiguashca (eds), *Force and Legitimacy in World Politics* (Cambridge: Cambridge University Press).

Mueller, J. (2006) 'Vietnam and Iraq', in J. Dumbrell and D. Ryan (eds), *Vietnam in Iraq*, (London: Routledge).

Myers, R. J. (1996) 'Notes on the Just War Theory: Whose Justice, Which Wars?', *Ethics and International Affairs*, 116–30.

Nardin, T. (ed.) (1998) *The Ethics of War and Peace: Religious and Secular Perspectives* (Princeton: Princeton University Press).

Nardin, T. (2002) 'Ethical Traditions in International Affairs', in T. Nardin and D. R. Mapel (eds), *Traditions of International Ethics* (Cambridge: Cambridge University Press).

Nardin, T. (2003) 'The Moral Basis for Humanitarian Intervention', in A. Lang (ed.), *Just Intervention* (Washington DC: Georgetown University Press).

Nardin, T. (2005) 'Response to "Ending Tyranny in Iraq": Humanitarian Imperialism', *Ethics and International Affairs*, 19:2, 21–6.

NATO (1999) 'Statement by the North Atlantic Council on Kosovo', press release 99(12), 30 January [online] http://www.nato.int/docu/pr/1999/p99-012e.htm (accessed 26 February 2009).

NATO (2011) 'We Answered the Call: The End of Operation Unified Protector', NATO News, 31 October, [online] http://www.nato.int/cps/en/natolive/news_80435.htm (accessed 2 September 2012).

New York Times (1998) 'Clinton in Africa; Clinton's Painful Words of Sorrow and Chagrin', *New York Times*, 26 March.

New York Times (1999) 'Conflict in the Balkans', Foreign Desk, *New York Times*, 25 March.

Niebuhr, R. (1932) *Moral Man and Immoral Society: A Study in Ethics and Politics* (New York: Charles Scribners).

Nolan, C. J. (2006) 'Great Powers and International Society' in W. Bain (ed.) *The Empire of Security and the Safety of the People* (London: Routledge).

Number 10 (2003) 'Legal Basis for the Use of Force Against Iraq', Number 10.Gov.UK, 17 March [online] http://webarchive.nationalarchives.gov.uk/+/http:/www.number10.gov.uk/Page3287 (accessed 26 September 2012).

Obama, O. Cameron, D. and Sarkozy, N. (2011) 'Libya's Pathway to Peace', *The New York Times*, 14 April [online] http://www.nytimes.com/2011/04/15/opinion/15iht-ed libya15.html (accessed 2 September 2012).

O'Connell, M.E. (2011) 'Responsibility to Peace: A Critique of R2P', in P. Cunliffe (ed.) *Critical Perspectives on the Responsibility to Protect* (London: Routledge)

O'Donovan, O. (2003) *The Just War Revisited* (Cambridge: Cambridge University Press).

O'Driscoll, C. (2008) *Renegotiation of the Just War Tradition and the Right to War in the Twenty-First Century* (Basingstoke: Palgrave Macmillan).

O'Fahey, R. S. (2008) *The Darfur Sultanate: A History* (London: Hurst).

O'Reilly, F. (2004) 'Environmental Degradation as a Cause of Conflict in Darfur', Conference Proceeding, Khartoum, December, University for Peace [online] http://www.unsudanig.org/darfurjam/trackII/data/cluster/development/Environmental%20Degradation%20as%20a%20cause%20of%20conflict%20in%20Darfur%20(.pdf#page=23 (accessed 26 February 2009).

O'Tuathail, G. (1996) 'An Anti-Geopolitical Eye: Maggie O'Kane in Bosnia, 1992–93', *Gender, Place an Culture*, 3:2, 171–85.

OIC (Organisation of Islamic Conference) (2011) 'OIC in the News', 22 February, [online] http://www.oic-oci.org/data/inthenews/en/OIC_Site3(10).pdf (accessed 2 September 2012).

Oppenheim, L. (2006) *International Law: A Treatise* (London: Lawbook Exchange).

Orend, B. (2000) 'Jus Post Bellum', *Journal of Social Philosophy*, 31, 1, 117–37.

Orford, A. (2003) *Reading Humanitarian Intervention* (Cambridge: Cambridge University Press).

Orford, A. (2009) 'A Jurisprudence of the Limit', in Anne Orford (ed.) *International Law and its Others* (Cambridge: Cambridge University Press).

Orford, A. (2011) *International Authority and the Responsibility to Protect* (Cambridge: Cambridge University Press).

Osiander, A. (1994) *The State System of Europe, 1640–1990* (Oxford: Oxford University Press).

Owens, P. (2004) 'Xenophilia, Gender and Sentimental Humanitarianism', *Alternatives*, 29, 285–304.

Pangle, T. and Ahrensdorf, P. (1999) *Justice Among Nations: On the Moral Basis of Power and Peace* (Kansas: University Press of Kansas).

Pape, R. (2012) 'When Duty Calls: A Pragmatic Standard of Humanitarian Intervention' *International Security*, 37, 1, 41–80.

Parsi, V. E. (2006) *The Inevitable Alliance: Europe and the United States Beyond Iraq* (Basingstoke and New York: Palgrave Macmillan).

Pasic, A. and Weiss, T. (2003) 'The Politics of Rescue: Yugoslavia's Wars and the Humanitarian Impulse', in A. Lang (ed.), *Just Intervention* (Washington, DC: Georgetown University Press).

Pattison, J. (2007) 'Humanitarian Intervention and International Law: The Moral Importance of an Intervener's Legal Status', *Critical Review of International Social and Political Philosophy*, 10:3, 301–19.

Pattison, J. (2010) *Humanitarian Intervention and the Responsibility to Protect* (Oxford: Oxford University Press).

Pavkovic, A. (2003) 'Humanitarian Intervention in Nationalist Conflicts', in A. Jokic (ed.), *Lessons of Kosovo: The Dangers of Humanitarian Intervention* (Ontario: Broadview Press).

Pesic, V. (1996) 'The War for Ethnic States', in N. Popov (ed.), *The Road to War in Serbia* (New York: CEU Press).

Peters, A. (2009) 'Humanity as the A and Ω of Sovereignty', *The European Journal of International Law*, 20/3, 513–544.

Pogge, T. (1994) 'Cosmopolitanism and Sovereignty', in C. Brown (ed.), *Political Restructuring in Europe: Ethical Perspectives* (London: Routledge).

Power, S. (2001) 'By-standers to Genocide', *Atlantic*, September [online] http://www.theatlantic.com/doc/200109/power-genocide (accessed 2 May 2009).

Project for a New American Century (1998) 'Open Letter to President William J. Clinton', 26 January [online] http://www.newamericancentury.org/iraqclintonletter.htm (accessed 2 May 2009).

Prokopijevic, M. (2004) 'Humanitarian Intervention', in G. Meggle (ed.), *Ethics of Humanitarian Intervention* (Frankfurt: Ontas).

Prunier, G. (1997) *The Rwanda Crisis: History of a Genocide* (New York: Colombia University Press).

Prunier, G. (2005) *Darfur: The Ambiguous Genocide* (Ithaca, NY: Cornell University Press).

Rabinow, P. (ed.) (1984) *The Foucault Reader* (New York: Pantheon).

Ramcharan. B.G. (2008) *Preventive Diplomacy at the UN* (Indiana: Indiana University Press)

Reed, C. and Ryall, D. (2007) 'Introduction', in C. Reed and D. Ryall (eds), *The Price of Peace* (Cambridge: Cambridge University Press).

Reeves, E. (2005) 'Genocide by Attrition: Agony in Darfur', *Dissent*, Winter.

Reinhold, T. (2010) 'The Responsibility to Protect: Much Ado About Nothing?', *Review of International Studies*, 36, 55–78.

Reinold, T. (2012) *Sovereignty and the Responsibility to Protect* (London: Routledge).

Reisman, M. (2000) 'Unilateral Action and the Transformations of the World Constitutive Process: The Special Problem of Humanitarian Intervention', *European Journal of International Law*, 11:1, 3–18.

Rengger, N. (2002) 'On the Just War Tradition in the Twenty First Century', *International Affairs*, 78:2, 353–63.

Rengger, N. (2005) 'The Judgment of War: On the Idea of Legitimate Force in World Politics', in D. Armstrong, T. Farrell and B. Maiguashca (eds), *Force and Legitimacy in World Politics* (Cambridge: Cambridge University Press).

Reus-Smit, C. (2005) 'Liberal Hierarchy and the License to Use Force', in D. Armstrong, T. Farrell and B. Maiguashca (eds), *Force and Legitimacy in World Politics* (Cambridge: Cambridge University Press).

Reuters (2008) 'Interview – Myanmar Must Act Now to Clear Red Tape', *Reuters*, 7 May [online] http://www.reuters.com/article/2008/05/07/idUSBKK328448 (accessed 13 December 2012).

Reuters (2012) 'Syrian Death Toll Now Tops 30,000: Activist Group', *Reuters*, 26 September [online] http://www.reuters.com/article/2012/09/26/us-syria-crisis-toll-idUSBRE88P12Y 20120926 (accessed 19 October 2012).

Rice, C. (2000) 'Promoting the National Interest', *Foreign Affairs*, 79:1, 45–78.

Rice, S. (2005) 'Why Darfur Can't be Left to Africa', *Washington Post*, 7 August [online] http://www.brookings.edu/articles/2005/0807africa_rice.aspx (accessed February 2009).

Richmond, O. (2005) 'UN Peacebuilding Operations and the Dilemma of the Peacebuilding Consensus', in A. Bellamy and P. Williams (eds), *Peace Operations and the Global Order* (London: Routledge).

Rieff, D. (2004) 'Kosovo: The End of an Era?' in F. Weissman (ed.), *In the Shadow of 'Just Wars': Violence, Politics and Humanitarian Action* (London: Hurst).

Rieff, D. (2006) 'A Nation of Pre-emptors?', *New York Times Magazine*, 15 January.

Roberts, A. (1999) 'NATO's "Humanitarian War" over Kosovo', *Survival*, 41, 102–23.

Roberts, A. (2002) 'The So-Called "Right" of Humanitarian Intervention', in *Yearbook of International Humanitarian Law 2000*, 3 (The Hague: T.M.C. Asser).

Roberts, A. (2006) 'The United Nations and Humanitarian Intervention', in J. Welsh (ed.), *Humanitarian Intervention and International Relations* (Oxford: Oxford University Press).

Robertson, G. (2002) *Crimes Against Humanity* (London: Penguin).

Rodin, D. (2002) *War and Self-Defence* (Oxford: Clarendon Press).

Rodley, N. and Cali, B. (2007) 'Kosovo Revisited: Humanitarian Intervention on the Fault Lines of International Law', *Human Rights Law Review*, 7: 2, 275–97.

Rogers, P. (2008) *Why We Are Losing the War on Terror* (London: Polity).

Roper, J. (2006) 'Europe's Vietnam Syndrome: America and the Quagmire of Iraq', in J. Dumbrell and D. Ryan (eds), *Vietnam in Iraq* (London: Routledge).

Rosenberg, J. (1994) *Empire of Civil Society* (London: Verso).

Rosenthal, J. H. (1995) 'Biography, Ethics and Statecraft', in C. J. Nolan (ed.), *Ethics and Statecraft: The Moral Dimensions of International Affairs* (Westport, Conn.: Praeger).

Roth, K. (2000) 'Bombs Report off Target', *Guardian*, 12 January, 21.

Rupert, M. (2007) 'Marxism and Critical Theory', in T. Dunne, M. Kurki and S. Smith (eds), *International Relations Theories: Discipline and Diversity* (Oxford: Oxford University Press).

Russett, B. Starr, H. and Kinsella, D. (2000) *World Politics: The Menu for Choice* (New York: St Martins Press).

Rutledge, I. (2005) *Addicted to Oil* (London: I.B. Taurus).

Ryan, D. (2007) '"Vietnam", Victory Culture and Iraq', in J. Dumbrell and D. Ryan (eds), *Vietnam in Iraq* (London: Routledge).

Said, E. (1993) *Culture and Imperialism* (London, Chatto & Windus).

Sands, P. (2006) *Lawless World* (London: Penguin).

Santini, R. (2011) 'The Transatlantic Relationship After the Arab Uprisings: Stronger in North Africa, Shakier in the Middle East?", Brookings Institution, 9 June 2011.

SaveDarfur (2007) 'About US: Frequently Asked Questions' [online] http://www.savedarfur.org/pages/faq/#1 (accessed 2 November 2007).

Schabas, W. (2000) *Genocide in International Law: The Crimes of Crimes* (Cambridge: Cambridge University Press).

Schachter, O. (1991) *International Law in Theory and Practice* (London: Martinus Nijhoff).

Scheffer, D. (2009) 'Atrocity Crimes: Framing the Responsibility to Protect', in R.H. Cooper and J.V. Kohler (eds.) *Responsibility to Protect: The Global Moral Compact for the 21st Century* (Basingstoke and New York: Palgrave Macmillan).

Scheipers, S. (2009) *Negotiating Sovereignty and Human Rights* (Manchester: Manchester University Press).

Schmitt, C. (1996) *The Concept of the Political*, trans. G. Schwab (Chicago: University of Chicago Press).

Schmitt, M. (2011) 'Wings Over Libya: The No-Fly Zone in Legal Perspective', *The Yale Journal of International Law Online*, 36, 45–58.

Sciolino, E. (2007) 'A Surprising Choice for France's Foreign Minister', *New York Times*, 18 May.

Sciolino, E. and Bronner, E. (1999) 'Crisis in the Balkans', *New York Times*, 18 April, 3.

Seybolt, T. (2007) *Humanitarian Military Intervention: The Conditions for Success and Failure* (Oxford: Oxford University Press).

Shaw, M. (1994) *Global Civil Society and International Relations* (London: Polity).

Shawcross, W. (2001) *Deliver Us From Evil* (London: Bloomsbury).

Shue, H. (2003) 'Bombing to Rescue? NATO's 1999 bombing of Serbia', in D. Chatterjee and D. Scheid (eds), *Ethics and Foreign Intervention* (Cambridge: Cambridge University Press).

Simma, B. (1999) 'NATO, the UN and the Use of Force', *European Journal of International Law*, 10:1, 1–22.

Simpson, G. (2004) *Great Powers and Outlaw States* (Cambridge: Cambridge University Press).

Singh, R. (2006) 'The Bush Doctrine', in M. Buckley and R. Singh (eds), *The Bush Doctrine and the War on Terrorism* (London, Routledge).

Slaughter, A. M. (1995) 'International Law in a World of Liberal States', *European Journal of International Law*, 6, 503–38.

Slaughter, A. M. (2003) 'Good Reasons for Going Around the UN', *New York Times*, 18 March.

Slaughter, A. M. (2011a) 'Wilsonianism in the 21st Century', in G.J. Ikenberry, T.J. Knock, A-M. Slaughter and T. Smith, *The Crisis of American Foreign Policy* (New Jersey, Princeton University Press)

Slaughter, A. M. (2011b) 'A Day to Celebrate, but Hard Work Ahead', *Foreign Policy*, March 18. [online] http://www.foreignpolicy.com/articles/2011/03/18/does_the_world_belong_in_libyas_war?page=0,7 (accessed 12 June 2011).

Slim, H. (2004) 'Dithering over Darfur?', *International Affairs*, 80:5, 811–28.

Smith, B. (2011) 'The Arab Uprisings', House of Commons Library, Research Paper 11/73, 11 November.

Smith, M. (1998) 'Humanitarian Intervention: An Overview of Ethical Issues', *Ethics and International Affairs*, 12:1, 63–79.

Sørensen, G. (2001) *Changes in Statehood: The Transformation of International Relations* (Basingstoke and New York: Palgrave Macmillan).

Spykman, N. (1942) *America's Strategy in World Politics* (New York: Harcourt, Brace).

Stahn, C. (2007) 'Responsibility to Protect: Political Rhetoric or Emerging Legal Norm?', *American Journal of International Law*, 101:1, 99–120.

Starr, H. (1995) 'International Law and International Order', in C. Kegley (ed.), *Controversies in International Relations Theory* (New York: St Martin's Press).

Steans, J. and Pettiford, L. (2005) *Introduction to International Relations* (London: Pearson Longmans).

Stephan, A. and Robertson, G. (2003) 'An "Arab" More than a "Muslim" Democracy Gap', *Journal of Democracy*, 14:3, 30–44.

Straus, S. (2005) 'Darfur and the Genocide Debate', *Foreign Affairs*, 81:4, 123–33.

Strauss, E. (2009) *The Emperor's New Clothes?: The UN and the Implementation of the Responsibility to Protect* (Baden-Baden: Nomos Verlagsges).

Stromseth, J. (2005) 'Rethinking Humanitarian Intervention', in J. L. Holzgrefe and R. Keohane (eds), *Humanitarian Intervention* (Cambridge: Cambridge University Press).

Sulyok, G. (2003) 'The Theory of Humanitarian Intervention with Special Regard to NATO's Kosovo Mission', in F. Bieber and Z. Daskalovski (eds), *Understanding the War in Kosovo* (London: Frank Cass).

Sutterlin, J. (2003) *The United Nations and the Maintenance of International Security* (Westport, Conn.: Praeger).

Tanguy, J. (2003) 'Redefining Sovereignty and Intervention', *Ethics and International Affairs*, 17:1, 141–8.

Tesón, F. (1988) *Humanitarian Intervention: An Enquiry into Law and Morality* (New York: Transnational).

Tesón, F. (1996) 'Collective Humanitarian Intervention', *Michigan Journal of International Law*, 17, 323–71.

Tesón, F. (2005a) 'The Liberal Case for Humanitarian Intervention', in L May, E. Rove and S. Viner (eds), *The Morality of War: Classical and Contemporary Readings* (Upper Saddle River, NJ: Pearson).

Tesón, F. (2005b) 'Ending Tyranny in Iraq', *Ethics and International Affairs*, 19:2, 1–20.

Thakur, R. (2004) 'Developing Countries and the Intervention-Sovereignty Debate', in R.M. Price, and M.W. Zacher (eds.) *The United Nations and Global Security* (New York: Palgrave Macmillan).

Thakur, R. (2006) 'The Responsibility to Protect', in R. Thakur and W. P. S. Sidhu (eds), *The Iraq Crisis and World Order: Structural, Institutional and Normative Challenges* (New York: United Nations University Press).

Thakur, R. (2011) 'Has R2P Worked in Libya?', *Canberra Times*, 19 September.

Thakur, R. and Sidhu, W. P. S. (2006) 'Iraq's Challenge to World Order', in R. Thakur and W. P. S. Sidhu (eds), *The Iraq Crisis and World Order: Structural, Institutional and Normative Challenges* (New York: United Nations University Press).

Thomas, N. and Tow, W. (2002) 'The Utility of Human Security: Sovereignty and Humanitarian Intervention', *Security Dialogue*, 33:2, 127–40.

Thomas, R. (2003) 'Wars, Humanitarian Intervention and International Law', in R. Thomas (ed.), *Yugoslavia Unraveled: Sovereignty, Self Determination, Intervention* (Oxford: Lexington).

Thompson, J. (1992) *Justice and World Order: A Philosophical Enquiry* (London: Routledge).

Thucydides (1972 [431 BC]) *History of the Peloponnesian War*, trans. R. Warner (London: Penguin).

Tilly, C. (1990) *Coercion, Capital and European States* (Oxford: Blackwell).

Tomasky, M. (2011) 'Gaddafi's Speech', *The Guardian*, 17 March. [online] http://www.guardian.co.uk/commentisfree/michaeltomasky/2011/mar/17/usforeignpolicy-united nations-libya-it-will-start-fast (accessed 2 September 2012)

Tooke, J. (1965) *The Just War in Aquinas and Grotius* (London: SPCK).

Tucker, R. (1960) *The Just War: A Study on Contemporary Doctrine* (Baltimore, MD: Johns Hopkins University Press).

Tyler, P. (2003) 'Threats and Responses: News Analysis; A New Power in the Streets', *New York Times*, 17 February.

Tyner, J. (2006) *The Business of War* (Aldershot: Ashgate).

United Nations (1999) 'Report of the Independent Inquiry into the Actions of the United Nations During the 1994 Genocide in Rwanda', S/1999/1257, 15 December [online] http://www.un.org/News/dh/latest/rwanda.htm (accessed 2 May 2009).

UN Commission on Global Governance (1995) *Our Global Neighbourhood* (Oxford: Oxford University Press).

UN General Assembly (1993) 'Vienna Declaration and Programme of Action', A/CONF.157/23, 12 July [online] http://www.unhchr.ch/huridocda/huridoca.nsf/(Symbol)/A.CONF.157.23.En (accessed 26 February 2009).

UN General Assembly (2000) 'United Nations Millennium Declaration', 55/2, 8 September [online] http://www.un.org/millennium/declaration/ares552e.htm (accessed 26 February 2009).

UN General Assembly (2005) *Outcome Document* for 2005 World Summit, A/60/L.1, 15 September [online] http://www.who.int/hiv/universalaccess 2010/worldsummit.pdf (accessed 26 February 2009).

UN General Assembly (2008) 'Human Rights Situations that Require the Council's Attention: Report of the Special Rapporteur on the Situation of Human Rights in the Sudan, Sima Samar', A/HRC/9/13, 2 September [online] http://www.reliefweb.int/rw/RWFiles2008.nsf/FilesByRWDocUnidFilename/EGUA-7JJNR2-full_report.pdf/$File/full_report.pdf (accessed 24 September, 2008).

UNHCR (UN High Commissioner for Human Rights) (2004) 'Report of the United Nations High Commissioner for Human Rights and Follow-Up to the World Conference on Human Rights: Situation of Human Rights in the Darfur region of Sudan', E/CN.4/2005/3, 7 May [online] http://www.unhchr.ch/huridocda/huridoca.nsf/AllSymbols/863D14602AA82CAEC1256EA80038E268/$File/G0414221.doc?OpenElement (accessed 12 October 2007).

UN High-Level Panel on Threats, Challenges and Change (2004) *A More Secure World: Our Shared Responsibility*, 2 December [online] http://www.un. org/secureworld/report.pdf (accessed 25 September 2012).

UN Human Rights Council (2007) 'Report of the High-Level Mission on the Situation of Human Rights in Darfur pursuant to Human Rights Council decision S-4/101', A/HRC/4/80, 9 March.

UN Press Release (2012) 'UN Secretary-General Special Adviser on the Prevention of Genocide Francis Deng, and Special Adviser on the Responsibility to Protect Ed Luck, on the Situation in Libya', 22 February, [online] http://www.un.org/en/preventgenocide/adviser/pdf/OSAPG,%20Special%20Advisers%20Statement%20on%20Libya,%2022%20February%202011.pdf (accessed 2 September 2012).

UNSC (UN Security Council) (1992) 'S/PV.3145', 3 December, [online] http://daccess-dds-ny.un.org/doc/UNDOC/PRO/N92/621/12/PDF/N9262112. pdf?OpenElement (accessed 2 September 2012).

UNSC (UN Security Council) (1994) 'Letter Dated 15 April 1994 from the Permanent Representative of Belgium to the United Nations Addressed to the President of the Security Council', S/1994/446, 15 April.

UNSC (UN Security Council) (2004) 5015th Meeting, 30 July, S/PV.5015 [online] http://daccessdds.un.org/doc/UNDOC/PRO/N04/445/15/PDF/N0444515.pdf?OpenElement (accessed 27 September 2012).

UNSC (UN Security Council) (2011) 'Security Council 6498th Meeting', S/PV.6498, 17 March [online] http://responsibilitytoprotect.org/Security% 20Council%20meeting%20on% 20the%20situation%20in%20Lybia%2017%20March%202011.pdf (accessed 12 September 2012).

United States Department of State (2004) 'The Crisis in Darfur: Secretary Colin Powell, Testimony before the Senate Foreign Relations Committee', 9 September [online] www.ithaca.edu/faculty/cduncan/375/powell.doc (accessed 11 September 2012).

Uvin, P. (1998) *Aiding Violence: The Development Enterprise in Rwanda* (West Hartford, CT: Kumarian).

Uvin, P. (1999) 'Ethnicity and Power in Burundi and Rwanda: Different Paths to Mass Violence', *Comparative Politics*, 31:3, 253–71.

Uvin, P. (2001) 'Reading the Rwandan Genocide', *International Studies Review*, 3:3, 75–99.

Valentino, B. (2011) 'The True Costs of Humanitarian Intervention', *Foreign Affairs*, 90:6, 60–73.

Vandewalle, D. (2006) *A History of Modern Libya* (Cambridge: Cambridge University Press).

Venezuela (2012) 'Statement by Ambassador Jorge Valero: Debate on "Responsibility While Protecting"', February 21 [online] http://www.globalr2p.org/media/pdf/VenezuelaRWP.pdf (accessed September 2012).

Vincent, J. (1974) *Non Intervention and International Order* (Princeton, NJ: Princeton University Press).

Vincent, J. (1986) *Human Rights and International Relations* (Cambridge: Cambridge University Press).

Voeten, E. (2008) 'Delegation and the Nature of Security Council Authority', in B. Cronin and I. Hurd (eds), *The UN Security Council and the Politics of International Authority* (London: Routledge).

Walker, R. B. J. (2003) 'Polis, Cosmopolis, Politics', *Alternatives*, 28, 267–86.

Wallerstein, I. (1974) *The Modern World System* (New York: Academic Press).

Wall Street Journal (1992) 'Everybody's Business', editorial, *Wall Street Journal*, 24 August.

Waltz, K. (1979) *Theory of International Politics* (Toronto: McGraw-Hill).

Waltz, K. (1981) 'The Spread of Nuclear Weapons: More May Be Better', *Adelphi Papers*, 171 (London: International Institute for Strategic Studies).

Waltz, K. (1991) 'Realist Thought and Neo-realist Theory', in R. L. Rothstein (ed.), *The Evolution of Theory in International Relations* (Columbia, SC: University of South Carolina Press).

Walzer, M. (1992a) *Just and Unjust Wars* (New York: Basic Books).

Walzer, M. (1992b) 'The Argument about Humanitarian Intervention', in N. Mills and K. Brunner (eds), *The New Killing Fields* (New York: Basic Books).

Walzer, M. (2006) *Just and Unjust Wars*, rev. edn (New York: Basic Books).

Walzer, M. (2011) 'The Case Against Our Attack on Libya', *The New Republic*, 20 March, [online] http://www.tnr.com/article/world/85509/the-case-against-our-attack-libya (accessed 2 September 2012).

Watts, A. (2001) 'The Importance of International Law', in M. Byers (ed.), *The Role of International Law in International Politics* (Oxford: Oxford University Press).

Weber, C. (1995) *Simulating Sovereignty: Intervention, the State and Symbolic Exchange* (Cambridge: Cambridge University Press).

Wedgewood, R. (2003) 'Legal Authority Exists for Strike on Iraq', *Financial Times*, 14 March.

Wedgewood, R. (2006) 'The Multinational Action in Iraq and International Law', in R. Thakur and W. P. S. Sidhu (eds), *The Iraq Crisis and World Order: Structural, Institutional and Normative Challenges* (New York: United Nations University Press).

Weigel, G. (2007) 'The Development of Just War Thinking in the post-Cold War World', in C. Reed and D. Ryall (eds), *The Price of Peace* (Cambridge: Cambridge University Press).

Weiss, T. (1999) 'Principles, Politics and Humanitarian Action' *Ethics and International Affairs*, 13, 1–22.

Weiss, T. (2007a) *Humanitarian Intervention*, 2nd edn 2010 (London: Polity).

Weiss, T. (2007b) 'Halting Genocide: Rhetoric versus Reality', *Genocide Studies and Prevention*, 2/1, 7–30.

Weiss, T. (2009) *What's Wrong With the United Nations and How to Fix It* (Cambridge: Polity).

Weiss, T. (2011) 'R2P Alive and Well After Libya', *Ethics and International Affairs*, 25/3, 1-6. [online] http://www.carnegiecouncil.org/resources/journal index.html (accessed September 2011).

Weller, M. (1999) *The Crisis in Kosovo 1989–1999* (Cambridge: Documents and Analysis Publishing).

Welsh, J. (ed.) (2006) *Humanitarian Intervention and International Relations* (Oxford: Oxford University Press).

Welsh, J. (2011) 'Civilian Protection in Libya: Putting Coercion and Controversy Back into RtoP', *Ethics and International Affairs*, 25/3, 1-8. [online] http://www.carnegiecouncil.org/resources/journal/index.html (accessed September 2011).

Wesley, M. (2006) 'The New Interventionism and the Invasion of Iraq', in M. Heazle and I. Islam (eds), *Beyond the Iraq War: The Promises, Pitfalls and Perils of External Interventionism* (Cheltenham: Edward Elgar).

Western, J. and Goldstein, J. (2011) 'Humanitarian Intervention Comes of Age' *Foreign Affairs*, 90:6, 48–59.

Wheeler, N. (1992) 'Pluralist or Solidarist Conceptions of International Society: Bull and Vincent on Humanitarian Intervention', *Millennium*, 21:3, 463–87.

Wheeler, N. (1997a) 'Guardian Angel or Global Gangster?' *Political Studies*, 44:1, 123–35.

Wheeler, N. (1997b) 'Agency, Humanitarianism and Intervention', *International Political Science Review*, 18, 1, 9–25.

Wheeler, N. (2002) *Saving Strangers: Humanitarian Intervention in International Society* (Oxford: Oxford University Press).

Wheeler, N. (2003) 'Humanitarian Intervention after September 11, 2001', in A. Lang (ed.), *Just Intervention* (Washington, DC: Georgetown University Press).

Wheeler, N. (2005) 'A Victory for Common Humanity? The Responsibility to Protect after the 2005 World Summit', *Journal of International Law and International Relations*, 2:1, 95–106.

Wheeler, N. (2006) 'The Humanitarian Responsibilities of Sovereignty', in J. Welsh (ed.), *Humanitarian Intervention and International Relations* (Oxford: Oxford University Press).

Wheeler, N. and Dunne, T. (1998) 'Good International Citizenship: A Third Way for British Foreign Policy', *International Affairs*, 74:4, 847–70.

Wheeler, N. and Dunne, T. (2001) 'East Timor and the New Humanitarian Interventionism', *International Affairs*, 77/4, 805–27.

Wheeler, N. and Morris, J. (2006) 'Justifying the Iraq War as a Humanitarian Intervention: The Cure is Worse then the Disease' in R. Thakur and W. P. S. Sidhu (eds), *The Iraq Crisis and World Order: Structural, Institutional and Normative Challenges* (New York: United Nations University Press).

White, N. (2000) 'The Legality of Bombing in the Name of Humanity', *Journal of Conflict and Security Law*, 5:1, 27–43.

White, N. (2004) 'The Will and Authority of the Security Council after Iraq', *Leiden Journal of International Law*, 17: 4, 645–72.

White House (2002a) 'President Delivers State of the Union Address', 29 January [online] http://www.whitehouse.gov/news/releases/2002/01/20020129-11. html (accessed 15 June 2008).

White House (2002b) 'Vice President speaks at VFW 103rd National Convention', 26 August [online] http://www.whitehouse.gov/news/releases/2002/08/ 20020826. html (accessed 15 June 2008).

White House (2003a) 'President Says Saddam Hussein Must Leave Iraq Within 48 Hours: Remarks by the President in Address to the Nation', 17 March [online] www.whitehouse.gov/news/releases/2003/03/20030317-7.html (accessed 15 June 2008).

White House (2003b) 'President Discusses Beginning of Operation Iraqi Freedom', White House press release, 22 March [online] http://www.whitehouse.govnews/releases/2003/03/20030322.html (accessed 4 October 2007).

White House (2003c) 'President Announces End to Major Combat Operations', 1 May [online] http://www.whitehouse.gov/news/releases/2003/05/20030501-15.html (accessed 15 June 2008).

White House (2004a) 'President Addresses the Nation in Prime Time Press Conference', 13 April [online] http://www.whitehouse.gov/news/releases/ 2004/04/20040413-20.html (accessed 4 October 2007).

White House (2004b) 'President Speaks to the United Nations General Assembly', White House press release, 21 September [online] http://www.whitehouse.gov/news/releases/2004/09/20040921-3.html (accessed 12 December 2008).

White House (2004c) 'President and Prime Minister Blair Discussed Iraq, Middle East', press release, 12 November [online] http://www.whitehouse.gov/news/releases/2004/11/20041112-5.html (accessed 15 June 2008).

White House (2011) 'Remarks by the President in Address to the Nation on Libya', 28 March, [online] http://www.whitehouse.gov/the-press-office/2011/03/28/ remarks-president-address-nation-libya (accessed 2 September 2012).

Whitman, J. (2005) 'Humanitarian Intervention in an Era of Pre-emptive Self-defence', *Security Dialogue*, 36:3, 259–74.

Wight, M. (1966a) 'Why Is There no International Theory?' in H. Butterfield and M. Wight (eds), *Diplomatic Investigations: Essays in the Theory of International Politics* (Cambridge, MA: Harvard University Press).

Wight, M. (1966b) 'Western Values in International Relations', in H. Butterfield and M. Wight (eds), *Diplomatic Investigations: Essays in the Theory of International Politics* (Cambridge, Mass.: Harvard University Press).

Wight , M. (1979a) *Power Politics* (Harmondsworth: Penguin).

Wight, M. (1979b) *International Theory: The Three Traditions*, ed. G. Wight and B. Porter (Leicester: Leicester University Press).

Williams, M. (2005) 'What is the National Interest? The Neoconservative Challenge in IR Theory', *European Journal of International Relations*, 11:3, 307–33.

Williams, M. (2007) *Realism Reconsidered* (Oxford: Oxford University Press).

Williams, P. (2005) 'Peace Operations and the International Financial Institutions: Insights from Rwanda and Sierra Leone', in P. Williams and A. Bellamy (eds), *Peace Operations and the Global Order* (Oxford: Routledge).

Williams, P. (2007) 'From Non-Intervention to Non-Indifference: The Origins and Development of the African Union's Security Culture', *African Affairs* 106:423, 253–79.

Williams, P. (ed.) (2008) *Security Studies: An Introduction* (London: Routledge).

Williams, P. (2011) 'The Road to Humanitarian War in Libya', *Global Responsibility to Protect*, 3:2, 248–59.

Williams, P. and Bellamy, A. (2005) 'The Responsibility to Protect and the Crisis in Darfur', *Security Dialogue*, 36:1, 27–47.

Wolf, M. (2005) 'The Case for Optimism: A Response', in D. Held (ed.), *Debating Globalization* (London: Polity).

Wood, E. M. (2000) 'Kosovo and the New Imperialism', in T. Ali (ed.), *Masters of the Universe? NATO's Balkan Crusade* (London: Verso).

Woodhouse, T. and Ramsbotham, O. (2005) 'Cosmopolitan Peacekeeping and the Global Order', *International Peacekeeping*, 12:2, 139–56.

Wright, R. (2006) *A Short History of Progress* (Edinburgh: Canongate).

Yom, S. (2005) 'Civil Society and Democratization in the Arab World', *Middle East Review of International Affairs*, 9:4, 14–33.

Young, I. (2000) 'Violence Against Power: Critical Thoughts on Humanitarian Intervention', in D. Chatterjee and D. Scheid (eds), *Ethics and Foreign Intervention* (Cambridge: Cambridge University Press).

Young, M. B. (2006) 'The Vietnam Laughter Track', in J. Dumbrell and D. Ryan (eds) *Vietnam in Iraq* (London: Routledge).

Zakaria, F. (1992) 'Is Realism Finished?' *The National Interest*, Winter. 30.

Zaum, D (2007) *The Sovereignty Paradox: The Norms and Politics of International Statebuilding* (Oxford: Oxford University Press).

Zolo, D. (1997) *Cosmopolis* (Cambridge: Polity Press).

Index

Printed and bound in Great Britain by
CPI Antony Rowe, Chippenham and Eastbourne